Mici
&
202 258 5399

PSYCHOTHERAPY
THEORIES
AND
TECHNIQUES

---※---

A READER

PSYCHOTHERAPY
THEORIES
AND
TECHNIQUES

A READER

Edited by
GARY R. VANDENBOS, EDWARD MEIDENBAUER,
and JULIA FRANK-McNEIL

American Psychological Association • Washington, DC

Copyright © 2014 by the American Psychological Association. All rights reserved. Except as permitted under the United States Copyright Act of 1976, no part of this publication may be reproduced or distributed in any form or by any means, including, but not limited to, the process of scanning and digitization, or stored in a database or retrieval system, without the prior written permission of the publisher.

First Printing, October 2013
Second Printing, July 2016

Published by
American Psychological Association
750 First Street, NE
Washington, DC 20002
www.apa.org

To order
APA Order Department
P.O. Box 92984
Washington, DC 20090-2984
Tel: (800) 374-2721; Direct: (202) 336-5510
Fax: (202) 336-5502; TDD/TTY: (202) 336-6123
Online: www.apa.org/pubs/books
E-mail: order@apa.org

In the U.K., Europe, Africa, and the Middle East, copies may be ordered from
American Psychological Association
3 Henrietta Street
Covent Garden, London
WC2E 8LU England

Typeset in Goudy by Circle Graphics, Inc., Columbia, MD

Printer: United Book Press, Baltimore, MD
Cover Designer: Mercury Publishing Services, Inc., Rockville, MD

The opinions and statements published are the responsibility of the authors, and such opinions and statements do not necessarily represent the policies of the American Psychological Association.

Library of Congress Cataloging-in-Publication Data

Psychotherapy theories and techniques : a reader / edited by Gary R. VandenBos, Edward Meidenbauer, and Julia Frank-McNeil. — First edition.
    pages cm
  Includes bibliographical references and index.
  ISBN 978-1-4338-1619-2 — ISBN 1-4338-1619-9 1. Psychotherapy. 2. Psychotherapy—Philosophy. 3. Psychotherapy—Methodology. I. VandenBos, Gary R., editor of compilation.
II. Meidenbauer, Edward, editor of compilation. III. Frank-McNeil, Julia, editor of compilation.
  RC480.5.P785 2014
  616.89'14—dc23
                                2013020747

British Library Cataloguing-in-Publication Data

A CIP record is available from the British Library.

Printed in the United States of America
First Edition

http://dx.doi.org/10.1037/14295-000

CONTENTS

Preface... *ix*

How to Use This Book With PsycTHERAPY, APA's Database of
Psychotherapy Demonstration Videos.. *xi*

Chapter 1.   Acceptance and Commitment Therapy........................... 3
Steven C. Hayes and Jason Lillis

Chapter 2.   Acceptance and Commitment Therapy Process 11
Steven C. Hayes and Jason Lillis

Chapter 3.   Behavior Therapy.. 19
Martin M. Antony and Lizabeth Roemer

Chapter 4.   Behavior Therapy Process... 29
Martin M. Antony and Lizabeth Roemer

Chapter 5.   Brief Dynamic Therapy... 35
Hanna Levenson

Chapter 6.   Brief Dynamic Therapy Process 43
             Hanna Levenson

Chapter 7.   Cognitive Therapy 57
             Keith S. Dobson

Chapter 8.   Cognitive Therapy Process 67
             Keith S. Dobson

Chapter 9.   Cognitive–Behavioral Therapy 79
             Michelle G. Craske

Chapter 10.   Cognitive–Behavioral Therapy Process 87
             Michelle G. Craske

Chapter 11.   Constructivist Therapy 97
             Vittorio F. Guidano

Chapter 12.   Constructivist Therapy Process 107
             Greg J. Neimeyer

Chapter 13.   Emotion-Focused Therapy 117
             Leslie S. Greenberg

Chapter 14.   Emotion-Focused Therapy Process 125
             Leslie S. Greenberg

Chapter 15.   Existential Therapy 139
             Kirk J. Schneider and Orah T. Krug

Chapter 16.   Existential Therapy Process 149
             Kirk J. Schneider and Orah T. Krug

Chapter 17.   Family Therapy 155
             William J. Doherty and Susan H. McDaniel

Chapter 18.   Family Therapy Process 165
             William J. Doherty and Susan H. McDaniel

Chapter 19.   Feminist Therapy 173
             Laura S. Brown

Chapter 20.   Feminist Therapy Process 181
             Laura S. Brown

Chapter 21.   Gestalt Therapy.. 187
               Derek Truscott

Chapter 22.   Gestalt Therapy Process... 195
               Uwe Strümpfel and Rhonda Goldman

Chapter 23.   Multicultural Therapy... 203
               Lillian Comas-Díaz

Chapter 24.   Multicultural Therapy Process 213
               Lillian Comas-Díaz

Chapter 25.   Narrative Therapy... 231
               Stephen Madigan

Chapter 26.   Narrative Therapy Process 241
               Stephen Madigan

Chapter 27.   Person-Centered Therapy 251
               David J. Cain

Chapter 28.   Person-Centered Therapy Process 261
               David J. Cain

Chapter 29.   Psychoanalytic Therapy 271
               Jeremy D. Safran

Chapter 30.   Psychoanalytic Therapy Process 281
               Jeremy D. Safran

Chapter 31.   Rational Emotive Behavior Therapy 289
               Albert Ellis and Debbie Joffe Ellis

Chapter 32.   Rational Emotive Behavior Therapy Process.............. 299
               Albert Ellis and Debbie Joffe Ellis

Chapter 33.   Reality Therapy.. 307
               Robert E. Wubbolding

Chapter 34.   Reality Therapy Process 317
               Robert E. Wubbolding

Chapter 35.   Relational–Cultural Therapy.. 325
               Judith V. Jordan

Chapter 36.   Relational–Cultural Therapy Process 335
               Judith V. Jordan

Chapter 37.   Schema Therapy... 345
               Lawrence P. Riso and Carolina McBride

Chapter 38.   Schema Therapy Process.................................... 351
               Lawrence P. Riso, Rachel E. Maddux,
               and Noelle Turini Santorelli

Index 357

PREFACE

Whether you are a student in a clinical training program or a seasoned practitioner, you may find it difficult to grasp the full range of psychotherapy theories or to become even partially acquainted with the plethora of associated techniques. My hope is that this book will be of assistance. This is a reader—a compendium of excerpts of previously published work. We chose to create this reader to provide access to some of the best writing the American Psychological Association (APA) has published on clinical theories and techniques in psychotherapy. The book surveys the great variety of orientations practiced today and provides not a complete explanation of each but rather a glimpse of these orientations at their richest—neither distilled into pat definitions nor tidily packaged into bullet points and takeaway phrases. Instead, short encounters with the best writing on each approach, afford the reader a look at the way psychotherapy is practiced today.

For every psychotherapeutic approach we have included an excerpt on theory and an excerpt on the therapeutic process. At the end of the excerpt on the therapy process we have included a list of techniques associated with that approach to therapy. Some of these techniques appear in the excerpts; others do not appear there. All are well-known interventions used by practitioners of the orientation in question.

In addition, we have provided guidance on where to find video examples of the techniques in our database of psychotherapy demonstrations, PsycTHERAPY. Although PsycTHERAPY is a product quite different from the individual videos in the APA Psychotherapy Video Series, it was created for the same purpose: training and educating psychotherapists. Just as the APA Psychotherapy Video Series has its companion books—from *The Anatomy of Psychotherapy: Viewer's Guide to the APA Psychotherapy Videotape Series* to the more recent *Exploring Three Approaches to Psychotherapy*—this book may be considered as a companion to PsycTHERAPY.

Readers will find that viewing the video clips listed in the chapter appendixes will augment the glimpse into psychotherapy practice provided by the text excerpts. APA created its various psychotherapy video products because there is no better way to demonstrate the timing, the look, the feel of a technique than to capture it in video. In one way, the excerpts and the video clips may be seen as serving the same purpose. That is, just as we have captured a segment of our best writing on theory and technique in this book, we have also captured segments of our videos that best demonstrate some of the techniques for each of these theories. The technique lists are a road map to finding these video clips.

Psychotherapy Theories and Techniques may be enjoyed on its own, without the use of the videos, as an overview and introduction to the many psychotherapies that exist today. The technique lists will be useful in that they neatly identify the key techniques associated with each approach. Our recommendation is to use the book in combination with PsycTHERAPY by first reading the excerpts for each approach and then viewing all of the associated video clips. This will give a vivid introduction to each orientation—not a full one, not one meant to provide the background necessary to take up practice of the approach—but certainly enough of an introduction to get a good sense of what each of these orientations is about.

Observant readers will notice that many of the excerpts in this volume come from chapters in the APA Theories of Psychotherapy book series. If the writing intrigues you, I suggest going to the original books themselves to read more, as they provide a succinct introduction to the history, theory, and therapeutic process of the major approaches. Whatever further reading this volume inspires, my hope is that *Psychotherapy Theories and Techniques: A Reader* will provide a glimpse of the breadth, depth, and richness of psychotherapy as it is practiced today.

Gary R. VandenBos, PhD
APA Publisher

HOW TO USE THIS BOOK
WITH PsycTHERAPY, APA'S
DATABASE OF PSYCHOTHERAPY
DEMONSTRATION VIDEOS

Psychotherapy Theories and Techniques: A Reader contains 38 chapters, each made up of an excerpt from previously published work from the American Psychological Association (APA). The chapters are paired up: The first chapter in each pair is an excerpt on a psychotherapy theory, and the second chapter is on psychotherapy technique. After the second chapter in each pair, there is an appendix of techniques associated with the approach discussed in that pair of chapters.

The appendices contain not only the list of techniques but also information about where to find a video example of those techniques in PsycTHERAPY, APA's premier database of psychotherapy demonstration videos. PsycTHERAPY contains hundreds of streaming videos of therapy demonstrations, each approximately 45 minutes long. All of the videos in PsycTHERAPY have been carefully tagged with metadata, making the videos findable by therapist, approach, therapy topic, and index terms. In addition, each video has been transcribed, and the transcripts may be searched as well. None of the videos appear in the APA Psychotherapy Video Series, but they were created in conjunction with that series.

The chapter appendices contain the following information for each technique as well as where to find it in PsycTHERAPY:

1. Technique name
2. Video title: the video in which the technique appears
3. Video identifying number: A 12-digit number uniquely identifying the video in PsycTHERAPY
4. Time at which technique occurs: The beginning and end times for when exactly the technique is demonstrated in the video

To locate a technique in PsycTHERAPY, use the following steps:

1. Open PsycTHERAPY in your browser (http://psyctherapy.apa.org).
2. Accept the disclaimer terms.
3. Enter the video identifying number in the Quick Search box in the upper right (alternatively, enter the video title in this search box).
4. Click "Go." This will bring you to the search result page, where the video should appear.
5. Open the video page. Click on the "Clips" tab above the transcript pane.
6. A clip with the name of the technique will be provided here.

Rather than searching for the video for each technique, it may be easier to simply find the playlist associated with a given list of techniques. For each list of techniques, there is a playlist in PsycTHERAPY that collects all of the video clips of these techniques in one place. To locate a playlist of all of the technique demonstrations in an appendix, use the following steps:

1. Open PsycTHERAPY in your browser (http://psyctherapy.apa.org) and accept the disclaimer terms.
2. Click on "Playlists" in the blue navigation bar at the top of the screen.
3. There will be a featured playlist for every one of the approaches in the *Psychotherapy Theories and Techniques* book.
4. Click on the playlist you are looking for (e.g., "Behavioral Therapy Techniques").
5. Click "Play All Items" or click on an individual title in the playlist to go directly to that technique clip.

PSYCHOTHERAPY
THEORIES
AND
TECHNIQUES

A READER

1

ACCEPTANCE AND COMMITMENT THERAPY

STEVEN C. HAYES AND JASON LILLIS

The goal of acceptance and commitment therapy (ACT) is the creation of psychological flexibility. The psychological flexibility model underneath ACT emphasizes six specific processes that promote psychopathology and needless human limitation, and six related processes that promote psychological health and human flourishing.

PSYCHOLOGICAL FLEXIBILITY

Psychological flexibility is the process of contacting the present moment fully as a conscious human being and persisting or changing behavior in the service of chosen values. That skill is argued to be composed of the following processes.

Excerpted from *Acceptance and Commitment Therapy* (2012), from Chapter 3, "Theory," pp. 41–50. Copyright 2012 by the American Psychological Association. Used with permission of the authors.

http://dx.doi.org/10.1037/14295-001
Psychotherapy Theories and Techniques: A Reader, G. R. VandenBos, E. Meidenbauer, and J. Frank-McNeil (Editors)
Copyright © 2014 by the American Psychological Association. All rights reserved.

Cognitive Fusion Versus Defusion

If thinking is learned and regulated by arbitrary stimuli, it will always be difficult, if not impossible, to fully eliminate thoughts we do not like. There is no process called *unlearning*, and it is hard to eliminate all the cues for certain thoughts. Indeed, trying to do so creates such cues (Wenzlaff & Wegner, 2000). If a client with obsessive–compulsive disorder tries hard not to think of a disturbing image, for example, the frequency of that image is almost certain to increase, as all of the various distraction cues used become related to the very image being avoided and begin to evoke it.

In relational frame theory (RFT), some contextual cues regulate the emergence of relationships between events, but other cues regulate the *functions* of related events. ACT tends to emphasize interventions that change the functional context, not the relational context.

Suppose a person learns that another name for a favorite candy is "jumjaw." Even a single exposure to that training could establish a mutual relation between these two events that may last a lifetime. But that is only half the story. It is possible to undermine the automatic functions of cognitive relations by altering the functional context. We do that in ordinary ways when we, for example, imagine tasting a jumjaw versus looking at one, but this insight from RFT can be used to clinical effect by changing the literal context of thoughts. Suppose a person is struggling with food urges that revolve around the thought "I want a jumjaw." We might diminish the behavioral impact of that thought by saying it aloud in the voice of Donald Duck, or repeating the word jumjaw out loud until it loses all meaning, or noting that "I am having the thought I want a jumjaw" (this is called *word repletion*). These functional changes are arguably easier and more reliable than the difficult work of changing the occurrence of thoughts. ACT takes advantage of this insight and focuses particularly on the alternation of functional contexts that determine the behavioral impact of verbal/cognitive events.

Cognitive Fusion

Cognitive fusion (or what we will often just call *fusion* for short) is a process in which verbal events have a strong behavioral impact beyond other sources of regulation because they occur in a context of literal meaning. In some external situations, fusion with thought is not harmful to human functioning. A person trying to repair a broken bicycle needs to understand cognitively what is broken and how to fix it; being continuously aware of the process of thinking, in order to increase the psychological distance between the person and his or her thoughts, would likely not add to the effectiveness of this process. Suppose it is clear on inspection that a chain link is damaged.

Thinking "I'm having the thought that the chain link is damaged," would be of little help. The chain is damaged. Judgments about why it is damaged will likely help fix it.

That picture changes dramatically when the focus of what is being addressed is not amenable to problem solving. A person who is suffering is not like a bicycle with a broken chain. The emotions and thoughts being struggled with are historical. Some are deeply conditioned, and those aspects of history will not be changed. In such circumstances, ACT practitioners are likely to try to change the *functions* of experiences rather than their occurrence. Cognitive defusion is a classic method of that kind. We will examine this in a somewhat extended example.

Imagine a person who feels insecure, guilt-ridden, and self-critical. Decades earlier, her mother was very demanding and tried to motivate more attention from her daughter by using criticism and blame. Hayes (2009) shows a client in exactly that situation. We use another client as an example here. We refer to her throughout by the name "Sarah." The transcript entries for Sarah in this volume are edited for clarity, space, and confidentiality, but the actual word-for-word interactions can be seen on the DVD.[1]

Sarah was seen by Steve Hayes in 2008. Sarah is in her early 60s and is returning to therapy. She has chronic health problems due to lung disease. She helps care for her elderly mother, and the relationship is very conflicted. Her mother has always been extremely demanding and critical:

> *Sarah:* Her standards for "if you love me"—well, she has criteria. "If you love me, you'd ____."
>
> *Therapist:* Right, and then there is a list.
>
> *Sarah:* And I can do nice things for her, and she notices them, but it's still not enough. You should never say no. You should never say, "I've gotta go." You should always be there to do whatever she wants.

This is not a new pattern. It turns out that even as a young child, Sarah constantly heard, as she put it, "'This should be this and this should be that.'" Sarah observes, "It impressed me that my mother was full of 'shoulds.'" The pressure to conform and to serve her mother's needs went all the way up to such judgmental and critical statements as, "and you call yourself a Christian."

---

[1]The DVD, which can be purchased at http://www.apa.org/pubs/books/, is titled *Acceptance and Commitment Therapy* and is copyrighted by the American Psychological Association. It is important to note that the client's name and other identifying information have been changed here to protect her confidentiality. The reader who watches the DVD may notice some discrepancies.

The result of this history is that it is hard to set reasonable limits without feeling bad about it:

Sarah: I feel bad if I'm not concerned about what my mother needs for her happiness. And so this is kind of painful. I go over here, "But I wanna be a good Christian, I wanna be, you know, good to my mother and love her," but then I'm not responsible for making all of her moments happy. So it feels like a heavy burden.

Therapist: Yeah. Even as you say it, you kind of winced.

Sarah: And even, you know, I got caller ID so I can see when it was her. So that way if I didn't think I could emotionally handle it, I just wouldn't. But even now every time her name comes up on the caller ID, I have *feelings*. I feel overburdened.

Therapist: And sometimes when you don't answer and she's called?

Sarah: You know what? I don't do that so much because I *still* do it to myself. Then I'm thinking, "Oh, what if this time it was something really important?" I've had to deal with a lot of guilt.

Fusion with judgment and self-criticism is extremely painful, but worse than that, it pulls for ineffective actions. Let's apply the same mode of mind to this situation as one might apply to the broken bicycle. The indication that something is broken is the emotional result of the history we have been describing (e.g., "I feel a heavy burden" or "I feel a lot of guilt"). The broken link in the chain is like the negative self-judgment that leads to guilt and an inability to set reasonable limits. This pattern is historical—she was taught to do it. During the session, the client realized how she too often "goes with the shoulds"—directed at herself and her mother. In one of these moments, she declared, "That's scary. The very thing you have hated in someone else, then you start becoming that."

The problem is that, as the person tries to fix the "broken bicycle" of their own history, this very effort can amplify the thoughts and feelings this history produces. It is easy to end up in the paradoxical and unworkable situation of trying judgmentally to eliminate judgment ("I shouldn't say should!"). Difficult thoughts can become even more central. Real behavior change can be put on hold while a war within is fought. Sarah knows this:

Therapist: If you start arguing with them logically, difficult thoughts and feelings can become even more central.

Sarah: I know! Isn't that something?!

In an ACT model, the problem is not automatic thoughts. It's that there is no distance between the person and predictions, judgments, and interpretations. Fusion itself is the problem. Fusion then restricts the ability to be moved by contact with direct experience. This exchange shows the process clearly:

> *Therapist:* And when it's happening, when these thoughts—these "should" thoughts—get going, are they up here, right on you? [Therapist holds his hand right in front of his face.] Or are they sort of out there? [Therapist holds his hand a couple of feet away from his face.]
>
> *Sarah:* No, they're right up there on me.
>
> *Therapist:* They're right up on you.
>
> *Sarah:* Almost like I can't breathe.
>
> *Therapist:* Almost like you can't . . . Oh, yeah.
>
> *Sarah:* And when I'm talking to her on the phone like *that* she can be telling me something interesting and I *still* don't wanna talk to her. I mean I don't hate her, but her voice and her mannerisms annoy me.

The effects of fusion as seen in this case are typical. Fusion feeds a problem-solving mode of mind, but treating our inner life that way turns life from a process to be experienced into a problem to be solved.

Defusion

In ACT, therapy itself is viewed as a different context for verbal/cognitive events; the goal is to establish a verbal community that changes how the client *interacts with* or *relates to* thoughts, feelings, and bodily sensations. The main goal is to undermine the excessive literal quality of evaluations and judgments and to relate to them instead as merely aspects of ongoing experience. That is the essence of *defusion*. Exercises, metaphors, and other methods are used to help the client to be able to see that a thought is more like a coffee cup than a lens; that is, it is something one can look *at*, not merely look *from*. In that posture, thoughts need not regulate actions other than mere noticing. They can, if they are helpful, or not, if they are not. The issue is workability toward a goal, not literal "truth."

Let's return to Sarah and show a method for how thoughts can be looked *at*, not *from*.

> *Therapist:* So let's just see if we could sort of take some of that burden off without having to take off the programming. Like, let's just look at how easy it is to get things programmed. If you've got this judgmental critical streak going, sometimes you probably even hear these words in your mother's voice, and I bet you they are so deeply in your head that . . .

Sarah: You're right.

Therapist: Okay, so let's just see how fast it happens. I'm gonna give you three numbers to remember. If you remember them, the people who are doing this filming, they're giving me money, and if you remember them a week from now I'll give you $10,000. Here are the numbers—1, 2, 3. Now if I come back and say, "What are the numbers?" what are you gonna say?

Sarah: The numbers are 1, 2, 3.

Therapist: Oh! Good for you; $10,000. So if I say, "What are the numbers?" you'll say?

Sarah: 1, 2, 3.

Therapist: There's no $10,000. I fibbed. [laughter] If I came back next week, do you suppose you could remember those?

Sarah: I think so.

Therapist: Next month?

Sarah: Probably.

Therapist: It's even possible, possible, next year?

Sarah: Yes.

Therapist: What if a very old man who is bald came up on your deathbed and said, "Sarah, what are the numbers?" Is even that possible?

Sarah: It's possible.

Therapist: I've said it twice. Your mother said these judgmental things to you a hundred times.

Sarah: Daily.

Therapist: They will never leave your head. There's no place for them to go. When you're interacting with her, this voice shows up. What are the numbers?

Sarah: 1, 2, 3.

Therapist: And if I get angry with my mother, then I'm . . .

Sarah: Bad. Oh, I see what you are saying! That's why that guilt and judgment just keep coming up!

The What Are the Numbers? exercise is a classic ACT cognitive defusion method. When the person sees how easy it is to program a human mind, conditioned thoughts take on less literal meaning. Having "1, 2, 3" come to

id'd
unhelpful
thoughts
first

mind (perhaps even for life!) means nothing about Sarah other than that she has a history. This is experientially obvious after this exercise. Yet Sarah is taking "I'm bad" literally, as if it means that there is something wrong with her and that something needs to be changed. By metaphorical extension, she now sees that it too could say nothing more about her than that she has a history. In such a moment, the thought "I'm bad" is being looked *at*, not looked *from*.

There are hundreds of specific ACT defusion methods such as the What Are the Numbers? exercise. We have already mentioned *word repletion*, adding "I am having the thought that ___" before difficult thoughts, saying thoughts in unusual voices, or distilling difficult thoughts down to a word and saying it out loud a number of times. The point is not to ridicule thoughts but rather to be able to notice thought as an ongoing process in the moment. Defusion methods can rapidly reduce the believability and distress produced by thoughts. Some well-researched defusion methods are as short as 30 seconds long (e.g., Masuda et al., 2009).

A common objection to our arguments about defusion versus content change in thinking is that if deliberate change or elimination is difficult, unreliable, or risky, traditional cognitive restructuring should not work or should even be harmful. In fact, there is little evidence that cognitive restructuring is an effective component of traditional cognitive behavior therapy (for a review of that evidence, see Longmore & Worrell, 2007). But why isn't it harmful? Some studies suggest that it is (Haeffel, 2010), but we expect it is usually neutral because detecting and trying to change thoughts can do both positive and negative things. It contains an elementary distancing component that arguably has a defusion effect (noticing your thoughts is a key facet of defusion, an argument similar to that being made by mindfulness researchers in cognitive therapy; see Segal, Teasdale, & Williams, 2004). In addition, thinking about how to change thoughts can encourage greater cognitive flexibility just by generating multiple cognitive variants to consider. Indeed, ACT sometimes uses this process by encouraging clients to formulate their self-narrative in several different ways as a defusion method (Hayes, Strosahl, & Wilson, 1999). ACT theory suggests that negative effects from cognitive restructuring would come from consequences such as greater entanglement with difficult thoughts, increased cues for them, greater chance of thought suppression, or amplification of a neurotic self-focus. These unintended effects would vary with the skill of the clinician (skilled cognitive therapists are trained to avoid most of them) and the propensity of individuals to engage in them. Thus, some individuals would benefit, some would be harmed, and on the whole it would be a wash.

REFERENCES

Haeffel, G. J. (2010). When self-help is no help: Traditional cognitive skills training does not prevent depressive symptoms in people who ruminate. *Behaviour Research and Therapy, 48,* 152–157. doi:10.1016/j.brat.2009.09.016

Hayes, S. C. (2009). *Acceptance and commitment therapy* [DVD]. Washington, DC: American Psychological Association.

Hayes, S. C., Strosahl, K. D., & Wilson, K. G. (1999). *Acceptance and commitment therapy: An experiential approach to behavior change.* New York, NY: Guilford Press.

Longmore, R. J., & Worrell, M. (2007). Do we need to challenge thoughts in cognitive behavior therapy? *Clinical Psychology Review, 27,* 173–187. doi:10.1016/j.cpr.2006.08.001

Masuda, A., Hayes, S. C., Twohig, M. P., Drossel, C., Lillis, J., & Washio, Y. (2009). A parametric study of cognitive defusion and the believability and discomfort of negative self-relevant thoughts. *Behavior Modification, 33,* 250–262. doi:10.1177/0145445508326259

Segal, Z. V., Teasdale, J. D., & Williams, J. M. G. (2004). Mindfulness-based cognitive therapy: Theoretical rationale and empirical status. In S. C. Hayes, V. M. Follette, & M. M. Linehan (Eds.), *Mindfulness and acceptance: Expanding the cognitive-behavioral tradition* (pp. 45–65). New York, NY: Guilford Press.

Wenzlaff, R. M., & Wegner, D. M. (2000). Thought suppression. *Annual Review of Psychology, 51,* 59–91. doi:10.1146/annurev.psych.51.1.59

2

ACCEPTANCE AND COMMITMENT THERAPY PROCESS

STEVEN C. HAYES AND JASON LILLIS

DEFUSION

Have you ever had the thought deep down that you're a horrible person or there is something really wrong with you? Perhaps you came by that thought honestly; maybe somebody told you that, your dad screamed it at you, or you derived it on the basis of painful and traumatic events in your life. It is possible that this thought will be with you from time to time for the rest of your life, at times powerfully so, and could be triggered by just about anything that happens to you. Trying to get it out of your mind means you have to focus on it. It means you have to treat it as important. As you do so, you

Excerpted from *Acceptance and Commitment Therapy* (2012), from Chapter 4, "The Therapy Process," pp. 81–86. Copyright 2012 by the American Psychological Association. Used with permission of the authors.

http://dx.doi.org/10.1037/14295-002
Psychotherapy Theories and Techniques: A Reader, G. R. VandenBos, E. Meidenbauer, and J. Frank-McNeil (Editors)
Copyright © 2014 by the American Psychological Association. All rights reserved.

make it more central, you connect it to more events, and you devote more life moments to it. As a result, you might actually make it more frequent, amplifying its impact on your behavior. Treating thoughts literally is called *cognitive fusion*, and it is a primary target of acceptance and commitment therapy (ACT).

Imagine being in a place where you can have whatever thoughts you have, more as you might watch the dialogue in a movie or a play. You can have the thought, "There's something wrong with me," and, without having to change or get rid of it, you can determine its impact on your life. As you experience that thought with perspective, awareness, and curiosity, that is what you are doing. That is the goal of defusion work.

Fusion is so pervasive that the signs of it are often hard to notice. There may be a loss of your sense of being present, like in a daydream; a sense of being caught up in your thoughts, as though your mind were working overtime; a sense of busyness, comparison, and evaluation. Maybe you're often looking to the future or thinking about the past, as opposed to being connected to the now; there may be a sense of struggling to clarify things. Conversely, defusion contains a sense of lightness, flexibility, presence, consciousness, and playfulness. There is a sense that you have the freedom to direct your behavior without the dominance of certain thoughts. Defusion is simply seeing your thoughts as thoughts, so that what you do is determined more by your choices and less by automatic language processes.

In the subsections that follow, we discuss examples of cognitive fusion processes and techniques designed to address these processes in an attempt to change the context in which thoughts occur. There are hundreds of defusion methods in the ACT literature—these are just a few examples.

Ubiquity

Thoughts are ubiquitous; they are always hanging around. Sometimes they are big or small, loud or soft, good or bad, scary, happy, strange, and so on. But they are there, and they often pull us out of the present moment. It can be useful to simply call this process out and get it in the room. You might consider naming your mind and the mind of your client, noting that there are "four of us" in the room. Or you might refer to the mind as a "word-generating machine" that is constantly churning out thoughts, commenting on everything, judging, having opinions, causing a ruckus. The natural tendency is to look at the world from our thoughts. Defusion allows us to look *at* our thoughts rather than *from* them. *(or through them)*

Watching your thoughts without involvement is inherently defusing. Many mindfulness exercises fit the bill. The Thoughts on Clouds exercise is an example:

> I'd like you to close your eyes and simply follow the sound of my voice. Try to focus your attention on your breathing, and notice as each breath enters and exits your nose or mouth. . . . And now I want you to imagine sitting in a lush field. . . . Notice the trees and foliage, see the blue sky, try to become aware of your surroundings and really see yourself there. . . . And now I want you to lie down and look up to the sky and notice that there are clouds moving at a steady pace across the sky. . . . See if you can focus your attention on your thoughts, and as you become aware of a thought, put it on a cloud and watch it float across the sky. . . . Try to put each thought you have on a cloud and watch it as it goes by. . . . If you notice that you are no longer viewing the clouds from afar, but rather are caught up in a thought, gently bring yourself back to the field, lying down, gazing up at the clouds, and put each thought, one by one, on a cloud.

When you debrief this exercise, it is a good idea to check in with the client about his or her general experiences first. If the client was unable to perform the exercise, some more basic mindfulness training might be needed. Assuming the client was able to follow the exercise, you might want to discuss the experience of watching thoughts versus being caught up in thoughts. Typically clients are able to watch their thoughts for a while but then get caught up in a sticky thought (something personal or with emotional valence) or a process thought (e.g., "Am I doing this right?"), or perhaps worries about the future or past. This distinction is key because you are trying to teach the client to be able to notice the process of thinking. Nobody is able to do this all the time, nor would that be desirable; rather, it is important to be able to catch oneself entangled in thought, so that fusion or defusion can be used on a basis of workability rather than automaticity.

Literality

Swimming in a stream of thoughts, as we often do, we tend to experience our thoughts as being literally true. ACT calls this the *context of literality*, and it can contribute greatly to suffering. We become like a person so lost in a movie that the threats to the characters seem like personal threats: each sudden sound eliciting a startle, each creak on the stairs evoking an urge to flee. We are like that with our mental sounds and creaks because we've forgotten that they are in large part echoes of moments gone by.

If we treat thoughts as literal, then we must be invested in their content. For example, if you have the thought "I am a horrible person," and you take that thought to be literally true, then it makes sense that you would do anything to try and not have that thought or change that thought in some way to make it possible for you to exist in the world and not be a horrible person. However, if you can step back from the screen and notice that there is a "you" and there is also a thought, maybe there is some room there for you to just have that thought as it is, without struggle.

ACT uses a variety of techniques to undermine the literality of thoughts. For example, clients might be asked to imagine that their negative thoughts (e.g., "I'm a failure," "I can't do anything right") are like a radio station that can't be shut off—it's bad news radio, all bad news all the time! They can also imagine a barrage of negative thoughts as pop-up ads from hell. They can't get a spam blocker for these! Another method is to have clients say their thoughts in silly voices, or say them very slow or very fast, or in the voice of themselves as children. Thoughts can be distilled into a single word and said rapidly aloud for 20 to 30 seconds.

It is important not to use these methods to ridicule thoughts. You can explain it to the client like this:

> When you start seeing thoughts the way you would see things like a billboard or a pop-up ad or radio voice, or when you change how you interact with thoughts by speaking them slowly or singing them, or having a puppet say it to you, it gives you just a little space to look at them and use what is useful in them. It's like stepping away from the computer screen. Then maybe this thought is also just a thought, and not necessarily anything that you have to do anything about, and certainly not something that you have to turn over your life to.

Automaticity

Say whatever words come to mind when I give you these partial phrases: "Only the good die . . . [young]" or "A picture is worth . . . [a thousand words]" or "Blondes have more . . . [fun]." These words come as a package in our history. If the words are painful (try this one: "I pretend to be a good person but deep down I'm _____"), we might try to erase them, but all we are doing is adding to them. Try it with any of these statements and you will notice that another word appears and you are initially pleased because it is not ____ [put in the forbidden word], until you realize that "___ is not ___" is yet another relation. There is no healthy eraser. This can be exactly like what is going on with clients. It can help to see how this game is impossible to win:

Therapist:	Tell me, as a child did you believe in Santa Claus?
Client:	Sure. We put cookies out and everything, I'd write a wish list.
Therapist:	Do you still believe in Santa Claus?
Client:	Of course not, but it's fun for the kids.
Therapist:	Yeah. And when you see a rainbow reaching the ground, what's over there?
Client:	[chuckles] A pot of gold.
Therapist:	Funny, everyone says that. Not a pile of gold, not a pot of silver, but a pot of gold. Ever gone digging for it?
Client:	[laughs] No.
Therapist:	Back to Christmas for a moment. When you walk through the toy store in mid-December, what do you see?
Client:	Santa, all the Christmas stuff, elves, reindeer.
Therapist:	And what does that make you think of?
Client:	Santa's toy factory at the North Pole.
Therapist:	Now you don't believe in this stuff, right? But it still comes up. And when you see a rainbow, what pops up in your mind?
Client:	A pot of gold.
Therapist:	Where did these thoughts come from?
Client:	I suppose we're told this stuff when we are kids, by our parents, other people.
Therapist:	And this idea, you haven't done well enough in your life, that you've failed as a person. Where did that come from?
Client:	I don't know, same place, I guess, stuff I've heard, stuff I've put together over the years.
Therapist:	Yeah. And tell me, how would we get rid of the thought of a pot of gold, or the elves?
Client:	Don't know, I guess we don't.
Therapist:	So what about this other stuff—I've failed. . . . I'm not good enough, nothing I do is ever quite good enough, and all the dozens of variations?

[handwritten margin note: like what are the Numbers?]

A classic ACT technique is the What Are the Numbers? exercise we described in the case of Sarah in the chapter on the theory behind ACT. If clients get a sense of the point, the exercise itself can be used as a form of communication: Why should we take our own thoughts so seriously, when they may be nothing more than conditioned events? How silly is it that we are at the whim of their showing up at any time? The point is not to convince clients that their thoughts are wrong, or useless, or silly, but to offer a context in which they can notice that thoughts can be automatic. Maybe your client needn't give such importance to those thoughts or engage in a struggle to change or get rid of them but, rather, can make room for them and let them be, while choosing to live his or her life.

This was done later in the work with Sarah, when discussing her anger and frustration with her mother (it is also worth noting that she is now spontaneously using more defused language as the result of the previous defusion interventions):

Therapist: It's something almost like "I'm bad for feeling that."

Sarah: Yeah. That's it. I think that's the bottom line. I mean all the other sentences come but the bottom-line sentence is "and that means, I'm bad."

Therapist: OK, [offering a tissue] so here comes "I'm bad." What are the numbers?

Sarah: 1, 2, 3.

Therapist: And if I get angry I'm . . . ?

Sarah: Bad.

Therapist: OK, here we go. We'll just let that be there like that [laying the tissue on her knee]. Is that your enemy? Does that have to change before you can be there with yourself and allow yourself to feel what you feel even when your mind says you can't? It's just your conditioning. What are the numbers?

APPENDIX 2.1: ACCEPTANCE AND COMMITMENT THERAPY TECHNIQUES

Technique	Video title	Video identifying number	Time at which technique occurs
Defusion technique	Grief Work With Acceptance and Commitment Therapy	777700245-001 *6*	36:07–41:39
Focused exercise	Grief Work With Acceptance and Commitment Therapy	777700245-001 *1*	03:19–05:18
Guided meditation	Working With Depression and Anxiety With Acceptance and Commitment Therapy	777700244-001 *1*	03:46–15:49
Exposure	Grief Work With Acceptance and Commitment Therapy	777700245-001 *4*	20:56–24:46
Accepting where you are	Grief Work With Acceptance and Commitment Therapy	777700245-001 *2*	08:42–17:35
Acceptance work	Grief Work With Acceptance and Commitment Therapy	777700245-001 *3*	14:56–19:13
Mindfulness exercise	Working With Depression and Anxiety With Acceptance and Commitment Therapy	777700244-001 *1*	03:46–15:49
Noticing breath	Working With Depression and Anxiety With Acceptance and Commitment Therapy	777700244-001 *2*	04:08–10:01
Observer exercise	Grief Work With Acceptance and Commitment Therapy	777700245-001 *5*	25:00–26:06
Uncovering core values	Working With Depression and Anxiety With Acceptance and Commitment Therapy	777700244-001 *3*	20:15–31:43

245 12:53

3

BEHAVIOR THERAPY

MARTIN M. ANTONY AND LIZABETH ROEMER

Reviews of behavior therapy often focus more on the techniques than on the theory underlying them. However, to conduct behavior therapy skillfully, one must understand the conceptual basis and intention of the specific techniques, beginning with the overarching goals of behavior therapy.

GOALS OF BEHAVIOR THERAPIES

The overarching goal of behavior therapies is to help clients develop flexible behavioral repertoires that are sensitive to environmental contingencies and are maximally effective for the individual (e.g., Drossel, Rummel, & Fisher, 2009). From a behavioral perspective, a wide range of clinical

Excerpted from *Behavior Therapy* (2011) from Chapter 3, "Theory," pp. 15–24. Copyright 2011 by the American Psychological Association. Used with permission of the authors.

http://dx.doi.org/10.1037/14295-003
Psychotherapy Theories and Techniques: A Reader, G. R. VandenBos, E. Meidenbauer, and J. Frank-McNeil (Editors)
Copyright © 2014 by the American Psychological Association. All rights reserved.

problems are seen as evidence of habitual, stuck patterns of responding that have developed over time because of associations and contingencies in the environment (which can also include the internal environment, e.g., physical sensations, thoughts, imagery) that maintained these patterns in a given context. Therapy is therefore focused on identifying the factors that are currently maintaining the difficulties in question and on intervening to reduce problematic behaviors and responses and increase more flexible, adaptive behaviors and responses. A central focus is on broadening behavioral repertoires and encouraging alternative, adaptive repertoires that will enhance well-being and functioning, rather than on symptom reduction (Drossel et al., 2009). That is, the intent is to help clients engage in a range of behaviors that are likely to help them function in their lives rather than solely to reduce their anxiety or depressive symptoms.

An initial goal, therefore, is the careful assessment and analysis of presenting problems to determine the contexts in which they occur, the stimuli that trigger their occurrence, and the consequences that maintain them. This functional analysis helps the client and the therapist to see the ways in which problematic patterns of responding emerge in response to specific cues and are maintained by specific consequences. It also helps to determine whether problematic responses can be understood as resulting from learned associations, reinforcing consequences, or skills deficits, which will have implications for intervention. This analysis also helps to determine how multiple problems interact so that treatment targets can be chosen that will optimize positive outcomes by influencing more than one presenting problem. Although people often think of cues and contingencies as explaining only overt, simplistic behavior problems, such as phobias, these same models can be used to understand more complex patterns of responding, such as those that underlie relationship difficulties. For instance, a client who presents for treatment because of relationship concerns might first be asked to monitor when concerning interactions with a partner occur. Functional analysis may reveal that the client has developed a habit of responding to perceived instances of rejection (which take the behavioral form of the client's partner being focused on something else or seeming distant) by feeling hurt and vulnerable. The client may habitually respond to these feelings by expressing anger through criticism or storming out of the room, behaviors that are reinforced by the initial reduction in hurt and vulnerability that the client experiences. However, these behaviors increase the partner's tendency to withdraw, thus perpetuating the problematic cycle of interaction. This analysis provides several potential targets for intervention: the client's learned emotional response to the partner's behavior and the client's behavioral responses to feeling hurt and vulnerable. If the couple were in treatment together, a functional analysis of the partner's behavior would also be conducted, providing additional targets for intervention.

In behavior therapy, the therapist and client collaboratively set specific treatment goals and the therapist shares with the client the model of how these goals will be met. Therapy is active in that the client engages in exercises both within and between sessions designed to develop and strengthen new learning and new patterns of responding and to weaken old, habitual ways of responding. Given the emphasis on new learning, practice is an essential part of treatment, requiring the client to actively engage with the treatment. *Actively engaging* means that it is essential that the client agree with the rationale for and goals of treatment. Therapists need to be sensitive to indications that the conceptualization and plan make sense to the client. As in all treatments, the therapist should be attuned to and familiar with both general cultural views that may affect how a client views health, clinical problems, and goals for treatment and the specific perspective of a client and his or her family. These perspectives should all shape the developing conceptualization and plan.

Behavior therapy is flexible and iterative. Therapists and clients are continually evaluating the impact of interventions and the continued relevance of stated goals. Alterations are made to treatment plans on the basis of the effects of interventions, the feasibility of specific interventions for a given individual, and changing external circumstances. The scientific basis of behavior therapy makes continual hypothesis testing an explicit characteristic of this approach to treatment. The findings from a functional analysis are always treated as a working hypothesis, and ongoing assessment and reflection are used to reevaluate and revise these models and intervention plans in order to promote optimal functioning for the individual.

Thus, the goals of behavior therapy are idiographic and are determined and refined collaboratively in the therapeutic relationship. An overarching goal of flexible, adaptive functioning is consistent across clients and presenting problems, but the specifics of what this will look like for a given individual depend on the context and what is most important to the client. Behavior therapists are careful not to assume that they know what is optimal functioning for an individual, but instead aim to help the individual examine his or her life to determine what will be optimal for her or him.

KEY CONCEPTS IN BEHAVIOR THERAPIES

Behavior therapy is a broad category that encompasses a wide range of intervention strategies, as well as variability in theoretical emphases. Behavior therapists incorporate various behavioral approaches (e.g., cognitive, mindfulness based) to differing degrees. Also, because behavior therapists emphasize the importance of scientific inquiry, theories that underlie these approaches are constantly being refined on the basis of scientific study and discovery. However, several shared theoretical assumptions characterize therapy based in the behavioral tradition. In this chapter, we provide an overview of these theoretical assumptions and also discuss some of the points of disparity among behavior therapists.

Theory plays an important role in behavior therapies that is often overlooked. The importance that behaviorists (and cognitive behaviorists) place on empirical study has led to the development of numerous manualized treatments that can be subjected to careful, controlled evaluation to examine the efficacy of a specific approach. Although this approach has many advantages, one disadvantage is that it can give the impression that behavior therapy is a collection of techniques rather than a coherent way of understanding human behavior and optimizing human functioning. An emphasis on technique can leave clinicians who are implementing interventions at a loss when aspects of a specific strategy do not fit well with a given client. A clear understanding of the theory underlying specific strategies helps therapists to flexibly implement treatments, responding to individual clients' needs while remaining consistent with the underlying model of the treatment. For instance, strategies can be adjusted so that they are more culturally consistent for a given client while still corresponding to the intervention's initial intent. For example, relaxation imagery that incorporates other people may be more resonant for individuals who identify themselves in relation to others than solitary images that are more commonly used, leading these individuals to practice using imagery more regularly and benefit more from treatment (La Roche, D'Angelo, Gualdron, & Leavell, 2006).

All Behavior Serves a Function

A central assumption of behavior therapists is that problematic patterns of behavior happen for a reason. That is, even behaviors that seem to be destructive or clearly harmful to an individual, such as substance dependence, deliberate self-harm, or an abusive relationship, make sense in the context of an individual's learning history. In the context of behavior therapy, the term *behavior* applies to a wide range of client responses, including thoughts, physiological responses, emotional responses, and covert behaviors as well as overt behaviors. Using a behavioral conceptualization, even responses that seem irrational, such as extreme anxiety in response to apparently nonthreatening cues or guilt and shame in response to apparently benign interpersonal exchanges, happen because of biological predispositions and prior learning experiences that have shaped a client to have certain types of responses to particular stimuli. In this way, puzzling behaviors can actually be explained and understood because of previous learning experiences (which we describe in more detail shortly).

Thus, a central goal in behavior therapies is to determine the potential function of presenting problems. This determination serves several purposes in therapy. First, as the therapist and client work together to understand why the client is repeatedly having responses or engaging in behaviors that she or he sees as problematic, these puzzling responses begin to make more sense and seem less baffling. More important, the client often experiences a reduction in self-blame and criticism as a result of this increased understanding of why she or he is responding in this way. For instance, clients with a long-standing history of anxiety often experience relief when the fight-or-flight response, paths to learning fear, and the natural but fear-maintaining response of avoidance are explained to them. Although this understanding alone is often not enough to alter responding, it does often help to reduce the criticism, judgment, and shame that can exacerbate anxious responding and further interfere with relationships and general functioning.

Although the validation that comes with a behavioral conceptualization is likely an active ingredient in behavior therapies, a more important goal is the identification of targets for intervention and strategies that will promote new learning that is more adaptive and growth enhancing. An understanding of principles of learning (described more fully in the next section) is an important foundation in developing intervention strategies that will most efficiently lead to robust new learning.

BEHAVIOR IS LEARNED; NEW BEHAVIOR CAN BE LEARNED THROUGH EARLY CUE DETECTION AND PRACTICE

Behavior therapies are based on an assumption that individuals have learned to respond and act in the ways they habitually respond and act through identifiable principles of learning. Behavior therapies evolved from experimental research that detailed these learning principles. Modern behavior therapies are similarly informed by newer developments in experimental research that have identified complexities in principles of learning (e.g., Bouton, Mineka, & Barlow, 2001; Craske et al., 2008). An in-depth discussion of these principles and complexities is beyond the scope of this book (see Bouton, Woods, Moody, Sunsay, & García-Gutiérrez, 2006; Craske & Mystkowski, 2006; O'Donohue & Fisher, 2009), but we provide a summary so that therapists can use these principles to guide implementation of behavior therapies.

Learning Through Association

Both humans and animals learn to associate stimuli that frequently appear together. *Classical conditioning* refers to the process through which a previously neutral stimulus becomes associated with a stimulus that evokes certain responses (either aversive or appetitive). Through being repeatedly paired with an unconditioned stimulus (US) that naturally evokes a given response, the conditioned stimulus (CS) becomes a cue for the US and elicits similar or related responses. This process is clearly evolutionarily adaptive in that organisms learn that the presence of certain stimuli indicates that a threat is likely to appear or that something desirable is likely to appear, and respond accordingly. Once a stimulus has been conditioned, it can lead to new learning by being paired with another previously neutral stimulus, which will in turn come to be associated with the CS and elicit similar or related responses.[1] Through this process of higher order conditioning, more stimuli come to be associated with undesirable or desirable events. Also, through stimulus generalization, stimuli that are similar to the CS also become learned cues, so that eventually a broad range of stimuli are associated and evoke similar responses. For instance, a learned fear of a bright red shirt might lead an individual to respond with anxiety or fear to anything red in the environment.

A client, Monique, can be used to illustrate these principles. Monique presented for therapy reporting that she was anxious and uneasy in social situations. A functional analysis, including monitoring of her symptoms and exploration of specific incidents of anxiety during the previous week, revealed that she responded with physiological arousal and anxious thoughts when she interacted with people who looked or sounded critical. She described her father as extremely critical when she was growing up and stated that he would often turn his attention to other people or walk away after he had criticized her for something. In this example, this withdrawal of attention and affection from a parent was a US that would have naturally elicited fear in a child. Its pairing with criticism from her father led Monique to respond to her father's criticism with anxiety because she anticipated the removal of his attention and affection. Gradually, these associations generalized, and she came to have similar responses to any instances of perceived criticism, leading her to feel anxious in a broad range of social situations.

People are particularly prone to learning threatening cues because it is evolutionarily adaptive to identify markers for potential harm and danger so

---

[1]Initially, this learning process was thought to involve learning a response to a stimulus because that stimulus had been associated with another stimulus that automatically elicited that response. However, an extensive body of research has demonstrated that an association is learned between the previously neutral stimulus and the US and that associations are also learned regarding the context in which these pairings take place (Rescorla, 1988). In addition, conditioning can result in a different response to the CS than the response to the US, one that is preparatory for the potential occurrence of the US and matched to the properties of the CS (Rescorla, 1988). Although classical conditioning continues to often be described in terms of learning responses, the term *learned associations* is a technically more accurate description of this type of learning.

that individuals can avoid this harm or danger. In addition, some individuals are probably biologically predisposed to learn threat more easily and robustly and are therefore more prone to anxiety (e.g., Lonsdorf et al., 2009). Prior experiences with threat, or modeling of fear behavior by significant role models, may also make it more likely that an individual will easily learn to fear cues, and those responses will generalize (Mineka & Zinbarg, 2006). Biology, prior experiences, and modeling likely play a role in other kinds of learning, such as the reinforcing properties of alcohol and drugs (e.g., Enoch, 2007).

Initial models of associative learning identified the conditions under which learned associations (to CSs) could be extinguished such that an organism no longer responded to the CS as though it were associated with the US. Further study has indicated that the term *extinction* is a misnomer because associations are not, in fact, unlearned. Instead, new, competing, nonthreatening associations are learned. So, in the case of fear conditioning, repeated exposure to the CS in the absence of the US will lead to a new, nonthreatening association to the CS, such that fear is no longer the predominant response. Extinction can therefore be thought of as *inhibitory learning* (Craske et al., 2008) in that an association that inhibits the previous association is learned. Rescorla and Wagner (1972) noted that learning is an adjustment that occurs when there is a discrepancy between the outcome that is expected and the outcome that occurs. So extinction trials promote new learning in that the expected association does not occur, so that the CS comes to be associated with "not US" instead of the US.

Bouton et al. (2006) reviewed the literature that suggests that conditioned associations, as well as conditions that are likely to make extinction or inhibitory learning more robust, are not unlearned. Animal research has demonstrated that even after extensive extinction of fearful associations, the continued presence of these associations is demonstrated by (a) a renewal effect, in which a learned association to a CS returns when the CS is presented in a different context from the extinction trials; (b) spontaneous recovery, in which a learned association to a CS returns after the passage of time; (c) reinstatement, in which a learned association to a CS returns after the US is presented alone and the CS is presented later; and (d) rapid reacquisition, in which an association to a previously extinguished CS is learned much more rapidly in new conditioning trials. All of these phenomena suggest that a learned fearful association is maintained despite successful extinction. Bouton et al. interpreted these findings as evidence that extinction learning is context specific, which makes sense from an evolutionary standpoint—people learn cues for fear easily, and generalize them, yet learning of inhibitory responses to feared stimuli is more context specific. This serves an important survival function in that individuals will not prematurely learn that a given stimulus is safe simply because it was safe in a specific context. However, it makes it more likely that learned fears will recur, making it important for therapists to address relapse prevention in therapy, so that clients are prepared for these recurrences and are able to continue to approach feared stimuli to promote more robust extinction learned across multiple contexts. Researchers have also suggested that the presence of retrieval cues during extinction trials will help extinction (or inhibitory learning) generalize to novel contexts (Craske et al., 2008).

Although associative learning is often described in terms of learned associations to external stimuli, there is also extensive evidence that organisms learn associations to internal stimuli as well (for an extensive review of this literature in the context of panic disorder, see Bouton et al., 2001). As a result, people's own internal sensations can become threat cues, leading them to respond with anxiety, which strengthens the cue, potentially leading to a spiral of anxiety or panic. From a behavioral perspective, thoughts can also become associated with a US. As such, thoughts or memories of a traumatic event can elicit posttraumatic responses, even in the absence of the event itself. Thoughts can also have appetitive associations, so that a thought of a drink can lead to a powerful conditioned response of craving for an individual addicted to alcohol. Because these internal cues are beyond people's instrumental control (they cannot avoid thoughts of drinking or anxious sensations completely), these associations are particularly likely to lead to clinical problems. As such, learning new associations to these cues is often an important target of treatment (as is learning not to respond to them behaviorally).

REFERENCES

Bouton, M. E., Mineka, S., & Barlow, D. H. (2001). A modern learning theory perspective on the etiology of panic disorder. *Psychological Review, 108*, 4–32. doi:10.1037/0033-295X.108.1.4

Bouton, M. E., Woods, A. M., Moody, E. W., Sunsay, C., & García-Gutiérrez, A. (2006). Counteracting the context-dependence of extinction: Relapse and tests of some relapse prevention methods. In M. G. Craske, D. Hermans, & D. Vansteenwegen (Eds.), *Fear and learning: From basic processes to clinical implications* (pp. 175–196). Washington, DC: American Psychological Association. doi:10.1037/11474-009

Craske, M. G., Kircanski, K., Zelikowsky, M., Mystkowski, J., Chowdhury, N., & Baker, A. (2008). Optimizing inhibitory learning during exposure therapy. *Behaviour Research and Therapy, 46*, 5–27. doi:10.1016/j.brat.2007.10.003

Craske, M. G., & Mystkowski, J. L. (2006). Exposure therapy and extinction: Clinical studies. In M. G. Craske, D. Hermans, & D. Vansteenwegen (Eds.), *Fear and learning: From basic processes to clinical implications* (pp. 217–233). Washington, DC: American Psychological Association. doi:10.1037/11474-011

Drossel, C., Rummel, C., & Fisher, J. E. (2009). Assessment and cognitive behavior therapy: Functional analysis as key process. In W. T. O'Donohue & J. E. Fisher (Eds.), *General principles and empirically supported techniques of cognitive behavior therapy* (pp. 15–41). Hoboken, NJ: Wiley.

Enoch, M. (2007). Genetics, stress, and risk for addiction. In M. Al'Absi (Ed.), *Stress and addiction: Psychological and biological mechanisms* (pp. 127–146). San Diego, CA: Elsevier. doi:10.1016/B978-012370632-4/50009-7

La Roche, M. J., D'Angelo, E., Gualdron, L., & Leavell, J. (2006). Culturally sensitive guided imagery for allocentric Latinos: A pilot study. *Psychotherapy: Theory, Research, Practice, Training, 43*, 555–560. doi:10.1037/0033-3204.43.4.555

Lonsdorf, T. B., Weike, A. I., Nikamo, P., Schalling, M., Hamm, A. O., & Öhman, A. (2009). Genetic gating of human fear learning and extinction: Possible implications for gene-environment interaction in anxiety disorder. *Psychological Science, 20*, 198–206. doi:10.1111/j.1467-9280.2009.02280.x

Mineka, S., & Zinbarg, R. (2006). A contemporary learning theory perspective on the etiology of anxiety disorders: It's not what you thought it was. *American Psychologist, 61*, 10–26. doi:10.1037/0003-066X.61.1.10

O'Donohue, W. T., & Fisher, J. E. (Eds.). (2009). *General principles and empirically supported techniques of cognitive behavior therapy*. Hoboken, NJ: Wiley.

Rescorla, R. A. (1988). Pavlovian conditioning: It's not what you think it is. *American Psychologist, 43*, 151–160. doi:10.1037/0003-066X.43.3.151

Rescorla, R. A., & Wagner, A. R. (1972). A theory of Pavlovian conditioning: Variations in the effectiveness of reinforcement and nonreinforcement. In A. H. Black & W. F. Prokasy (Eds.), *Classical conditioning II: Current research and theory* (pp. 64–99). New York, NY: Appleton Century Crofts.

4

BEHAVIOR THERAPY PROCESS

MARTIN M. ANTONY AND LIZABETH ROEMER

EXPOSURE-BASED STRATEGIES

In the context of behavior therapy, the term *exposure* refers to the repeated and systematic confrontation of feared stimuli (Moscovitch, Antony, & Swinson, 2009). Many behavior therapists consider it to be an essential component of behavioral treatment for most anxiety disorders, as well as for certain related conditions. It has long been established in research with animals and humans that repeated exposure leads to a reduction in fear responding. Habituation is often cited in the literature as a mechanism to explain how exposure works, although the pattern of change seen in exposure is not consistent with what one might expect after habituation (Moscovitch et al., 2009). For example, in habituation (as it is typically defined) no new

Excerpted from *Behavior Therapy* (2011) from Chapter 4, "The Therapy Process," pp. 59–63. Copyright 2011 by the American Psychological Association. Used with permission of the authors.

http://dx.doi.org/10.1037/14295-004
Psychotherapy Theories and Techniques: A Reader, G. R. VandenBos, E. Meidenbauer, and J. Frank-McNeil (Editors)
Copyright © 2014 by the American Psychological Association. All rights reserved.

learning occurs, and there is a full reinstatement of the response after a short break; neither of these is true in the case of exposure (Tryon, 2005). Rather, models relying on the occurrence of new inhibitory associative learning or extinction seem to explain the effects of exposure much better than habituation models (for reviews, see Moscovitch et al., 2009; Tryon, 2005).

The contemporary behavior therapy literature typically refers to three types of exposure: in vivo exposure, imaginal exposure, and interoceptive exposure. *In vivo exposure* involves exposure to external situations and objects in real life (e.g., entering social situations to reduce anxiety around other people, practicing driving to overcome a fear of driving), while minimizing any forms of avoidance, such as distraction. It is a standard component of evidence-based treatments for specific phobias, social anxiety disorder, agoraphobia, obsessive–compulsive disorder (OCD), posttraumatic stress disorder (PTSD), and other problems in which an individual has an exaggerated fear of some external object or situation. Typically, the difficulty of exposures is increased gradually across sessions, although some forms of exposure therapy involve confronting the most frightening stimuli right from the start (a process sometimes referred to as *flooding*).

Imaginal exposure involves exposure in imagination to thoughts, memories, imagery, impulses, and other cognitive stimuli and is most often used in evidence-based treatments for OCD (e.g., exposure to obsessional thoughts of stabbing a loved one) and PTSD (e.g., exposure to a feared traumatic memory). Imaginal exposure may involve having the client describe a feared stimulus aloud or in writing or having the client listen to a verbal description of the feared stimulus, either in the form of an audio recording or described out loud by the therapist. The therapist encourages the client to imagine the stimulus vividly, with all of her or his senses, to maximize the new associative learning that takes place (i.e., the nonfearful associations to the range of conditioned stimuli present).

Interoceptive exposure involves purposely experiencing feared physical sensations until they are no longer frightening. It is used most often in the treatment of panic disorder. Examples of commonly used interoceptive exposure exercises include breathing through a straw to induce breathlessness, spinning in a chair to induce dizziness, and hyperventilation to induce breathlessness and dizziness.

Exposure may involve other stimuli as well. For example, exposure to visual stimuli in photos or on video is often used in the treatment of blood and needle phobias (Antony & Watling, 2006) and fears of certain animals, such as snakes, spiders, bugs, and rodents (Antony & McCabe, 2005). Exposure using computer-generated stimuli in virtual reality is also increasingly being used for the treatment of certain phobias and other anxiety disorders (Parsons & Rizzo, 2008).

Because behavioral models for disorders have begun to focus particularly on the role of avoidance of emotions (e.g., Barlow, Allen, & Choate, 2004; Mennin & Fresco, 2010) in maintaining difficulties, explicit exposure to emotional responses (which has always been a part of exposure-based treatment) has been proposed as an effective intervention. Therapists might ask clients to imagine emotional situations or view emotionally evocative film clips to reduce avoidance of their own emotional responses.

GUIDELINES FOR EFFECTIVE EXPOSURE

A number of factors have been found to affect outcomes after exposure-based treatments. First, exposure seems to work best when it is predictable (i.e., the client knows what is going to happen and when it is going to happen) and when it is under the client's control (i.e., the client controls the intensity and duration of the practice; see Antony & Swinson, 2000). Second, exposure works best when sessions are prolonged. Two-hour exposures have been found to be more effective than 30-minute exposures (Stern & Marks, 1973). However, contrary to previous assumptions, it may not be necessary for fear to decrease in any particular exposure session for a client to show improvement across sessions (Craske & Mystkowski, 2006). Third, exposure seems to work best when practices are not too spread out, particularly early in treatment (Foa, Jameson, Turner, & Payne, 1980). A number of other variables can influence the outcomes of exposure, including the extent to which the context of exposure is varied and the extent to which safety behaviors (e.g., distraction) are used during exposure practices (for a review, see Abramowitz, Deacon, & Whiteside, 2011; Antony & Swinson, 2000).

EXPOSURE HIERARCHIES

Before starting exposure therapy, the therapist and client typically develop an exposure hierarchy, which is subsequently used to guide exposure practices. The hierarchy usually includes 10 to 15 situations. Each item is rated in terms of how much fear it would typically generate and how likely the client would be to avoid the situation, using a Likert-type scale (e.g., ranging from 0 to 100, where 0 = *no fear or avoidance* and 100 = *maximum fear and avoidance*). Ratings are used to determine the order of items, such that the most difficult items are at the top of the list and the less difficult items are at the bottom. Table 4.1, "Exposure Hierarchy for Social Anxiety Disorder," includes an example of an exposure hierarchy for an individual with a diagnosis of social anxiety disorder.

TABLE 4.1.
Exposure Hierarchy for Social Anxiety Disorder

Item	Description	Fear	Avoidance
1	Attend Rick's birthday party, where I will not know anyone except for Rick.	100	100
2	Arrange for a date with a woman I met online.	100	100
3	Eat dinner in a fancy restaurant with a single woman whom I do not know well.	100	100
4	Have lunch with three coworkers in a casual restaurant.	90	100
5	Have lunch with Rick in a casual restaurant.	80	80
6	Participate three times in a single weekly staff meeting at work.	75	90
7	Ask different people at the mall for directions (repeat for 45 min).	60	60
8	Talk to coworkers on Monday about what I did on the weekend.	50	50
9	Talk to women online through a web-based dating service.	50	50
10	Sit on a crowded bus for 45 min and make eye contact with other passengers.	45	50
11	Get my hair cut and chat with the stylist.	40	40
12	Go for a walk in my neighborhood, during the day, on a Saturday.	40	40
13	Order a pizza by phone.	25	25

Note. Fear and avoidance are rated on scales ranging from 0 to 100. *Fear* refers to the level of fear that a client expects to experience if he or she were to practice the item. *Avoidance* refers to the likelihood that he or she would avoid the situation.

RESPONSE PREVENTION

Response prevention refers to the inhibition or blocking of a learned behavioral response to a stimulus, with the goal of breaking the association between the stimulus and the response (Nock, 2005). The process may be facilitated by physically preventing the unwanted behavior (e.g., turning off the main water source so a client with OCD cannot wash his or her hands) or using reinforcement for not engaging in the unwanted behavior (e.g., complimenting a client for his or her success at refraining from nail biting).

Response prevention is most often discussed in the context of treating OCD, in which it is also referred to as *ritual prevention*. Compulsive rituals are believed to have the same functions as safety behaviors, avoidance, and escape—namely, to prevent the occurrence of harm and to reduce fear, anxiety, and distress. Compulsions are also thought to help maintain fear of relevant obsessional thoughts, situations, and objects. Therefore, along with exposure to feared stimuli, individuals with OCD are typically encouraged to prevent their compulsive rituals.

In addition to the treatment of OCD, response prevention is used to reduce the occurrence of safety behaviors in other anxiety-based disorders and to reduce problematic impulsive behaviors (e.g., hair pulling in trichotillomania).

REFERENCES

Abramowitz, J. S., Deacon, B. J., & Whiteside, S. P. H. (2011). *Exposure therapy for anxiety: Principles and practice*. New York, NY: Guilford Press.

Antony, M. M., & McCabe, R. E. (2005). *Overcoming animal and insect phobias: How to conquer fear of dogs, snakes, rodents, bees, spiders, and more*. Oakland, CA: New Harbinger.

Antony, M. M., & Swinson, R. P. (2000). *Phobic disorders and panic in adults: A guide to assessment and treatment*. Washington, DC: American Psychological Association. doi:10.1037/10348-000

Antony, M. M., & Watling, M. A. (2006). *Overcoming medical phobias: How to conquer fear of blood, needles, doctors, and dentists*. Oakland, CA: New Harbinger.

Barlow, D. H., Allen, L. B., & Choate, M. L. (2004). Toward a unified treatment for emotional disorders. *Behavior Therapy, 35*, 205–230. doi:10.1016/S0005-7894(04)80036-4

Craske, M. G., & Mystkowski, J. L. (2006). Exposure therapy and extinction: Clinical studies. In M. G. Craske, D. Hermans, & D. Vansteenwegen (Eds.), *Fear and learning: From basic processes to clinical implications* (pp. 217–233). Washington, DC: American Psychological Association. doi:10.1037/11474-011

Foa, E. B., Jameson, J. S., Turner, R. M., & Payne, L. L. (1980). Massed vs. spaced exposure sessions in the treatment of agoraphobia. *Behaviour Research and Therapy, 18*, 333–338. doi:10.1016/0005-7967(80)90092-3

Mennin, D. S., & Fresco, D. M. (2010). Emotion regulation as an integrative framework for understanding and treating psychopathology. In A. M. Kring & D. M. Sloan (Eds.), *Emotion regulation and psychopathology: A transdiagnostic approach to etiology and treatment* (pp. 356–379). New York, NY: Guilford Press.

Moscovitch, D. A., Antony, M. M., & Swinson, R. P. (2009). Exposure-based treatments for anxiety disorders: Theory and process. In M. M. Antony & M. B. Stein (Eds.), *Oxford handbook of anxiety and related disorders* (pp. 461–475). New York, NY: Oxford University Press.

Nock, M. K. (2005). Response prevention. In M. Hersen & J. Rosqvist (Eds.), *Encyclopedia of behavior modification and cognitive behavior therapy: Vol. 1. Adult clinical applications* (pp. 489–493). Thousand Oaks, CA: Sage.

Parsons, T. D., & Rizzo, A. A. (2008). Affective outcomes of virtual reality exposure therapy for anxiety and specific phobias: A meta-analysis. *Journal of Behavior Therapy and Experimental Psychiatry, 39*, 250–261. doi:10.1016/j.jbtep.2007.07.007

Stern, R., & Marks, I. (1973). Brief and prolonged flooding: A comparison in agoraphobic patients. *Archives of General Psychiatry, 28*, 270–276.

Tryon, W. W. (2005). Possible mechanisms for why desensitization and exposure therapy work. *Clinical Psychology Review, 25*, 67–95. doi:10.1016/j.cpr.2004.08.005

APPENDIX 4.1: BEHAVIOR THERAPY TECHNIQUES

Technique	Video title	Video identifying number	Time at which technique occurs
Self-monitoring	A Challenging Behavioral Assessment With a Client Who (Maybe) Wants to Quit Smoking	777700019-001	2:57–4:50
Psychoeducation	Quitting Smoking With Multi-component Behavioral Treatment	777700018-001	19:29–20:50
Exposure-based strategies	Exposure Therapy for Obsessive-Compulsive Disorder	777700163-001	25:00–39:11
Response prevention	Exposure Therapy for Obsessive-Compulsive Disorder	777700163-001	25:00–39:11
Reinforcement	A Challenging Behavioral Assessment With a Client Who (Maybe) Wants to Quit Smoking	777700019-001	9:55–10:40
Relaxation	Quitting Smoking With Multi-component Behavioral Treatment	777700018-001	45:20–47:44
Problem-solving training	Quitting Smoking With Multi-component Behavioral Treatment	777700018-001	22:45–25:17
Stimulus control procedures	Quitting Smoking With Multi-component Behavioral Treatment	777700018-001	28:05–29:54

5

BRIEF DYNAMIC THERAPY

HANNA LEVENSON

attachmt : motiv
I/R : frame
Exper/aff : process of change

The integrative view of time-limited dynamic psychotherapy (TLDP) intertwines three substantive approaches that have complex, overlapping historic and clinical perspectives, each one pertaining to a different focus of the clinical work. The first leg of this theoretical stool is *attachment theory*, which provides the motivational rationale for the therapy. From attachment theory, one can answer the questions "Why do people behave as they do?" "What is necessary for mental health, and how does mental illness occur?" The second support comes from *interpersonal–relational theory*, which forms the frame or platform for the therapy. "What is the medium in which the therapy occurs?" The third leg emphasizes the *experiential–affective component*, which is concerned with the process of change. "What needs to shift for change to occur?" When I am working clinically, I experienced these three perspectives

Excerpted from *Brief Dynamic Therapy* (2010), from Chapter 3, "Theory," pp. 29–36. Copyright 2010 by the American Psychological Association. Used with permission of the author.

http://dx.doi.org/10.1037/14295-005

Psychotherapy Theories and Techniques: A Reader, G. R. VandenBos, E. Meidenbauer, and J. Frank-McNeil (Editors)
Copyright © 2014 by the American Psychological Association. All rights reserved.

as inseparable and reinforcing one another—all contributing to support a stable base from which to do therapy.[1] In the next section each component will be examined so that the reader can better understand my current perspectives on the theory and practice of TLDP.

ATTACHMENT THEORY

Attachment in Infancy

Attachment theory maintains that infants manifest an instinctive behavioral repertoire (the attachment behavioral system) in the service of maintaining physical closeness to caregivers. From an attachment perspective, we are hardwired to gravitate toward "older and wiser" others particularly during times of stress or threat. Moreover, we are genetically programmed to solicit attention from our caregivers on whom we are dependent because our very existence depends on this vital bond. Infants' ability to elicit such attention is then maintained through a *mutual feedback loop* in which caregivers (usually initially mothers) are socially reinforced by their infants for engaging in attentional behaviors (e.g., the infant's steady gaze reinforces the mother's cooing and staring back, which then encourages the infant to fixate on her face and engage in smiling behaviors that again results in more rapt attention from mother). There is ample research to indicate that some of an infant's ability to imitate the social behavior of another (e.g., stick out one's tongue after seeing the mother stick out her tongue) and to respond to social cues from a caregiver is not learned and is already available in the infant's behavioral repertoire just a few hours after birth (Meltzoff & Moore, 1977).

The literature on attachment theory and its application to understanding human development is enormous and spans nearly 40 years (Obegi & Berant, 2008). John Bowlby's classic trilogy on attachment, separation, and loss (1969, 1973, 1980) highlighted the importance of the emotional quality of early childhood for understanding psychopathology. Through observations, consultations, and the empirical/theoretical literature that existed at the time, Bowlby concluded that

> the young child's hunger for his [sic] mother's love and presence is as great as his hunger for food, and that in consequence her absence inevitably generates a powerful sense of loss and anger. . . . Thus we reached the

---

[1]Each of these three components has been identified as an empirically supported, therapeutic change principle in the modern practice of psychotherapy (e.g., Castonguay & Beutler, 2005; Neborsky, 2006).

conclusion that loss of mother-figure, either by itself or in combination with other variables yet to be clearly identified, is capable of generating responses and processes that are of the greatest interest to psychopathology. (1969, p. xiii)[2]

Bowlby noticed that infants had a large repertoire of behaviors to keep their mothers close and interactive. He believed the infant had acquired this behavioral repertoire gradually over the course of evolution; those infants who could connect had a better chance of passing on their DNA to future generations. "Bowlby viewed the human infant's reliance on, and emotional bond with, its mother to be the result of a *fundamental instinctual behavioral system* that, unlike Freud's sexual libido concept, was relational without being sexual" (Mikulincer & Shaver, 2007, p. 7, emphasis added).

Attachment Patterns

While attachment originally pertained to an infant's proximity seeking, Bowlby later wrote of how the attachment needs and behaviors continue throughout the life cycle, with adults turning to other adults, especially in times of stress. As he stated in his treatise on healthy human development, *A Secure Base* (1988), "All of us, *from the cradle to the grave*, are happiest when life is organized as a series of excursions, long or short, from the secure base provided by our attachment figure(s)" (p. 62, emphasis added). We probably have no stronger example of this in modern times than when so many people in the Twin Towers on 9/11, when faced with a certain, horrific death, reached for their cell phones for the sole purpose of making contact with loved ones.

The analysts called Bowlby a behaviorist (the ultimate condemnation, no doubt) because of his interest in animal research and in observing the actual behavior of children. But quite to the contrary, the behaviorists would have nothing to do with his ideas. During this time, John Watson, for example, was cautioning parents not to reward crying children with attention. "Never hug and kiss them . . . never let them sit in your lap. If you must, kiss them once on the forehead when they say goodnight" (Watson, 1928, as quoted by Lewis, Amini, & Lannon, 2001, p. 71).

Ainsworth, an American colleague of Bowlby's, developed an experimental procedure to assess the attachment patterns of infants called the "Strange Situation" (Ainsworth, 1969). In this situation, infants came with

---

[2]When Bowlby heard Harry Harlow speak at an American Psychological Association Convention in 1958, he immediately saw the relevancy of Harlow's work with rhesus monkeys who preferred a "cloth mother," even though they were fed by a wire mesh "mother" (Karen, 1998).

their mothers into a room with a one-way mirror. The infants would spend some time in the room with their mothers, an experimenter, and a variety of toys. At some point the mother would leave the child alone with the experimenter who recorded the child's behavior. When the mother came back a short time later, the child's behavior was again noted. Infants who were classified as *secure* were able to use their mothers as a home base as they explored their new surroundings. When their mothers left, they were obviously distressed, but they were able to be soothed by her return and resume constructive play. Children who were classified as *avoidant* exhibited little visible distress when their mothers left and did not greet her upon her return. They seemed more interested in the toys, but their play was not particularly creative.[3] These children were thought to have deactivated their attachment system. The children labeled as *anxious–ambivalent* looked distressed even when they entered the room with their mothers. When their mothers left, they cried and were visibly angry. At reunion, these children were not able to be comforted and remained hyperaroused, unable to return to their play activities.

Internal Working Models

Bowlby's formulations about the significance of internal working models help therapists understand how patterns of attachment might be maintained over time.[4] He postulated that "an internal psychological organization with a number of highly specific features, which include representational models of the self and of attachment figure(s)" (1988, p. 29), develops over time and is built up through a series of experiences with caregivers throughout one's early life. Thus the child not only has an internalized set of expectancies about how he or she will be treated by others, but also an internalized model of how one sees, feels about, and treats one's self that is a reflection of how one has been treated by others.

Bowlby postulated that a securely attached child (i.e., a child who has been responded to by caregivers in a contingent, helpful, and loving manner whether distressed or contented) comes to expect that there are no aspects of the self that cannot be noticed, responded to, and dealt with. However, children who are not securely attached (i.e., who have been responded to sporadically, noncontingently, inadequately, or inappropriately) learn that when they are under threat, they cannot count on others to keep them safe.

---

[3]It should be noted that while the avoidant children did not appear distressed, measurements of their physiology showed high degrees of activation. Thus, with children and adults classified as avoidant, there is often marked internal distress with behavioral suppression.

[4]According to Mikulincer and Shaver (2007), the term *working* models was to connote two ideas: (a) the models are heuristic—that is, they are pragmatically useful in predicting likely outcomes, and (b) the models are provisional—that is, they are changeable as in a *working* title (p. 15).

insecure

Insecurely attached children get a ~~quadruple whammy~~. First, they have models of self and/or others that are negative; second, they also have considerable difficulty self-correcting these harmful internalized models because of difficulties cognitively and emotionally perceiving disconfirmatory incoming information; third, since their working models or templates are derived and perpetuated out of awareness, they continue to be at their mercy. I am reminded of the saying that a fish has no idea of water. So it is with working models. They have an enormous impact on our lives, but we take them for granted as the way life is. Wachtel (2008) points out a fourth way insecurely attached children are affected. The stability of their internal working models persists in part because the ongoing interactions with the very people who gave rise to these experiences also persist (e.g., parents who were harsh toward their child as an infant are harsh when the child is a toddler and harsh when the child is an adolescent).

Adult Attachment

How does one understand the relevancy of attachment theory for adults? As Bowlby stated, attachment is significant from "cradle to grave," but by the time people are adults, they normally do not need the proximity to another human being to survive. Adults feel secure when their attachment figures have confirmed "that (a) they are loved and lovable people, and (b) they are competent or have mastery over their environment" (Pietromonaco & Feldman Barrett, 2000, p. 167). Over the years, this builds up a sense of _felt security_ that individuals internalize and carry with them throughout the life span (Stroufe & Waters, 1977).

Shaver and Mikulincer (2008) delineate the three critical functions necessary for a person to reach adult attachment figure status: (a) this person is sought out at times of stress, or this person's undesired leaving creates distress and protest; (b) this person creates a "safe haven" because he/she is a source of comfort, protection, or security; and (c) this person provides a "secure base" from which the adult can explore the world, take risks, and pursue self-development. Bowlby (1969/1982) acknowledged that a variety of people, personages (like God), or even institutions could be seen as attachment figures. In addition, the mental representations of these central figures (or of oneself) also can be a source of felt security and comfort. In a series of ingenious studies (see Shaver & Mikulincer, 2008), it has been demonstrated that activation of mental representations of attachment figures (e.g., asking people to visualize the faces of such figures) promotes a positive feeling, reduces painful or hurt feelings, and fosters empathy. (As a mini-experiment right now, the reader could take a moment and imagine seeing the face of someone who has provided comfort and security. Are you aware of having more positive feelings and an increased sense of well-being?)

Mary Main, a student of Ainsworth's, developed the Adult Attachment Interview (AAI; Main, Kaplan, & Cassidy, 1985) to explore the mental representations of adults' attachment as children to their parents. The AAI asks people to respond to specific questions about their relationships with their parents when they were young. For example, "Could you give me five adjectives or phrases to describe your relationship with your mother during childhood?" Those interviewed are then classified into one of three attachment styles— secure, dismissing, or preoccupied—corresponding to the three categories found for infants in the Strange Situation.

Secure adults describe their pasts (even those that were distressing) in a clear and coherent manner; dismissing adults give few examples of their relationships with parents and offer sparse, minimizing responses (e.g., "My relationship with my mother was fine"); and preoccupied adults' responses show an inability to pull back from their anger and/or anxiety, apparently overwhelmed by their feelings. Thus, the securely attached individuals demonstrate *autobiographical competence* (Holmes, 1993; Siegel, 1999); they are able to tell a coherent story of how the past affected them and why they are the way they are. Furthermore, they are able to *mentalize* (Fonagy & Target, 2006); they can "interpret others' minds, which in turn fostered the ability to read and understand one's own mental states, especially those mental states that are based on emotions" (Jurist & Meehan, 2008, p. 72). Such autobiographical competence and the ability to mentalize have been hypothesized to be central to affect regulation and mental health in general.[5]

Attachment-Based Therapy

Although there is no specific "attachment therapy" for adults, the relevance of attachment theory for therapeutic formulation and intervention is enormous. Bowlby (1988) outlined five therapeutic tasks—all revolving around the therapist's role of providing "conditions in which his [sic] patient can explore his representational models of himself and his attachment figures with a view to reappraising and restructuring them in the light of the *new understanding* he acquires and the *new experiences* he has in the therapeutic relationship" (p. 138, emphasis added). Specifically, the therapist must: (a) provide a secure base, a "trusted companion," so that the painful aspects

---

[5]Siegel and Hartzell (2003) wrote a book for parents to help them understand that they could promote their children's mental health by "making sense" of their own lives in a way that is coherent—a way that tells a story of how the past affected them and why they are the way they are in the present. Siegel (1999) believes that such coherence leads to neural integration and facilitates raising securely attached children.

of one's life can be examined; (b) assist exploration of expectations and biases in forming connections with others; (c) encourage consideration of how early parenting experiences are related to current functioning; (d) help the patient see the past for what it is and help him or her to imagine healthier alternative ways of acting and thinking; and (e) help examine the therapeutic relationship as the patient's working models of self and other play out in the therapy. In fact, Bowlby felt that examining the transference and countertransference in the here and now of the sessions should be the main focus of therapy, with explorations of the patient's past delved into only as they are useful in helping one understand current ways of feeling and coping with one's interpersonal world. It is in this context that Bowlby specifically mentioned the work of Strupp and Binder (1984) in his 1988 book, *A Secure Base*, stating that TLDP contains many of the same ideas on therapeutic process that he has outlined.

REFERENCES

Ainsworth, M. D. S. (1969). Object relations, dependency and attachment: A theoretical review of the infant–mother relationship. *Child Development, 40,* 969–1025. doi:10.2307/1127008

Bowlby, J. (1969). *Attachment and loss: Vol. 1. Attachment.* New York, NY: Basic Books.

Bowlby, J. (1973). *Attachment and loss: Vol. 2. Separation anxiety and anger.* New York, NY: Basic Books.

Bowlby, J. (1980). *Attachment and loss: Vol. 3. Loss, sadness, and depression.* New York, NY: Basic Books.

Bowlby, J. (1982). *Attachment and loss: Vol. 1. Attachment* (2nd ed.). New York, NY: Basic Books.

Bowlby, J. (1988). *A secure base: Clinical applications of attachment theory.* London, England: Routledge.

Castonguay, L. G., & Beutler, L. E. (Eds.). (2005). *Principles of therapeutic change that work.* New York, NY: Oxford University Press.

Fonagy, P., & Target, M. (2006). The mentalization-focused approach to self pathology. *Journal of Personality Disorders, 20,* 544–576. doi:10.1521/pedi.2006.20.6.544

Holmes, J. (1993). *John Bowlby and attachment theory.* London, England: Routledge.

Jurist, E. L., & Meehan, K. B. (2008). Attachment, mentalization, and reflective functioning. In J. H. Obegi & E. Berant (Eds.), *Attachment theory and research in clinical work with adults* (pp. 71–93). New York, NY: Guilford Press.

Karen, R. (1998). *Becoming attached: First relationships and how they shape our capacity to love.* New York, NY: Oxford University Press.

Lewis, T., Amini, F., & Lannon, R. (2001). *A general theory of love*. New York, NY: Vintage Books.

Main, M., Kaplan, N., & Cassidy, J. (1985). Security in infancy, childhood, and adulthood: A move to the level of representation. *Monographs of the Society for Research in Child Development, 50*, 66–104. doi:10.2307/3333827

Meltzoff, A. N., & Moore, M. K. (1977). Imitation of facial and manual gestures by human neonates. *Science, 198*, 75–78. doi:10.1126/science.198.4312.75

Mikulincer, M., & Shaver, P. R. (2007). *Attachment in adulthood: Structure, dynamics, and change*. New York, NY: Guilford Press.

Neborsky, R. J. (2006). Brain, mind, and dyadic change processes. *Journal of Clinical Psychology, 62*, 523–538. doi:10.1002/jclp.20246

Obegi, J. H., & Berant, E. (2008). Introduction. In J. H. Obegi & E. Berant (Eds.), *Attachment theory and research in clinical work with adults* (pp. 1–14). New York, NY: Guilford Press.

Pietromonaco, P. R., & Feldman Barrett, L. (2000). The internal working models concept: What do we really know about the self in relation to others? *Review of General Psychology, 4*, 155–175. doi:10.1037/1089-2680.4.2.155

Shaver, P. R., & Mikulincer, M. (2008). An overview of adult attachment theory. In J. H. Obegi & E. Berant (Eds.), *Attachment theory and research in clinical work with adults* (pp. 17–45). New York, NY: Guilford Press.

Siegel, D. J. (1999). *The developing mind: Toward a neurobiology of interpersonal experience*. New York, NY: Guilford Press.

Siegel, D. J., & Hartzell, M. (2003). *Parenting from the inside out: How a deeper self-understanding can help you raise children who thrive*. New York, NY: Tarcher/Putnam.

Stroufe, L. A., & Waters, E. (1977). Attachment as an organizational construct. *Child Development, 48*, 1184–1199. doi:10.2307/1128475

 Strupp, H. H., & Binder, J. L. (1984). *Psychotherapy in a new key: A guide to time-limited dynamic psychotherapy*. New York, NY: Basic Books.

Wachtel, P. L. (2008). *Relational theory and the practice of psychotherapy*. New York, NY: Guilford Press.

6

BRIEF DYNAMIC THERAPY PROCESS

HANNA LEVENSON

MAINTAINING THE THERAPEUTIC RELATIONSHIP

In time-limited dynamic psychotherapy (TLDP), as with most clinical approaches, managing the therapeutic relationship is a critical competency (Binder, 2004). To strengthen the therapeutic alliance, the TLDP therapist engages clients from a respectful and nonjudgmental stance, validates their feelings and perceptions, and invites their collaboration in the process (Strategy 1).

It is critical in this relationally based approach that the therapist shows evidence of listening receptively to what the client is saying. This receptivity may be communicated by body position, facial expression, and head nodding (Strategy 2). Many of these are culturally determined. In a brief therapy in

Excerpted from *Brief Dynamic Therapy* (2010), from Chapter 4, "The Therapy Process," pp. 81–94. Copyright 2010 by the American Psychological Association. Used with permission of the author.

http://dx.doi.org/10.1037/14295-006
Psychotherapy Theories and Techniques: A Reader, G. R. VandenBos, E. Meidenbauer, and J. Frank-McNeil (Editors)
Copyright © 2014 by the American Psychological Association. All rights reserved.

general and in TLDP in particular, it is critical to assess, use, and comment on the strengths of the client to foster change (Strategy 3). Often clients are the last to know about their own capacities. No one has ever commented on them, elicited them, admired them; therefore, clients are often blind to their own cognitive, emotional, and relational resources. Highlighting their internal and external resources can often build a strong positive alliance.

In Strategy 4 the therapist addresses "obstacles" (e.g., coming late) and "opportunities" (e.g., willingness to be vulnerable) that might influence the therapeutic process. In psychoanalytically oriented therapies, "overt or covert opposition to the therapist, the counseling process, or the therapist's agenda" (Bischoff & Tracey, 1995, p. 488) has been called *resistance*. Resistance from the perspective of TLDP, on the other hand, is viewed within the interpersonal sphere—as one of a number of transactions between therapist and client (Levenson, 1995). The assumption is that clients are doing what they believe is necessary to maintain their personal integrity, ingrained perceptions of themselves, and interpersonal connectedness. Resistance in this light reflects the clients' attempts to do the best they can given how they construe the world. For example, a client might miss a session following the session when she has cried in the hour because she is so worried that the therapist will perceive her as too needy.

Thus, when TLDP therapists feel as if they have hit a wall of resistance from the client, they can stand back, appreciate the attachment-based significance of the wall, and invite the client to look at possible "good" reasons to have the wall. Such an approach often avoids power plays with hostile clients and helps to promote empathy and collaboration.

ACCESSING AND PROCESSING EMOTION

No matter what else the therapist may do in the therapy, he or she is trying to relate to clients in the here and now of the therapeutic relationship from a deeply empathic place, helping to keep clients in an emotionally receptive "working space" through what has been called *dyadic regulation* (e.g., Tronick, 1989). Such transactions are hypothesized to be beneficial in and of themselves in that they permit emotional processing and the modulation of goal-directed behaviors and adaptive strategies. However, as pointed out by Binder (2004) and others (e.g., Henry, Strupp, Butler, Schacht, & Binder, 1993), helping clients stay emotionally regulated (Strategy 5) is easier said than done when one is interacting with powerful interpersonal dynamics that dysregulate the therapist's own emotional state. Thus, this strategy is more of a desired optimum therapeutic stance that will usually be manifested through several other specific interventions.

For Strategy 6, the therapist actively encourages clients to experience and express affect in the session. Activating the emotional fabric of the person's cyclical maladaptive pattern (CMP) is critical in changing it. As Greenberg is fond of saying, "You must arrive at a place before you can leave it." From experiential theory, research, and practice, we know that emotional arousal and expression are necessary precursors of change (e.g., Greenberg, 2002; Johnson, 2004). Similarly the therapist helps clients become aware of emotions on the edge of awareness and helps them deepen their emotional experience (Strategy 7). However, mere ventilation of emotions is not enough, and the therapist must help clients label their emotional experience and tune into its goal-directed significance (Strategy 8). In particular, the TLDP therapist is invested in focusing on the client's accessing, experiencing, and deepening any attachment-related feelings specifically related to the person's CMP (Strategy 9).

EMPATHIC EXPLORATION

Open-ended questions (Strategy 10) and inquiring into the personal meanings of the clients' words (Strategy 11) as well as asking for concrete details (Strategy 12) all help the therapist understand the client's world from the inside out. It is not unusual when I am listening to the client talk in a global fashion about a disturbing (or rewarding) interaction with another person ("She just really ticked me off!") to ask them to slow the action down so that I can understand the details of the situation—both in terms of external transactions and internal, visceral responses.[1] Often clients are quite surprised to see all the steps (e.g., attributions of self and other) that have led them to their reaction that often feels as if it "just happens."

FOCUSED INQUIRY

Throughout the therapy, the TLDP therapist attempts to maintain a circumscribed line of inquiry and stays on the focus unless there are dramatic indications to the contrary (Strategy 13). Such a focusing, however, should not be done in a dogmatic or controlling manner. Binder (2004) defines problem formulation and focusing to be one of the five competencies in conducting good interpersonal–psychodynamic therapy. Maintaining a focus is the most commonly mentioned feature defining brief dynamic therapy. The

---

[1] It is quite ironic that often my feedback to trainees learning to work briefly is to "slow down" the process.

TLDP therapist uses the emotional–interpersonal goals derived from the formulation to keep the therapy on track. Such focusing is critical in a brief therapy that demands making the best use of time.

RELATIONSHIP FOCUS

The TLDP therapist encourages clients to talk about their relationships with others (including with the therapist). Focusing on relevant thoughts, feelings, and beliefs associated with such transactions is of paramount importance (Strategy 14). Much of the therapeutic work will focus on the clients' relationships *outside of the sessions* (unless a negative process emanating from within the sessions needs to be addressed directly). Similarly, the therapist helps clients explore their perceptions of how the therapist might be acting, feeling, or thinking about them (Strategy 15). In this way, the therapeutic relationship is examined as a here-and-now microcosm of what might happen with others.

In a reciprocal fashion, it can often be helpful for therapists to self-disclose their countertransference in response to clients' specific behaviors (Strategy 16). Of course the therapist is always self-disclosing inadvertently through gestures, voice quality, facial expression, etc. Self-disclosure is "not an option; it is an inevitability" (Aron, 1991, p. 40). But here I am talking about the therapist's *self-involving disclosures*—statements in the present tense that describe the therapist's reactions to some aspect of the client's CMP (McCarthy & Betz, 1978). In this way the therapist can open up other possibilities in the clients' perceptions of others and help clients appreciate their impact on others. In TLDP therapists need to become comfortable with comprehending their own internal processes and then deciding when, where, and how to share these with clients. TLDP advocates limited self-disclosure specifically designed to give clients more information about the dynamics involved in relating to others. Such disclosures can be narrowly seen as a manifestation of the therapist's *clinical honesty* (Wilkinson & Gabbard, 1993, p. 282).

In particular, the therapist focuses on his or her reactions to the client that are particularly relevant for the client's CMP. It should be noted that the therapist's sharing such reactions is not only helpful for bringing into awareness negative aspects when there are reenactments, but also for recognizing when there are *positive shifts* in the quality of the interaction. For example, after Mrs. Follette (the guarded client described earlier) allowed herself to be more open in session, the therapist shared that he felt closer to her. The reader is referred to Levenson (1995) for a discussion of this type of interactive self-disclosure as distinguished from other types of disclosures.

Related to self-disclosing strategies is *metacommunication* (Strategy 17). From an interpersonalist position (Kiesler, 1996), metacommunication involves discussing and processing what occurs in the here-and-now client–therapist relationship that involves both therapist and client. For example, "It seems, Mr. Johnson, as you get quieter and quieter, I become more and more reassuring. I am not sure what is happening here, but can we take a look at what this feels like for both of us?" Muran's (2001) expansion of the definition of metacommunication to include *intrapersonal* aspects (i.e., communication with parts of the self) is also useful. From an attachment point of view, metacommunication can be pivotal in providing corrective emotional experiences, shifts in self-awareness, and richer narratives of the self in relation to self and others.

While much of the therapy will be devoted to examining the clients' issues in their relationships outside the therapy (especially for those with more flexible working models), the therapist's observations about manifestations of the CMP (not necessarily full-blown reenactments) *in the sessions* provides an in vivo understanding of the client's behaviors and stimulus value. By ascertaining how an interpersonal pattern has emerged in the therapeutic relationship, the client has, perhaps for the first time, the opportunity to examine the nature of such behaviors in a relatively safe environment.

I want to make a comment here about the use of *transference interpretations*, since they have been a standard intervention strategy for psychodynamic therapists in both short- and long-term therapies (although intersubjective, two-person approaches like TLDP shy away from using them). When therapists are "analyzing the transference," they are linking emotionally charged interactions with past significant others (usually parents) with what is happening in present transactions between therapist and client, rather than making observations about the ongoing therapeutic process. For example, if I would have *explained* to Mr. Johnson that "you want me to nurture and take care of you in ways you didn't get from your parents," this would be an example of a transference interpretation.

Kasper, Hill, and Kivlighan (2008) differentiate between immediacy (her term for metacommunication) and transference interpretations in a similar manner:

> Immediacy seeks to promote the *here-and-now awareness* of problematic interpersonal patterns and to create a corrective emotional experience by establishing new interpersonal patterns. By contrast, transference interpretations seek to promote the client's awareness of the existence and insight into the origin of displaced interactional patterns by *providing an explanation* or reason for the behaviors. (p. 282, emphasis added)

I very much like quoting Strupp's admonition that the supply of transference interpretations far exceeds the demand. A few go a long way. In part I have placed a major focus in TLDP on experiential learning and empathic attunement, because of the deleterious effect repeated transference interpretations can have on psychotherapeutic process and outcome. Clients often experience such interventions as blaming and/or belittling (Henry, Schacht, Strupp, Butler, & Binder, 1993; Piper, Azim, Joyce, & McCallum, 1991). There is convincing empirical evidence that questions the heretofore prominent role transference interpretations have played in psychodynamic interventions (Henry, Schacht, et al., 1993; Høglend, Johannsson, Marble, Bøgwald, & Amlo, 2007; Piper et al., 1991).

EXPLORATION OF MALADAPTIVE CYCLICAL PATTERNS

In Strategy 18, the therapist helps clients explore their introjects (how they feel about and treat themselves) and how these relate to their interpersonal patterns (CMPs). Inquiring about how one feels about oneself during certain interpersonal behaviors (especially those that are attachment-related) links one's sense of self with transactions with others. As I say to Ann in the clinical case to follow, "How do you feel about yourself when you cry yourself to sleep, making sure that your boyfriend does not hear you?"

The therapist then helps clients put all of the aforementioned emotional–interpersonal information of self and others into describing a cyclical pattern (Strategy 19). For example:

> So when you feel so alone and depressed, and expect no one will be there for you, you make sure that you present yourself as "together," "cool," and not "needy." Is that right? The problem is that others get the message that you don't want their attention, and so they leave you alone. Yes? You see people aren't there for you, and you then tell yourself that no one would want to be with someone so needy, and this makes you feel more depressed, and the whole cycle begins again. Do I have that right?

It is very important at this stage that the therapist be as specific as possible and slowly review each component of the pattern, checking it out with clients at each linking, soliciting their elaboration and emotional confirmation.

Once the pattern has been recognized, the therapist refers to the CMP throughout the therapy and, at each link, helps the client access, experience, and deepen the attachment-related feelings (Strategy 20). The therapist focuses on previously warded-off, unacknowledged, disowned, or disavowed attachment-related feelings and/or primary emotions specifically relevant to the CMP. The therapist confronts blocks in experiencing by using experiential techniques such as arousal, heightening, and empathic conjecture (Johnson, 2004). In this way, the client comes to understand the deeper, attachment-based needs that drive the maladaptive cycle and begins to appreciate how this working model has colored his or her worldview.

When appropriate, the therapist then links the need for disowning these primary emotions to the clients' early experiences (Strategy 21). The clients come to understand how they perceived these basic core emotions as undesirable by caregivers; therefore, these emotions were suppressed and finally disowned so that early attachments would not be threatened. The therapist can help depathologize the client's current behavior and symptoms by explaining how they were a way to survive emotionally as a child, but now they serve no useful purpose and may even be alienating.

Over time, the therapist helps the client incorporate more core feelings (Fosha, 2000) and more adaptive thoughts and behaviors into a new coherent narrative that opens up an expanded sense of self and a wider repertoire of actions, leading to greater intrapersonal and interpersonal health (Strategy 22). Going back to our example of Mr. Johnson, by the end of therapy, he was able to talk about how he had to squelch his angry feelings as a child to avoid being beaten by his alcoholic father—a very different narrative than when he entered therapy and shamefully saw himself as weak. In his last session, Mr. Johnson said he now felt entitled to be angry—"honest anger."

PROMOTING CHANGE DIRECTLY

One of the most important TLDP treatment strategies is providing opportunities for clients to have new experiences in session that are designed to help undermine their CMPs (Strategy 23). Therapists should seize opportunities to expand or deepen experiences that disconfirm clients' intrapersonal and interpersonal schemata. The therapist makes clear and repeated efforts to promote such experiential learning (e.g., facilitating new behaviors that the client sees as "risky"). With sufficient quality and/or quantity of these experiences, clients can foster healthier internalized working models of relationships. In this way TLDP promotes change by altering the basic infrastructure of the client's transactional world, which then reverberates to influence the concept of self.

Going back to our case of Mr. Johnson, at one point in the sixth session, he was complaining that he could not think and participate in the therapy because he had not eaten breakfast. When I asked him what he wanted to do, he was confused by my question. Of course he would finish the session! Upon further inquiry, I learned that he thought I would be angry if he left the session early to get something to eat, and he would want to avoid my anger at all costs. When I simply stated back to him that it seemed he was choosing to remain in the session and be uncomfortable hoping not to displease me, he said he would go get some food if *I* thought it were a good idea. I expressed my curiosity about his leaving the decision up to me by stating in a puzzled tone, "If *I* thought it was a good idea?"

A short while later, Mr. Johnson said he felt better and would finish the session. However, in the next session a similar dynamic (but with different content) arose, and that time, Mr. Johnson announced that he wanted to leave the session early to attend to his personal needs (i.e., take a stool softener so he would not be constipated later that evening when his children came to visit). Rather than interpreting what I thought was going on at an unconscious level, I simply told Mr. Johnson I would look forward to seeing him at our usual time next week. Mr. Johnson's stating his own needs over what he imagined were my wishes (that he should stay in the session no matter what) had been a big risk for him because, as I learned later, he thought I was going to throw him out of therapy if he were not "compliant." Being aware that he was directly verbalizing his own needs (for once in his life), taking a chance that I would disapprove and might even retaliate, and then finding out that his assertiveness did not jeopardize our relationship was a major new intrapersonal *and* interpersonal experience for Mr. Johnson.

However, I do not want to give the impression that in TLDP the therapist tries to create that *one* new experience that totally realigns the client's affective and cognitive world. Rather, new experiences should be encountered throughout the therapy—sometimes as almost imperceptible nuances embedded in the relationship context. In our long-term follow-up study of clients who have received TLDP (Bein, Levenson, & Overstreet, 1994), many clients described that one of the biggest benefits they got from therapy was having the opportunity to be more in touch with their emotions as they related in new and healthier ways to their therapists.

Unlike many long-term psychodynamic models, in TLDP the therapist may give directives to help clients foster their growth *outside of the session* (Strategy 24). Giving homework, for example, is very compatible with the TLDP approach. However, before making any such assignments, the TLDP therapist must carefully weigh the implications of such directives to make sure they are not a subtle reenactment of the client's dysfunctional pattern. For example, asking Mr. Johnson to take assertiveness training classes may sound like a good idea on the surface. But if it is something he does because he feels he must do whatever I say in order to stay in my good graces, the homework assignment just serves to feed his attachment fears and compliant security operations—ultimately making sure he has yet another dysfunctional interpersonal interaction.

Strategy 25 involves the therapist's introducing and discussing the time-limited or brief nature of the therapy. The brief therapist does not do this just at the end of the treatment. At the beginning of the work and periodically throughout, the TLDP therapist comments on the limits on the time and/ or scope of the work. TLDP, however, is not one of those models (like that of Mann, 1973) that emphasizes the finiteness of time in order to precipitate change. Rather, it is thought of as the backdrop against which dysfunctional patterns take center stage. As termination approaches, one can expect to see the client's anxiety about loss handled in ways characteristic for that particular person given his or her CMP. Painful emotions associated with previous losses can be evoked. However, the TLDP therapist does not stray from the overarching goals of the treatment.

Given the TLDP systems framework, when one person (the client) changes, other people's responses are affected, usually reinforcing the client's positive changes. As previously mentioned, I think of the therapeutic work continuing after the sessions have ended. For example, with Mr. Johnson, where there used to be a vicious dysfunctional cycle, now there was more of a victorious cycle filled with energy and joy. As a consequence of his feeling more powerful in the world, he began socializing more. He experienced himself as more alive and involved in life; his self-pity and depressive thinking were dramatically decreased. Now that he was a happier person, his adult children enjoyed being around him more, which only served to quiet his fears of abandonment and reinforce his sense of security. A year after he ended treatment, during a follow-up interview (done by another therapist), I learned that Mr. Johnson had moved into a house owned by two other people. After living there a short time, he had been instrumental in setting up a rule that if any tension occurred among the housemates, they would sit down at the dining room table and talk about it after dinner. For a man who had been so conflict-avoidant, this was a clearly a sign of further growth. The therapy continued in Mr. Johnson's life, although the sessions had ended a year ago.

How does the therapist make a good decision about knowing when a client is "ready" to end?[2] As one of the originators of single-session therapy,

---

[2] I have found that having an explicit ending date (rather than a fixed number of sessions or a brief therapy defined by a limited focus) works best for training. With a fixed date, therapists-in-training are forced to confront their "resistances" to working briefly (Hoyt, 1985)—for example, fears of being seen as withholding, the need to be needed, and overconcern for "successful" termination. Also when I do group supervision with a specific termination date, all the trainees are roughly on the same page—beginning and ending together. Without such a structure, I have found that beginning brief therapists often find "good reasons" for extending the length of the therapy.

Michael Hoyt (Hoyt, Rosenbaum, & Talmon, 1992), has said to me, "Clients are not 'done'; they are not baked like a cake!" In brief therapy, we are clearly not looking for therapeutic perfectionism. All of the loose ends are not tied together. However, since brief therapy often ends while the client usually is in the midst of changing, I have six sets of questions to help guide beginning brief therapists in making termination decisions as the therapy is proceeding:[3]

- Has the client evidenced interactional changes with significant others in his or her life? Are these transactions more rewarding?
- Does the client evidence more emotional fluidity within himself or herself? Does the client report a fuller experience of self?
- Has the client had a new experience (or a series of new experiences) of himself or herself and the therapist within the therapy?
- Has there been a change in the level on which the therapist and client are relating (usually from parent–child to adult–adult)?
- Has the therapist's countertransferential reaction to the client shifted (usually from negative to positive)?
- Does the client manifest some understanding about his or her dynamics and the role he or she needed to play to maintain them?

If the answer to most of these questions is no, then I do not consider that the client has had an adequate course of TLDP. The therapist should consider why this has been the case and weigh the possible benefits of using another therapeutic model, another course of TLDP, a different therapist, nonpsychological interventions, and so forth.

REFERENCES

Aron, L. (1991). The patient's experience of the analyst's subjectivity. *Psychoanalytic Dialogues, 1,* 29–51. doi:10.1080/10481889109538884

Bein, E., Levenson, H., & Overstreet, D. (1994, June). Outcome and follow-up data from the VAST project. In H. Levenson (Chair), *Outcome and follow-up data in brief dynamic therapy.* Symposium conducted at the annual international meeting of the Society for Psychotherapy Research, York, England.

Binder, J. L. (2004). *Key competencies in brief dynamic psychotherapy: Clinical practice beyond the manual.* New York, NY: Guilford Press.

---

[3]Unfortunately, in today's managed care environment, the decision of when to end therapy is often not made collaboratively between therapist and client. Instead it may be a decision made by an administrative person or limited by one's insurance coverage to a specified number of sessions for specific diagnoses. See Levenson and Burg (2000) for a discussion of the effect of these economic influences on professional training and patient care.

Bischoff, M. M., & Tracey, T. J. G. (1995). Client resistance as predicted by therapist behavior: A study of sequential dependence. *Journal of Counseling Psychology, 42*, 487–495. doi:10.1037/0022-0167.42.4.487

Fosha, D. (2000). *The transforming power of affect: A model for accelerated change*. New York, NY: Basic Books.

Greenberg, L. S. (2002). *Emotion-focused therapy: Coaching clients to work through their feelings*. Washington, DC: American Psychological Association. doi:10.1037/10447-000

Henry, W. P., Schacht, T. E., Strupp, H. H., Butler, S. F., & Binder, J. L. (1993). Effects of training in time-limited dynamic psychotherapy: Mediators of therapists' responses to training. *Journal of Consulting and Clinical Psychology, 61*, 441–447. doi:10.1037/0022-006X.61.3.441

Henry, W. P., Strupp, H. H., Butler, S. F., Schacht, T. E., & Binder, J. L. (1993). Effects of training in time-limited dynamic psychotherapy: Changes in therapist behavior. *Journal of Consulting and Clinical Psychology, 61*, 434–440. doi:10.1037/0022-006X.61.3.434

Høglend, P., Johansson, P., Marble, A., Bøgwald, K., & Amlo, S. (2007). Moderators of the effects of transference interpretations on brief dynamic psychotherapy. *Psychotherapy Research, 17*, 160–171. doi:10.1080/10503300701194206

Hoyt, M. F. (1985). Therapist resistances to short-term dynamic psychotherapy. *Journal of the American Academy of Psychoanalysis, 13*, 93–112.

Hoyt, M. F., Rosenbaum, R., & Talmon, M. (1992). Planned single-session psychotherapy. In S. H. Budman, M. F. Hoyt, & S. Friedman (Eds.), *The first session in brief therapy* (pp. 59–86). New York, NY: Guilford Press.

Johnson, S. M. (2004). *The practice of emotionally focused couple therapy: Creating connection* (2nd ed.). New York, NY: Brunner-Routledge.

Kasper, L. B., Hill, C. E., & Kivlighan, D. M., Jr. (2008). Therapist immediacy in brief psychotherapy: Case study I. *Psychotherapy Theory, Research, Practice, Training, 45*, 281–297. doi:10.1037/a0013305

Kiesler, D. J. (1996). *Contemporary interpersonal theory and research: Personality, psychopathology, and psychotherapy*. New York, NY: Wiley.

Levenson, H. (1995). *Time-limited dynamic psychotherapy: A guide to clinical practice*. New York, NY: Basic Books.

Levenson, H., & Burg, J. (2000). Training psychologists in the era of managed care. In A. J. Kent & M. Hersen (Eds.), *A psychologist's proactive guide to managed mental health care* (pp. 113–140). Hillsdale, NJ: Erlbaum.

Mann, J. (1973). *Time-limited psychotherapy*. Cambridge, MA: Harvard University Press.

McCarthy, P. R., & Betz, N. E. (1978). Differential effects of self-disclosing versus self-involving counselor statements. *Journal of Counseling Psychology, 25*, 251–256. doi:10.1037/0022-0167.25.4.251

Muran, J. C. (2001). A final note: Meditations on "both/and." In J. C. Muran (Ed.), *Self-relations in the psychotherapy process* (pp. 347–372). Washington, DC: American Psychological Association. doi:10.1037/10391-014

Piper, W. E., Azim, H. F. A., Joyce, A. S., & McCallum, M. (1991). Transference interpretations, therapeutic alliance, and outcome in short-term individual psychotherapy. *Archives of General Psychiatry, 48,* 946–953. doi:10.1001/archpsyc.1991.01810340078010

Tronick, E. Z. (1989). Emotions and emotional communication in infants. *American Psychologist, 44,* 112–119. doi:10.1037/0003-066X.44.2.112

Wilkinson, S. M., & Gabbard, G. O. (1993). Therapeutic self-disclosure with borderline patients. *Journal of Psychotherapy Practice and Research, 2,* 282–295.

APPENDIX 6.1: BRIEF DYNAMIC THERAPY TECHNIQUES

Technique	Video title	Video identifying number	Time at which technique occurs
Reflection	Time-Limited Dynamic Psychotherapy, Client 2	777700414-001	00:56–01:40
Interpretation	Time-Limited Dynamic Psychotherapy, Client 2	777700414-001	18:30–20:24
Clarification	Time-Limited Dynamic Psychotherapy, Client 2	777700414-001	00:29–00:50
Confrontation	Brief Dynamic Therapy With a Young Man	777700045-001	27:10–28:34
Talking about patterns between client and therapist	Time-Limited Dynamic Psychotherapy, Client 1	777700413-001	42:29–44:14
Engaging clients	Time-Limited Dynamic Psychotherapy, Client 2	777700414-001	00:02–00:39
Listening receptively	Time-Limited Dynamic Psychotherapy, Client 2	777700414-001	00:56–01:27
Assess, use, and comment on strengths of client	Time-Limited Dynamic Psychotherapy, Client 2	777700414-001	09:44–10:49
Helping client stay emotionally regulated	Time-Limited Dynamic Psychotherapy, Client 1	777700413-001	31:00–32:15
Help clients become aware of emotions	Time-Limited Dynamic Psychotherapy, Client 2	777700414-001	10:50–11:23
Help clients label emotions	Brief Dynamic Therapy With a Young Man	777700045-001	29:03–31:04
Open-ended questions	Time-Limited Dynamic Psychotherapy, Client 2	777700414-001	02:09–02:17
Inquiring into personal meanings of client's words	Time-Limited Dynamic Psychotherapy, Client 3	777700415-001	16:01–18:41
Asking for concrete details	Time-Limited Dynamic Psychotherapy, Client 2	777700414-001	03:37–03:42
Maintain circumscribed line of inquiry	Brief Dynamic Therapy With a Young Woman	777700043-001	00:56–07:01
Focus on relevant thoughts, feelings, and beliefs	Time-Limited Dynamic Psychotherapy, Client 2	777700414-001	08:09–14:25

(continues)

Technique	Video title	Video identifying number	Time at which technique occurs
Explore perceptions of how therapist might be feeling or acting	Time-Limited Dynamic Psychotherapy, Client 3	777700415-001	29:40–32:07
Self-disclose counter-transference in response to client's specific behaviors	Time-Limited Dynamic Psychotherapy, Client 1	777700413-001	42:29–44:14
Metacommunication (here and now)	Time-Limited Dynamic Psychotherapy, Client 1	777700413-001	29:03–30:21
Explore client's introjects	Time-Limited Dynamic Psychotherapy, Client 3	777700415-001	15:24–17:04
Describe cyclical pattern	Time-Limited Dynamic Psychotherapy, Client 1	777700413-001	02:37–07:53
Help client assess, experience, and deepen attach-ment-related feelings	Time-Limited Dynamic Psychotherapy, Client 1	777700413-001	13:50–17:35
Providing opportu-nities for clients to have new experiences	Time-Limited Dynamic Psychotherapy, Client 3	777700415-001	41:14–43:48
Direct client to foster growth outside the sessions	Brief Dynamic Therapy With a Woman Considering Divorce	777700044-001	44:41–47:45
Discuss time-limited or brief nature of therapy	Time-Limited Dynamic Psychotherapy, Client 2	777700414-001	00:01–00:28

7

COGNITIVE THERAPY

KEITH S. DOBSON

It has been argued that cognitive therapy is based on a *realist* model of human functioning (Held, 1995). According to this model, events occur in the real world, irrespective of whether someone perceives their occurrence and whether they are perceived accurately. From this epistemological underpinning, it can be argued that human adjustment is reflected by optimal accuracy in perception of the world, and by implication, human maladjustment is reflected by lack of accurate correspondence between perception and actual events—or by misperception of the world. Consistent with this perspective, human adjustment can also be defined as the extent to which the individual accurately appraises his or her environment and is therefore able to cope with the demands of that environment.

Excerpted from *Cognitive Therapy* (2012), from Chapter 3, "Theory," pp. 11–25. Copyright 2012 by the American Psychological Association. Used with permission of the author.

http://dx.doi.org/10.1037/14295-007

Psychotherapy Theories and Techniques: A Reader, G. R. VandenBos, E. Meidenbauer, and J. Frank-McNeil (Editors)

Copyright © 2014 by the American Psychological Association. All rights reserved.

The realist viewpoint can be contrasted with a *constructivist* perspective, which holds that the existence of an objective, external reality is wrong or, at the least, a weak and untestable premise. In the first instance, a *radical constructivist* perspective would be that the external world does not exist; that all that can and does exist is what we perceive and experience. In this sense, any one person's reality is uniquely situated in space and time, so that it is neither the same reality that that person "knew" yesterday nor the same reality that he or she will experience in the future. A somewhat weaker version of the constructivist perspective is that it is irrelevant whether an external reality exists because humans are fallible in their perception. As such, we will never know what "reality" is in any event, since our perceptions and experiences are always limited by the possible range of human experience, by our history and development experiences, and by our current state, which might either enhance or limit our possible set of experiences.

From a constructivist perspective, human adjustment is not defined by the *correspondence* between perception and the real world, but rather by the *coherence* or integrity of experience. Also from this perspective, language does not reflect our experience of the world, but it literally defines the world and how it can be perceived: "In a constructivist view, human beings are denied any direct access to an immediate reality beyond *language*, defined broadly as the entire repertory of symbolic utterances and actions afforded to us by our culture" (Neimeyer, 1995, p. 15, italics in original).

Realist and constructivist perspectives have often been contrasted, especially with regard to the epistemological underpinnings of each perspective and their attendant research methodologies (Mahoney, 1991). In particular, whereas a realist perspective is consistent with logical positivism and quantitative science, constructivism eschews a universal perspective on science and instead supports the use of qualitative methods in research, situated within the experience of individuals, who are in turn considered to be situated within a unique historical, cultural, and personal context (Guidano, 1984).

Cognitive therapy has been primarily associated with a realist perspective and epistemology. Evidence in support of this claim can be found in many writings. For example, cognitive therapists have discussed the individual as a "personal scientist" (Arnkoff, 1980; Mahoney, 1977) who seeks knowledge of the world and who can accurately perceive that reality or can have distorted perceptions. Some of the better-known techniques of cognitive therapy teach patients to recognize biases and distortions in perception and to have more realistic perceptions, so that the patient can solve problems in a "realistic" manner. In those instances in which it might not be clear whether the patient's perceptions are accurate or if there is simply not enough information, cognitive therapists may work with patients to gather "evidence" and discuss the implications of this new information. Cognitive therapists are comfortable with scales and measurement tools that have been developed through group and quantitative research; they also rely on diagnosis and research evidence, and they incorporate ideas related to evidence-based treatment (Dobson & Dobson, 2009) into case conceptualization and planning.

Other features of cognitive therapy are actually more consistent with constructivism. For example, cognitive therapists recognize that individuals have unique cultural, historical, and personal backgrounds, which shape the meanings that they assign to their experience: "The cognitive perspective posits . . . the dual existence of an objective reality and a personal, subjective, phenomenological reality" (Alford & Beck, 1997, p. 23). Put otherwise, the cognitive model posits that an individual's perceptions and appraisals are based in part on the objective nature of the event or experience, as might be experienced by anyone in that situation, and in part on the unique ways of knowing, language, and developmental experiences of the individual.

NATURE OF COGNITION

Within the overall cognitive model of human experience, distinctions are made among different types of cognition or thought. Various typologies or conceptualizations of cognition have arisen, but two are of particular relevance here: the *information processing model* and the *cognitive model of cognition*.

The information processing model of cognition is consistent with the idea that objective reality occurs and can be attended to, perceived, known, and stored in memory. A series of aspects of this cognitive system, including cognitive structures, content, processes, and products, have been distinguished (Ingram & Kendall, 1986; Kendall & Ingram, 1987). Each of these aspects is discussed next.

Cognitive structures represent the organization of long-term memories, which are held within the mind. These structures are composed of specific memories, situated at a specific place and time (sometimes referred to as *episodic* or *autobiographical* memory), as well as organized, linguistically based collections of memories (sometimes referred to as *semantic memory*). Semantic memory is the symbolic representation of the formal knowledge that is collected through experience and tends to be shared among people within a certain culture and during a historical period. By definition, however, autobiographical memory is unique and based on personal experience.

Both autobiographical and semantic memories are themselves structured. For example, they comprise different aspects of memory, including sensory aspects of knowledge and experience, but they also comprise linguistic, emotional, and even potentially bodily or behavioral aspects of knowledge. These memories are also hierarchically organized. For example, the autobiographical memory of "mother" will comprise a number of different events or interactions, not only with "my mother" but "mothers" in general, and even "not mother" (i.e., experiences that differentiate mother and mothering from different other types of experiences, such as "father" and "fathering"). Semantic memories can be formally hierarchical, for example, in the way that "living organisms" is a superordinate construct that encompasses animals, which in turn encompasses mammals, which in turn encompasses dogs (among other animals), which in turn encompasses specific breeds or types of dogs.

Cognitive structures not only represent a repository for the storage of memories but also guide the processing of new information. New information is more easily processed if there is an existing template or structure into which it can be placed. It appears that existing cognitive structures can actually bias attention to and processing of new information so that new information fits within them. Thus, once cognitive structures are established, they tend to be self-confirming or self-maintaining.

Cognitive content can be defined as the actual material that is held within cognitive structures or is the object of new information processing. Cognitive content is as variable as the range of human experience and includes words, images, memories, sensory experiences, fantasies, and emotions. There is a tendency in the cognitive literature to assume that cognitive content must be subject to verbal mediation—it must be named, or at least be nameable. However, this assumption is somewhat controversial, as some cognitive theorists would argue that even emotional memories are part of the content that humans can experience.

Cognitive processes include the various mechanisms through which information flows through the information processing system. They include the various sensory and attentional processes through which new experiences enter the system. They are known not to be literal copies of the external world but are potentially biased by the emotional state of the person who is attending to the environment and to preexisting structures. Once information comes into attention, various processes can either amplify the information (e.g., rehearsal of information) or reduce its salience (e.g., selective forgetting). Furthermore, if information is transferred into long-term memory, either it can be assimilated into existing memory structures or, if the experience is unique or bizarre, accommodation of the memory structures might be required to enable the memory to be retained.

Several cognitive processes are associated with memory for cognitive structures. Certain biases or heuristics might either enhance or diminish the opportunity to recall certain information. Some memories may depend on the actual state of the person, so that they are best recalled when the person tries to remember in a state that is similar to when the information was first put into memory. Some memories appear to be lost or repressed but are later accessible. It even appears that memories can be changed or manipulated to some extent.

The final aspect of the information processing model is *cognitive products*. These products are the specific cognitions that result from the dynamic interplay among cognitive structures, content, and processes. They can take the form of specific ideas or reactions to events, memories of events, or thoughts about or reflections on different experiences. Some cognitive products may occur very quickly or "automatically" if they involve well-used cognitive structures and processes, whereas others may only result from reflection and consideration. Cognitive products also exist in different forms, such as verbal utterances, images, or even emotional memories.

In contrast to the information processing model of cognition, as reflected in the constructs of structure, process, content, and product, the cognitive model of cognition was formulated specifically in the context of cognitive therapy. This model makes use of some of the same principles and processes as the information processing model, but the terminology is more specific, and the model is more attuned to the needs of a clinically useful way to consider these constructs. This model has been presented in graphical form in various sources (Alford & Beck, 1997; Dobson & Dobson, 2009).

According to the cognitive model, individuals possess cognitive structures, which are a composite of both formal (semantic) and personal (autobiographical or episodic) knowledge and experience. Various terms have been used to refer to these structures, but the most common are *beliefs* and *schemas*. Within the cognitive model, schemas are seen as both *reactive*, in that they respond to and incorporate new information, and *proactive*, in that they influence which types of situations a person might be willing to enter, the information that is attended to in different situations or contexts, and even the range of experiences an individual is able to have.

Because the schema construct is broad, there have been efforts to identify the possible content of schemas in various disorders. For example, in an early article about depression, A. T. Beck, Rush, Shaw, and Emery (1979) discussed the *cognitive triad*, which consists of beliefs about the self, the world, and the future. They went on to specify typical or characteristic beliefs that a depressed person has in each of these three domains. Specifically, they suggested that depressed persons view themselves as "losers," that they are "helpless" in the world, and that the future is "hopeless." Over time, this model has been presented in various ways. In one recent model, core beliefs and schemas interact dynamically with critical incidents or triggers to activate assumptions or behavior rules, as well as automatic thoughts, which then lead to the symptoms of depression.

Key schemas have been similarly identified in other disorders, such as the idea that the world is "dangerous" in anxiety disorders (A. T. Beck & Emery, 1985) or that other people are "hostile" for people with anger problems (A. T. Beck, 1999). Models either have been or are being developed for a wide range of disorders and clinical problems (Tarrier, 2006).

It has been argued that schemas may also follow common patterns that cut across disorders. A. T. Beck, Epstein, Harrison, and Emery (1983) identified the two schema themes of sociotropy and autonomy to reflect this idea and developed the Sociotropy–Autonomy Scale (SAS) to measure these constructs. From this perspective, sociotropy reflects an interpersonal dependency and the personal belief that one needs interpersonal relations and support to function. Sociotropic persons are vulnerable to anxiety if their interpersonal relationships are threatened or to depression if these relationships are actually disrupted or broken. In contrast, autonomous persons tend to define themselves in terms of their individual achievements, accomplishments, and degree of independence or autonomy. Autonomous persons become anxious if their autonomy is threatened and depressed if they suffer a blow to their sense of achievement or accomplishment. These constructs are not specific to a particular disorder but cut across different emotional response patterns.

Considerable research has been done to validate the SAS and to demonstrate its predictive validity. In general, the internal reliability and factor structure of the SAS have been substantiated (Bieling, Beck, & Brown, 2000, 2004; Ross & Clark, 1993). Research has also demonstrated that the dimension of Sociotropy interacts with interpersonal difficulties to predict depression, although the evidence in support of the construct of Autonomy has been somewhat more elusive to obtain (Bieling & Alden, 2001; Coyne & Whiffen, 1995; Raghavan, Le, & Berenbaum, 2002; Robins, Bagby, Rector, Lynch, & Kennedy, 1997).

A schema model has been developed in the context of personality disorders (Young, 1990; Young, Klosko, & Weishaar, 2003). This model lists 18 different negative or dysfunctional early maladaptive schemas (EMSs). These constructs are divided into five broad domains: abandonment/instability, mistrust/abuse, emotional deprivation, defectiveness/shame, and social isolation/alienation. The specific EMSs are fairly closely related to different personality disorders in some instances, as for example in the area of "dependence/incompetence," which is similar to the idea of dependent personality disorder, as defined in the *Diagnostic and Statistical Manual of Mental Disorders* (4th ed.; American Psychiatric Association, 2000). In other instances, however, EMSs reflect broad and stable dimensions of functioning that potentially cut across disorders. For example, "failure" is likely a personal schema seen in a number of different disorders.

Young and colleagues (Young, 1990; Young et al., 2003) have developed different scales to assess these schema dimensions. The Schema Questionnaire and its short form have been subjected to several psychometric studies, and despite the fairly complex nature of the scale, results have been generally positive (Lee, Taylor, & Dunn, 1999; Schmidt, Joiner, Young, & Telch, 1995). The short form of the Schema Questionnaire also has good internal reliability and factor structure (Welburn, Coristine, Dagg, Pontefract, & Jordan, 2002). The predictive value of these scales has yet to be fully evaluated, however.

Hypothetically, schemas develop naturally and spontaneously in everyone as major mechanisms that are used in making sense of the world and our lived experiences. Furthermore, every person has schemas in many different areas, some of which may be positive and some of which might be negative, depending on developmental experiences. One of the more difficult assumptions related to the schema model, however, is that schemas lie relatively dormant until primed or activated by a relevant situation or trigger. So, for example, a person who has a strong interpersonal dependency schema will function well and appear to be functionally independent, unless his or her interpersonal relationships are threatened, at which time negative thoughts, emotions, and behaviors might all be demonstrated. The assumption of "silent schemas" has been expressed as a diathesis–stress process, in that schemas represent a diathesis or vulnerability toward distress or dysfunctional behavior, but only when activated by a relevant stressor (Coyne & Whiffen, 1995; Robins & Block, 1989).

Once a schema is activated by a trigger or situation, the cognitive model holds that the information that the individual is experiencing is appraised. Appraisals can be benign or potentially positive, depending on the nature of the event and the corresponding schemas. Most of the focus in cognitive therapy, however, is on more insidious and negative appraisals. A. T. Beck et al. (1979) argued that in psychopathology, negative appraisals tend to be relatively reflexive and "automatic," as they reflect overlearned reactions to various types of situations. Although these appraisals or "automatic thoughts" are often made without conscious effort or deliberation, they can be brought to awareness and evaluated with appropriate training and skills.

The concept of automatic thoughts actually encompasses different aspects of the information processing model of cognition. The actual thoughts are the product of information processing, which includes attention to the trigger or stimulus situation, thoughts about the situation (e.g., rumination, distorted appraisals), appraisals of the meaning of the situation as mediated by the schemas, and the production of a cognitive product, which is the thought itself. Cognitive theorists have elucidated a variety of possible ways in which situations can be misperceived or distorted to yield negative outcomes (A. T. Beck et al., 1979; J. S. Beck, 1995). Patients use these cognitive distortions selectively, in ways that help to maintain the integrity and stability of schemas, even sometimes at the risk of emotional health.

REFERENCES

Alford, B. A., & Beck, A. T. (1997). *The integrative power of cognitive therapy*. New York, NY: Guilford Press.

American Psychiatric Association. (2000). *Diagnostic and statistical manual of mental disorders* (4th ed., text rev.). Washington, DC: Author.

Arnkoff, D. B. (1980). Psychotherapy from the perspective of cognitive theory. In J. M. Mahoney (Ed.), *Psychotherapy process: Current issues and future directions* (pp. 339–361). New York, NY: Plenum Press.

Beck, A. T. (1999). *Prisoners of hate: The cognitive basis of anger, hostility, and violence*. New York, NY: HarperCollins.

Beck, A. T., & Emery, G. (1985). *Anxiety disorders and phobias: A cognitive perspective*. New York, NY: Basic Books.

Beck, A. T., Epstein, N., Harrison, R. P., & Emery, G. (1983). *Development of the Sociotropy–Autonomy Scale: A measure of personality factors in psychopathology. Preliminary write-up*. Philadelphia: University of Pennsylvania, Department of Psychiatry.

Beck, A. T., Rush, A. J., Shaw, B. F., & Emery, G. (1979). *Cognitive therapy of depression*. New York, NY: Guilford Press.

Beck, J. S. (1995). *Cognitive therapy: Basics and beyond*. New York, NY: Guilford Press.

Bieling, P. J., & Alden, L. E. (2001). Sociotropy, autonomy, and the interpersonal model of depression: An integration. *Cognitive Therapy and Research, 25*, 167–184. doi:10.1023/A:1026491108540

Bieling, P. J., Beck, A. T., & Brown, G. K. (2000). The Sociotropy–Autonomy Scale: Structure and implications. *Cognitive Therapy and Research, 24*, 763–780. doi:10.1023/A:1005599714224

Bieling, P. J., Beck, A. T., & Brown, G. K. (2004). Stability and change of sociotropy and autonomy subscales in cognitive therapy of depression. *Journal of Cognitive Psychotherapy, 18*, 135–148. doi:10.1891/jcop.18.2.135.65962

Coyne, J. C., & Whiffen, V. E. (1995). Issues in personality as diathesis for depression: The case of sociotropy–dependency and autonomy–self-criticism. *Psychological Bulletin, 118*, 358–378. doi:10.1037/0033-2909.118.3.358

Dobson, D. J. G., & Dobson, K. S. (2009). *Evidence-based practice of cognitive-behavioral therapy*. New York, NY: Guilford Press.

Guidano, V. F. (1984). A constructivist outline of cognitive processes. In M. A. Reda & M. J. Mahoney (Eds.), *Cognitive psychotherapies: Recent developments in theory, research, and practice* (pp. 31–45). Cambridge, MA: Ballinger.

Held, B. S. (1995). *Back to reality: A critique of postmodern theory in psychotherapy.* New York, NY: Norton.

Ingram, R. E., & Kendall, P. C. (1986). Cognitive clinical psychology: Implications of an information processing perspective. In R. E. Ingram (Ed.), *Information processing approaches to clinical psychology* (pp. 3–21). London, England: Academic Press.

Kendall, P. C., & Ingram, R. E. (1987). The future for cognitive assessment of anxiety: Let's get specific. In L. Michelson & L. M. Ascher (Eds.), *Anxiety and stress disorders: Cognitive-behavioral assessment and treatment* (pp. 89–104). New York, NY: Guilford Press.

Lee, C. W., Taylor, G., & Dunn, J. (1999). Factor structure of the Schema Questionnaire in a large clinical sample. *Cognitive Therapy and Research, 23,* 441–451. doi:10.1023/A:1018712202933

Mahoney, M. J. (1977). Personal science: A cognitive learning therapy. In A. Ellis & R. M. Greiger (Eds.), *Handbook of rational-emotive therapy* (pp. 352–368). New York, NY: Springer.

Mahoney, M. J. (1991). *Human change processes: The scientific foundations of psychotherapy.* New York, NY: Basic Books.

Neimeyer, R. A. (1995). Constructivist psychotherapies: Features, foundations, and future directions. In R. A. Neimeyer & M. J. Mahoney (Eds.), *Constructivism in psychotherapy* (pp. 11–38). Washington, DC: American Psychological Association. doi:10.1037/10170-001

Raghavan, C., Le, H., & Berenbaum, H. (2002). Predicting dysphoria and hostility using the diathesis–stress model of sociotropy and autonomy in a contextualized stress setting. *Cognitive Therapy and Research, 26,* 231–244. doi:10.1023/A:1014525920767

Robins, C. J., Bagby, R. M., Rector, N. A., Lynch, T. R., & Kennedy, S. H. (1997). Sociotropy, autonomy, and patterns of symptoms in patients with major depression: A comparison of dimensional and categorical approaches. *Cognitive Therapy and Research, 21,* 285–300. doi:10.1023/A:1021874415967

Robins, C. J., & Block, P. (1989). Cognitive theories of depression viewed from a diathesis–stress perspective: Evaluations of the models of Beck and of Abramson, Seligman, and Teasdale. *Cognitive Therapy and Research, 13,* 297–313. doi:10.1007/BF01173475

Ross, L. R., & Clark, D. A. (1993). *A psychometric revision of Beck's Sociotropy–Autonomy Scale.* Poster session presented at the annual meeting of the Canadian Psychological Association, Montreal, Canada.

Schmidt, N. B., Joiner, T. E., Jr., Young, J. E., & Telch, M. J. (1995). The Schema Questionnaire: Investigation of psychometric properties and the hierarchical structure of a measure of maladaptive schemas. *Cognitive Therapy and Research, 19*, 295–321. doi:10.1007/BF02230402

Tarrier, N. (Ed.). (2006). *Case formulation in cognitive behaviour therapy: The treatment of challenging and complex cases*. New York, NY: Routledge.

Welburn, K., Coristine, M., Dagg, P., Pontefract, A., & Jordan, S. (2002). The Schema Questionnaire–Short Form: Factor analysis and relationship between schemas and symptoms. *Cognitive Therapy and Research, 26*, 519–530. doi:10.1023/A:1016231902020

Young, J. E. (1990). *Cognitive therapy for personality disorders: A schema-focused approach*. Sarasota, FL: Professional Resource Exchange.

Young, J. E., Klosko, J. S., & Weishaar, M. E. (2003). *Schema therapy: A practitioner's guide*. New York, NY: Guilford Press.

8

COGNITIVE THERAPY PROCESS

KEITH S. DOBSON

Once automatic thoughts are being consistently reported in treatment, appropriate interventions can be selected. Three broad classes of interventions for negative automatic thoughts can be distinguished by the manner in which the patient might answer the following three questions:

1. What evidence supports or does not support the automatic thought?
2. What are the viable alternative thoughts in this situation?
3. What meaning is attached to the automatic thought?

The interventions associated with each of these three questions are discussed next.

Excerpted from *Cognitive Therapy* (2012), from Chapter 4, "The Therapy Process," pp. 64–76. Copyright 2012 by the American Psychological Association. Used with permission of the author.

http://dx.doi.org/10.1037/14295-008
Psychotherapy Theories and Techniques: A Reader, G. R. VandenBos, E. Meidenbauer, and J. Frank-McNeil (Editors)
Copyright © 2014 by the American Psychological Association. All rights reserved.

EVIDENCE-BASED INTERVENTIONS
FOR AUTOMATIC THOUGHTS

In general, the first set of interventions that a cognitive therapist will consider relates to the match or mismatch between the automatic thought and the situation or trigger. Patients with various diagnoses characteristically distort or misperceive events or their own experiences in a manner that is consistent with their core beliefs and current problems. For example, patients with anxiety tend to overstate the danger of situations they face or might underestimate their ability to cope. Angry people often overstate the intention of another person with little supporting evidence. Therefore, identifying distorted or exaggerated thoughts is a regular feature of cognitive therapy for various disorders.

The general belief in cognitive therapy is that patients perceive the world and themselves in a manner consistent with their core beliefs and schemas. Schemas not only affect how we view events that have already occurred but also lead us to look for information in new situations that is consistent with our core beliefs and to engage in different behaviors that tend to reinforce our beliefs. Also as noted previously, the cognitive model presumes that real events occur and may be perceived accurately or be distorted. The degree of discrepancy between the actual event and the perception of it is a direct reflection of the degree of psychopathology experienced by the patient.

If the therapist comes to understand that the patient is engaging in cognitive distortions, either through reviewing thought records or other analyses of the negative thoughts that the patient brings to therapy, he or she may discuss the process of cognitive distortions with the patient. The therapist would educate the patient about the proactive nature of core beliefs and note that distortion is a normal process for anyone with a particular set of core beliefs. For example, a woman with social anxiety disorder likely has the perception that other people are critical, which leads her to reduce her social engagement, to perceive criticism from other people when it may not be intended, and generally to perpetuate her belief about the critical nature of others. Providing a rationale of this type to patients can allow them to understand why they might distort social interactions. An understanding of this process can also help patients in searching for distortive processes in the future.

A cognitive therapist who chooses to intervene in cognitive distortions might provide the patient with a list of cognitive distortions and a definition of each distortion. The patient might then be encouraged to examine his or her automatic thoughts and to explore with the therapist whether any of these thoughts are distorted. Some patients enjoy this investigative process, which can allow them to distance themselves from the momentary experience of the situation and to look at the "facts of the matter" more dispassionately. Some patients enjoy the process of labeling their own cognitive distortions because it gives them a shorthand way to think about their negative thought processes.

If the patient demonstrates a clear and repeated type of cognitive distortion, the cognitive therapist might discuss it at length with the patient. For example, many patients with anxiety disorders engage in fortune-telling and make negative predictions about what will happen if they confront their feared object or situation. The therapist can discuss the cognitive, emotional, and behavioral consequences of negative fortune-telling, and once the patient concurs, the therapist and patient can design a behavioral experiment to test the predictions that are being made by the patient. In the case of depression, a characteristic cognitive distortion is that of making negative attributions for failure (in particular, blaming oneself for negative outcomes). If the therapist observes this attributional pattern, he or she can spend time with the patient in observing the facts of the situation to determine whether negative attributions are warranted.

A number of specific interventions have been developed for the evidence-based approach to negative automatic thoughts. In some cases, the intervention consists of asking the patient for more details about the trigger or situation that precipitated the negative thoughts. The therapist then listens for distortions in the patient's perceptions and through a series of questions contrasts the facts of the matter with the perceptions. If skillfully done, this type of Socratic questioning will identify for the patient where he or she has exaggerated or misperceived the situation and will allow the patient to modify the automatic thoughts to be more consistent with the facts. In instances where insufficient evidence exists to fully judge the accuracy of the thought, homework may be developed to collect more information.

Negative fortune-telling is a common distortion. Often, based on the negative prediction, a patient may fail to engage in a particular social task or other behavior; indeed, avoidance patterns almost always have some degree of negative fortune-telling associated with them. For example, a patient who expects his partner to get angry with him in certain situations may purposely avoid getting into those situations. When this type of negative automatic thought emerges, the patient can undertake a homework assignment in which he or she makes a prediction (ideally, a specific and time-limited prediction that can be evaluated against the evidence), then goes out and collects information to evaluate the accuracy of the prediction. Such assignments are ideal in the context of cognitive therapy because they may identify exaggerated negative predictions by the patient and allow the patient to modify such predictions in the future. In instances where the outcome is partially negative, graduated thinking and degrees of success or failure can be discussed. And even in instances where the outcomes are as negative as the patient had predicted, the patient can still congratulate himself or herself for having explored the situation that has been previously avoided. In addition, knowing the actual outcomes will allow the therapist and patient to discuss more effective problem-solving strategies for use in the future.

As noted above, another fairly common type of cognitive distortion is negative attribution. Negative attributions occur regularly in patients with depression: They often blame themselves for perceived failure. Negative attributions also emerge in anger-related problems when the patient makes negative attributions toward other people in the social environment (e.g., "He did it to me, and on purpose"). Attributional biases are relatively easy to evaluate using evidence-based strategies. In the context of depression, overly negative attributions for failure can often be identified. Sometimes just drawing such biases to the attention of patients with depression can allow them to examine other causes for different outcomes and to blame themselves less for failure. As they make positive changes during treatment, depressed patients can use positive attributional biases to give themselves credit for the advances that they have made. Indeed, a general strategy in cognitive therapy is to encourage internal attributions for positive changes made over the course of therapy.

Labeling is yet another type of cognitive distortion that lends itself to an evidence-based intervention. People engage in labeling as a shorthand way to describe themselves or others. Labels are often extreme and, almost by definition, categorical. When the cognitive therapist hears a patient engaging in labeling, he or she can undertake a series of interventions. First, the therapist may inquire about the actual behaviors or attributes of a person that the patient uses as cues to make the label. Often a particular feature or behavior is being noted and other aspects of a person's behavior are ignored. Developing a broader perception of a person may undermine the labeling process. Second, the process of asking about the actual behaviors allows for a more complete description of the person, including not only the associated negative attributes but also his or her positive attributes or characteristics. Third, when the behaviors rather than the label are described, it often becomes clear that the person does not *always* do whatever the patient has noticed in applying the label. The awareness of variability allows for discussion about the extent to which that person engages in various activities and for a more graduated and evidence-based perception of the person.

Evidence-based strategies have recently been used with regard to delusions. Whereas in the past it was thought that formal delusional experiences could not be evaluated (since by definition they are out of contact with reality), more recent clinical experience and trials have shown that delusions can be subjected to evidence-based intervention (Beck, Rector, Stolar, & Grant, 2009). This type of intervention follows a series of steps: The particular delusional belief is identified, its consequences are named, predictions based on the delusional belief are made, and then evidence-based strategies are used to test the predictions. Recent clinical work suggests that evidence-based approaches can undermine the confidence that patients have in their deluded beliefs and, if the experiment is effective, can undermine a delusional idea (Kingdon & Turkington, 2005).

The following dialogue exemplifies how a cognitive therapist might work with a patient using evidence-based techniques:

Therapist: As you speak, I get the impression that you might sometimes not just react to the situation you are in, but also to your own way of thinking about things.

Patient: I'm not sure what you mean.

Therapist: Well, earlier you told me that you started to cry when you heard that your friend may have cancer.

Patient: Yes, of course.

Therapist: So what idea did you have, do you think, that made you so sad?

Patient: I imagined her husband and their children trying to get by without her. She has always been the strength in the family, and I just can't imagine them doing very well.

Therapist: So, in your mind, it is like you already have your friend dead and buried. But what did she actually tell you? Did she say she had cancer?

Patient: Well, no, not exactly. She told me she had a lump in her breast, and that she was going to see her doctor right away. I know that breast cancer is pretty serious.

Therapist: Do women have this problem without having cancer?

Patient: I suppose so.

Therapist: And if it was breast cancer, what is the survival rate?

Patient: I don't actually know.

Therapist: So, I think that I understand your compassion and concern about your friend and her family, but is it possible that you have maybe overreacted to what you actually know?

Patient: Well, when you put it this way, I guess so. But I was really upset, so naturally I just thought of the worst possibility.

In all of the evidence-based strategies listed above, it is insufficient for the therapist to have the evidence to undermine a given negative automatic thought. It is imperative for the patient to recognize the evidence that is needed to undermine the thought. An effective question that can be asked of the patient in designing experiments or evaluating evidence is, "What information or evidence would it take for you to change your mind?" Having elaborated the patient's requirement for evidence to modify the automatic thought, the therapist and patient can then work to that end. For the therapist to simply contradict the patient's automatic thoughts or to tell him or her the "truth" about a matter is rarely of much use because the patient's perspective is the critical ingredient in changing the emotional and behavioral outcomes of the initial perception.

ALTERNATIVE-BASED INTERVENTIONS

The second class of interventions in working with negative thoughts is the examination of alternatives. In some cases, having reviewed the evidence related to a negative automatic thought, it becomes apparent that the original thought is not justified. The patient can be asked for a more accurate rendition of the situation. A simple strategy to urge this type of alternative thinking is to inquire whether the patient can think about the event in another way. The tactic of encouraging alternative perspectives may illustrate for the patient how locked in and rigid certain types of thinking are. This exercise allows patients to look at the situation from another person's perspective or from their own perspective as if they were not as distressed.

A more formal strategy to encourage alternative responses to negative automatic thoughts is the rational role play in which the therapist asks the patient to state out loud his or her automatic thoughts. The therapist then verbalizes each statement and encourages the patient to respond, similar in form to a debate or a role play among alternative thoughts. If the patient struggles with this exercise, the therapist may role-play the alternative responses to the original negative thoughts to provide possible ways to "talk back" to these thoughts. The therapist should assess the believability of these alternatives so that the patient can either accept or reject them. If the therapist does take the step of responding to the negative automatic thoughts, it is necessary to reverse this role play so that the patient has the opportunity to respond in an alternative manner to his or her original negative thoughts. This type of role play exercise can be repeated across sessions until the patient is fluent with the process of responding to negative thoughts. The rational role play technique can incorporate elements of an evidence-based response, but the alternatives must be credible to the patient, even if no evidence exists to support or refute the alternative thoughts.

Another strategy to examine reasonable alternatives to negative automatic thoughts involves homework in which the patient identifies *possible* alternative thoughts, even in the absence of particular evidence and even if the alternatives do not seem credible. The homework assignment is not to find out whether the original thought was true but rather to poll friends and colleagues about alternative ways to view the situation. The strategy of polling encourages the patient to learn about perspectives that may be viable alternatives to the original negative thought. If the therapist is aware of a particular resource or system to capture such alternatives, this kind of perspective taking might be extended by using various media or other information sources. For example, in *Feeling Good* (Burns, 1980), different types of alternative perspectives are provided for difficult thoughts in several chapters. In addition, movies or books might aid in this type of perspective taking.

Another strategy for generating alternatives to negative thoughts is to treat the process as a problem-solving exercise. In problem-solving therapy (D'Zurilla & Nezu, 2007), the technique for overcoming problems involves generating as many ways to solve a problem as possible. During problem solving, the patient is encouraged to withhold any judgments about the "correct" or optimal response until the largest possible number of alternatives has been generated. In like fashion, cognitive therapists can encourage the patient to generate many alternative thoughts to the particular situation, and the therapist and patient can together review the viability of the alternative perspectives. This exercise also can be useful in assessing the patient's ability to think about situations in different ways. If necessary, the therapist can prompt or encourage different ways of thinking about situations. In general, however, a cognitive therapist will tend not to provide alternative perspectives unless the patient is willing to entertain the suggestions as reasonable alternatives. Again, the purpose of looking at alternative thoughts is not to generate ideas that the therapist can believe but rather to develop alternatives that are credible to the patient.

The use of humor is another strategy to encourage alternative perspectives to a negative thought. Jokes and humor often require a sudden shift in perspective. For example, many jokes are set up so that the listener expects a certain kind of dialogue or communication; a twist in perspective or radical shift in what is being communicated creates humor. If the therapeutic relationship is sound and if patients have shown any predilection toward humor, subtle jokes about the patients' original negative thoughts can encourage them to look at alternatives. If humor is used as a cognitive therapy technique, being clear that the humor is directed toward the thoughts rather than the patients is critical. Belief by patients that the therapist is making fun of them or is not taking their problems seriously can lead to a therapeutic rupture. Humor should be used judiciously and typically later in the process of therapy, once the patient is feeling better than when he or she first came to therapy and when the therapist is confident in the therapeutic relationship.

Another technique to encourage alternative thoughts is to ask the patient how useful or adaptive the original negative thought was. The intent is not to look at the accuracy or the viability of the negative thought but rather at its value or utility in the patient's life. In some cases, a negative thought might be accurate, but holding on to it is not helpful with respect to the patient's ongoing relationships or longer term personal goals (e.g., "Yes, he hurt your pride. How helpful is it, though, to harbor resentment toward men in general? Doesn't this reaction get in the way of making new relationships?"). In such cases, patients can be asked about the value of retaining this thought to encourage them to hold on to it less tightly so that alternative thoughts can be entertained.

The question about the value of holding on to a particular thought may lead to a broader discussion about the meaning that the thought has for the patient. A patient may say that he cannot let go of a particular thought even though he knows that it is problematic because to do so would have a particular meaning for him. For example, a patient might hang on to hurt feelings that were precipitated by a relationship rejection long after the other person has started new relationships. On inquiry, it may turn out that he has this reaction because giving up hurt feelings would signal to him that the relationship is over and that he is alone. The discussion can then lead to a deeper discussion about the meanings associated with particular negative thoughts, as is described below.

Emotional reasoning is a type of negative thought that lends itself to an examination of alternatives. Emotional reasoning occurs when people use their emotional response to a situation to justify the automatic thought that led to the response. For example, after an altercation the patient may say " I felt horrible, so she must have really insulted me badly." If the therapist hears this type of distortion, the logical error of affirming an antecedent based on a consequence can be discussed. The therapist can also use this opportunity to generate alternative thoughts or reactions to the situation as thought experiments. For example, the therapist can ask questions such as "How might somebody else have responded to this situation?" or "How might you have responded to this situation, if you weren't feeling the way that you are at present?" The therapist can help the patient recognize that thoughts do not establish facts; thoughts are just thoughts and can be evaluated in their own right.

Which of the above methods is most effective in generating credible alternatives to the original negative thought? Unfortunately, discovering which of these interventions will be effective with a particular patient, or at what time over the course of therapy it will be effective, is often a matter of trial and error. Fortunately, cognitive therapists have generated many interventions, so if one attempt does not work, an alternative strategy may be effective.

Sometimes it is useful to step back from the actual interventions and discuss with the patient the general idea of looking at the evidence and the alternatives to negative thoughts. Such a discussion has an educational aspect and provides a framework for the patient to think about his or her negative thoughts. The discussion also signals the therapist's desire to help the patient develop more adaptive ways to respond to difficult situations and to give the patient the freedom to approach difficult people and situations in more productive ways.

Cognitive restructuring techniques such as those described above often can be done through simple therapeutic dialogue—the thrust and parry of verbal exchange in psychotherapy. However, it is also possible to formalize these strategies through written experiments. A number of techniques have been developed in this regard. For example, a relatively easy strategy for looking at alternative thoughts is through the use of a flash card. If the patient has a repetitive negative thought or behavioral pattern to which a more adaptive and viable alternative can be generated, the original negative thought can be written on the top part of the flash card and the more viable alternative on the bottom. The card can be posted in a visible location for the patient, such as on the refrigerator at home or on a bulletin board at work, so that when the original negative thought occurs, the alternative is readily available. A similar technique is called TIC-TOC. In TIC-TOC, if a patient has a recurring negative thought that can be counteracted by a viable and reasonable alternative, the patient can be encouraged to think about the image of a pendulum clock, so that when the first TIC (task-interfering cognition) occurs, it can be replaced with a TOC (task-oriented cognition).

Perhaps the best-known formal technique for modifying automatic thoughts is the use of an expanded dysfunctional thought record (DTR). Figure 8.1 presents an example of a complete DTR. Columns have been added for the identification of cognitive distortions in the figure, the correction of negative thoughts (which can be achieved through evidence review, the generation of reasonable alternatives, or a combination), and the emotional and behavioral outcomes of the alternative thoughts. This type of DTR allows the patient and therapist to work through various difficult situations and negative thoughts, to explore them fully, and to formally write down the method for changing these thoughts. In many cases of cognitive therapy, several sessions will be spent working through DTRs to ensure that the patient has the techniques well in hand. In addition to having these forms preprinted, free-form diary formats, handwritten sheets, or computerized thought records may be used. Regardless of the type of form, the key is to have the methods readily available for use by patients. The cognitive therapist should use the format that will work in the patient's life.

Date/time	Situation	Automatic thoughts (Believability rating, 0–100)	Emotions (Intensity rating, 0–100)	Behaviors	Distortions	Responses to automatic thoughts (Believability rating, 0–100)	Emotions (Intensity rating, 0–100)	Behaviors
May 17, 8:30 p.m.	My husband was home late from work again, after saying he would not be. This is the fifth time this month.	Where is he? (50)	Anxiety (50)			I do not know. (100)	Anxiety (50)	Reading a book with the TV on in the background.
		He is having an affair. (85)	Anger (50) Sadness 30		Arbitrary inference	I do not have any evidence to know. He seems loving enough when home. (80)	Anger (30)	
		Maybe he has had an accident. (25)	Anxiety (20)	Watching TV for accident reports.	Arbitrary inference	If there was an accident, the police would phone. (70)	Worry (10)	
		His work is too demanding. (60)	Anger (50)		Maximization Ignoring the positive	He says he enjoys his work. (90)	Anger (20)	
		If he loved me, he would at least call. (90)	Sadness (50) Loneliness (70) Anger (80)	Check to see if phone line is working.	Arbitrary inference	Phoning would not prove his love for me. (80)	Loneliness (40) Love (50)	

Figure 8.1. Completed dysfunctional thought record.

REFERENCES

Beck, A. T., Rector, N. A., Stolar, N., & Grant, P. (2009). *Schizophrenia: Cognitive theory, research, and therapy.* New York, NY: Guilford Press.

Burns, D. D. (1980). *Feeling good: The new mood therapy.* New York, NY: Morrow.

D'Zurilla, T. J., & Nezu, A. M. (2007). *Problem-solving therapy: A positive approach to clinical intervention* (3rd ed.). New York, NY: Springer.

Kingdon, D. G., & Turkington, D. (2005). *Cognitive therapy of schizophrenia.* New York, NY: Guilford Press.

APPENDIX 8.1: COGNITIVE THERAPY TECHNIQUES

Technique	Video title	Video identifying number	Time at which technique occurs
Homework	Cognitive Therapy to Control Compulsions (Session 3 of 6)	777700389-001	33:58–37:43
Collaborative empiricism	Cognitive Therapy to Control Compulsions (Session 2 of 6)	777700388-001	41:20–43:50
Psychoeducation	Cognitive Therapy to Control Compulsions (Session 4 of 6)	777700390-001	39:40–43:30
Automatic thoughts: Evidence-based interventions	Cognitive Therapy to Control Compulsions (Session 5 of 6)	777700391-001	32:32–38:17
Automatic thoughts: Alternative interventions	Cognitive Therapy to Control Compulsions (Session 2 of 6)	777700388-001	27:42–29:40
Flash cards	Cognitive Therapy to Control Compulsions (Session 4 of 6)	777700390-001	31:15–35:30
Dysfunctional thought record	Learning to Overcome Automatic Negative Thoughts	777700126-001	43:28–45:10
Thinking about an event in a different way	Cognitive Therapy to Control Compulsions (Session 4 of 6)	777700390-001	28:18–30:25
Encouraging positive thoughts	Cognitive Therapy to Control Compulsions (Session 4 of 6)	777700390-001	19:17–20:03
Meaning-based intervention (downward arrow)	Cognitive Therapy to Control Compulsions (Session 1 of 6)	777700387-001	23:18–26:33
Data log	Cognitive Therapy to Control Compulsions (Session 1 of 6)	777700387-001	36:10–38:10
Public declaration	Cognitive Therapy to Control Compulsions (Session 2 of 6)	777700388-001	3:02–4:34
Behavioral enactment	Cognitive Therapy to Control Compulsions (Session 3 of 6)	777700389-001	36:20–39:18
Confrontation and exploration	Cognitive Therapy to Control Compulsions (Session 3 of 6)	777700389-001	31:57–33:38
Acceptance: recognizing relapse	Pathological Gambling Prevention	777700114-001	29:33–30:28

(continues)

Acceptance: Coping with difficult people or situations	Cognitive Therapy to Control Compulsions (Session 5 of 6)	777700391-001	29:30–31:28
Acceptance: Tolerating emotional distress	Cognitive Therapy to Control Compulsions (Session 5 of 6)	777700391-001	15:20–16:23
Relaxation	Developing an Exercise Plan	777700002-001	19:27–22:50
De-escalation of conflict	Cognitive Behavioral Therapy for Anxiety Disorders	777700026-001	41:12–42:17
Mindfulness and meditation	Treating Substance Abuse Problems Through Mindfulness and Meditation	777700067-001	25:10–43:10
Cognitive reinterpretation	Cognitive Therapy to Control Compulsions (Session 4 of 6)	777700390-001	13:30–17:23
Therapy notebook		777700392-001	39:37–41:18
Fading of treatment sessions	Cognitive Therapy to Control Compulsions (Session 4 of 6)	777700390-001	25:50–26:55
Self session	Cognitive Behavioral Therapy for Anxiety Disorders	777700227-001	42:45–45:15

9

COGNITIVE–BEHAVIORAL THERAPY

MICHELLE G. CRASKE

The principles and theories that underlie cognitive–behavioral therapy (CBT) derive from several different sources that have become interweaved with each other as CBT has developed from its initial behavioral routes to the contemporary cognitive–behavioral integration. The more behaviorally oriented clinician will draw mainly from learning theory in conceptualizing a presenting problem and formulating a treatment plan, whereas the more cognitively oriented clinician will favor the theory and principles of cognitive appraisal. The cognitive–behavioral clinician can comfortably draw from both learning theories (including social learning theory) and cognitive appraisal theory to conceptualize a problem and formulate a treatment plan.

Excerpted from *Cognitive–Behavioral Therapy* (2010), from Chapter 3, "Theory," pp. 19–26. Copyright 2010 by the American Psychological Association. Used with permission of the author.

http://dx.doi.org/10.1037/14295-009

Psychotherapy Theories and Techniques: A Reader, G. R. VandenBos, E. Meidenbauer, and J. Frank-McNeil (Editors)

Copyright © 2014 by the American Psychological Association. All rights reserved.

GOALS

Broadly speaking, the goal of CBT is to achieve symptom reduction and improvement in quality of life through the replacement of maladaptive emotional, behavioral, and cognitive response chains with more adaptive responses. Underlying this goal is the notion that problem behaviors, cognitions, and emotions have been acquired at least in part through experience and learning and therefore are open to modification through new experience and learning.[1] The target of CBT is to teach new ways of responding and to develop new learning experiences that together promote more adaptive patterns of behavioral, affective, and cognitive responding. Also, these changes are attempted within relatively brief periods of time; in other words, CBT aims to be not only problem-focused but also time limited.

Another goal of CBT is for long-term positive effects that are self-maintaining. Thus, learning experiences are repeated, and new ways of responding are practiced over a sufficient number of occasions and contexts that they become the major determinants and preferred methods of responding in the long term, independent of the therapy context. In this way, CBT aims to tool clients with their own repertoire of skills for dealing with problematic situations and thereby become less and less dependent on, and eventually autonomous from, the therapist.

These two overarching goals are achieved within the framework of a set of guiding principles of behavioral theory and science and cognitive theory (and more recently, cognitive science) for conceptualizing presenting problems and formulating intervention strategies. These principles drive another goal, which is to use an individually based functional analysis of the causal relations among cognitions, behaviors, emotions, and environmental and cultural contexts for tailoring intervention strategies specifically to the needs of a given problem. Thus, rather than assuming that one standard treatment fits all, CBT is based on careful observation and understanding of each individual's presenting problem. Functional analysis refers to an analysis of not only the instrumental antecedents and consequences, but also which stimuli are producing which conditional responses (CRs), which cognitions are contributing to behaviors and emotions, and within which environmental and cultural contexts these occur. The therapist and client then make an informed choice about which methods for behavioral and cognitive change to use from a variety of different intervention strategies.

Another goal is to have a flexible approach to implementation, which is facilitated by ongoing evaluation and modification of intervention strategies

---

[1]Genetic endowments and temperament are viewed as additional contributing factors to problem behaviors, cognitions, and emotions.

as appropriate. Linked with this is the aim of engaging the client in the process of experimentation and ongoing evaluation of the effectiveness of the chosen interventions. Evaluation not only permits revision to the intervention strategies where necessary but provides an assessment of overall progress. Overall progress is measured by agreed-upon markers between the client and the therapist, and when the evidence indicates lack of progress, consideration is given to alternative treatment methods. Clearly, this entails therapist–client collaboration in formulating and implementing a treatment plan and a highly active orientation on the part of the client.

LEARNING THEORY: CLASSICAL CONDITIONING

Classical (or respondent) conditioning depends on innately evocative stimuli (unconditioned stimulus [US]) producing an unconditional, reflexive response (UR), such as when physical injury reflexively produces a pain grimace. When a neutral stimulus is paired with the US, the neutral stimulus becomes a conditional stimulus (CS) with powers to elicit a CR that resembles the original UR (Pavlov, 1927). For example, in the case of persons undergoing chemotherapy (US) that causes them to vomit (UR), the nurse may become a CS by association with administration of the chemotherapy. Consequently, sight of the nurse may produce conditional nausea in the patient even before the chemotherapy is administered the next time. Furthermore, through a process of generalization, the CR may begin to emerge in reaction to stimuli similar to the original CS. Following from the preceding example, generalization may result in conditional nausea in response to seeing the medical clinic or administrative staff. In addition, Pavlov (1927) demonstrated that if the CS is presented enough times without the US, the CR lessens or extinguishes. Continuing the example, once the chemotherapy course has completed, repeated visits to the clinic for checkups would result in an eventual diminution of the conditional nausea response.

The principles of aversive classical conditioning are applied mostly to anxiety disorders. Early theorizing of fears and phobias relied on *contiguous* classical conditioning models in which a neutral stimulus develops conditional fear-provoking properties simply by virtue of close temporal pairing with an aversive stimulus. Examples would include ridicule and rejection by a peer group leading to conditional fear (i.e., phobia) of social situations or barking by a ferocious dog leading to phobias of dogs. These early theories were criticized for being too simplistic (e.g., Rachman, 1978), especially as not everyone who undergoes an aversive experience develops a phobia. That is, not everyone who is ridiculed by a peer group develops social phobia, and not everyone who is barked at by a ferocious dog develops a phobia of dogs.

Recent revisions to classical conditioning models of fear and anxiety (see Mineka & Zinbarg, 2006, for a review) correct the earlier pitfalls.

The newer models continue to emphasize the role of aversive experiences in the formation of conditional anxiety responses, but instead of being limited to direct experience with negative events, they extend to conditioning through vicarious observation of negative events or even informational transmission about negative events (see Mineka & Zinbarg, 2006, for citations of supportive research). For example, observing someone else be physically injured and/or be terrified in a car accident may be sufficient for the development of a conditional fear of motor vehicles, as would being told about the dangers of driving and the high likelihood of fatal car accidents. Vicarious and informational transmission of conditioning represents the incorporation of cognitive processes into classical conditioning models. The newer conditioning models also recognize that a myriad of constitutional, contextual, and postevent factors moderate the likelihood of developing a conditional phobia after an aversive event. Constitutional factors (or individual difference variables) include temperament. For example, individuals who tend to be more nervous in general are believed to be more likely to develop a conditional phobia after a negative experience than less "neurotic" individuals who undergo the same negative experience. Another constitutional factor is personal history of experience with the stimulus that is subsequently paired with an aversive event, as prior positive experience may buffer against the development of a conditional phobia. For example, the effects of observing one parent react fearfully to heights may be buffered by having previously observed other family members react without fear to heights. Recognition of individual difference factors addresses the earlier criticism that not everyone who undergoes an aversive experience develops a phobia; rather, certain individuals are prone to developing conditional phobic responses following an aversive experience as a function of their temperament and life experience.

Contextual factors at the time of the aversive experience include intensity and controllability: More intense and less controllable negative events are more likely to generate conditional fear than less intense and/or more controllable negative events. According to these premises, individuals trapped for a lengthy period of time inside an elevator stuck between floors would be more likely to develop a conditional fear of elevators than the person who can escape from a stuck elevator relatively quickly. Similarly, soldiers at the front line of combat would be more likely to develop conditional fear than those further away. Another contextual factor pertains to principles of preparedness, or the innate propensity to rapidly acquire conditional fear of stimuli that posed threat to our early ancestors (Seligman, 1971). Examples of such stimuli are heights, closed-in spaces from which it is difficult to escape, reptiles, and signals of rejection from one's group. Thus, as a species, humans are more likely to develop long-lasting conditional fears following negative experiences in prepared situations (e.g., being laughed at by peers) compared to other, "non-prepared" situations (e.g., being shocked by an electric outlet). Preparedness is believed to account for the nonrandomness of phobias, or the fact that some objects or situations are much more likely to become feared than other objects.

Following conditioning, a variety of postevent processes may influence the persistence of conditional fear, including additional aversive experiences, expectancies for aversive outcomes (Davey, 2006), and avoidant responding. For example, the child who is teased by a peer group, then ruminates about being teased, expects further teasing, and avoids the peer group is more likely to develop social anxiety than the child who undergoes the same teasing but returns to the peer group the next day. In sum, recent models of classical conditioning recognize that the development of an excessive and chronic conditional fear is not explained by a specific aversive event in isolation but by an interaction among predisposing features, the aversive event, and reactions to the event.

The classical conditioning model is also applicable to disorders related to substance use, in which the principles of appetitive conditioning apply as well as aversive conditioning. Appetitive conditioning refers to conditioning with a US that produces an innately positive response, whereas aversive conditioning refers to conditioning with a US that produces an innately negative response. In the case of substance use disorders, euphoria serves as an innately positive UR to the drug. Over time, environmental stimuli present during the euphoric state become conditional. These environmental stimuli may be the locations in which the drugs are usually consumed or the people with whom drug taking normally occurs. Consequently, the environmental stimuli elicit conditional urges or cravings to take more of the drug. Known as the *conditioned appetitive motivational model of craving* (Stewart, de Wit, & Eikelboom, 1984), this model explains the difficulties experienced when recovering drug users return to the environments in which they originally developed their drug dependence. That is, just seeing a group of friends with whom drugs used to be taken may be enough to produce cravings for the drugs, even though the drugs themselves are not present.

Siegel (1978) proposed the conditional compensatory response model, a classical conditioning model of drug tolerance. In this model, environmental stimuli associated with drug intake become associated with the drug's effect on the body and elicit a CR that is opposite to the effect of the drug, driven by an automatic drive for body homeostasis. As this CR increases in magnitude with continued drug use, the drug's effects decrease and tolerance increases. Finally, aversive classical conditioning has been evoked as an additional mechanism by which stimuli associated with the unpleasant periods of drug withdrawal elicit withdrawal-like symptoms. For example, if withdrawal is typically experienced upon waking from sleep, then waking may elicit conditioned withdrawal symptoms that in turn could drive continued drug use to minimize withdrawal effects.

PRINCIPLES OF TREATMENT

The treatment model that derives from classical conditioning states that behaviors and emotions can be changed by disrupting the associations that have formed between a cue (CS) and either an aversive or a pleasant outcome (US). In learning theory, this is referred to as extinction. Conditioning involves pairings of the CS with the US; extinction involves repeated presentations of the CS without the US. The corresponding treatment is referred to as exposure therapy; in this therapy, the client repeatedly faces the object of fear (in the case of anxiety disorders) or the drug-related cue (in the case of substance use disorders) in the absence of an aversive or a pleasant outcome. As an example, individuals with social anxiety would be encouraged to repeatedly enter social situations without being ridiculed or rejected, or individuals with posttraumatic stress disorder would be encouraged to repeatedly enter places where they were previously traumatized without being retraumatized. As another example, individuals who drink alcohol excessively would be exposed to substance cues (e.g., sight or smell of alcohol) and prevented from consuming the alcohol so that the CS is repeatedly presented in the absence of reinforcement that comes from the consumption of the drug. This is called cue exposure.

Several mechanisms are believed to underlie extinction and thereby exposure therapy. One such mechanism is habituation (or decreased response strength simply as a function of repeated exposure). Another mechanism, inhibitory learning, is considered to be even more central to extinction (Myers & Davis, 2007). Inhibitory learning means that the original association between a CS and aversive event is not erased throughout extinction, but rather a new inhibitory association (or expectancy) is developed. For example, as a result of exposure therapy for fear of dogs, an original "excitatory" association between a dog and ferocious barking would be complemented by a new "inhibitory" association between a dog and the absence of ferocious barking. Consequently, as a result of exposure therapy, two sets of associations exist in memory. Once exposure therapy is over, the level of fear that is expressed when a dog is encountered in daily life will depend on which set of associations is evoked. Interestingly, basic research by Bouton and colleagues (reviewed in Bouton, Woods, Moody, Sunsay, & Garcia-Gutierrez, 2006) indicates that context is important in determining which set of associations is evoked. If the previously feared stimulus is encountered in a context that is similar to the extinction/exposure therapy context, then the inhibitory association will be more likely to be activated, resulting in minimal fear. However, if the previously feared stimulus is encountered in a context distinctly different from the extinction/exposure therapy context, then the original excitatory association is more likely to be activated, resulting in more fear. Following the example of dog phobia, assume that the exposure treatment was conducted in a dog training center. Then, once treatment is over, a dog is encountered on a neighborhood sidewalk, a context that is distinctly different from the dog training center. On the sidewalk, the original excitatory fear association is more likely to be activated than the new inhibitory association that was developed throughout exposure treatment, resulting in the expression of fear.

Thus, a change in context is presumed to at least partially account for the return of fear that sometimes occurs following exposure therapy for anxiety disorders (Craske et al., 2008) and relapse following treatment for substance use disorders (e.g., Collins & Brandon, 2002). In addition to context, other factors can also reactivate the original excitatory association. One such factor is being exposed to a new negative experience. Thus, persons who are successfully treated for their fear of dogs may have their fear return if they are subsequently involved in a car accident (in learning theory this is called *reinstatement*) or if they are barked at by another ferocious dog (termed *reacquisition*).

Innovative strategies are now being tested for enhancing new inhibitory associations throughout exposure therapy (see Craske et al., 2008, for a review). In addition, attention is being given to ways of enhancing the retrievability of new inhibitory associations once exposure therapy is completed, and thereby decreasing relapse, such as conducting exposure therapy in multiple contexts. Another is to provide retrieval cues that remind clients, when they are outside of the therapy context, of the new learning that took place in the therapy context or at least recommend to clients that they actively try to remember what they learned when in the therapy context (see Craske et al., 2008).

Another key concept associated with extinction of CRs is safety signals, or conditional inhibitors that predict the absence of the aversive stimulus. When the conditional inhibitor is present, the CS is not paired with the US; when the conditional inhibitor is not present, the CS is paired with the US. In the experimental literature, safety signals alleviate distress to the CS in the short term, but when no longer present, fear to the CS returns (Lovibond, Davis, & O'Flaherty, 2000). Common safety signals for anxiety disorder clients are the presence of another person, therapists, medications, food, or drink. Thus, clients with panic disorder and agoraphobia may feel relatively comfortable walking around a shopping mall with a bottle of medication in their pocket (even if the medication is never taken) but report being anxious in the shopping mall when without the bottle of medication. Conditional inhibitors have been shown to interfere with extinction learning in human experimental studies (e.g., Lovibond et al., 2000).

REFERENCES

Bouton, M. E., Woods, A. M., Moody, E. W., Sunsay, C., & Garcia-Gutierrez, A. (2006). Counteracting the context-dependence of extinction: Relapse and tests of some relapse prevention methods. In M. G. Craske, D. Hermans, & D. Vansteenwegen (Eds.), *Fear and learning: From basic processes to clinical implications* (pp. 175–196). Washington, DC: American Psychological Association.

Collins, B. N., & Brandon, T. H. (2002). Effects of extinction context and retrieval cues on alcohol cue reactivity among nonalcoholic drinkers. *Journal of Consulting and Clinical Psychology, 70*, 390–397. doi:10.1037/0022-006X.70.2.390

Craske, M. G., Kircanksi, K., Zelikowsky, M., Mystkowski, J., Chowdhury, N., & Baker, A. (2008). Optimizing inhibitory learning during exposure therapy. *Behaviour Research and Therapy, 46*, 5–27. doi:10.1016/j.brat.2007.10.003

Davey, G. C. L. (2006). Cognitive mechanisms in fear acquisition and maintenance. In M. G. Craske, D. Hermans, & D. Vansteenwegen (Eds.), *Fear and learning: From basic processes to clinical implications* (pp. 99–116). Washington, DC: American Psychological Association.

Lovibond, P. F., Davis, N. R., & O'Flaherty, A. S. (2000). Protection from extinction in human fear conditioning. *Behaviour Research and Therapy, 38*, 967–983. doi:10.1016/S0005-7967(99)00121-7

Mineka, S., & Zinbarg, R. (2006). A contemporary learning theory perspective on the etiology of anxiety disorder: It's not what you thought it was. *American Psychologist, 61*, 10–26. doi:10.1037/0003-066X.61.1.10

Myers, K. M., & Davis, M. (2007). Mechanisms of fear extinction. *Molecular Psychiatry, 12*, 120–150. doi:10.1038/sj.mp.4001939

Pavlov, I. P. (1927). *Conditioned reflexes* (G. V. Anrep, Trans). London, England: Oxford University Press.

Rachman, S. (1978). *Fear and courage.* San Francisco, CA: Freeman.

Seligman, M. E. P. (1971). Phobias and preparedness. *Behavior Therapy, 2*, 307–320. doi:10.1016/S0005-7894(71)80064-3

Siegel, S. (1978). Tolerance to the hyperthermic effect of morphine in the rat is a learned response. *Journal of Comparative and Physiological Psychology, 92*, 1137–1149. doi:10.1037/h0077525

Stewart, J., de Wit, H., & Eikelboom, R. (1984). Role of unconditioned and conditioned drug effects in the self-administration of opiates and stimulants. *Psychological Review, 91*(2), 251–268. doi:10.1037/0033-295x.91.2.251

10

COGNITIVE–BEHAVIORAL THERAPY PROCESS

MICHELLE G. CRASKE

SKILL- AND REINFORCEMENT-BASED STRATEGIES

Self-Monitoring

In cognitive–behavioral therapy (CBT), self-monitoring is a tool for evaluating the functional relations among thoughts, behaviors, and emotions, and their antecedents and consequences, as they occur (vs. retrospective report). Self-monitoring is particularly valuable for recording subjective experience, such as appraisals (e.g., "My friends must think I am a fool.") and levels of subjective distress. Moreover, self-monitoring is useful for behaviors or physiological events that are difficult to record otherwise because they occur infrequently (e.g., occasional panic attacks) or under conditions that

Excerpted from *Cognitive–Behavioral Therapy* (2010), from Chapter 4, "The Therapy Process," pp. 62–71. Copyright 2010 by the American Psychological Association. Used with permission of the author.

http://dx.doi.org/10.1037/14295-010
Psychotherapy Theories and Techniques: A Reader, G. R. VandenBos, E. Meidenbauer, and J. Frank-McNeil (Editors)
Copyright © 2014 by the American Psychological Association. All rights reserved.

are difficult to replicate in the presence of the therapist (e.g., compulsive rituals that are dependent on the home environment; Craske & Tsao, 1999). Overall, self-monitoring is used widely across a large array of disorders and behavioral problems.

Self-monitoring begins with a rationale that emphasizes the importance of a personal scientist model of learning to observe one's own reactions. Then, clients are trained to use objective terms and anchors rather than affective-laden terms. For example, clients with panic disorder are trained to record the intensity of their symptoms on 0- to 10-point scales in place of using a general description of how "bad" the panic attack felt. The objectivity of recording is presumed to enhance its effectiveness. Then, clients are taught what, when, where, and how to record. Various types of recording exist, but the most common are event recording, or whether an event occurs during a period of recording (e.g., did a panic attack occur today), and frequency recording, or recording every event during the period of recording (e.g., every panic attack during the day).

Diaries are the most common form of recording, although counters or palm tops can be used. Data are then transformed into graphs, to demonstrate change over time (such as frequency of panic attacks per week, or average number of calories consumed per day). Feedback from the therapist about self-monitoring positively influences compliance with self-monitoring. In addition, therapists can use the self-monitoring data to emphasize progress or to identify previously undetailed functional relations among cognitions, behaviors, and emotions that are worthy of targeting in treatment.

The underlying mechanisms of self-monitoring are not entirely clear, although increased awareness of the problem behavior and/or its antecedents and consequences may facilitate motivation to change (Heidt & Marx, 2003). Additionally, recording the frequency of behaviors over the course of therapy may provide reinforcement as positive behavioral changes are noted. Also, self-monitoring may provide a cue or reminder for engaging in newly acquired cognitive and behavioral skills.

Rarely is there an outright contraindication to self-monitoring, although the method of monitoring is often modified to suit particular needs and offset potential pitfalls. For example, the person with obsessive–compulsive or perfectionistic tendencies may benefit from limit setting or tightly abbreviated forms of self-monitoring. Occasionally, negative affect can be worsened as it is monitored. For example, monitoring negative affect may activate negative self-evaluation; something that may be then addressed by cognitive restructuring of the negative self-evaluation. Self-monitoring in general will be more difficult for the person who lacks motivation and in turn serves to "confirm" a sense of failure in those persons who already judge themselves to be failures and cannot even succeed at self-monitoring (Heidt & Marx, 2003). In the latter case, problem solving and behavioral activation may be helpful approaches for increasing engagement in self-monitoring.

Relaxation

Relaxation has been a mainstay of behavioral treatments and encompasses an array of strategies, including autogenic training (Schultz & Luthe, 1959), progressive muscle relaxation training (Jacobson, 1938), breathing retraining (e.g., Kraft & Hoogduin, 1984), and various forms of meditation and yoga. Progressive muscle relaxation is a commonly used methodology, although in its condensed form of 8 to 15 sessions as standardized by Bernstein and Borkovec (1973) relative to the lengthy training (30–50 sessions) originally developed by Jacobson (1938). Progressive muscle relaxation training involves tensing and relaxing major muscle groups in progression, followed by deepening relaxation through slow breathing and/or imagery. The data show that muscle relaxation is anxiety reducing overall (e.g., Lang, Melamed, & Hart, 1970). Relaxation has been used for sleep disturbance, headache, hypertension, asthma, alcohol usage, hyperactivity, and various forms of anxiety, as well as other disorders.

The procedure involves progressive tensing (for 10 s) and relaxing (for 15–20 s) the following muscle groups: dominant hand and forearm, dominant bicep, nondominant hand and forearm, nondominant bicep, forehead, upper cheeks and nose, lower cheeks and jaws, neck and throat, chest/shoulders and upper back, abdominal region, dominant thigh, dominant calf, dominant foot, nondominant thigh, nondominant calf, nondominant foot.

After a rationale is provided, the client's current emotional state is measured for purpose of comparison with the state that is achieved after relaxation. This can be done using a simple 0 to 100 visual analogue scale or a more sophisticated behavioral relaxation scale (Poppen, 1998). The latter scale also provides a precise definition of the targeted state of each body area to be achieved during relaxation. Next, the therapist provides a verbal description and then models the relaxed and tensed postures for each muscle area. The client then imitates the therapist while the latter provides feedback. The entire set of tensing and relaxing exercises are completed with therapist guidance. The client then practices the procedure daily between therapy sessions. Over sessions, the number of muscle groups can be reduced (from 16 to 8 to 4 muscle groups). Furthermore, cue-controlled relaxation is sometimes used, in which the state of relaxation between each tensing is paired with the word "relax"; that word then becomes a conditional cue that eventually elicits conditional relaxed sensations in isolation of the entire set of tensing and releasing exercises.

One mechanism underlying relaxation training is enhanced discrimination between feelings of relaxation and tension, achieved through paying attention to the sensations associated with each state during the training. The assumption is that clients then are better able to detect tension in their daily lives (Ferguson, 2003). Second, the training is presumed to build a skill for how to evoke the relaxation response as a means of self-control when experiencing tension in daily life. The physiological intent is for relaxation to activate more parasympathetic activity and thereby slow sympathetic autonomic processes such as heart rate and sweating. However, as with other relaxation techniques, such as breathing retraining, the mechanism may pertain more to a sense of control or other cognitive variables than to actual physiological change (e.g., Garssen, de Ruiter, & van Dyck, 1992).

When relaxation is paired with a biofeedback signal, as is used in the treatment of headache or chronic pain, another mechanism is brought to bear, that being shaping through reinforcement. That is, changes in physiological responding are achieved by continuous raising of the criterion (such as larger reductions in muscle tension) and reinforcement for each successful attainment of the criterion in the form of the biofeedback signal. Again, however, others suggest that perceptions of control may be equally if not more accountable for the effectiveness of biofeedback, since use of bogus biofeedback signals is as effective as veridical feedback (e.g., Rains, 2008). As an example, Mary had suffered from chronic tension headaches for many years. She was first taught progressive muscle relaxation training, including cue-controlled relaxation, which she practiced twice daily in relaxing environments for three weeks. Then, while continuing to use progressive muscle relaxation as a daily exercise, she simultaneously used the cue-controlled element of relaxation within the context of six weekly biofeedback sessions as she learned to progressively lower her muscle tension. As a result of this training, Mary's self-monitoring of headache activity indicated that it had decreased by approximately one half since the two weeks before treatment initiated.

The skill of relaxation is most often employed for states of heightened autonomic arousal that interfere with quality of life or therapy progress, or as a coping skill to actively face challenging situations. Relaxation has been shown to be particularly helpful in the treatment of phobias and anxiety disorders, preparing for surgery and other medical procedures, and coping with chronic pain. It is also incorporated into treatments that focus on emotion regulation, as in dialectical behavior therapy for borderline personality disorder (Linehan, 1994). Occasionally, negative reactions can be produced by relaxation, such as relaxation-induced anxiety (Heide & Borkovec, 1983). The latter involves intrusive thoughts, fears of losing control, and the experience of unusual and therefore anxiety-producing bodily sensations (such as depersonalization). However, rather than being a contraindication to continued relaxation, discussion of the processes and continued exposure to relaxation and its associated states can be an effective tool for managing relaxation-induced anxiety.

Behavioral Rehearsal of Social Skills and Assertiveness

In behavioral rehearsal of social skills and assertiveness, a set of skills is taught through instruction, modeling, and role play and feedback, as therapist and client play out different roles. Social skills include nonverbal (e.g., facial expressions, body movements, affective displays) as well as verbal components (e.g., refusing requests from others that seem unreasonable, and making requests; Dow, 1994).

An initial step is evaluation of skills in social and assertive situations, usually complementing the client's self-report by observational methodology, such as through role plays with the therapist or direct observation of client behaviors in the natural environment. A rationale then is provided that emphasizes how learning social and assertive skills will help clients to achieve personal control and respect for self and others, which in turn will contribute to the attainment of their own life goals. A hierarchy of behaviors is then devised for the purposes of role playing and behavioral rehearsal. For example, assertive requests for behavior change in others include a statement of the negative impact of the current behavior, provision of a specific and reasonable alternative behavior, and a statement of the likely positive impact of the new behavior on both parties.

Then, the therapist directly models the specific skill or presents the skill through another model, such as through the use of video. Modeling can involve a mastery approach, in which the model performs the desired behavior with confidence and competency. Alternatively, modeling can involve a coping approach, in which the model initially displays some trepidation and error followed by increasing skill. The latter approach may be particularly helpful for clients who are hesitant or fearful (e.g., Naugle & Maher, 2003). The client then rehearses the behavior.[1] Typically, clients are asked to evaluate their own performance first before the therapist reinforces their efforts, provides verbal feedback regarding execution of the skill, and shapes behavioral approximations. Videotaping sometimes can be helpful in this regard. Following mastery in-session, homework is assigned to practice the new behaviors in real-life situations between treatment sessions. Consideration also is given to realistic performance expectations and the value of self-reinforcement for continued rehearsal and practice.

---

[1]There are some occasions when modeling and overt rehearsal are not appropriate, such as when addressing skills associated with sexual intimacy; in these cases, covert or imaginal rehearsal is used instead.

A subset of social skills training is communication training for couples in distress. The assumption is that either couples lack the communication skills for negotiating conflict, and/or for reasons of stimulus control of behaviors, effective communication skills are not being used in the context of interpersonal tension. Couples communication training involves speaker/listener skills to understand and validate the partner's perspective. The therapist defines each skill. Listening skills include parroting (i.e., repeat), paraphrasing (i.e., rephrase), reflection (i.e., discern emotional meaning of speaker's message), and validation (i.e., convey that speaker's message is understandable). Speaking skills include learning to make succinct statements, to clarify and express accurate feeling statements, and to level (i.e., to express the core underlying feelings associated with a problem; e.g., Gottman et al., 1976). Then, the therapist provides reinforcement and corrective feedback to the couple as each practice using these skills to communicate in the therapy setting. Homework is to practice the same skills in their daily life between sessions.

In terms of mechanisms, behavioral rehearsal itself relies on principles of reinforcement and shaping. The new behavior is reinforced by the therapist. Once achieved, skills of communication and assertiveness may function as reciprocal inhibitors of conditional fear in social situations and/or contribute to extinction of conditional responses (CRs) by devaluing the expectancy of the unconditioned stimulus (i.e., increased assertiveness lessens fear of negative reactions from others). Additionally, the same skills may function to overcome deficits in behavioral repertoires (e.g., McFall & Marston, 1970). The new or modified behaviors are expected to result in an increase in positive reinforcers and decrease in punishers from the social environment, thereby improving overall mood and life satisfaction and functioning. Finally, implementation of these newly acquired skills may raise self-efficacy and decrease negative beliefs about oneself and the world.

Behavioral rehearsal of social skills and assertiveness is particularly helpful when there are clear deficits in these skills (e.g., pervasive developmental disorders, psychosis, or extreme social anxiety or avoidant personality disorder), or their rate of expression is limited overall or limited in certain contexts (due to anxiety or depression, for example). Assertiveness training should be implemented in a culturally responsive manner. This involves consideration of cultural values pertaining to independence and autonomy. CBT in general and assertiveness training in particular is permeated with European/North American norms that place high value on independence and autonomy (see Hays & Iwamasa, 2006). Assertiveness may conflict with values of collectivism and the importance of family in Asian, Arabic, Latino, African American, and other cultures. Culturally sensitive modifications to assertiveness include prefacing assertive communication with traditional forms of deference and respect (e.g., Organista, 2006), or by replacing assertiveness with other CBT strategies, such as problem solving.

Problem-Solving Training

Problem solving is a skill that has been implemented for a wide array of difficulties, including anxiety, depression, couples conflict, and stress management. In general, clients are taught a set of skills for approaching problems of everyday living. Steps involved in problem solving include problem definition and formulation, generation of alternatives, decision making, and verification.

D'Zurilla and Nezu (1999) identified two main targets of treatment: the orientation toward problem solving and the style of problem solving. The goals of problem-solving training are to increase positive and decrease negative *problem-solving orientation* and to foster a rational problem-solving style that minimizes maladaptive styles of being impulsive or careless or avoiding problems. Thus, training begins with steps of problem-solving orientation to develop positive self-efficacy beliefs, such as by reverse-advocacy role play that encourages clients to recognize their overly negative beliefs through contrast and by visualization of successfully resolving a problem and being reinforced as a result. The orientation phase also includes recognition that problems are a normal part of human existence and ways of identifying problems as they occur, such as by using negative emotions as a cue for recognizing that a problem exists and to observe what is occurring in the environment that is causing the emotions.

For the *style of problem solving phase,* clients are first trained in problem definition. This involves gathering information about the problem, objectively and concisely defining the problem, separating facts from assumptions, identifying the features that make the situation problematic, and setting realistic goals (Nezu, Nezu, & Lombardo, 2003). Next, alternatives are developed by generating as many solutions as possible, deferring judgment until a full list is generated, and then developing a list of action plans for the enactment of each solution. In the decision-making phase, a cost benefit analysis is conducted of each solution to identify the ones that are most likely to be successful and to be implemented. Effective solutions, or solutions that are likely to be successful and lead to the most positive and least negative consequences, are then selected. The final step is implementing the action plan associated with the most effective solution, and evaluating the success of its implementation along with troubleshooting and modification where necessary.

Problem solving is essentially a skill-building intervention. The mechanisms underlying problem solving include reinforcement from skills acquisition and from the success with which the problem solving resolves pending problems. In addition, by facing problematic situations rather than avoiding them, a type of exposure is being conducted that may lead to extinction of CRs. Furthermore, changes in cognitive appraisals and assumptions are involved in the problem orientation phase of the procedure. Also, successful implementation of problem solving may raise self-efficacy and provide evidence that disconfirms negative beliefs about the self and the world.

REFERENCES

Bernstein, D. A., & Borkovec, T. D. (1973). *Progressive relaxation training: A manual for the helping professions*. Champaign, IL: Research Press.

Craske, M. G., & Tsao, J. C. I. (1999). Self-monitoring with panic and anxiety disorders. *Psychological Assessment, 11*, 466–479. doi:10.1037/1040-3590.11.4.466

Dow, M. G. (1994). Social inadequacy and social skills. In L. W. Craighead, W. E. Craighead, A. E. Kazdin, & M. J. Mahoney (Eds.), *Cognitive and behavioral interventions: An empirical approach to mental health problems* (pp. 123–140). Boston, MA: Allyn & Bacon.

D'Zurilla, T. J., & Nezu, A. M. (1999). *Problem-solving therapy: A social competence approach to clinical intervention* (2nd ed.). New York, NY: Springer.

Ferguson, K. E. (2003). Relaxation. In W. O'Donohue, J. E. Fisher, & S. C. Hayes (Eds.), *Cognitive behavior therapy: Applying empirically supported techniques in your practice* (pp. 330–340). Hoboken, NJ: Wiley.

Garssen, B., de Ruiter, C., & van Dyck, R. (1992). Breathing retraining: A rational placebo? *Clinical Psychology Review, 12*, 141–153. doi:10.1016/0272-7358(92)90111-K

Gottman, J., Notarius, C., Markman, H., Bank, S., Yoppi, B., & Rubin, M. E. (1976). Behavior exchange theory and marital decision making. *Journal of Personality and Social Psychology, 34*, 14–23. doi:10.1037//0022-3514.34.1.14

Hays, P. A., & Iwamasa, G. Y. (2006). *Culturally responsive cognitive–behavioral therapy: Assessment, practice, and supervision*. Washington, DC: American Psychological Association.

Heide, F. J., & Borkovec, T. D. (1983). Relaxation-induced anxiety: Paradoxical anxiety enhancement due to relaxation training. *Journal of Consulting and Clinical Psychology, 51*, 171–182. doi:10.1037/0022-006X.51.2.171

Heidt, J. M., & Marx, B. P. (2003). Self-monitoring as a treatment vehicle. In W. O'Donohue, J. E. Fisher, & S. C. Hayes (Eds.), *Cognitive behavior therapy: Applying empirically supported techniques in your practice* (pp. 361–367). New York, NY: Wiley.

Jacobson, E. (1938). *Progressive muscle relaxation*. Chicago, IL: University of Chicago Press.

Kraft, A. R., & Hoogduin, C. A. (1984). The hyperventilation syndrome: A pilot study on the effectiveness of treatment. *British Journal of Psychiatry, 145,* 538–542. doi:10.1192/bjp.145.5.538

Lang, P. J., Melamed, B. G., & Hart, J. (1970). A psychophysiological analysis of fear modification using an automated desensitization procedure. *Journal of Abnormal Psychology, 76,* 220–234. doi:10.1037/h0029875

Linehan, M. M. (1994). Case consultation: A borderline dilemma [Comment]. *Suicide and Life-Threatening Behavior, 24,* 192–198.

McFall, R. M., & Marston, A. R. (1970). An experimental investigation of behavior rehearsal in assertive training. *Journal of Abnormal Psychology, 76,* 295–303. doi:10.1037/h0030112

Naugle, A. E., & Maher, S. (2003). Modeling and behavioral rehearsal. In W. O'Donohue, J. E. Fisher, & S. C. Hayes (Eds.), *Cognitive behavior therapy: Applying empirically supported techniques in your practice* (pp. 238–246). Hoboken, NJ: Wiley.

Nezu, A. M., Nezu, C. M., & Lombardo, E. (2003). Problem-solving therapy. In W. O'Donohue, J. E. Fisher, & S. C. Hayes (Eds.), *Cognitive behavior therapy: Applying empirically supported techniques in your practice* (pp. 301–307). Hoboken, NJ: Wiley.

Organista, K. C. (2006). Cognitive–behavioral therapy with Latinos and Latinas. In P. A. Hays & G. Y. Iwamasa (Eds.), *Culturally responsive cognitive–behavioral therapy: Assessment, practice, and supervision* (pp. 73–96). Washington, DC: American Psychological Association.

Poppen, R. (1998). *Behavioral relaxation training and assessment* (2nd ed.). Thousand Oaks, CA: Sage.

Rains, J. C. (2008). Change mechanisms in EMG biofeedback training: Cognitive changes underlying improvements in tension headaches. *Headache, 48,* 735–736. doi:10.1111/j.1526-4610.2008.01119_1.x

Schultz, J. H., & Luthe, W. (1959). *Autogenic training: A psychophysiologic approach to psychotherapy.* Oxford, England: Grune & Stratton.

APPENDIX 10.1: COGNITIVE–BEHAVIORAL THERAPY TECHNIQUES

Technique	Video title	Video identifying number	Time at which technique occurs
Self-monitoring	Developing an Exercise Plan	777700002-001	26:15–28:52
Relaxation	Developing an Exercise Plan	777700002-001	19:27–22:50
Behavioral rehearsal of social skills and assertiveness	Learning to Overcome Automatic Negative Thoughts	777700126-001	38:24–43:06
Problem-solving training	Developing an Exercise Plan	777700002-001	4:05–9:10
Behavioral contracting	Pathological Gambling Prevention	777700114-001	34:39–37:10
Exposure therapy	Learning to Overcome Automatic Negative Thoughts	777700126-001	31:05–42:20
Response prevention	Cognitive Behavioral Therapy for Anxiety Disorders	777700227-001	21:30–24:33
Homework	Cognitive Behavioral Therapy for Anxiety Disorders	777700026-001	42:43–46:25
Collaborative empiricism	Learning to Overcome Automatic Negative Thoughts	777700126-001	24:34–26:30
Automatic thoughts: Evidence-based interventions	Learning to Overcome Automatic Negative Thoughts	777700126-001	25:09–31:43
Automatic thoughts: Alternative interventions	Developing an Exercise Plan	777700002-001	9:08–9:54
Cognitive reinterpretation	Cognitive Behavioral Therapy for Anxiety Disorders	777700026-001	29:15–34:38

11

CONSTRUCTIVIST THERAPY

VITTORIO F. GUIDANO

Contemporary cognitive psychology is still dominated by rationalist and objectivist perspectives, which have traditionally avoided or devalued the phenomenological realm and the complex nature of lived human experience. When reality is assumed to be an objective external order that exists independently from people's observations of it—an assumption common to objectivism, realism, and traditional rationalism—it is inevitable that people will overlook their own characteristics and processes as observers. The only possible themes of investigation in an objectivist world are to refine or perfect one's perceptions of that world and to modify one's mental representations in ways that reflect improved "contact" or compliance with objective reality.

Excerpted from Robert A. Neimeyer and Michael J. Mahoney (Eds.), *Constructivism in Psychotherapy* (2000), from Chapter 5, "Constructivist Psychotherapy: A Theoretical Framework," pp. 93–100. Copyright 2000 by the American Psychological Association. Used with permission of the author.

http://dx.doi.org/10.1037/14295-011
Psychotherapy Theories and Techniques: A Reader, G. R. VandenBos, E. Meidenbauer, and J. Frank-McNeil (Editors)
Copyright © 2014 by the American Psychological Association. All rights reserved.

A constructivist approach entails significant changes in these initial assumptions and in the possible themes of investigation. From such a non-objectivist perspective, an essential task becomes understanding how people's characteristics as observers are involved in the process of observing, as well as how people otherwise participate in cocreating the dynamic personal realities to which they individually respond. This shift leads necessarily to a radical change in traditional formulations of human experience, human knowing, and professional helping.

BASIC FEATURES OF HUMAN EXPERIENCE

A proper framework for investigating such a problem, it seems, should rest on two basic points. One is the assumption of an evolutionary epistemological perspective—that is, a perspective that is based in the continuing study of evolving knowledge and knowing systems. Given that, as human beings, we cannot escape our particular way of being—which is fleshbound and animal—such a stance requires a central acknowledgment of the embodiment of human experience. The second basic point in this framework is that the ordering of our world is inseparable from our experiencing of it. We do, in fact, "experience it," or, more accurately, we "experience." The "it" is an objectification, however, and hence, implies a distancing between the experiencer and the living moment.

What is important to emphasize here is that there is no outside, impartial viewpoint capable of analyzing individual knowledge independent of the individual exhibiting this knowledge; there is no "God's eye point of view" (Putnam, 1981). Hence, knowledge should be considered from an ontological and epistemological perspective in which knowing, consciousness, and all other aspects of human experience are seen from the point of view of the experiencing subject. How an individual experiences is affected by the self-knowledge that he or she has been able to conjure. On the basis of these premises, I outline here some of the basic features inherent to the nature and the structure of human experience, with the aim of deriving from them a consistent methodology and strategy of intervention for cognitive therapy (cf. Guidano, 1991, 1995).

Experiencing and Explaining

Given that we can perceive the reality in which we live only from within our perceiving order, we always find ourselves, as human beings, in the immediacy of our ongoing praxis of living, which is the absolute primary ontological condition. The praxis of living is one of those dimensions that is difficult (perhaps impossible) to put into words. It is the "living of living," if you will, or the "practice of practicing," which is a life-span project for all of us. Maturana (1986) pointed out the following:

> In these circumstances, whatever we say about how anything happens takes place in the praxis of our living as a comment, as a reflection, as reformulation; in short, as an explanation of the praxis of our living, and as such it does not replace or constitute the praxis of living that it purports to explain. (pp. 3–4)

Human experience, therefore, appears as the emerging product of a process of mutual regulation continuously alternating between experiencing and explaining—that is, a process in which ongoing patterns of activity (immediate experience) become subject to linguistic distinctions and are reordered in terms of symbolic propositions distributed across conceptual networks. The level of symbolic reordering (explanation) makes possible new categories of experience, such as true–false, real–unreal, right–wrong, and subjective–objective, to name a few. This interdependence between subjective and objective, emotioning and cognizing, experiencing and explaining, and so forth, is constitutive of any human knowing process, just as is feeling ourselves to be alive.

In humans, as in all mammals (and especially all primates), affective-emotional activity corresponds to and depends on immediate and irrefutable apprehensions of the world. Hence, from a purely ontological point of view, feelings can never be "mistaken." It is through feelings that we experience our way of being in the world. In other words, we always are as we feel (Olafson, 1988). At the level of immediate experiencing, it is not possible to distinguish between perception and illusion (Maturana, 1986). For example, the perturbing feeling of having seen a ghost is, for the subject who is feeling it, a momentarily real and inescapable experience. Only by shifting to the level of "languaging" can the individual explain the felt experience in a variety of alternative manners, such as its having been a trick of light or an illusion, thereby making the experience consistent with his or her current appraisal of the world. In other words, errors can be noticed only a posteriori (after the experience) and depend on the point of view that we, as observers, take in reordering our experiencing. All rational-cognitive reordering involves expanding the coherence of symbolic rules to make the flow of immediate experience more consistent with the continuity of one's current appraisal of the world.

Rather than representing an already given reality according to a logic of external correspondence, knowledge is the continuous construction and reconstruction of a world by the ordering individual in an attempt to make ongoing experiences consistent (Arciero, 1989; Arciero & Mahoney, 1989; Maturana, 1988; Varela, 1987; Winograd & Flores, 1986).

Self and the Emotional Realm of Intersubjectivity

The evolutionary development of humans and their environments has always been fundamentally intersubjective. This is a relatively recent realization in global thinking. In fact, the phenomenon of "globalization" has sometimes been likened to the shrinking of the planet, bringing all of its inhabitants into more extensive contact. Most pertinent for this discussion is the fact that we humans are undeniably social beings. We need others (who, in turn, need us), and we participate in communities of identity and otherness that are crucial to our mutual well-being and development. We live in a complex interpersonal reality primarily structured and made consistent by language. Among other things, this fact implies that any knowledge of oneself and the world is always dependent on and relative to knowledge of others. The increasing complexity of the interpersonal dimension has afforded humans a range of skills in intersubjective learning (e.g., imitation and modeling) paralleled by an increase in the capacity for self-individuation (Kummer, 1979; Passingham, 1982). In fact the ability to discriminate among individual others appears to be hardwired in primate organization, as evidenced by the central role of the face in the primate emotional system (Ekman, 1993; Reynolds, 1981). Hence, facial recognition has emerged as a neocortical process whose evolutionary progression closely parallels the emergence of a more complex interpersonal realm (e.g., closer mother–infant relationship and competition and social bonds) that requires incremental capacities for attunement with others' behaviors and intentions in order to viably adapt.

Facial recognition should therefore be regarded as a self-referent ordering of intersubjective experience that facilitates the possibility of self-individuation. On the one hand, the ability to discriminate between individual others allows one to anticipate their perceptions of one's action, thus improving interactional synchrony and reciprocity. On the other hand, simulating how others will interpret one's actions entails the capacity to view oneself from the perceived perspective of others. This enhances the possibilities for self-bordering (i.e., setting one's own psychological boundaries) and self-individuation.

The human dimension of intersubjectivity is a prerequisite for individuation and self-recognition (Gallup & Suarez, 1986), bringing about the differentiation of a sense of self—both as subject and as object. Language, in fact, affords the ability to make distinctions and references regarding the flow of immediate experience, making it possible to at least symbolically distinguish the self that is experiencing from the self that is appraising those experiences.

The experience of "being a self" is something intertwined with and arising from the endless flowing of one's praxis of living so that, as Gadamer

(1976) explained, "the self that we are does not possess itself: one could say that it happens" (p. 55). In other words, the experiencing–explaining interdependence that underlies self-understanding is matched by an endless process of circularity between the immediate experience of oneself (the acting and experiencing I) and the sense of self that continually emerges as a result of abstractly self-referencing the ongoing experience (the observing and appraising *me*; James, 1890/1989; Mead, 1934; Smith, 1978, 1985). The self as subject (*I*) and the self as object (*me*) therefore represent the irreducible dimensions of a selfhood dynamic whose directionality depends on the continuous flow of our praxis of living. Indeed, the acting and experiencing I is always one step ahead of the current evaluation of the situation, and the appraising me becomes a continuous process of reordering one's conscious self-image.

Consider an emotional realm inherent to an intersubjective reality in which adaptation always transforms itself into a social relationship (e.g., the mother–infant bond). In a space–time dimension apprehensible in terms of proximity and distance from a safe base of emotional attachment, psychobiological attunement of and to caregivers allows the newborn human to order its sensory inflow into feelings that become recognizable only within an approach–avoidance continuum. In such a space–time dimension, attachment comes to exert a primary role in differentiating a range of decodable emotional tonalities (a) by regulating the rhythmic oscillation between arousal-inducing (exploration and play) and arousal-reducing (security and clinging) psychophysiological patterns and (b) by exerting a secondary role of modulating fear and anger by alternating between these same patterns (Fox & Davidson, 1984; Reynolds, 1981; Schore, 1994; Suomi, 1984). Alternatively, within an intersubjective reality, attachment exerts an organizational role in the development of a sense of self both as subject and as object.

Whereas the newborn's attunement to a synchronous source of regularities organizes his or her sensory inflow into a stream of recurrent psychophysiological rhythms, the emotional aspects of attachment transform feeling tonalities into specific emotional modules. Through regularities drawn from caregivers' behaviors and affective messages, the infant can begin to construct basic feelings that are inseparable from early perceptions, actions, and memories. The emergence of subjective experience is matched by the perception that one is an entity differentiated from other objects and people in the surrounding world. In other words, the initially ambivalent experience of being a self emerges with varying constraints of definition as a result of intersubjective experiences, especially those associated with intense emotional activity. Psychophysiological rhythms and emotional schemata become basic ingredients of infantile consciousness, a consciousness that is truly and fundamentally affective in nature and quality (Buck, 1984; Emde, 1984; Izard, 1980; Schore,

1994). The self-feeling immediately and tacitly perceived as an inner kinesthetic sense of I is therefore primarily organized around prototypical emotional
schemata differentiated out of emotional reciprocity with caregivers.

The I comes to see himself or herself as a me (i.e., like other surrounding people) only through the consciousness that caregivers have of his or
her behavior. Anticipating others' perceptions of one's actions facilitates the
recognition of ongoing patterns of emotional schemata out of the stream of
recurrent inner states, structuring them into specific emotional experiences
connected to related intentions and goal-oriented behaviors. Evidence suggests that infants' perceptions of themselves, although dependent on their
caregivers' behavior, are not confined to those situations in which their parents attempt to meet their basic needs. Indeed, it appears that parental imitation of infant behavior is very common from the earliest periods (Bretherton
& Waters, 1985; Harter, 1983), and it is therefore very likely that such imi-
tations are essential cues that allow the infant to recognize or internalize
as his or her own those characteristics and attitudes that caregivers perceive
as belonging to the infant as a person. In other words, self-consciousness
emerges from a self-recognizability made possible only by the empathic ability to take the attitude of others onto oneself, subsequently elaborating a
conscious self-image that consists of emotionally etching the profile of the
me out of the experienced I.

Selfhood Dynamics and Life-Span Development

Individual life-span development should be regarded as a *hortogenetic*
progression, meaning that it is an open-ended, spiraling process in which the
continuous reordering of selfhood dynamics results in the emergence of more
structured and integrated patterns of internal complexity. Self-regulating
abilities reflect a dynamic equilibrium known as "order through fluctuations" (Brent, 1978; Dell & Goolishian, 1981; Prigogine, 1976). That is,
continuous—both progressive and regressive—shifts of the point of equilibrium in I–me dynamics provide a scaffolding that enables one to maintain a
coherent continuity of experiencing while allowing the assimilation of the
perturbations that emerge from that experiencing. I now take a look at two
essential variables involved in this lifelong process: the role of awareness in
regulating and modulating challenging perturbations and the role of emotional activity in triggering them.

In strictly ontological terms, being aware of oneself means reaching
an explanation for the ongoing experience of being a unique, irreducible,
and often unpredictable I. Hence, awareness is a reflexive process for self-
referencing immediate experience (I) in order to amplify consistent aspects
of the perceived me while inhibiting discrepant aspects. Because the acting

and experiencing I is always one step ahead of the current appraisal of the me, each person is in a position where it is possible to experience much more than the minimum required at that moment to maintain his or her own self-image consistency in that particular situation. As a consequence, the ability to manipulate immediate experiencing while self-referencing and reordering becomes essential. This ability is necessary to direct conscious attention in ways that contrast with the selected appraisal of the current situation. In this sense, one can say that no self-awareness can be viable without a necessary level of self-deception. Thus, it follows that excessive self-deception lowers the accuracy of decoding immediate experiencing (possibly to critical levels of uncontrollability), whereas limited self-deception, by failing to reject extraneous information, complicates the self-referencing process exponentially such that levels of complexity in selfhood dynamics are difficult to manage. Hence, any individual, although having critical emotional tonalities in immediate experiencing, is also endowed with specific self-deceiving abilities designed to manipulate their decoding so that it is consistent with the quality of awareness they have reached thus far. Through such procedures, individuals can appraise critical feelings and make them intelligible without questioning the total validity of the currently existing self-image.

Alternatively, attachment to significant others, although it shifts toward a more abstract level with maturation, maintains its fundamental interdependence with selfhood dynamics throughout the life span. This shift, it seems, explains the crucial role of affectivity in triggering significant perturbations. Although attachment is central to the stable differentiation of a sense of self, new patterns of attachment emerge (e.g., intimate love relationships) throughout maturational stages during adulthood, attachments that function to confirm, support, and further expand the pattern of self-coherence that has thus far been structured. It follows naturally that the influence of early attachments is subsequently manifested in later styles of attachment, which continue to differentiate along the entire developmental pathway (Bretherton, 1985). Indeed, the continuity of attachment throughout the life span is understandable if one considers that the perception of certain affective relationships as being unique to the self begins early in life and that subsequent adult bonds of love seem to grow out of these very first attachments (Hazan & Shaver, 1987; Marris, 1982; Shaver, Hazan, & Bradshaw, 1988; Weiss, 1982). Just as unique primary bonds seem to be necessary prerequisites for "perceiving a world" and "recognizing one's being in it," so in adulthood—though at a different level of abstraction—is building a unique relationship with a significant other an important way for one to perceive a consistent sense of uniqueness in his or her "being in the world." Hence, if working models of attachment figures are interdependent with ongoing patterns of self-perception, it is clear that any perceived modification of these models is matched by intense perturbations in immediate experiencing; these disruptions can trigger the emergence of I–me discrepancies, which in turn can challenge the current appraisal of the self. In fact, the importance of a balanced interplay of the individual's network of unique relationships throughout the life span is currently supported by evidence from various sources. First, life-events research has shown that the most disrupting emotions a person can experience in life are those triggered in the course of establishing, maintaining, and dissolving such relationships (Bowlby, 1977; Brown, 1982; Hafner, 1986; Henderson, Byme, & Duncan-Jones, 1981). Second, recent epidemiological evidence has shown how the "social network index" should be regarded as a significant predictor of health on the basis of findings suggesting that social and affective isolation is a major risk factor for morbidity and mortality (House, Landis, & Umberson, 1988).

REFERENCES

Arciero, G. (1989, October). *From epistemology to ontology: A new age of cognition.* Paper presented at the annual meeting of the American Association for the Advancement of Science, San Francisco, CA.

Arciero, G., & Mahoney, M. J. (1989). *Understanding and psychotherapy.* Unpublished manuscript, University of California, Santa Barbara.

Bowlby, J. (1977). The making and breaking of affectional bonds: I. Etiology and psychopathology in the light of attachment theory. *British Journal of Psychiatry, 130,* 201–210.

Brent, S. B. (1978). Prigogine's model for self-organization in nonequilibrium systems: Its relevance for developmental psychology. *Human Development, 21,* 374–387. doi:10.1159/000272417

Bretherton, I. (1985). Attachment theory: Retrospect and prospect. In I. Bretherton & E. Waters (Eds.), *Growing points of attachment theory and research* (pp. 3–35). Chicago, IL: University of Chicago Press.

Bretherton, I., & Waters, E. (Eds.). (1985). *Growing points of attachment theory and research.* Chicago, IL: University of Chicago Press.

Brown, G. W. (1982). Early loss and depression. In C. M. Parkes & J. Stevenson-Hinde (Eds.), *The place of attachment in human behavior* (pp. 232–268). London, England: Tavistock.

Buck, R. (1984). *The communication of emotion.* New York, NY: Guilford Press.

Dell, P. E, & Goolishian, H. A. (1981). Order through fluctuation: An evolutionary epistemology for human systems. *Australian Journal of Family Therapy, 2,* 175–184.

Ekman, P. (1993). Facial expression and emotion. *American Psychologist, 48,* 384–392. doi:10.1037/0003-066X.48.4.384

Emde, R. N. (1984). Levels of meaning for infants' emotions: A biosocial view. In K. R. Scherer & P. Ekman (Eds.), *Approaches to emotion* (pp. 77–107). Hillsdale, NJ: Erlbaum.

Fox, N. A., & Davidson, R. J. (Eds.). (1984). *The psychobiology of affective development*. Hillsdale, NJ: Erlbaum.

Gadamer, H. G. (1976). *Philosophical hermeneutics*. Berkeley: University of California Press.

Gallup, E. E., & Suarez, S. (1986). Self-awareness and the emergence of mind in humans and other primates. In J. Suls & A. G. Greenwald (Eds.), *Psychological perspectives on the self* (Vol. 3, pp. 23–36). Hillsdale, NJ: Erlbaum.

Guidano, V. E (1991). *The self in process*. New York, NY: Guilford Press.

Guidano, V. E. (1995). Self-observation in constructivist psychotherapy. In R. A. Neimeyer & M. J. Mahoney (Eds.), *Constructivism in psychotherapy* (pp. 155–168). Washington, DC: American Psychological Association.

Hafner, R. J. (1986). *Marriage and mental illness*. New York, NY: Guilford Press.

Harter, S. (1983). Development perspectives on the self-system. In E. M. Hetherington (Ed.), *Handbook of child psychology* (Vol. 4, pp. 275–385). New York, NY: Wiley.

Hazan, C., & Shaver, P. (1987). Romantic love conceptualized as an attachment process. *Journal of Personality and Social Psychology, 52,* 511–524. doi:10.1037/0022-3514.52.3.511

Henderson, S., Byme, D. G., & Duncan-Jones, P. (1981). *Neurosis and the social environment*. San Diego, CA: Academic Press.

House, J. S., Landis, K. R., & Umberson, D. (1988, July 29). Social relationships and health. *Science, 241,* 540–545. doi:10.1126/science.3399889

Izard, C. E. (1980). The emergence of emotions and the development of consciousness in infancy. In J. M. Davidson & R. J. Davidson (Eds.), *The psychobiology of consciousness* (pp. 193–216). New York, NY: Plenum Press.

James, W. (1989). The consciousness of self. In *Principles of psychology* (Vol. 1). New York, NY: Holt, Rinehart & Winston. (Original work published 1890)

Kummer, H. (1979). On the value of social relationships to nonhuman primates: A heuristic scheme. In M. Von Cranach, K. Foppa, W. Lepenies, & D. Ploog (Eds.), *Human ethology* (pp. 381–395). Cambridge, England: Cambridge University Press.

Marris, P. (1982). Attachment and society. In C. M. Parkes & J. Stevenson-Hinde (Eds.), *The place of attachment in human behavior* (pp. 185–201). London, England: Tavistock.

Maturana, H. (1986). *Ontology of observing: The biological foundations of self-consciousness and the physical domain of existence*. Unpublished manuscript, University of Chile, Santiago.

Maturana, H. (1988). Reality: The search for objectivity, or the quest for a compelling argument. *Irish Journal of Psychology, 9,* 25–82. doi:10.1080/03033910.1988.10557705

Mead, G. H. (1934). *Mind, self, and society.* Chicago, IL: University of Chicago Press.

Olafson, A. E. (1988). *Heidegger and the philosophy of mind.* New Haven, CT: Yale University Press.

Passingham, R. (1982). *The human primate.* New York, NY: Freeman.

Prigogine, I. (1976). Order through fluctuations: Self-organization and social systems. In E. Jantsch & C. H. Waddington (Eds.), *Evolution and consciousness: Human systems in transition* (pp. 93–133). Reading, MA: Addison-Wesley.

Putnam, H. (1981). *Reason, truth and history.* Cambridge, England: Cambridge University Press.

Reynolds, P. C. (1981). *On the evolution of human behavior.* Los Angeles: University of California Press.

Schore, A. N. (1994). *Affect regulation and the origin of the self: The neurobiology of emotional development.* Hillsdale, NJ: Erlbaum.

Shaver, P., Hazan, C., & Bradshaw, D. (1988). Love as attachment. In R. J. Stenberg & M. L. Barnes (Eds.), *The psychology of love* (pp. 68–99). New Haven, CT: Yale University Press.

Smith, M. B. (1978). What it means to be human. In R. Fitzgerald (Ed.), *What it means to be human* (pp. 49–64). Elmsford, NY: Pergamon Press.

Smith, M. B. (1985). The metaphorical basis of selfhood. In A. J. Marsella, G. DeVos, & E. L. K. Hsu (Eds.), *Culture and self: Asian and Western perspectives* (pp. 56–88). London, England: Tavistock.

Suomi, S. G. (1984). The development of affect in rhesus monkeys. In N. A. Fox & R. J. Davidson (Eds.), *The psychobiology of affective development* (pp. 119–159). Hillsdale, NJ: Erlbaum.

Varela, E. (1987). Laying down a path in walking. In W. I. Thompson (Ed.), *Gaia, a way of knowing: Political implications of the new biology* (pp. 48–64). Great Barrington, MA: Lindisfarne Press.

Weiss, R. S. (1982) . Attachment in adult life. In C. M. Parkes & J. Stevenson-Hinde (Eds.), *The place of attachment in human behavior* (pp. 171–183). London, England: Tavistock.

Winograd, T., & Flores, F. (1986). *Understanding computers and cognition.* Norwood, NJ: Ablex.

12

CONSTRUCTIVIST THERAPY PROCESS

GREG J. NEIMEYER

Presenting problems represent windows onto the client's system of constructions. Clients' "effort after meaning"—as Bartlett (1932) so aptly phrased it—assures that they have struggled to understand the nature of their experience prior to therapy, and their presence in therapy speaks to the difficulty they have encountered along the way. When participating in a constructivist form of therapy, neither client nor therapist can enjoy the familiar moorings that anchor more realist or rationalist forms of therapy (see Mahoney & Lyddon, 1988; G. J. Neimeyer & Neimeyer, 1993; Parry & Doan, 1994). Gone is the certainty of a single "best," "right," or "functional" form of thinking, feeling, or behaving. Gone, too, is the directive, disputational comportment associated with that certainty, replaced by a more tentative,

Excerpted from Robert A. Neimeyer and Michael J. Mahoney (Eds.), *Constructivism in Psychotherapy* (2000), from Chapter 6, "The Challenge of Change," pp. 112–119. Copyright 2000 by the American Psychological Association. Used with permission of the author.

http://dx.doi.org/10.1037/14295-012
Psychotherapy Theories and Techniques: A Reader, G. R. VandenBos, E. Meidenbauer, and J. Frank-McNeil (Editors)
Copyright © 2014 by the American Psychological Association. All rights reserved.

patient struggle aimed at developing a constructive process of exploration from within the individual (see Clark, 1989, 1993) that may lead to a more viable and developmentally progressive understanding of the world (Lyddon & Alford, 1993; R. A. Neimeyer, 1995).

There are many ways to encourage this kind of exploration and experimentation. For most constructivists, the nature of the therapeutic relationship itself is a figural feature in this process (Guidano, 1991; Lyddon & Alford, 1993; Mahoney, 1991). This relationship supports and contextualizes various forms of direct and indirect intervention. As Kelly (1969c) has noted,

> the relationships between therapist and client and the techniques they employ may be as varied as the whole human repertory of relationships and techniques. . . . It is the orchestration of techniques and the utilization of relationships in the on-going process of living and profiting from experience that makes psychotherapy a contribution to human life. (p. 223)

Constructivist approaches have contributed significantly in both of these regards, placing inflection on the nature of interpersonal and therapeutic bonds on the one hand, and sponsoring a wide variety of novel methods of intervention on the other. Mirror time, streaming, fixed-role therapy, controlled elaboration, tightening and loosening techniques, interpersonal transaction groups, bipolar sculptures, personal epilogues, repertory grid techniques, systemic bowties, time and place binding, laddering, and various forms of journaling have all emerged from constructivist traditions—and these are just a few techniques (see Mahoney, 1991; G. J. Neimeyer, 1993; R. A. Neimeyer & Neimeyer, 1987).

Still, constructivists are wary of an exclusive dedication to technique, preferring instead to emphasize the critical role of the therapeutic relationship in enabling and initiating human change. "I am not against technique," noted Mahoney (1991, p. 253), in a sentiment shared by many constructivists, "I am against technolatry."

This caveat contextualizes the discussion of methods that follows. All methods, all techniques, and all forms of intervention necessarily evolve from and reside within the context of a given relationship in a given time and place (Efran & Clarfield, 1993). In this sense, techniques can be regarded as coconstructed meaning rituals—vehicles for punctuating, initiating, or reorganizing experience—and, as such, they hold no power apart from the social and cultural contexts that inform them. Human change follows less from the application of a given technique per se than from the meaning that follows from its use in the therapeutic process. In a direct sense, therefore, a technique does not "do" anything for a person; rather, the person does something with the technique.

CONSTRUCTING A LIFELINE

For constructivists, psychotherapeutic technique occurs in relational contexts. For that reason, in most constructivist therapies a premium is placed on forging an intimate therapeutic bond between client and therapist. This bond enables them to participate jointly in conjuring a variety of alternative worlds to be explored and elaborated. These twin processes—exploration and elaboration—serve as the linchpins of the psychotherapeutic process, and both follow from the development of a strong working relationship.

Forging a Bond

Like Bowlby's (1988) "secure base," constructivists regard the thera-peutic relationship as a kind of home base, or emotional tether, for the client to use in his or her personal exploration (Guidano, 1991). Although the ways in which this type of attachment may be formed can be quite varied, they converge in providing a kind of secure, permissive acceptance. Adopting what Kelly (1955) has referred to as a "credulous approach," the therapist takes the client's perspective seriously and respects it, even though she or he may not choose to be bound by it. Part of this credu-lous approach implies acceptance of the client, although acceptance takes on special meaning in this context: It is understood as a willingness to use the client's personal knowledge system, to see the problem and the world through his or her eyes, though not necessarily to be encapsulated by it. To this is added an attitude of inquiry—a curiosity or fascination with the client's perspective and its implications. From this the therapist develops a form of collaborative empiricism, establishing a working relationship that conveys a willingness to conjoin the client in an exploratory process that may seek to test or transcend the limitations of the client's personal worldview.

This kind of therapeutic relationship is qualitatively distinct from other forms of therapeutic alliances. As Kelly (1969b) observed,

> instead of assuming, on the one hand, that the therapist is obliged to bring the client's thinking into line, or, on the other, that the client will mysteriously bring his own thinking into line once he has been given the proper setting, we can take the stand that client and therapist are conjoining in an exploratory venture. The therapist assumes neither the position of judge nor that of the sympathetic bystander. He is sincere about this; he is willing to learn along with his client. He is the client's fellow researcher who seeks first to understand, and then to examine, and finally to assist the client in subjecting alternatives to experimental test and revision. (p. 82)

The constructivist therapist's attitude, therefore, is more inquisitive than disputational, more approving than disapproving, and more exploratory than demonstrative.

Beyond this, specific permission is sometimes given to remove the limits on what can be said and done in the therapy room. The therapist might emphasize, for example, that "this therapy room is a special kind of place for you. Here you can say things, express feelings and thoughts, and act out things that you might never even consider, much less do, in the outside world." This kind of explicit permissiveness again underscores the security of the therapeutic arena, and it begins to conjure the image of a hypothetical, "as if" world (Vaihinger, 1924) in which the client may fashion and test new meanings and behaviors.

Conjuring a World

Even as the nascent therapeutic world is conjured into existence, its function is already being partially fulfilled. Because it is a hypothetical place, a make-believe world, the client can feel free to experiment with changes without necessarily jeopardizing or assaulting existing meaning structures. New perspectives can be tried on without shedding present constructions, thereby circumventing much of the threat and anxiety associated with significant personal change.

A recent development in cosmetology provides a metaphorical marker for the power of this pretend world and illustrates its utility in facilitating personal change. Developed a few years ago, this technological advance enables cosmetologists to project the image of their clients' faces into a limitless assortment of different hairstyles. These projections transport people into whole new identities in swift succession, enabling them to peer out from within their make-believe worlds under the guise of a cast of different characters. From the copious curls of Dolly Parton to the shorn scalp of Sinead O'Connor, from the flowing tresses of Crystal Gayle to the boyish coiffure of Lady Di, these computer-generated images permit a sort of smorgasbord sampling of identities, a playful means of engaging and disengaging a parade of alter egos without risking the more terminal, steely feel of actual scissors to scalp.

As a kind of metaphor for constructivist psychotherapy, this procedure pairs the exploratory, experiential features of significant change with important identity safeguards that protect extant personal meaning. After all, the comic value of Bill Clinton adopting the dreadlocks of Bob Marley or the electrified look of Don King would be matched only by the sheer terror that would, for Clinton, accompany that actual transformation. Radical reconstruction of current meanings, particularly those central to the self, is customarily and understandably resisted.

For most constructivists, the self constitutes an organized meaning unit, and events that signal profound changes in that system are threatening. Variously referred to as "personal construct systems" (Kelly, 1955), "personal meaning organizations" (Guidano, 1991), "cognitive structures" (Liotti, 1987), and "core ordering processes" (Mahoney, 1991), these interconnected networks of meaning are taken to constitute the individual. By jeopardizing the integrity of this worldview, change—particularly significant, core role change (Kelly, 1955)—produces massive threat and anxiety. In response, the individual understandably develops a self-protective approach that is commonly recast as "resistance" within the therapeutic context. "A cognitive structure that attributes meaning and causal relationships to an important class of emotional experiences," noted Liotti (1987, p. 95), "will be quite resistant to change if the individual does not develop alternative meaning structures." This self-protective theory of resistance is common to many diverse constructivist approaches (Guidano, 1991; Kelly, 1955; Liotti, 1987; Mahoney, 1991), and the development of a secure, "pretend world" in therapy is one means of cultivating these alternative meaning structures.

Central to this pretend world is the language of hypothesis. "There is something in stating a new outlook in the form of a hypothesis," noted Kelly (1969a, p. 156), "that leaves the person himself intact and whole." The use of this language, the development and exploration of alternative meanings, can occur alongside of rather than instead of existing meanings. It is the security associated with the preservation of existing meanings that often enables the exploration of new ones. Kelly (1969a) has characterized threat as

> the experience that occurs at the moment when we stand on the brink of profound change in ourselves and can see just enough of what lies ahead to know that so much of what we are now will be left behind forever, once we take that next step. (p. 156)

It is precisely at this point that the language of hypothesis can be most helpful, preserving the integrity of the client's current understandings, but momentarily suspending them as well, while alternative possibilities are explored. Having bracketed present perspectives, the person is free to envision alternative possibilities, to experience fresh perspectives from behind an assortment of masks. And these masks, Kelly (1969a) observed wryly, "have a way of sticking to our faces when worn too long" (p. 158).

For the constructivist psychotherapist, therefore, alternative perspectives are encouraged. Forged and tested within an as-if world, these various viewpoints are designed to dislodge the client from a strict allegiance to any single belief or conviction. "The psychologist is at his best," observed Kelly (1969a), "when he speaks the language of hypothesis rather than imposes psychological certainties on his clients" (p. 154).

That being said, techniques for encouraging this hypothetical exploration and personal revision must enable the client's active participation in the
process of meaning making. In this regard, constructivist psychotherapy is an
engaging, interactive vehicle for the negotiation of new meanings. Meaning
is made through action, through participation, and through concrete and
representational manipulations of the world. These manipulations yield novel
experience, that is, perceived invalidations of present systems of knowing
that require active efforts of meaning making to render them sensible within
a coherent meaning structure (see Mahoney, 1991). This kind of "continuous
self-reordering," noted Guidano (1991), "is inherently characterized, moment
by moment, by a series of possible 'I'/'Me' discrepancies, that is, perceived
gaps between immediate experience and self-consciousness that challenge
ongoing patterns of self-control" (p. 69). One important means of fostering
this kind of exploratory self-reordering is through various forms of interpersonal
enactments.

Conducting the Exploration

Mahoney (1991) has noted "the importance of active exploratory
behavior on the part of the changing individual," emphasizing that "there
can be no real learning without novelty—that is, without a challenge to or
elaboration of what has become familiar" (p. 19). Enactments, various forms of
interpersonal role plays, constitute one important vehicle for introducing this
novelty. Enactments can vary from very brief, unstructured, casual scenarios
all the way to the formalized and enduring role plays that constitute fixed-role
therapies. Regardless of their brevity or length, their spontaneity or formality,
all enactment procedures share a common set of goals. Foremost among these
is to provide for elaboration of the clients' personal worldview while protecting
their core role structures from premature invalidation, to buffer them from
assault until they are better able to consider abandoning them.

Casual enactments are brief, informal role plays designed to give the
client an opportunity to experiment by trying on a part to see what it is like.
Rarely more than a few minutes duration each, these enactments are aimed
at discovery rather than demonstration, at exploration rather than rehearsal.
An enactment is "designed, like a good experiment, to give the experimenter
and his colleagues a chance to observe its outcomes" (Kelly, 1955, p. 1166).

Casual enactments have several salient features. Although brief, they
can nonetheless present potent opportunities for discovery, even when they
involve little or no actual conversation. Moreover, they foster a fleet-footed
fluidity by enabling the client to move quickly among multiple perspectives.

Unverbalized casual enactments can be as potent as their more verbal
counterparts. Clients often profit immensely from a brief enactment that casts

them in a role that they are wholly unable or unwilling to enact or express in any overt way. "Just sitting there and feeling that he is cast in a certain part, or that he is perceived as being in a certain part," noted Kelly (1955), "is, in itself, a form of adventure which he is not likely to pass off lightly" (p. 1147).

One of my recent experiences with the potency of Kelly's (1955) insight came in an early session with "David," a client in his late 20s who was referred to me with alcoholism and alcohol-related difficulties. David had experienced several run-ins with the law at the time, having lost his driver's license and been placed on probation for a weapons violation in the process. He had returned home to live with his parents because his life had been so "out of control," and he was contemplating a return to his private apartment. He spoke openly about how concerned his parents were about him and how they feared that returning to his apartment would again give him the license to drink that he could not exercise in their home. He was frustrated and angry that they did not trust him, and he felt a growing impasse that he could not resolve: either stay with them and sacrifice his adult freedoms, or return to his apartment and disappoint and provoke his parents, potentially jeopardizing their support of him.

I immediately cast David in his mother's role, pointed to a nearby empty chair, and said "Tell David what concerns you have. Tell him about your fears and worries for him." David, portraying his mother, talked fluidly for several minutes, detailing a set of concerns undoubtedly familiar to him. I then asked him to sit in the other chair and respond, as David, to his mom's concerns. He sat frozen. "I can't. I can't say anything!" he said. "I mean, she's right, I've always started drinking when I got by myself and that started the cycle down. I mean, what can I tell her?" As he spoke, he flushed with emotion and turned to talk about how he was unwilling to provide her with the kind of false assurances that he had in the past. He spoke, too, of how justified her concerns were and how unjustified his own anger and frustration with her was, saying that "This has nothing to do with Mom in a sense, I mean, I've got to find some way of handling this thing myself." From here we turned to talking about possible safeguards, ways that he could reduce the ever-present temptation to start drinking and provide some tentative assurances to himself, as well as to his mother, en route.

In this and other uses of casual enactment, the client can be asked to shift perspectives. This provides one means of developing a contextual shift as discussed by Efran and Clarfield (1993). I have used a wide variety of such enactments productively in my practice, and Kelly (1955) has detailed a number of possibilities in this regard. In one form of enactment, for example, the client is asked to report to the therapist as if he or she were the client's best (real or imagined) friend. Simple prompts like "What concerns do you have about him or her?" or "What do you see going on from your perspective?" can initiate the enactment and help breathe life into the interaction. Another approach is to have the client portray the part of the therapist while the therapist enacts the part of another therapist who is being consulted about the client. This offers the additional advantage of indicating something about the client's constructions of the therapist and of the nature of the therapeutic enterprise. Yet another enactment that can have powerful effects is to ask the client to enact an admired or respected person, parent or otherwise, who has served as a source of inspiration or in the role of wise council for the client. In this variation, I typically ask clients to stand up, close their eyes, and imagine adopting the voice, movement, and mannerisms of that person. When they open their eyes they are to introduce the client and talk about specific aspects of the pride and concerns that they have regarding them. As with most casual enactments, roles can then be reversed to enable the client to shift perspectives within the same context or scenario.

In addition to brief, casual enactments, more elaborate enactment procedures can also be formulated within the therapeutic arena. Among the most elaborate of these is Kelly's (1955) fixed-role therapy. Like other enactments, the purpose of fixed-role therapy is primarily exploratory, to help dislodge the client from his or her adherence to an extant perspective by encouraging the adoption of an alternative one. Unlike the enactments described above, however, fixed-role therapy involves systematically developing a new, alternative identity, rather than simply co-opting an already available perspective.

REFERENCES

Bartlett, E. C. (1932). *Remembering*. Cambridge, England: Cambridge University Press.

Bowlby, J. (1988). *A secure base*. New York, NY: Basic Books.

Clark, K. M. (1989). Creation of meaning: An emotional processing task in psychotherapy. *Psychotherapy: Theory, Research, Practice, Training, 26*, 139–148. doi:10.1037/h0085412

Clark, K. M. (1993). Creation of meaning making in incest survivors. *Journal of Cognitive Psychotherapy, 7*, 195–203.

Efran, J. S., & Clarfield, L. E. (1993). Context: The fulcrum of constructivist psychotherapy. *Journal of Cognitive Psychotherapy: An International Quarterly, 7*, 173–182.

Guidano, V. E. (1991). *The self in process: Toward a post-rationalist cognitive therapy*. New York, NY: Guilford Press.

Kelly, G. A. (1955). *The psychology of personal constructs* (2 vols.). New York, NY: Norton.

Kelly, G. A. (1969a). The language of hypothesis: Man's psychological instrument. In B. Maher (Ed.), *Clinical psychology and personality: The selected papers of George Kelly* (pp. 147–163). New York, NY: Wiley.

Kelly, G. A. (1969b). Man's construction of his alternatives. In B. Maher (Ed.), *Clinical psychology and personality: The selected papers of George Kelly* (pp. 66–93). New York, NY: Wiley.

Kelly, G. A. (1969c). Psychotherapy and the nature of man. In B. Maher (Ed.), *Clinical psychology and personality: The selected papers of George Kelly* (pp. 207–223). New York, NY: Wiley.

Liotti, G. (1987). The resistance to change of cognitive structures: A counterproposal to psychoanalytic metapsychology. *Journal of Cognitive Psychotherapy: An International Quarterly, 1,* 87–104.

Lyddon, W. J., & Alford, D. J. (1993). Constructivist assessment: A developmental epistemic perspective. In G. J. Neimeyer (Ed.), *Casebook of constructivist assessment* (pp. 31–57). Newbury Park, CA: Sage.

Mahoney, M. J. (1991). *Human change processes: The scientific foundations of psychotherapy.* New York, NY: Basic Books.

Mahoney, M. J., & Lyddon, W. J. (1988). Recent developments in cognitive approaches to counseling and psychotherapy. *The Counseling Psychologist, 16,* 190–234. doi:10.1177/0011000088162001

Neimeyer, G. J. (1993). The challenge of change: Reflections on constructivist psychotherapy. *Journal of Cognitive Psychotherapy, 7,* 183–194.

Neimeyer, G. J., & Neimeyer, R. A. (1993). Defining the boundaries of constructivist assessment. In G. J. Neimeyer (Ed.), *Casebook of constructivist assessment* (pp. 1–30). Newbury Park, CA: Sage.

Neimeyer, R. A. (1995). An invitation to constructivist psychotherapies. In R. A. Neimeyer & M. J. Mahoney (Eds.), *Constructivism in psychotherapy* (pp. 1–8). Washington, DC: American Psychological Association.

Neimeyer, R. A., & Neimeyer, G. J. (Eds.). (1987). *Personal construct therapy casebook.* New York, NY: Springer.

Parry, A., & Doan, R. E. (1994). *Story re-visions: Narrative therapy in a postmodern world.* New York, NY: Guilford Press.

Vaihinger, H. (1924). *The philosophy of "as if."* Berlin, Germany: Reuther & Reichard.

APPENDIX 12.1: CONSTRUCTIVIST THERAPY TECHNIQUES

Technique	Video title	Video identifying number	Time at which technique occurs
Bipolar sculptures	Constructivist Therapy for Loss of a Father (Session 3 of 6)	777700234-001	29:35–29:59
Circular questions	Constructivist Therapy for Loss of a Father (Session 5 of 6)	777700251-001	10:34–11:26
Controlled elaboration	Constructivist Therapy With a Young Woman Grieving the Loss of Her Mother	777700056-001	26:36–28:55
Credulous approach	Constructivist Therapy With a Young Woman Grieving the Loss of Her Mother	777700056-001	19:52–20:15
Enactments	Constructivist Therapy With a Young Woman Grieving the Loss of Her Mother	777700056-001	7:15–9:54
Fixed-role therapy	Constructivist Therapy With a Young Woman Grieving the Loss of Her Mother	777700056-001	29:08–32:44
Laddering and other various forms of journaling	Constructivist Therapy With a Young Woman Grieving the Loss of Her Mother	777700056-001	4:56–5:27
Mirroring	Constructivist Therapy for Loss of a Father (Session 5 of 6)	777700251-001	27:44–29:28
Personal epilogues	Constructivist Therapy for Loss of a Father (Session 3 of 6)	777700234-001	39:20–39:32
Time and place binding	Constructivist Therapy for Loss of a Father (Session 1 of 6)	777700230-001	3:28–5:50

13

EMOTION-FOCUSED THERAPY

LESLIE S. GREENBERG

In emotion-focused therapy (EFT), emotion is viewed as fundamentally adaptive and as providing our basic mode of information processing, rapidly and automatically appraising situations for their relevance to our well-being and producing action tendencies to meet our needs. With the aid of emotions, people react automatically to their apprehension of patterns of sounds, sights, and smells and to other nonverbal signs of people's intentions in a way that has served us well as a species for centuries and as individuals for years. Fear-induced flight produces safety, disgust expels a noxious intrusion, and in sadness one calls out for the lost other. People respond emotionally, in an automatic fashion, to patterns of cues in their environment that signal novelty, comfort, loss, or humiliation.

Excerpted from *Emotion-Focused Therapy* (2011), from Chapter 3, "Theory," pp. 36–44. Copyright 2011 by the American Psychological Association. Used with permission of the author.

http://dx.doi.org/10.1037/14295-013

Psychotherapy Theories and Techniques: A Reader, G. R. VandenBos, E. Meidenbauer, and J. Frank-McNeil (Editors)
Copyright © 2014 by the American Psychological Association. All rights reserved.

Client emotions thus act as a kind of therapeutic compass, guiding the client and therapist as to what is important to the client and what needs are being met (or not met). A key principle of EFT is that emotions provide access to needs, wishes, or goals and the action tendencies associated with them. Thus, every feeling has a need, and every emotion scheme activation provides a direction for action, one that will promote need satisfaction. When a client acknowledges feeling sad, this statement conveys that their tacit processing has evaluated that they have lost something important to them, are in need of comfort, and probably want to cry out for the connection. By contrast, in couples therapy the expression of underlying adaptive emotions to the partner is seen as crucial in changing the partner's view of the self and emotion and its expression thereby changes negative interactions (Greenberg & Goldman, 2008).

Emotion is a brain phenomenon that is vastly different from thought. It has its own neurochemical and physiological basis and is a unique language in which the brain speaks. The limbic system, a part of the brain possessed by all mammals, is responsible for basic emotional responses. It governs many of the body's physiological processes and thereby influences physical health, the immune system, and most major body organs. Le Doux (1996) identified two different paths for producing emotion: the shorter and faster amygdala pathway, which sends automatic emergency signals to brain and body and produces gut responses, and the longer and slower neocortex pathway, which produces emotion mediated by thought. Clearly it was adaptive to respond quickly in some situations, but at other times better functioning resulted from the integration of cognition into an emotional response (by reflecting on emotion).

The developing cortex added to the emotion brain's adaptive wisdom a new form of emotional response. This new emotional response system used not only inherited emotional responses, like fear of the dark, but also learned signs of what had evoked emotion in a person's own life experience, like fear of one's father's impatient voice. Those *emotional memories* and organizations of lived emotional experience were formed into *emotion schemes* (Greenberg & Paivio, 1997; Greenberg, Rice, & Elliott, 1993; Oatley, 1992). Through these internal organizations or neural programs, people react automatically from their emotion systems, not only to inherited cues, such as looming shadows or comforting touch, but also to cues that they had learned were dangerous or life enhancing. These reactions are rapid and automatic.

EMOTION SCHEMES

Emotion schemes are at the base of the adult emotional response system. They are internal emotion memory structures that synthesize affective, motivational, cognitive, and behavioral elements into internal organizations that are activated rapidly, out of awareness, by relevant cues. Schemes are elicited by cues that match the input features of the scheme and produce experience and action as their output. Important life experiences, significant by virtue of having activated emotional responses, become coded into *emotion schematic memory*. The emotion scheme represents both the situation as construed and its emotional effect on the individual, and this is done in a predominantly wordless or imagistic script in the form of narrative. Thus, emotional memories of cuddling in one's mother's arms or being physically abused are coded as procedural memories of what happened and how this felt. The scheme represents an unfolding of an experience from the initial cue (e.g., a touch) to a sequence of moments of experience, with a beginning, middle, and end. The innate capacity for emotional response and experience thus evolves into core emotion schematic autobiographical memories with an internal narrative structure (Angus & Greenberg, 2011).

Emotion schematic learning makes emotions a flexible, adaptive processing system but also opens them to the possibility of becoming maladaptive. People not only flee from predators and get angry at violations of their territorial boundaries, but they also fear their boss's criticism and get angry at self-esteem violations. The important issue is that the emotionally motivated, basic mode of processing that is set in motion by scheme activation occurs out of awareness and influences conscious processing. Only after this basic mode of processing has been activated does the person begin to process more consciously for sources of danger and ultimately symbolizes in words the appraised danger and generates ways of coping with it. Thus, the activation of a fear scheme sets a basic mode of processing for threat in motion, and this conscious processing works in the service of the affective goal activated by the scheme (safety in the case of fear). Emotion schematic processes can include linguistic components but often consist largely or entirely of preverbal elements (including bodily sensations, visual images, and even smells); emotion schemes are also oriented toward action to satisfy needs, goals, and concerns.

The development of schemes is best understood as the development of neural networks that represent the basic story of a lived experience. A network is shown in Figure 13.1. Here, a scheme of fear of failing, formed from the experience of having failed a mother's expectation, contains components of a visual image of the mother's face, a variety of nonverbal physiological and sensory aspects of those experiences, as well as the action tendency to withdraw and possibly, but not necessarily, a belief stated in language that the self is going to fail an expectation. The whole representation is an unfolding sequence as shown by the arrows leading from one node to the next. The most obvious therapeutic implication is that optimal emotional processing

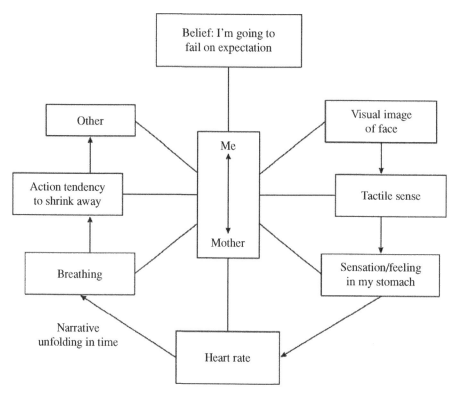

Figure 13.1. Emotion scheme.

involves activating the whole scheme and focusing on all of the narrative schematic elements. Particular difficulties occur when the person excludes all the elements from awareness, or neglects one or more types of elements, so that his or her experiencing is not processed fully or coherently.

Enduring change occurs through the synthesis of two or more existing schemes and the formation of higher level schemes (Piaget & Inhelder, 1973). In development, when opposing schemes are coactivated, compatible elements from the coactivated schemes synthesize to form new higher level schemes. For example, in a 1-year-old child, schemes of standing and falling can be dynamically synthesized into a higher level scheme for walking, by a process of dialectical synthesis (Greenberg & Pascual-Leone, 1995; Pascual-Leone, 1991); similarly, schemes of different emotional states can be synthesized to form new integrations. Thus, a schematic emotional memory of fear and withdrawal from prior abuse can be synthesized with current empowering anger against violation, which motivates approach rather than withdrawal, to form a new sense of confidence or assertion.

EMOTION GENERATION

The flow diagram in Figure 13.2 depicts the process of emotion generation; it can be used to think linearly about what is in reality a complex nonlinear and dynamic process. (A more representative form of a more complex dynamic process can be found in Greenberg & Pascual-Leone, 2001.) In this diagram, attention to a stimulus preconsciously activates an emotion scheme (or more accurately, a number of schemes) by the cues matching the releasers of a scheme. For example, a frown or a raised voice activates a fear scheme. In addition, certain automatic cognitive processing takes place along a separate and ultimately slower path that helps generate conscious appraisals in language. Each scheme includes its basic components of affect, action tendency, need, and cognition structured in a wordless narrative; the person experiences the other as a threat, the body tenses and prepares for escape, and negative beliefs about self become primed. With attention the activated scheme or schemes in turn may be symbolized in language giving rise to conscious emotion, the concern or desire, an action tendency and thought, and these combine, in the case of fear activation, to influence behavioral avoidance.

Note that in this model it is not cognitive appraisal in language that produces emotion; rather, it is a type of automatic pattern matching that releases the scheme that produces emotion. In this view, meaning appraisal

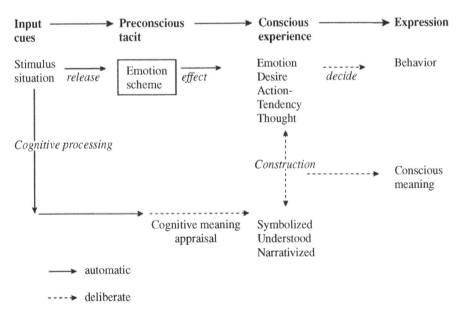

Figure 13.2. The dialectical construction of the self.

occurs at two levels. The first level is the rapid evaluation of patterns *matching* internal features of the emotion scheme where the evaluation is one of fit— for example, a frowning face rather than a more conscious cognitive appraisal of explicit meaning (this person is angry at me and I am in danger). The latter is generated by more automatic and deliberate cognitive processes. The cognitive level of meaning in language is influenced by and interacts with the experiential output of the emotion scheme. However, emotion scheme activation provides our basic mode of processing information and sets specific emotion-based scripts (e.g., seeking, safety, closeness, boundary protection) into motion, plus certain anticipatory expectations that guide ways of thinking. Emotion schemes themselves are not directly available to awareness but can only be accessed indirectly through the experiences they produce. EFT works to activate schemes, articulate their output in language, and then explore and reflect on this experience to create new meaning (Greenberg, 2002; Greenberg & Safran, 1987).

Emotion schemes thus provide implicit higher order organizations of experience based on biologically given emotional responses influenced by the person's history of lived emotional experience. The emotion schematic memory system is the central catalyst of self-organization. It is the generator of not only healthy states such as confidence, calm, and security but also of disordered self-organizations, such as anxious insecurity, shame-based worthlessness, or lonely abandonment. Emotion schemes and their activation are the final targets of intervention.

TYPES OF EMOTION

Not all emotion serves the same function. It is theoretically and clinically crucial to distinguish between different types of emotional experience and expression in order to guide intervention. Four types of emotional experience are outlined in this section.

The normal function of emotion is to rapidly process complex situational information, to provide feedback to the person about his or her reaction, and to prepare the person to take effective action. Such uncomplicated responses are referred to as *primary adaptive* emotion responses because the emotion is a direct reaction consistent with the immediate situation, and it helps the person take appropriate action. For example, if someone is threatening to harm your children, anger is an adaptive emotional response because it helps you take assertive (or if necessary, aggressive) action to end the threat. *Fear* is the adaptive emotional response to danger and prepares us to take action to avoid or reduce the danger, by freezing and monitoring, or, if necessary, by fleeing. *Shame*, on the other hand, signals that we have been exposed as having acted inappropriately and are at risk of being judged or rejected by others; it therefore motivates us to correct or hide in order to protect our social standing and relationships. Rapid, automatic responding of this kind helped our ancestors survive. Such responses are to be accessed and promoted. Not all emotions, however, are functional or fit the situation. The three types described in the following paragraphs generally are dysfunctional.

Maladaptive primary emotions are also direct reactions to situations, but they no longer help the person cope constructively with the situations that elicit them; rather, they interfere with effective functioning. These emotion responses generally involve overlearned responses, based on previous, often traumatic, experiences. For example, a fragile client may have learned when she was growing up that closeness was generally followed by physical or sexual abuse. Therefore, she will automatically respond to caring or closeness with anger and rejection as a potential violation.

Secondary reactive emotions follow some more primary response (i.e., they come second). Often people have emotional reactions to their initial primary adaptive emotion, so that it is replaced with a secondary emotion. This "reaction to the reaction" obscures or transforms the original emotion and leads to actions that are, again, not entirely appropriate to the current situation. For example, a man who encounters rejection and begins to feel sad or afraid may become either angry at the rejection (externally focused) or angry with himself for being afraid (self-focused), even when the anger is not functional or adaptive. Many secondary emotions obscure or defend against a painful primary emotion; others are emotional reactions to primary emotions. If the man feels ashamed of his fear, he experiences *secondary shame*. People can feel afraid of, or guilty about, their anger, ashamed of their sadness, or sad about their anxiety. Secondary emotions can also be responses to interceding thoughts—in other words, an emotion that is secondary to a thought (e.g., feeling anxious because of an expectation of rejection). Some emotions can be secondary to thought, but it is important to notice that this is symptomatic emotion and that the thought itself stems from a more primary mode of processing set in motion by a maladaptive emotion scheme, probably the fear of rejection. Although thought can produce emotion, not all emotion is produced by thought.

Instrumental emotions are emotions expressed to influence or control others. For example, crocodile tears may be expressed to elicit support, anger to dominate, and shame often is expressed deliberately to indicate that one is socially appropriate. A person may respond deliberately or out of habit, automatically or without full awareness. In either case, the display of emotion is independent of the person's original emotional response to the situation, although the expression may induce some form of internal emotional experience. These emotions are referred to as *manipulative* or *racket feelings*.

REFERENCES

Angus, L., & Greenberg, L. S. (2011). *Working with narrative in emotion-focused therapy: Changing stories, healing lives*. Washington, DC: American Psychological Association.

Greenberg, L. S. (2002). *Emotion-focused therapy: Coaching clients to work through their feelings*. doi:10.1037/10447-000

Greenberg, L. S., & Goldman, R. N. (2008). *Emotion-focused couples therapy: The dynamics of emotion, love, and power*. doi:10.1037/11750-000

Greenberg, L. S., & Paivio, S. C. (1997). *Working with emotions in psychotherapy*. New York, NY: Guilford Press.

Greenberg, L. S., & Pascual-Leone, J. (1995). A dialectical constructivist approach to experiential change. In R. A. Neimeyer & M. J. Mahoney (Eds.), *Constructivism in psychotherapy* (pp. 169–191). doi:10.1037/10170-008

Greenberg, L., & Pascual-Leone, J. (2001). A dialectical constructivist view of the creation of personal meaning. *Journal of Constructivist Psychology, 14*, 165–186. doi:10.1080/10720530151143539

Greenberg, L., Rice, L., & Elliott, R. (1993). *Facilitating emotional change*. New York, NY: Guilford Press.

Greenberg, L. S., & Safran, J. D. (1987). *Emotion in psychotherapy: Affect, cognition, and the process of change*. New York, NY: Guilford Press.

Le Doux, J. (1996). *The emotional brain: The mysterious underpinnings of emotional life*. New York, NY: Simon and Schuster.

Oatley, K. (1992). *Best laid schemes*. New York, NY: Cambridge University Press.

Pascual-Leone, J. (1991). Emotions, development, and psychotherapy: A dialectical constructivist perspective. In J. Safran & L. Greenberg (Eds.), *Emotion, psychotherapy, and change* (pp. 302–335). New York, NY: Guilford Press.

Piaget, J., & Inhelder, B. (1973). *Memory and intelligence*. London, England: Routledge and Kegan Paul.

14

EMOTION-FOCUSED THERAPY PROCESS

LESLIE S. GREENBERG

The two major tasks are helping people (a) with too little emotion access more emotion and (b) with too much emotion to contain their emotions. There are many possible ways of helping clients access feelings, including encouraging attention to bodily sensations that cue emotions, helping clients recall previous emotion episodes or situations that bring up particular feelings, and using vivid emotion cues, such as poignant words or images in communicating with clients. In addition, therapists can suggest that clients act as if they feel a certain way, or exaggerate and repeat phrases or gestures (e.g., speaking in a loud, angry voice; shaking one's fist). It also is important to help clients monitor their level of arousal in order to maintain the safety that allows emotion to arise. This latter strategy is very important because most people cut off access to their feelings if they sense that they are losing control.

Excerpted from *Emotion-Focused Therapy* (2011), from Chapter 4, "The Therapy Process," pp. 70–82. Copyright 2011 by the American Psychological Association. Used with permission of the author.

http://dx.doi.org/10.1037/14295-014
Psychotherapy Theories and Techniques: A Reader, G. R. VandenBos, E. Meidenbauer, and J. Frank-McNeil (Editors)
Copyright © 2014 by the American Psychological Association. All rights reserved.

Therapists often ask me what they should do to access emotion in constricted clients or to help regulate dysregulated clients. These questions are better posed as follows: In what kind of relationship will a therapist be able to help the client access or regulate emotion? The relationship always plays a key role in both accessing and influencing the type of emotion experienced and how it is processed. The assumption in emotion-focused therapy (EFT) is that the therapist is a potential agent in accessing emotion through affect attunement, in regulating emotion through interpersonal soothing, and in providing new emotional experiences through the relationship.

Types of empathy that help clients access and symbolize their emotions range from purely understanding empathic responses, through validating and evocative responses, to exploratory and conjectural responses as well as empathic refocusing (Elliott, Watson, Goldman, & Greenberg, 2004; Greenberg & Elliott, 1997). Empathic exploration is the fundamental mode of intervention in EFT and is a response that is focused on the leading edge of the client's experience—that which is most alive or poignant or implicit— to help it unfold. When a therapist's response is structured in such a way that it ends with a focus on what seems most alive in a client's statement, the client's attention is in turn focused on this aspect of his or her experience and more likely to differentiate this leading edge of his or her experience. By sensitively attending, moment by moment, to what is most poignant in clients' spoken and nonspoken (nonverbal) narrative, a therapist's verbal empathic exploration can help capture clients' experiences even more richly than the clients' descriptions. This helps clients symbolize previously implicit experience consciously in awareness.

Clients usually begin therapy by telling the story of their problem. EFT therapists start with empathy and encourage clients to focus inward and deepen their experience. If this does not deepen client experience, they move to focusing, guiding attention to the bodily felt sense. This often is followed later by more stimulating interventions such as chair dialogues and imagery work in which affect is heightened to bring it vividly into focal awareness.

The therapist encourages clients to bring their attention to their experiencing as it is bodily felt and to ask themselves, "What's problematic for me?" The therapist then helps the client verbalize the feeling, focus on the experiential effect this has, sense a problem as a whole, and let what is important come up from that bodily sensing. This is the focusing process and represents the basic style of engagement with internal experience that is being encouraged.

EFT therapists also help clients who feel overwhelmed or emotionally flooded develop adaptive strategies for containing emotion by using a range of possibilities, including observing and symbolizing the overwhelming feelings (e.g., meditatively creating a safe distance by adopting an observer's stance and describing one's fear as a black ball located in one's stomach). Offering support and understanding and encouraging clients to seek others' support and understanding are also helpful in regulating emotions, as is encouraging clients to organize their distressing emotions (e.g., by making a list of problems). Helping clients to engage in self-soothing is a crucial strategy. Here the therapist encourages relaxation, self-comfort, and self-care (e.g., "Try telling this other part of you, 'It's OK to feel sad'"). Helping clients in distress distract themselves (e.g., by counting backwards or going in imagination to a safe place) is another useful intervention for promoting regulation. If clients become overwhelmed in the session, the therapist can regulate their distress by suggesting that they breathe, put their feet on the ground, feel themselves in their chair, look at the therapist, and describe what they see.

Paradoxically, one of the most effective ways of helping clients contain emotion may actually be helping them to become aware of it, express it, and decide what to do about it as soon as it arises. This is because suppressing an emotion and doing nothing about it tend to generate more unwanted emotional intrusions, making it more overwhelming or frightening. One of the dilemmas for clients and therapists alike is knowing when to facilitate awareness and experience of emotion and when to regulate it. A helpful practical guideline, especially for people who experience overwhelming destructive emotions, is to be aware of how intense the feeling is and to use this as a guide to coping. Emotional approach and awareness should be used when the emotions are below some manageable level of arousal, say 70%, but distraction and regulation should be applied when they exceed this level and the emotions become unmanageable.

In addition to these general strategies for working with emotion, the different types of emotion described in Chapter 3 must be worked with in different ways. Primary adaptive emotions must be accessed and more fully allowed to provide information and action tendency. To help clients sort out if what they are feeling is a primary adaptive emotion, therapists respond empathically and act as surrogate information processors, offering symbols to describe feelings that clients can check against their experiences for fit. Therapists can help to assess whether an emotion is primary by asking, "Is this what your core feeling is at rock bottom?" or prompting them ("Check inside; see if this is your most basic feeling"). Maladaptive emotions are best handled by helping the client to approach, allow, tolerate, symbolize, regulate, and explore these emotions. After they have been accessed and accepted rather than avoided, they become amenable to change by accessing different underlying emotions (e.g., undoing maladaptive shame with anger, self-compassion, or pride) and by reflecting on them to make sense of them. Therapists help clients access these emotions by means of empathic exploration of, and empathic conjectures into, the client's deeper experience. To access maladaptive emotions, therapists might ask, "What is your most vulnerable feeling, one you have had from early on, ever since you can remember?" or "Does this feeling feel like a response to things that have happened in the past, or does it feel mainly like a response to what's happening now?" Other questions that are helpful are "Does this feel like a familiar stuck feeling?" and "Will this feeling help you deal with the situation?"

Secondary reactive emotions are best responded to with empathic exploration in order to discover the underlying primary emotions from which they are derived (e.g., primary fear under reactive anger). To get beneath the secondary emotions, therapists also might ask, "When you feel that, do you feel anything in addition to what you're most aware of feeling?" or "Take a minute and see if it feels like there is something else underneath that feeling." Instrumental emotions are best explored for their interpersonal function or intended impact on others. After conveying an understanding that the person feels sad or angry, the therapist might say, "I wonder if maybe you are trying make a point or tell this person something with this feeling?" People may recognize the intention in their emotional experience, be it their desire for self-protection or comfort or their attempt to dominate the other.

PRINCIPLES OF EMOTIONAL CHANGE

From the EFT perspective, change occurs by helping people make sense of their emotions through awareness, expression, regulation, reflection, transformation, and corrective experience of emotion in the context of an empathically attuned relationship that facilitates these processes. These empirically supported principles of emotional change (Greenberg, 2002) are discussed below in relation to working with emotion in therapy and not with reference to managing emotion in life. For example, in therapy it often is helpful to promote awareness, arousal, and expression of traumatic fear or unexpressed resentment to a significant other, whereas in life one might want to promote coping behaviors and regulation of affect.

Awareness

Increasing awareness of emotion is the most fundamental overall goal of treatment. When people know what they feel, they reconnect to their needs and are motivated to meet them. Increased emotional awareness is therapeutic in a variety of ways. Becoming aware of and symbolizing core emotional experience in words provide access both to the adaptive information and the action tendency in the emotion. It is important to note that emotional awareness is not thinking about feeling; it involves feeling the feeling in awareness. What is disowned or split off cannot change. When that which is disclaimed is felt, it changes. Only when emotion is felt does its articulation in language become an important component of its awareness. The goal is acceptance of emotion. Self-acceptance and self-awareness are interconnected. To truly know something about oneself, one must accept it.

Three important stages of emotion awareness of problematic emotions can be delineated. The first stage of change is awareness of emotion after the event, when a person is reflecting on what was felt in the past, which can serve as a basis for learning how to respond better in the future. This also may include awareness of the trigger of the emotional response. Much of insight-oriented therapy stops at step one, in which people understand why they acted in a particular way they regretted, but this does not help them to stop behaving that way or being triggered again by similar situations. The second stage is reduction in the length of time it takes an emotion to determine one's feelings. The third stage is recognizing the emergence of the emotion as it is arising and being able to head it off before it arises (e.g., one recognizes the impulse to anger or disappointment and can transform it before it emerges fully). Here one can see the impulse before the action. Finally, in the last stage of change the emotion is not triggered in the first instance.

Expression

Expressing emotion in therapy does not involve venting secondary emotion but rather overcoming avoidance to experience and being able to express previously constricted primary emotions (Greenberg & Safran, 1987). Expressive coping also may help one attend to and clarify central concerns and may serve to promote pursuit of goals. There can be no universal rule about the effectiveness of emotional expression, and the distinction between the role of expression in therapy, to reexperience and rework past problematic experience, versus expression in life must be maintained. The role of arousal and expression and the degree to which they could be useful in therapy (and in life) depend on what emotion is expressed, about what issue, how it is expressed, by whom, to whom, when and under what conditions, and in what way the emotional expression is followed by other experiences of affect and meaning. In daily life, expression of problematic emotions is often not helpful. In therapy, arousal and expression are necessary but not always sufficient for therapeutic progress.

Because of the strong human tendency to avoid experiencing and expressing painful emotions, clients must be encouraged to overcome avoidance and approach painful emotion in sessions by attending to their bodily experience, often in small steps. This may involve changing explicit beliefs (e.g., "Anger is dangerous" or "Men don't cry") governing their avoidance or helping them face their fear of dissolution (Greenberg & Bolger, 2001). Then clients must allow and tolerate being in live contact with their emotions. These two steps, approaching emotion and tolerating often uncomfortable emotion, are consistent with notions of exposure. Extensive research supports the effectiveness of exposure to previously avoided feelings for a sufficient length of time in reducing its negative effect (Foa & Jaycox, 1999). From the emotion-focused perspective, however, the emotional processing steps of approach, arousal, and tolerance of emotional experience are necessary but not sufficient for change of primary maladaptive emotions. Optimum emotional processing involves both the integration of cognition and affect (Greenberg, 2002; Greenberg & Pascual-Leone, 1995; Greenberg & Safran, 1987) and the transformation of affect, not only its tolerance (Greenberg, 2002). After contact with primary maladaptive emotional experience such as core shame or basic insecurity is achieved and the emotion is expressed, clients must also cognitively orient to that experience as information; symbolize it in awareness and explore, reflect on, and make sense of it; and finally transform it.

Regulation

The third principle of emotional processing involves the regulation of emotion. For some individuals, psychological disorders and situations emotions are under- or dysregulated (Linehan, 1993). An important issue in any treatment is what emotions are to be regulated; how they are to be regulated then becomes a central aspect of treatment. Emotions that require down-regulation generally are either secondary emotions, such as despair and hopelessness, or anxiety about anxiety or primary maladaptive emotions, such as the shame of being worthless, the anxiety of basic insecurity, and panic.

The first step in helping emotion regulation is the provision of a safe, calming, validating, and empathic environment. This helps soothe automatically generated underregulated distress (Bohart & Greenberg, 1997) and helps strengthen the self. This is followed by the teaching of emotion regulation and distress tolerance skills (Linehan, 1993) involving such things as identifying triggers, avoiding triggers, identifying and labeling emotions, allowing and tolerating emotions, establishing a working distance, increasing positive emotions, self-soothing, breathing, and seeking distraction. Forms of meditative practice and self-acceptance often are most helpful in achieving a working distance from overwhelming core emotions. The ability to regulate breathing and to observe one's emotions and let them come and go are important processes to help regulate emotional distress.

Another important aspect of regulation is developing clients' abilities to self-soothe and develop self-compassion. Emotion can be down-regulated by soothing at a variety of different levels of processing. Physiological soothing involves activation of the parasympathetic nervous system to regulate heart rate, breathing, and other sympathetic functions that speed up under stress. Promoting clients' abilities to receive and be compassionate to their emerging painful emotional experience is an important step toward tolerating emotion and self-soothing. Being able to soothe the self develops initially by internalization of the soothing functions of the protective other (Sroufe, 1996; Stern, 1985). Over time this is internalized and helps clients develop implicit self-soothing, the ability to regulate feelings automatically without deliberate effort.

Reflection

In addition to recognizing emotions and symbolizing them in words, promoting further reflection on emotional experience helps people make narrative sense of their experience and promotes its assimilation into their ongoing self-narratives. What we make of our emotional experience makes us who we are. Reflection helps to create new meaning and develop new narratives to understand experience (Goldman, Greenberg, & Pos, 2005; Greenberg & Angus, 2004; Greenberg & Pascual-Leone, 1997; Pennebaker, 1995). Pennebaker (1995) showed the positive effects of writing about emotional experience on autonomic nervous system activity, immune functioning, and physical and emotional health and concluded that through language, individuals are able to organize, structure, and ultimately assimilate both their emotional experiences and the events that may have provoked the emotions.

Exploration of emotional experience and reflection on what is discovered to form coherent narratives are other important processes in change. Reflection promotes understanding of the way in which the self is psychologically constructed and constituted. Narrative provides a cognitive organizing process, a type of temporal gestalt where the meaning of individual life events and actions is determined by a particular plot or theme. The story renders the experiences and memories of the client into a meaningful coherent story, orders our experience, and provides a sense of identity. Human beings long to experience their own sense of personal meaning and need to create meaning to overcome an existential vacuum.

Transformation

Probably the most important way of dealing with maladaptive emotion in therapy involves not mere exposure to the maladaptive emotion, nor its regulation, but its transformation by other emotions. This applies most specifically to transforming primary maladaptive emotions, such as fear and shame and the sadness of lonely abandonment, with other adaptive emotions (Greenberg, 2002). I suggest that maladaptive emotional states are best transformed by undoing them by activating other more adaptive emotional states. In EFT, an important goal is to arrive at maladaptive emotion, not for its good information and motivation but to make it accessible to transformation. In time, the coactivation of the more adaptive emotion, along with or in response to the maladaptive emotion, helps transform the maladaptive emotion. The paradox of the path to emotional change is that it needs to start not with trying to change emotion but with fully accepting the painful emotion. Emotions must be fully felt and their message heard before they are open to change by other emotions. A major premise guiding intervention in EFT is that if you do not accept yourself as you are, you cannot make yourself available for transformation. One cannot leave a place until one has arrived at it; for emotion, one has to feel it to heal it. Even those aspects of oneself one truly wants to change must first be accepted, even embraced. Self-transformation thus is always preceded by self-acceptance.

The process of changing emotion with emotion goes beyond ideas of catharsis, completion and letting go, exposure, extinction, or habituation, in that the maladaptive feeling is not purged, nor does it simply attenuate by the person feeling it; rather, another feeling is used to transform or undo it. Although dysregulated secondary emotions such as the fear and anxiety in phobias, obsessive compulsiveness, and panic and fear-laden intrusive images may be overcome by mere exposure, in many situations primary maladaptive emotions (e.g., the shame of feeling worthless, the anxiety of basic insecurity, and the sadness of abandonment) are best transformed by contact with other emotions. For example, change in primary maladaptive emotions such as core shame or fear of abandonment is brought about by the coactivation of an incompatible, more adaptive experience such as empowering anger and pride or compassion for the self to the same situations. The new emotion undoes the old response rather than attenuating it (Fredrickson, 2001). This involves more than simply feeling or facing the feeling, which leads to its diminishment; rather, the withdrawal of tendencies primary maladaptive fear or shame (for example) is transformed into staying in contact by activating the approach tendencies in anger or comfort-seeking sadness.

In therapy, maladaptive fear of abandonment or annihilation from past childhood maltreatment, once aroused in the present, can be transformed into security by the activation of more empowering, boundary-establishing emotions of adaptive anger or disgust at the maltreatment that were felt in the past but not expressed, or by evoking the previously inaccessible softer soothing feelings of sadness and need for comfort or compassion toward the self. Similarly, maladaptive anger can be undone by adaptive sadness. Maladaptive shame, which was internalized from the contempt of others, can be transformed by accessing both anger at violation at the abuse one suffered, by self-compassion, and by accessing pride and self-worth; anger at being unfairly treated or thwarted is an antidote to hopelessness and helplessness. The tendency to shrink into the ground in shame or collapse in helplessness can be transformed by the thrusting forward tendency in presently accessed anger at violation. Withdrawal emotions from one side of the brain are replaced with approach emotions from another part of the brain or vice versa (Davidson, 2000a, 2000b). After the alternate emotion has been accessed, it transforms or undoes the original state and a new state is forged. Often a period of regulation or calming of the maladaptive emotion in need of change, and making sense of it, is needed before the activation of an opposing transforming emotion.

How does the therapist help the client access new emotions to change emotions? A number of ways have been outlined (Greenberg, 2002). Therapists can help the client access new subdominant emotions occurring in the present by a variety of means, including shifting attention to emotions that are currently being expressed but are only "on the periphery" of a client's awareness—or, when no other emotion is present, focusing on what is needed, and thereby mobilizing a new emotion (Greenberg, 2002). The newly accessed, alternate feelings are resources in the personality that help change the maladaptive state. These new feelings either were felt in the original situation but not expressed or are felt now as an adaptive response to the old situation. Bringing out implicit adaptive anger at a perpetrator can help change maladaptive fear in a trauma victim. When the tendency to run away in fear is combined with the tendency of angry individuals to thrust forward, this leads to a new relational position of holding the abuser accountable for wrongdoing while seeing oneself as having deserved protection, rather than feeling guilty and unsafe. It also is essential both to symbolize, explore, and differentiate the primary maladaptive emotion (in this case fear), and regulate it by breathing and calming, before cultivating access to the new more adaptive emotion (in this case anger).

Other methods of accessing new emotion involve using enactment and imagery to evoke new emotions, remembering a time an emotion was felt, changing how the client views things, or expressing an emotion for the client (Greenberg, 2002). Once accessed, these new emotional resources begin to undo the psycho-affective motor program previously determining the person's mode of processing. New emotional states enable people to challenge the validity of perceptions of self and other connected to maladaptive emotion, weakening its hold on them. Accessing adaptive needs acts automatically as disconfirmation of maladaptive feelings and beliefs.

In my view, enduring emotional change of maladaptive emotional responses thus occurs by generating a new emotional response, not through a process of insight or understanding but by generating new responses to old situations and incorporating these into memory. EFT works on the basic principle that people must first arrive at a place before they can leave it. Maladaptive emotion schematic memories of past childhood losses and traumas are activated in the therapy session in order to change these by memory reconstruction. Introducing new present experience into currently activated memories of past events has been shown to lead to memory transformation by the assimilation of new material into past memories (Nadel & Bohbot, 2001). By being activated in the present, the old memories are restructured by the new experience of both being in the context of a safe relationship and by the coactivation of more adaptive emotional responses and new adult resources and understanding to cope with the old situation. The memories are reconsolidated in a new way by incorporating these new elements. The past can in fact be changed—at least the memories of it can be!

Corrective Emotional Experience

New lived experiences with another person (often the therapist) are especially important in providing an interpersonal corrective emotional experience. Experiences that provide interpersonal soothing, disconfirm pathogenic beliefs, or offer new success experience can correct previously established interpersonal patterns. An experience in which a client faces shame in a therapeutic context and experiences acceptance, rather than the expected contempt or denigration, has the power to change the feeling of shame. Having one's anger accepted by the therapist rather than rejected leads to new ways of being. Now the client can express vulnerability or anger with the therapist without being punished and can assert without being censured. The undeniable reality of this new emotional experience allows clients to experience that they are no longer powerless children facing powerful adults. Corrective emotional experiences in EFT occur predominantly in the therapeutic relationship, although success experience in the world is also encouraged.

The goal in EFT is for clients, with the help of more favorable circumstances in therapy, to experience mastery in reexperiencing emotions they could not handle in the past. The client then undergoes a corrective emotional experience that repairs the damaging influence of previous relational experiences. Corrective interpersonal emotional experiences also occur generally throughout the therapeutic process, whenever the patient experiences the therapist as attuning to and validating the client's inner world. Overall, the genuine relationship between the patient and the therapist, as well as its constancy, is a corrective emotional experience.

REFERENCES

Bohart, A. C., & Greenberg, L. S. (1997). Empathy: Where are we and where do we go from here? In A. C. Bohart & L. S. Greenberg (Eds.), *Empathy reconsidered: New directions in psychotherapy* (pp. 419–449). doi:10.1037/10226-031

Davidson, R. (2000a). Affective style, mood and anxiety disorders: An affective neuroscience approach. In R. Davidson (Ed.), *Anxiety, depression and emotion* (pp. 88–108). Oxford, England: Oxford University Press.

Davidson, R. (2000b). Affective style, psychopathology, and resilience: Brain mechanisms and plasticity. *American Psychologist, 55*, 1196–1214. doi:10.1037/0003-066X.55.11.1196

Elliott, R., Watson, J. E., Goldman, R. N., & Greenberg, L. S. (2004). *Learning emotion-focused therapy: The process–experiential approach to change*. doi:10.1037/10725-000

Foa, E. B., & Jaycox, L. H. (1999). Cognitive-behavioral theory and treatment of posttraumatic stress disorder. In D. Spiegel (Ed.), *Efficacy and cost-effectiveness of psychotherapy* (pp. 23–61). Washington, DC: American Psychiatric Publishing.

Fredrickson, B. L. (2001). The role of positive emotions in positive psychology: The broaden-and-build theory of positive emotions. *American Psychologist, 56*, 218–226. doi:10.1037/0003-066X.56.3.218

Goldman, R. H., Greenberg, L. S., & Pos, A. E. (2005). Depth of emotional experience and outcome. *Psychotherapy Research, 15*, 248–260. doi:10.1080/10503300512331385188

Greenberg, L., & Angus, L. (2004). The contributions of emotion processes to narrative change in psychotherapy: A dialectical constructivist approach. In L. Angus & J. McLeod (Eds.), *Handbook of narrative psychotherapy: Practice, theory, and research* (pp. 331–349). Thousand Oaks, CA: Sage.

Greenberg, L., & Bolger, L. (2001). An emotion-focused approach to the over-regulation of emotion and emotional pain. *In-Session, 57*, 197–212.

Greenberg, L. S. (2002). *Emotion-focused therapy: Coaching clients to work through their feelings*. doi:10.1037/10447-000

Greenberg, L. S., & Elliott, R. (1997). Varieties of empathic responding. In A. C. Bohart & L. S. Greenberg (Eds.), *Empathy reconsidered: New directions in psychotherapy* (pp. 167–186). doi:10.1037/10226-007

Greenberg, L. S., & Pascual-Leone, J. (1995). A dialectical constructivist approach to experiential change. In R. A. Neimeyer & M. J. Mahoney (Eds.), *Constructivism in psychotherapy* (pp. 169–191). doi:10.1037/10170-008

Greenberg, L. S., & Pascual-Leone, J. (1997). Emotion in the creation of personal meaning. In M. J. Power & C. R. Brewin (Eds.), *The transformation of meaning in psychological therapies: Integrating theory and practice* (pp. 157–173). Hoboken, NJ: Wiley.

Greenberg, L. S., & Safran, J. D. (1987). *Emotion in psychotherapy: Affect, cognition, and the process of change*. New York, NY: Guilford Press.

Linehan, M. M. (1993). *Cognitive-behavioral treatment of borderline personality disorder*. New York, NY: Guilford Press.

Nadel, L., & Bohbot, V. (2001). Consolidation of memory. *Hippocampus, 11*, 56–60. doi:10.1002/1098-1063(2001)11:1<56::AID-HIPO1020>3.0.CO;2-O

Pennebaker, J. W. (1995). *Emotion, disclosure, and health*. doi:10.1037/10182-000

Sroufe, L. A. (1996). *Emotional development: The organization of emotional life in the early years. Cambridge studies in social and emotional development*. New York, NY; Cambridge University Press. doi:10.1017/CBO9780511527661

Stern, D. (1985). *The interpersonal world of the infant*. New York, NY: Basic Books.

APPENDIX 14.1: EMOTION-FOCUSED THERAPY TECHNIQUES

Technique	Video title	Video identifying number	Time at which technique occurs
Understanding empathic responses	Rebuilding Communication Skills With Emotion Focused Couple Therapy (Session 5 of 6)	777700151-001	6:44–7:53
Validating and evocative responses	Rebuilding Communication Skills With Emotion Focused Couple Therapy (Session 5 of 6)	777700151-001	17:14–17:55
Exploratory and conjectural responses	Rebuilding Communication Skills With Emotion Focused Couple Therapy (Session 5 of 6)	777700151-001	14:11–16:21
Empathic refocusing	Working Through Depression With Emotion-Focused Therapy (Session 1 of 2)	777700051-001	18:57–20:24
Focusing	Rebuilding Communication Skills With Emotion Focused Couple Therapy (Session 5 of 6)	777700151-001	19:33–21:38
Reflection	Rebuilding Communication Skills With Emotion Focused Couple Therapy (Session 5 of 6)	777700151-001	42:58–43:56
Shifting attention to peripheral emotion	Working Through Depression With Emotion-Focused Therapy (Session 1 of 2)	777700051-001	20:24–21:41
Enactment	Rebuilding Communication Skills With Emotion Focused Couple Therapy (Session 6 of 6)	777700154-001	21:07–32:08
Imagery	Working Through Depression With Emotion-Focused Therapy	777700053-001	22:53–26:04
Remembering a time emotion was felt	Rebuilding Communication Skills With Emotion Focused Couple Therapy (Session 5 of 6)	777700151-001	31:10–32:16
Expressing an emotion for a client	Rebuilding Communication Skills With Emotion Focused Couple Therapy (Session 6 of 6)	777700154-001	25:56–27:10
Systematic evocative unfolding	Working Through Depression With Emotion-Focused Therapy (Session 1 of 2)	777700051-001	27:31–34:54

(continues)

Technique	Video title	Video identifying number	Time at which technique occurs
Two-chair work	Balancing Spiritual and Practical Needs in the Decision to Divorce (Session 3 of 6)	777700141-001	12:10–26:52
Empty-chair dialogue	Working Through Depression With Emotion-Focused Therapy	777700053-001	30:49–43:53
Affirming empathic validation	Working Through Depression With Emotion-Focused Therapy	777700053-001	35:30–35:48
Offering support and understanding	Balancing Spiritual and Practical Needs in the Decision to Divorce (Session 3 of 6)	777700141-001	35:23–35:57
Encouraging clients to organize their distressing emotions	Rebuilding Communication Skills With Emotion-Focused Couple Therapy (Session 1 of 6)	777700138-001	14:09–21:31
Self-soothing	Working Through Depression With Emotion-Focused Therapy	777700053-001	42:03–45:48
Distraction	Working Through Depression With Emotion-Focused Therapy	777700053-001	41:43–42:00 (more grounding)

15

EXISTENTIAL THERAPY

KIRK J. SCHNEIDER AND ORAH T. KRUG

GOALS OF THE APPROACH

Freedom Within Limits

The aim of existential–humanistic (E–H) therapy is to "set clients free" (May, 1981, p. 19). Freedom is understood as the capacity for choice within the natural and self-imposed limits of living (Schneider, 2008). The natural limits of living refer to the inherent limitations of birth, heredity, age, and so forth, and the realities of living—often referred to as "the givens of existence"—such as death, separateness, and uncertainty. Self-imposed limits are the boundaries established by humans, such as culture, language, and lifestyle.

Excerpted from *Existential–Humanistic Therapy* (2010), from Chapter 3, "Theory," pp. 13–22. Copyright 2010 by the American Psychological Association. Used with permission of the author.

http://dx.doi.org/10.1037/14295-015

Psychotherapy Theories and Techniques: A Reader, G. R. VandenBos, E. Meidenbauer, and J. Frank-McNeil (Editors)

Copyright © 2014 by the American Psychological Association. All rights reserved.

The freedom to do or to act is probably the clearest freedom we possess. The freedom to be or to adopt attitudes toward situations is a less clear but even more fundamental freedom (May, 1981). Freedom to do is generally associated with external, physical decisions, whereas freedom to be is associated with internal, cognitive, and emotional stances. Within these freedoms we have a great capacity to create meaning in our lives—to conceptualize, imagine, invent, communicate, and physically and psychologically enlarge our worlds (Yalom, 1980). We also have the capacity to separate from others; to transcend our past; and to become distinct, unique, and heroic (Becker, 1973). Conversely, we can choose to restrain ourselves, to become passive, and to give ourselves over to others (May, 1981; Rank, 1936). We can choose to be a part of others or apart from others, a part of our possibilities or apart from our possibilities (Bugental & Kleiner, 1993).

Acknowledge Freedom's Limitations

Notwithstanding the vast possibilities, there are great limitations on all these freedoms. We can only do and be so much. Whatever we choose implies a relinquishment of something else (Bugental, 1987, p. 230). If we devote ourselves to scholarship, we relinquish a degree of athleticism. If we engage in wealth accumulation, we lessen our opportunities for spiritual pursuits. Moreover, every freedom has its price. If one stands out in a crowd, one becomes a larger target for criticism; if one acquires responsibility, one courts guilt; if one isolates oneself, one loses community; if one merges and fuses with others, one loses individuality, and so on (Becker, 1973; May, 1981). Finally, every freedom has its counterpart in destiny. May (1981) defines four kinds of destiny, or "givens" beyond our control: cosmic, genetic, cultural, and circumstantial. Cosmic destiny embraces the limitations of nature (e.g., earthquakes, climatic shifts); genetic destiny entails physiological dispositions (e.g., life span, temperament); cultural destiny addresses preconceived social patterns (e.g., language, birthrights); and circumstantial destiny pertains to sudden situational developments (e.g., oil spills, job layoffs). In short, our vast potentialities are matched by crushing vulnerabilities. We are semiaware, semicapable, in a world of dazzling incomprehensibility.

How, then, shall we deal with these clashing realities according to existential theorists, and what happens when we do not? Let us consider the latter first. The failure to acknowledge our freedom, according to existential theorists, results in the dysfunctional identification with limits, or repressed living (May, 1981). This dysfunctional identification forfeits the capacity to enliven, embolden, and enlarge one's perspective. The reticent wallflower, the pedantic bureaucrat, the paranoid reactionary, and the robotic conformist are illustrations of this polarity. The failure to acknowledge our limits, on the other hand, results in the sacrifice of our ability to discipline, discern, and prioritize life's chances (May, 1981). The aimless dabbler, the impulsive con man, the unbowed hedonist, and the power-hungry elitist exemplify this polarity.

Integrate Freedom and Limitation

The great question, of course, is how to help clients become emancipated from their polarized conditions and "experience their possibilities" as they engage their destinies (May, 1981, p. 20). Put another way, how do we help clients to *integrate* freedom and limits? This question strikes at the heart of another existential problem—that of identity. Whereas reprogramming clients' behaviors or helping them to understand the genesis of their polarized conditions leads to partially rejuvenated identities, for existential theorists, *experiential* encounters with these conditions are the great underappreciated complements to the aforementioned change processes (Schneider, 2007, 2008). The E–H practitioner believes that if life-limiting patterns are experienced in the present, then clients will be more willing and able to choose life-affirming patterns in the future. Put another way, the path to greater freedom is paradoxically found through an encounter with the ways in which we are bound (Krug, 2009).

The experiential modality for existential theorists embraces four basic dimensions: the immediate, the kinesthetic, the affective, and the profound or cosmic (Schneider, 2008). The road to a fuller, more vital identity, in other words, is to help clients experience their polarized conditions, to assist them to "embody" those conditions and their underlying fears and anxieties, and to help them attune, at the deepest levels, to the implications of what has been discovered. In so doing, E–H therapists help clients to respond to, as opposed to react against, panic-filled material. This work typically results in clients experiencing their polarized conditions as restrictive or self-limiting. Consequently, it not only allows clients to understand their part in the construction of their restrictive patterns, it also helps them accept the givens of existence that may have been avoided, denied, or repressed. However, for the E–H practitioner, responsibility assumption is not sufficient. It is simply preparatory for substantive change evidenced when clients choose more life-affirming patterns for themselves and with others. The net result, according to existential theorists, is an expanded sense of self, specifically an enhanced capacity for intimacy, meaning, and spiritual connection in one's life (Bugental, 1978; May, 1981).

An Illustration of This Process

The classic case of Mercedes, by Rollo May (1972), further illustrates this standpoint. Mercedes lived much of her life in subordination to others.

Her stepfather was a pimp and her mother a prostitute. Mercedes herself was coerced into prostitution to enable the family to subsist. Yet, Mercedes bristled at her subservient position. She harbored tremendous resentment toward her "clientele" and even more toward her "caretakers." She was frequently depressed, impaired in her love life, and unable to carry her pregnancies with her husband to full term. May utilized many approaches to help Mercedes confront and integrate her rage, which in his view portended her freedom. These efforts, however, invariably failed to spark her, until one day when he encountered her experientially. Instead of encouraging *her* to acknowledge her resentment, *he* acknowledged it for her. *He* vented his fury on her stepfather; *he* unleashed his indignation toward her mother; and *he* embodied the bitterness she had harbored. In turn, Mercedes was finally able to affirm and express these qualities—directly and bodily—in herself. The upshot, according to May, is that Mercedes integrated her freedom: She quit prostitution, revived her marriage, and carried her pregnancy to term.

Varied Interpretations of Experiential Encounter

The experiential mode is diversely interpreted by existential theorists. For example, Yalom (1980) appears to stress the immediate and affective elements of his interpersonal therapeutic contacts, but he refers little to kinesthetic components. Bugental (1987) stresses kinesthetic elements of his encounters— illuminating what is "implicitly present but unregarded" (Bugental, 1999, p. 25)—but places lesser emphasis on interpersonal implications of those elements (Krug, 2009). Tillich (1952) and Friedman (1995) accent the interpersonal dimension of therapeutic experiencing but convey little about the kinesthetic aspect.

There are also differences among existential theorists regarding verbal and nonverbal channels of communication. May (1983), Yalom (1980), and Friedman (1995), for example, rely relatively heavily on verbal interventions, whereas Bugental (1987), Gendlin (1996), and Laing (1967) draw upon comparatively nonverbal forms of mediation.

Finally, there are differences among existential theorists with regard to philosophical implications of therapeutic experiencing. Although most existential theorists agree that clients need to confront the underlying givens (or ultimate concerns) of human existence during the course of a typical therapy, the nature and specificity of these givens varies. Whereas Yalom (1980), for example, focuses on the need for clients to experientially confront death, freedom, isolation, or meaninglessness, Bugental provides a more elaborate schema: the need for clients to confront embodiment–change, finitude–contingency, action–responsibility, choice–relinquishment, separation–apartness, or relation–being a part of (Bugental & Kleiner, 1993). And whereas May (1981) unites these positions with his notion of freedom and destiny (or limitation), as previously suggested, there is only a vague explication of this synthesis in his work.

A Central Concern: The Present Moment

Despite these differences, each theorist shares a central concern—namely, how is this client in this moment coping with his or her awareness of being alive? The E–H theorists address this concern by focusing more on the implicit—moment to moment—processes in therapy than on explicit content. E–H theorists take an ahistorical approach; that is, the past is integral only insofar as it is alive, within the person, in the present moment. Moreover, E–H therapists seek to understand a person as a human being in the world, related to his or her physical, personal, and social worlds. It is assumed that a person is not simply a collection of drives and behavior patterns within an encapsulated self. It is further assumed that each person is more than the sum of his or her parts and that each person constructs a particular world from unique perceptions of the world. Finally, the E–H therapist assumes, as May (1983) suggests, that "the person and his world are a unitary, structural whole . . . two poles, self and world, are always dialectically related" (p. 122).

Consequently, the E–H theorist takes a step back from examining a person's drives and specific behavior patterns; with a wider scope, she or he understands these in the context of a person's relation to existence (May, 1958a, 1958b; Merleau-Ponty, 1962). These relations, which manifest as *structures*, are not abstract but actual, and though they may be obscured from conscious awareness, they are nevertheless evident (though perhaps implied) in the present moment. They express themselves through words spoken, and not through bodily gestures, vocal tones, dreams, and behavior patterns.

The Cultivation of Presence

The existential therapist aims to know the person who comes for therapy at this "structural" level. As May (1958a) states, "The grasping of the being of the other person occurs on a quite different level from our knowledge of specific things about him" (p. 38). In order to "grasp the being" of the client, and consequently help the client "grasp her being," the therapist must bring a full and genuine presence to the therapeutic encounter. The Latin root for *presence* is *prae* (before) + *esse* (to be); thus, *presence* means "to be before." Consequently, presence in a therapeutic setting can be understood as the capacity "to be before" or to be with one's being and/or "to be before" or to be with another human being.

Presence involves aspects of awareness, acceptance, availability, and expressiveness in both therapist and client. Presence implies that the encounter is real. For Martin Buber (1937/1970), it means that the person who is before one has ceased being an "it" and has become a "thou"; it means that we are all humans who include each other in each other's recognition. Indeed, as Gabriel Marcel (1951) suggests, intersubjective presence begins with "*we are*" as opposed to "*I think*." If one can be truly present with another, then a genuine encounter has occurred.

Even with this emphasis on presence, E–H theorists recognize the influence of the past in their present-centered encounters. They acknowledge, for example, the power of developmental deficits to impact therapeutic processes (Schneider, 2008; Yalom, 1980). However, the bases of those deficits and the contexts within which they are addressed differ significantly from those advanced by more conventional standpoints. For example, whereas psychoanalytically oriented theorists tend to view ruptures in early interpersonal relationships as the bases for developmental deficits, E–H-oriented theorists take a wider view. This view acknowledges those early ruptures but goes beyond them to embrace the fuller experience of rupture or estrangement before being itself (May, 1981; Schneider, 2008; Yalom, 1980). Put another way, whereas psychoanalytic theorists tend to focus on isolable family or physiological factors in the etiology of suffering, E–H theorists tend to home in on dimensions that are purported to underlie such factors, such as the experience of life's vastness, the terror of dissolving before, or, on the other hand, exploding into life's vastness and the struggle with the enigma of death (Becker, 1973; Schneider, 1993, 1999a, 1999b, 2008; Yalom, 1980).

Given this background, it may now be clearer why E–H theorists focus on here-and-now *experiences* of the past (as manifested in body posture, vocal tone, etc.) over discussions *about* the past. Whereas discussions can help clients to assimilate a specifiable event, such as an abuse memory, experiential awareness can help clients to assimilate the life stance, such as the sense of dissolution that both echoes and transcends the event.

For E–H theorists, accordingly, the deepest roots of trauma cannot simply be talked about or explained away; they must be rediscovered, felt, and lived through (Bugental, 1987; Krug, 2009; Schneider, 2008).

Four Core Aims

To sum, E–H theorists share four core aims: (a) to help clients to become more present to themselves and others; (b) to help them experience the ways in which they both mobilize and block themselves from fuller presence; (c) to help them take responsibility for the construction of their current lives; and

(d) to help them choose or actualize ways of being in their outside lives based on facing, not avoiding, the existential givens such as finiteness, ambiguity, and anxiety.

KEY CONCEPTS

Sense of Self

E–H psychology assumes that one does not experience a personality; one lives an experience. Moreover, E–H psychology assumes that lived experience is the basis on which one forms or creates a sense of self (May, 1975). E–H theorists' understanding of identity formation, or the "I am" experience, has been significantly influenced by May's perspective on human experience. His perspective focuses on awareness as an essence of being that has two dimensions. The first dimension is the fact of awareness: Every person is aware that she or he exists and consequently copes in various ways with this awareness. This is understood as the "existential predicament" and has been a major focus of existential philosophy and psychology (see Camus, 1955; Marcel, 1956; May, 1975, 1981; Sartre, 1956).

The second dimension focuses on how a person is aware and refers to the foundational structure of human experience—namely, how anxiety, which stems from awareness of existence, drives a person to create meaning through an ongoing dialectical process between the subjective and objective poles of reality. May (1975) asserts that this dialectical process of meaning making, which he calls "passion for form," is the essence of genuine creativity. May acknowledges that his principle of human experience is similar to the ideas of several great philosophers, one of whom is Alfred N. Whitehead.

Whitehead's philosophy is part of a philosophical tradition going back to Heraclitus that focuses on process. Reality is not an assortment of material things, which is the Aristotelian notion, but one of process. Nature is a process not a thing. A river is not a thing but a continuing flow. Therefore, human beings, being a part of nature, are understood as a matter of process, of activity, of change (Rescher, 2000).

In Whitehead's ontology every organism or "occasion of experience" is "a dipolar unity . . . that enfolds . . . the past . . . into the present . . . and orients the organism toward the future in a 'creative advance'" (de Quincy, 2002, p. 174). A significant aspect of the structure of experience is that the past is always flowing into the present moment. Another significant aspect is the ongoing shaping of experience into a pattern from the "welter of material" from the past and from the external world. Whitehead argues that a person is never simply aware of bare existence or thought. Awareness is a person's subjective reaction to his or her environment derived from a shaping of a welter of emotions, thoughts, hopes, fears, and valuations into a consistent pattern of feelings. According to Whitehead, this shaping results in a sense of unity or "I am." May (1975) specifically correlates his conceptualization of "passion for form" and its relationship to the formation of a sense of self or identity to Whitehead's "process of shaping" and the resulting "sense of unity":

> What I am calling passion for form is, if I understand Whitehead aright, a central aspect of what he is describing as the experience of identity. I am able to shape feelings, sensibilities, enjoyments, and hopes into a pattern that makes me aware of myself as a man or woman. But I cannot shape them into a pattern as a purely subjective act. I can do it only as I am related to the immediate objective world in which I live. (p. 135)

Whitehead's process perspective provides May, and existential psychotherapy, with a sound philosophical position from which to explain how a sense of identity is created. Identity is created not as a purely subjective act but only as a dialectical process with the objective world. By understanding the "I am" experience as an ongoing dialectical process between subjective and objective poles, E–H theorists and practitioners have a more complex understanding of how a sense of self or identity is created and maintained. This understanding can be like a road map for therapists, helping them to see more clearly in the living moment the ways in which their clients are forming their worlds. The road map also elucidates the significant role the therapist plays in helping a client reconstitute his or her world. Finally, the road map confirms in a concrete way a basic assumption of existential therapy, which is that human beings have the potential to grow and recreate themselves through ongoing creative practices.

REFERENCES

Becker, E. (1973). *Denial of death*. New York, NY: Free Press.

Buber, M. (1970). *I and thou* (W. Kaufmann, Trans.). New York, NY: Scribner's. (Original work published 1937)

Bugental, J. F. T. (1978). *Psychotherapy and process: The fundamentals of an existential–humanistic approach*. New York, NY: McGraw-Hill.

Bugental, J. F. T. (1987). *The art of the psychotherapist*. New York, NY: Norton.

Bugental, J. F. T. (1999). *Psychotherapy isn't what you think*. Phoenix, AZ: Zeig, Tucker, & Theisen.

Bugental, J. F. T., & Kleiner, R. (1993). Existential psychotherapies. In G. Stricker & J. R. Gold (Eds.), *Comprehensive handbook of psychotherapy integration* (pp. 101–112). New York, NY: Plenum Press.

Camus, A. (1955). *The myth of Sisyphus and other essays* (J. O'Brien, Trans.). New York, NY: Knopf.

de Quincey, C. (2002). *Radical nature: Rediscovering the soul of matter*. Montpelier, VT: Invisible Cities Press.

Friedman, M. (1995). The case of Dawn. In K. J. Schneider & R. May (Eds.), *The psychology of existence: An integrative, clinical perspective* (pp. 308–315). New York, NY: McGraw-Hill.

Gendlin, E. T. (1996). *Focusing-oriented psychotherapy*. New York, NY: Guilford Press.

Krug, O. T. (2009). James Bugental and Irvin Yalom: Two masters of existential therapy cultivate presence in the therapeutic encounter. *Journal of Humanistic Psychology, 49*(3), 329–354. doi:10.1177/0022167809334001

Laing, R. D. (1967). *The politics of experience*. New York, NY: Ballantine.

Marcel, G. (1951). *Mystery of being—Faith and reality*. Chicago, IL: Gateway Edition.

Marcel, G. (1956). *The philosophy of existentialism*. New York, NY: Philosophical Library.

May, R. (1958a). Contributions of existential psychotherapy. In R. May, E. Angel, & H. Ellenberger (Eds.), *Existence* (pp. 37–91). New York, NY: Basic Books.

May, R. (1958b). The origins and significance of the existential movement in psychology. In R. May, E. Angel, & H. Ellenberger (Eds.), *Existence* (pp. 3–36). New York, NY: Basic Books.

May, R. (1972). *Power and innocence*. New York, NY: Norton.

May, R. (1975). *The courage to create*. New York, NY: Norton.

May, R. (1981). *Freedom and destiny*. New York, NY: Norton.

May, R. (1983). *The discovery of being*. New York, NY: Norton.

Merleau-Ponty, M. (1962). *The phenomenology of perception* (C. Smith, Trans.). London, England: Routledge & Kegan Paul.

Rank, O. (1936). *Will therapy* (J. Taft, Trans.). New York, NY: Knopf.

Rescher, N. (2000). *Process philosophy: A survey of basic ideas*. Pittsburgh, PA: University of Pittsburgh Press.

Sartre, J. P. (1956). *Being and nothingness* (H. Barnes, Trans.). New York, NY: Philosophical Library.

Schneider, K. J. (1993). *Horror and the holy: Wisdom-teachings of the monster tale*. Chicago, IL: Open Court.

Schneider, K. J. (1999a). Clients deserve relationships, not merely "treatments." *American Psychologist, 54*, 206–207. doi:10.1037/0003-066X.54.3.206

Schneider, K. J. (1999b). *The paradoxical self: Toward an understanding of our contradictory nature* (2nd ed.). Amherst, NY: Humanity Books.

Schneider, K. J. (2007). The experiential liberation strategy of the existential–integrative model of therapy. *Journal of Contemporary Psychotherapy, 37,* 33–39. doi:10.1007/s10879-006-9032-y

Schneider, K. J. (2008). *Existential–integrative psychotherapy: Guideposts to the core of practice.* New York, NY: Routledge.

Tillich, P. (1952). *The courage to be.* New Haven, CT: Yale University Press.

Yalom, I. (1980). *Existential psychotherapy.* New York, NY: Basic Books.

Yalom, I. (1998). *The Yalom reader.* New York, NY: Basic Books.

16

EXISTENTIAL THERAPY PROCESS

KIRK J. SCHNEIDER AND ORAH T. KRUG

THE CULTIVATION AND ACTIVATION
OF INTRAPERSONAL PRESENCE

Bugental (1987) is representative of the intrapersonal tradition in existential–humanistic (E–H) therapy, although this characterization is far from discrete, and much about his approach can be considered interpersonal as well. Within the former tradition, however, Bugental outlines four basic practice strategies, or that which he terms "octaves" for activating clients' presence. These are listening, guiding, instructing, and requiring.

The first octave, listening, draws clients out and encourages them to keep talking so as to obtain their story without "contamination" by the therapist. Examples of listening include "getting the details" of clients' experiences and

Excerpted from *Existential–Humanistic Therapy* (2010), from Chapter 4, "The Therapy Process," pp. 39–44. Copyright 2010 by the American Psychological Association. Used with permission of the author.

http://dx.doi.org/10.1037/14295-016
Psychotherapy Theories and Techniques: A Reader, G. R. VandenBos, E. Meidenbauer, and J. Frank-McNeil (Editors)
Copyright © 2014 by the American Psychological Association. All rights reserved.

"listening to emotional catharsis, learning [clients' views of their] own life or . . . projected objectives" (Bugental, 1987, p. 71). The second octave, guiding, gives direction and support to clients' speech, keeps it on track, and brings out other aspects. Examples of guiding include exploration of clients' "understanding of a situation, relation, or problem; developing readiness to learn new aspects or get feedback" (Bugental, 1987, p. 71).

The third octave is instructing. Instructing transmits "information or directions having rational and/or objective support"; examples include "assignments, advising, coaching, describing a scenario of changed living," or reframing (Bugental, 1987, p. 71). Finally, the fourth octave is requiring, which brings a "therapist's personal and emotional resources to bear" to cause clients to change in some way; examples of requiring include "subjective feedback, praising, punishing [e.g., admonishing], rewarding," and "strong selling of [a] therapist's views" (Bugental, 1987, p. 71).

Listening and guiding comprise the lion's share of E–H activation of presence. Whereas instructing and requiring can certainly be useful from the E–H point of view, they are implemented in highly selective circumstances. For example, instructing may be very helpful to clients at early stages of therapy—those who have fragile emotional constitutions, such as victims of chronic abuse, or clients from authority-dependent cultures. Requiring, similarly, may be useful in these situations but also in the case of therapeutic impasses or entrenched client patterns, as we shall see. For the majority of E–H practice situations, however, listening and guiding are pivotal to the deepening, expanding, and consolidating of substantive client transformation.

May (1981) illustrates the value of listening with his notion of the pause. He writes,

> It is in the pause that people learn to listen to silence. We can hear the infinite number of sounds that we normally never hear at all—the unending hum and buzz of insects in a quiet summer field, a breeze blowing lightly through the golden hay . . . And suddenly we realize that this is *something*—the world of "silence" is populated by a myriad of creatures and a myriad of sounds. (May, 1981, p. 165)

The client, similarly, is almost invariably enlivened in the pause. As Bugental (1987, p. 70) suggests, it is in the therapist's silence at given junctures that abiding change can take root.

The provision of a working "space," a therapeutic pause, not only helps the therapist to understand but, most importantly, assists the client to vivify (or intensively elucidate) herself or himself. Vivification of a client's world is one of the cardinal tasks of E–H therapy. To the extent that clients can "see" close up the worlds in which they've lived, the obstacles they've created, and the strengths or resources they possess to overcome those obstacles, they can proceed to a foundational healing. Listening elucidates one of the most crucial realizations of vivification—the contours of a client's battle.

The client's battle—and virtually every client has one—becomes evident at the earliest stages of therapy. For some this battle takes the form of an interpersonal conflict, for others an intrapsychic split. To cite just a few examples, it may encompass the compulsion for and rejection of binge eating, a conflict with one's boss, or a struggle between squelched vocational potential and evolving aspirations. Regardless of the content of clients' battles, however, their form can be understood in terms of two basic valences—the part of themselves that endeavors to emerge and the part of themselves that endeavors to resist, oppose, or block themselves from emerging (Schneider, 1998). One can understand from this description of resistance and defenses that existential therapy is, as Yalom (1980) suggests, a kind of dynamic therapy that models its understanding of "forces in conflict" on Freud's dynamic model of mental functioning.

Whereas therapeutic listening acquaints and sometimes immerses clients in their battle, therapeutic guiding intensifies that contact. Therapeutic guiding can be further illustrated by encouragements to clients to personalize their dialogue—for instance, to give concrete examples of their difficulties, to speak in the first person, and to "own" or take responsibility for their remarks about others. Guiding is also illustrated by invitations to expand or embellish on given topics, such as in the suggestion "Can you say more?" or "How does it feel to make that statement?" or "What really matters about what you're saying?" Finally, guiding is exemplified by the notation of content/process discrepancies, such as "you smile as you vent your anger at him" or "notice how shallow your breathing is right now" (Bugental, 1987; Schneider, 2008).

Schneider (1998, 2008) has formulated a mode of guiding called guided or embodied meditation. This approach has proven pivotal for many clients, particularly those who battle over-intellectualization.[1] Embodied meditation begins with a simple grounding exercise, such as breathing awareness or progressive relaxation (usually assisted by the closing of the eyes). From there, it proceeds to an invitation to the client to become aware of his or her body. The therapist may then ask what, if any, tension areas are evident in the client's body. If the client identifies such an area, which often occurs, the therapist asks the client to describe, as richly and fully as possible, where the tension area is and what it feels like. Following this and assuming the client is able to

---

[1]Although several variations of embodied mediation have been shown to be highly effective with certain populations (e.g., see Gendlin, 1996; Leijssen, 2006), in the wrong hands they also can be debilitating. As with all approaches discussed in this volume, care must be taken to ensure that facilitation is preceded by appropriate training, skill development, and sensitivity to clients' needs.

proceed with the immersion, he or she is invited to place his or her hand on the affected area. (This somatic element can often be, although not necessarily, experientially critical.) Next, the client is encouraged to experientially associate to this contact. Prompts such as "What, if any, feelings, sensations, or images emerge as you make contact with this area?" can be of notable therapeutic value. Dr. Schneider reports having seen clients open emotional floodgates through this work, but he has also seen clients who feel overpowered by it. It is of utmost importance for the therapist to be acutely attuned while practicing this and other awareness-intensive modes.

Guidance is also illustrated by a variety of experimental formats that can be offered in E–H therapy. These experiments, including role-play, rehearsal, visualization, and experiential enactment (e.g., pillow-hitting, kinesthetic exercises), serve to liven emergent material and vivify or deepen the understanding of that material (Mahrer, 1996; Schneider, 2008; Serlin, 1996). The phrase "Truth exists only as it is produced in action" (Kierkegaard cited in May, 1958, p. 12) has much cachet in this context. When clients can enact (as appropriate) their anxieties, engage their aspirations, and simulate their encounters, they bring their battles into the room—in "living color"—for close and personal inspection.

While experimentation within the therapeutic setting is invaluable, experimentation outside the setting can be of equivalent or even superior benefit. After all, it is the life outside of therapy that counts most for clients, and it is in the service of this life that therapy proceeds. Experimentation outside of therapy, then, has two basic aims: (1) it reinforces intratherapy work, and (2) it implements that work in the most relevant setting possible—the lived experience. Accordingly, E–H therapists encourage clients to practice being aware and present in their outside lives. They may gently challenge clients to reflect on or write about problematic events, or they may propose an activity or therapeutic commitment (e.g., Alcoholics Anonymous or assigned readings). They may also challenge clients to do without a given activity or pattern. For example, Yalom (1980) challenged his promiscuous client Bruce to try living without a sexual partner for an extended period. This was a highly demanding exercise for Bruce, whose sexual compulsions were formidable and afforded no pause. Yet, after the exercise, Bruce reported rich therapeutic realizations, like the degree to which he felt empty in his life and the blind and compulsive measures he took to fill that emptiness. Emptiness, Yalom reported, subsequently became the next productive focus.

Prompts to clients to "slow down" or "stay with" charged or disturbing experience can also facilitate intensified self-awareness. We have known many a supervisee (and even seasoned colleague) who has had difficulties with this facilitation. They are superb at helping clients to reconnect with the parts of themselves they have shunted away, and they inspire deep somatic immersion in expressiveness, but they are left with one gaping question: "What do I do after the client is immersed?" The exasperation in this puzzlement is understandable. E–H work can seem tormenting. It can instigate profound moments of unalloyed pain. The last thing a therapist wishes to do in such a situation is to enable increased suffering or to hover in continued despair. And yet, given the client's desire and capacity for change, these are precisely the allowances that E–H therapists must provide, precisely the groundworks they must pursue. They must develop trust and a sense that the work will unfold (Welwood, 2001). Hence, what do we advise our supervisees and colleagues? We suggest that it is in their interest to trust—in particular, to trust that gentle prompts to "stay with" or "allow" intensive material will almost invariably lead to changes in that material. While these changes may not feel immediately welcome or gratifying—indeed, they may even feel regressive for a time—they do represent evolution, the "more" that every person is capable of experiencing.

REFERENCES

Bugental, J. F. T. (1987). *The art of the psychotherapist*. New York, NY: Norton.

Gendlin, E. T. (1996). *Focusing-oriented psychotherapy*. New York, NY: Guilford Press.

Leijssen, M. (2006). Validation of the body in psychotherapy. *Journal of Humanistic Psychology, 46*, 126–146. doi:10.1177/0022167805283782

Mahrer, A. R. (1996). *The complete guide to experiential psychotherapy*. New York, NY: Wiley.

May, R. (1958). The origins and significance of the existential movement in psychology. In R. May, E. Angel, & H. Ellenberger (Eds.), *Existence* (pp. 3–36). New York, NY: Basic Books.

May, R. (1981). *Freedom and destiny*. New York, NY: Norton.

Schneider, K. J. (1998). Existential processes. In L. S. Greenberg, J. C. Watson, & G. Lietaer (Eds.), *Handbook of experiential psychotherapy* (pp. 103–120). New York, NY: Guilford Press.

Schneider, K. J. (2008). *Existential–integrative psychotherapy: Guideposts to the core of practice*. New York, NY: Routledge.

Serlin, I. A. (1996). Kinesthetic imagining. *Journal of Humanistic Psychology, 36*(2), 25–33. doi:10.1177/00221678960362005

Welwood, J. (2001). The unfolding of experience: Psychotherapy and beyond. In K. J. Schneider, J. F. T. Bugental, & J. F. Pierson (Eds.), *The handbook of humanistic psychology: Leading edges in theory, practice, and research* (pp. 333–341). Thousand Oaks, CA: Sage.

Yalom, I. (1980). *Existential psychotherapy*. New York, NY: Basic Books.

APPENDIX 16.1: EXISTENTIAL THERAPY TECHNIQUES

Technique	Video title	Video identifying number	Time at which technique occurs
Listening	Existential–Humanistic Therapy for Life Satisfaction (1 of 4)	777700340-001	14:17–21:16
Guiding	Existential–Humanistic Therapy for Life Satisfaction (3 of 4)	777700342-001	17:52–21:29
Guided or embodied meditation	Existential–Integrative Psychotherapy With a Socially Anxious Young Adult Male Client	777700399-001	08:21–14:56
Role-play, rehearsal, visualization	Existential–Integrative Psychotherapy With a Socially Anxious Young Adult Male Client	777700399-001	21:01–27:33
Instructing	Existential–Humanistic Therapy for Life Satisfaction (1 of 4)	777700340-001	31:48–38:45
Requiring (subjective feedback, praising, punishing [e.g., admonishing])	Existential–Humanistic Therapy for Life Satisfaction (3 of 4)	777700342-001	27:34–33:46
Vivification	Existential–Humanistic Therapy for Life Satisfaction (3 of 4)	777700342-001	08:31–17:35

17

FAMILY THERAPY

WILLIAM J. DOHERTY AND SUSAN H. McDANIEL

Every theory has a set of driving questions it attempts to answer, and as theories develop over time, they usually extend their reach as new questions arise. Here are the original questions addressed by family therapy theories.

1. *How do individuals develop symptoms within families?* This was the primary question in the development of family therapy, with the initial focus on schizophrenia and then on a wide range of psychosocial problems, including depression, anxiety disorders, psychosomatic illness, childhood conduct disorders, and substance abuse disorders. When a "new" problem was identified, such as bulimia and borderline personality disorder, family therapy theorists set about understanding the problem in terms of its family context. Sometimes the emphasis is on how family dynamics lead to the onset of a particular problem (e.g., oppositional defiant disorder stemming from undermining between

Excerpted from *Family Therapy* (2010), from Chapter 3, "Theory," pp. 30–38. Copyright 2010 by the American Psychological Association. Used with permission of the authors.

http://dx.doi.org/10.1037/14295-017

Psychotherapy Theories and Techniques: A Reader, G. R. VandenBos, E. Meidenbauer, and J. Frank-McNeil (Editors)
Copyright © 2014 by the American Psychological Association. All rights reserved.

the parents), and sometimes the emphasis is on how the family comes to organize itself around the disorder and thereby perpetuate the problem (as in the case of anxiety disorders or alcoholism, in which the disorder might have preceded the formation of the family but family dynamics keep it going). All family therapy theories place a major emphasis on here-and-now family process, and some also emphasize longer term family of origin processes.

2. *How do families maintain levels of interpersonal connection that allow for both emotional bonding and individual autonomy?* Different theorists address this question in different ways. Bowen (1978) viewed the family as tending toward interpersonal enmeshment or overinvolvement; optimal functioning involves the fostering of differentiation of self and consequent ability to maintain emotional connections without loss of autonomy. Minuchin (1974) viewed the family as tending toward extremes of enmeshment or disengagement, with the former promoting family cohesion at the expense of the individual and the latter promoting the opposite. Minuchin also emphasized the importance of differentiated subsystems in the family; for example, a clear but flexible boundary separating the parental subsystem from the children's subsystem promotes separation within the context of interpersonal support. We discuss the term *boundary* more fully later in this chapter.

3. *How does family conflict become unmanageable?* For obvious reasons, family conflict is a major preoccupation of family therapy theories. A core approach to understanding family conflict relies on systems dynamics first identified by Bateson in the 1930s: the circular processes whereby negative interactions escalate symmetrically to destructive levels (Watzlawick, Beavin, & Jackson, 1967). For example, a father's coerciveness elicits rebellious responses by his son, which lead to further coerciveness from the father and heightened resistance from the son—and so the escalation continues. A second standard approach is to examine the role of third parties (triangular patterns) in maintaining irresolvable conflicts. A covert alliance between mother and son might underlie the sustained, overt conflict between father and son (Haley, 1976). A third approach to the question of unmanageable family conflict focuses on overall family systems properties such as overconnectedness or enmeshment, which would make serious conflict flow from attempts of family members to assert and protect their autonomy (Minuchin, 1974).

4. *How can families change dysfunctional patterns?* Here the primary focus has been on how therapists can assist families to change. Family therapists generally view the unit of systems change as one consisting of a therapist and a family (Haley, 1976). The therapist uses the therapeutic relationship to elicit new family patterns, which the family internalizes at home.

Dozens of other important questions about families are addressed by theory in family therapy. However, we think that most of them can be subsumed under the four we have delineated here.

CLASSIC CONCEPTS

Relatively few concepts are employed in all family therapy theories. Nevertheless, a number of concepts are in common parlance because of their status as classic, first-generation family therapy ideas. Although there are formal assessment tools for these and other family therapy concepts (Jordan, 2003), the complexity of family dynamics is such that few assessment tools can capture the subtleties of a particular family. Here we stress how family therapists see the family dynamics emerging in the clinical interview from history and direct observation of families in the therapy room.

1. *Cohesion and individuation.* Implicit or explicit in every theory of family functioning that has arisen from family therapy is the idea that optimal family functioning involves a precarious balance between group solidarity, often termed *cohesion,* and individual autonomy, often called *differentiation* (Olson, Russell, & Sprenkle, 1983). Families with too much connectedness raise children who are oversocialized and will have difficulty leaving home emotionally, and families with too much separateness raise children who are undersocialized and will have difficulty trusting others (Minuchin, 1974). In both cases, it is considered likely that some family members will show signs of psychosocial pathology.

Determining a family's levels of cohesion and individuation cannot be done without an understanding of the family's cultural context (McGoldrick, Giordano, & Garcia-Preto, 2005) and life cycle stage (Carter & McGoldrick, 2005). Some families are more intensely involved with one another as a reflection of their ethnicity, and families with young children are likely to be more engaged with one another than are families with young adult offspring. What family therapists look for are struggles over connection and autonomy (e.g., parent–adolescent conflict over rules), lack of nurturance and support for a dependent family member (e.g., an ill member who is not being cared for adequately), and the inability of a family member to make decisions and play independent roles in his or her cultural context (as when a young adult is not able to make friends and secure employment). In the therapy room, enmeshment can be seen in family members speaking for one another and reading one another's minds. Disengagement can be seen in family members' not responding to emotional cues and failing to connect with the process of healing and change.

2. *Adaptability.* Derived from the systems theory principle that successful organisms are continually adapting to their environment, the concept of family adaptability or flexibility is a cornerstone of family therapy theory (von Bertalanffy, 1976). It means the ability of a family to shift its beliefs and interactional styles in the face of developmental changes and environmental challenges that can create relational problems and psychosocial pathology in

family members. In articulating their circumplex model of family assessment, Olson et al. (1983) maintained that adaptability (flexibility) and cohesion (connectedness vs. separateness) are the two primary concepts in all systems theories of the family.

Family therapists see adaptability in how the family has coped with challenges in the past and how it rises to the challenge presented in therapy now. In adjusting to a divorce, some families form workable new patterns of shared parenting in different households, but others become paralyzed around coparental conflict and resistance of children to change. In dealing with a serious illness in an elderly parent, some families take on and share new caregiver roles; in other families, one child steps up while the others continue to relate to the parent as if nothing has changed.

3. *Boundaries*. This concept, which is most widely used in structural family therapy (Minuchin, 1974), has roots in systems theory. Every living organism has boundaries separating it from its environment, and complex organisms have internal boundaries demarcating subsystems such as cells and organs (von Bertalanffy, 1976). Minuchin defined boundaries as family rules determining who will participate in the family and its subsystems and how they will participate. Boundaries must be clear if family members are to know how to relate to one another and to the world. As described previously, family boundaries can be enmeshed—not enough protection of autonomy—or disengaged to the exclusion of appropriate contact between members of different subsystems. Pauline Boss's (2001) research demonstrates the consequences of this "boundary ambiguity," when family members are unclear as to who is in and out of the family and its subsystems. Clear boundaries also protect the integrity of subsystems within the family, such as the marital couple or the sibling group. They also allow for a balance of cohesion and individuation.

Family therapists see boundary violations in situations such as a father sharing confidences with his daughter about his relationship with the mother, or an adolescent boy becoming a quasi-spouse to his mother after the death of the father. Therapists see boundary ambiguity in situations when it's not clear whether a new stepparent is a "real" parent with authority or just the spouse of the real parent. In general, boundaries are one of the most useful concepts in family therapy.

4. *Triangles*. Triadic interactional configurations are at the heart of how family therapists think about problematic family interactions. Bowen (1978) defined a triangle as a "three-person emotional configuration" and saw triangles as the basic building block of any emotional system, including the family. Bowen proposed that two-person systems become unstable in the face of high anxiety, leading them to involve a third party—often the most vulnerable family member—to form a more stable triangle. For example, destabilizing marital conflict might become deflected into disagreement over parenting,

with the child's problems keeping the focus away from the original marital problem. This triangle endures during calmer periods, with emotional forces continually shifting back and forth among the threesome. In subsequent periods of high stress, according to Bowen, each family member tries for the outside position, leaving the conflict to be contained between the other two.

Family therapists see Bowen-type triangles in situations where a father might take the outside position during family conflict, leaving the arguments to occur between mother and child. In one case, the 12-year-old boy would curse his mother (but never his father) when he got angry at her, while the father stayed "neutral" and disengaged. Family therapists often focus on family secrets as a way to understand emotional triangles in a family—who is in the know on a family secret and who is cut out, and then who takes the heat when the secret is revealed.

5. *Coalitions*. This is a variation, out of structural and strategic family therapy, on the triangle concept that emphasizes negative alliances, termed coalitions, between two or more family members against another family member. Some coalitions involve the basic three parties in a triad, whereas other coalitions can involve larger groups, as when several adult children align with father in blaming mother for a parental divorce. The term *coalition* was used extensively by Minuchin (1974) in his discussion of three kinds of "rigid family triads." The first rigid triad, called *triangulation*, is the pattern in which a parent demands that the child take sides in a parental dispute. The second concept, *detouring*, is the pattern whereby parents maintain harmony by reinforcing a child's deviant behavior; focusing on the child's problems allows them to avoid dealing with their own conflict. Finally, intergenerational coalitions are deemed by Minuchin (1974), Haley (1976), and many other theorists to be a central dysfunctional pattern in families. These occur most commonly when one parent and a child take sides against another parent. This pattern can continue throughout life.

Family therapists see coalitions when a divorced mother tells her children that their (good enough) father cannot be trusted, when a father tells his adult daughter that her mother was never "affectionate" enough for him, and when an out-of-town daughter works with a frail parent to prevent a nursing home placement by allying behind the back of the in-town daughter who is responsible for the mother's care.

6. *Intergenerational transmission*. A key principle of family therapy is that family interaction patterns tend to repeat across generations and may create problems for subsequent generations. Although no family therapy theory would dispute this assumption, several theories strongly emphasize it. These include Bowen's theory (Bowen, 1978; Kerr & Bowen, 1988) and Boszormenyi-Nagy's theory of the family as an ethical group (Boszormenyi-Nagy & Spark, 1973). Boszormenyi-Nagy, for example, described how "destructive entitlement" is

passed on through generations when a child who feels deprived of attentive, responsible parenting grows up with a sense of being owed by the world and becomes an inattentive, nonresponsible parent to the next generation. Bowen described how patterns of "cutoffs" between family members can take hold over many generations as family members deal with their anxiety and conflict by amputating family relationships.

Family therapists often see intergenerational patterns of cutoffs between fathers and children, based in part on the fragility of male–female couple relationships. This challenge is especially common among low-income families facing employment and other environmental challenges (Edin & Kefalas, 2007). Despite feeling hurt by the underinvolvement of their fathers, children grow up to expect and repeat the pattern.

7. *Family belief systems.* Family therapists have always been concerned with how family members understand their problems. But it was not until the 1970s and 1980s that theories developed a more explicit emphasis on family beliefs systems. Kantor and Lehr (1975) and Constantine (1986) presented a theory of family paradigms, which are a family's fundamental worldview—its core beliefs and values about how the family should function. For example, how does the family view the larger world—as a safe place for the family to interact with via open boundaries or a dangerous place to be walled off as much as possible? The Milan model of family therapy developed an emphasis on particular family beliefs about the disturbed family member's symptom (Boscolo, Cecchin, Hoffman, & Penn, 1987). For example, adherents to the Milan model might hypothesize that family beliefs related to a child's obesity (family members agree he's just like his dad) may be tied into family dynamics that maintain the weight problem.

Nowadays, many therapists encounter differences between Western beliefs in mental health and those of non-Western immigrant families who view mental health problems as threatening and stigmatized in their communities. The advantage of seeing these beliefs as not just those of individuals but also of their families and communities is that the therapist is less apt to make the mistake of thinking that an individual family member can readily take on a new perspective. Forming a consensus with a family that its member's condition involves both emotional and physical components requires a respect for the power of family belief systems.

8. *Self processes.* This concept divides the family therapy field into two groups: those with an explicit theory of the self in addition to family process and those who remain exclusively at the level of family process. The major approaches to understanding the self in the family are object relations family therapy and Bowen's family therapy. James Framo (1981) was a pioneer in applying psychoanalytically derived object relations theory to family therapy. Object relations theory emphasizes how the self develops in relation

to significant others, especially parents (see also Scharff & Scharff, 1987). Problematic parent–child relations lead to internal splits in the child (e.g., good–bad, pride–shame) that are projected onto love objects as an adult. Thus, adult family members tend to see each other through lenses distorted by undeveloped parts of the self, which leads to efforts to turn each other into ideal parents who can complete the self. Idealization ends in disillusionment when the individual projects the disowned part of the self onto the family member. For example, a husband who is cut off from his own feelings of weakness and inadequacy projects them onto his wife and then tries to "fix" himself by "fixing" her.

In Bowen's theory, self-differentiation is the psychological prerequisite for healthy family functioning. Only a differentiated self can handle constructively the emotional intensity of family relations, without resorting to reactive or disengaged behavior. This differentiation process involves the progressive ability to separate thinking from emotional process and to maintain one's capacity to make free choices in social situations involving strong affect.

Family therapists are always working with multiple "selves" in the family and therefore have working models of the role of the self. But family therapists see the self in interpersonal terms, never as an "I" separate from a "we." The internal splits of the self are highly visible in the therapy room and thus can be worked with directly, as when successful parents of a struggling young adult child project their fears of failure onto the offspring—and do so right in the therapy hour where the therapist can help them own their fears. When the parents bounce back and forth between overprotection and desire to cut their child off from the family, the family therapist can work on their differentiation of self—how to be in supportive relationship with their child without fusion or disengagement. Richard Schwartz (1997) developed a model of internal family systems therapy where the therapist uses systemic principles to work with multiple "parts" of the individual patient's self that frequently mirror interpersonal conflicts.

9. *Family life cycle challenges.* All family interaction patterns occur in the context of where the family is in its life course, from a family in formation to a family in old age, rearing children versus launching children, divorcing and recombining in stepfamilies, and so forth. In the early decades of family therapy, family life cycle stage was an implicit rather than explicit emphasis. The work of Betty Carter and Monica McGoldrick (2005) brought work of family development scholars (Duvall, 1977; Hill, 1970) into the family therapy field. For example, it is not surprising that many families present for therapy when children are adolescents and the family is dealing with the challenge of managing to stay connected with parental leadership during a time when the adolescent requires more autonomy. Similarly, combining two

families with children in a stepfamily poses challenges that tax the ability of families to change while maintaining continuity with the past.

The original family life cycle models focused on the stages of the nuclear family, but the same ideas can be applied to the complexities of extended families. It is not uncommon in today's world of longevity for therapists to work with four-generational families where one of the generations is attending to the needs of three others! One family, for example, had a stressful nursing home placement of the great grandmother at the same time as a heart problem in her son in the next generation and a difficult pregnancy and health complication in the third generation, with a new baby in the fourth generation requiring extra attention because of an ill mother. Understanding the life cycle stages clashing here can be essential for the family therapist. Otherwise, the problems are seen as piecemeal and treated accordingly.

REFERENCES

Boscolo, L., Cecchin, G., Hoffman, L., & Penn, P. (1987). *Milan systemic family therapy*. New York, NY: Basic Books.

Boss, P. (2001). *Family stress management: A contextual approach* (2nd ed.). Newbury Park, CA: Sage.

Boszormenyi-Nagy, I., & Spark, G. M. (1973). *Invisible loyalties*. New York, NY: Harper & Row.

Bowen, M. (1978). *Family therapy in clinical practice*. New York, NY: Aronson.

Carter, B., & McGoldrick, M. (Eds.). (2005). *The expanded family life cycle: Individual, family and social perspectives* (3rd ed.). Needham Heights, MA: Allyn & Bacon.

Constantine, L. (1986). *Family paradigms*. New York, NY: Guilford Press.

Duvall, E. M. (1977). *Marriage and family development* (5th ed.). Philadelphia, PA: Lippincott.

Edin, K., & Kefalas, M. (2007). *Promises I can keep: Why poor women put motherhood before marriage*. Berkeley: University of California Press.

Framo, J. L. (1981). The integration of marital therapy with sessions with family of origin. In A. S. Gurman & D. P. Kniskern (Eds.), *Handbook of family therapy* (pp. 133–158). New York, NY: Brunner/Mazel.

Haley, J. (1976). *Problem-solving therapy*. San Francisco, CA: Jossey-Bass.

Hill, R. (1970). *Family development in three generations: A longitudinal study of changing family patterns of planning and achievement*. Cambridge, MA: Schenkman.

Jordan, K. (Ed.). (2003). *Handbook of couple and family assessment*. Hauppauge, NY: Nova Science.

Kantor, D., & Lehr, W. (1975). *Inside the family: Toward a theory of family process*. San Francisco, CA: Jossey-Bass.

Kerr, M. E., & Bowen, M. (1988). *Family evaluation: An approach based on Bowen theory.* New York, NY: Norton.

McGoldrick, M., Giordano, J., & Garcia-Preto, N. (Eds.). (2005). *Ethnicity and family therapy* (3rd ed.). New York, NY: Guilford Press.

Minuchin, S. (1974). *Families and family therapy.* Cambridge, MA: Harvard University Press.

Olson, D. H., Russell, C. S., & Sprenkle, D. H. (1983). Circumplex model of marital and family systems: VI. Theoretical update. *Family Process, 22,* 69–83. doi:10.1111/j.1545-5300.1983.00069.x

Scharff, D. E., & Scharff, J. S. (1987). *Object relations family therapy.* New York, NY: Basic Books.

Schwartz, R. C. (1997). *Internal family systems therapy.* New York, NY: Guilford Press.

von Bertalanffy, L. (1976). *General system theory* (2nd ed.). New York, NY: Braziller.

Watzlawick, P., Beavin, J. H., & Jackson, D. D. (1967). *Pragmatics of human communication.* New York, NY: Norton.

18

FAMILY THERAPY PROCESS

WILLIAM J. DOHERTY AND SUSAN H. McDANIEL

In family therapy, the relationship between family members, not the relationship between the therapist and the patient or family, is primary. In psychoanalysis or psychodynamic psychotherapy, the transference of the patient's introject of a parental figure onto the therapist becomes the grist for interpretation and exploration. In family therapy, it is the *actual* relationships that are the focus of treatment. Behavior therapists may talk with patients about how significant others reward progress or unwittingly reinforce symptoms. In family therapy, those positive and negative reinforcements are available for view in the therapy room directly. Because of this, the intimacy in the room is typically between family members rather than with the therapist.

Part of the challenge for the family therapist is developing what Ivan Boszormenyi-Nagy and Geraldine Spark (1973) termed *multilateral partiality*,

Excerpted from *Family Therapy* (2010), from Chapter 4, "The Therapy Process," pp. 54–60. Copyright 2010 by the American Psychological Association. Used with permission of the authors.

http://dx.doi.org/10.1037/14295-018
Psychotherapy Theories and Techniques: A Reader, G. R. VandenBos, E. Meidenbauer, and J. Frank-McNeil (Editors)
Copyright © 2014 by the American Psychological Association. All rights reserved.

or alliances with all members of the family. This term refers to the need for the family therapist to form strong relationships of trust and fairness with each member of the family, without taking sides and inadvertently forming a coalition with one member of the family against another (a professional version of an intergenerational coalition). This can be difficult when, for example, an adolescent is appealing and a parent appears to be too harsh. However, forming a warm bond with the adolescent while remaining cool with the parent only inflames the problem. Instead, the therapist is charged with finding something in each family member to connect with, recognizing that this kind of neutrality (or, better said, multipartial alliance) is part of the healing aspects of most family therapy. With multiple patients, there are inevitably multiple agendas. In the case of Jorge and Maria, the therapist worked to understand both party's positions—Jorge's worrying and Maria's advocacy for the relationship. By describing both positions respectfully, the therapist joined successfully with both members of the couple without siding with one against the other.

THE ROLE OF THE THERAPIST

The family therapist is in charge of the structure of treatment (Whitaker & Bumberry, 1988). This means that the therapist will organize the timing of the sessions, where and how they will occur, and who should come. He or she may suggest homework assignments to diagnose the problem and test the family's willingness to change.

The family therapist is also in charge of the communication in therapy. With more than one person, and sometimes many people, in the room, the therapist has many relationships to develop and manage. He or she becomes a kind of traffic cop—teaching family members to communicate without blame, listen respectfully to each other, acknowledge they heard what was said, and learn to deal with conflict, difference, and emotional intensity. The therapist wants to hear the individual and family stories, to understand their belief systems, and, like an applied anthropologist, to help the family find the solutions to their pain and their problems from within their culture and value systems.

The therapist may also be something of a teacher, educating or showing patients how their behavior affects each other. A common example of this is when a depressed patient is demanding and difficult when he feels badly so that his spouse distances from him, which only leads the patient to feel more depressed and be more difficult. Uncovering all these cycles, or cycles related to violence or child misbehavior or psychosomatic illness, can be foci of family therapy, helping the family to recognize the effect of each individual's behavior on the other.

THE ROLE OF THE PATIENT AND FAMILY

While the therapist is in charge of the treatment, the family is in charge of the initiative for change (Whitaker & Bumberry, 1988). It is critical that the therapist not become more invested and motivated in change than the family. Otherwise, a pursuer–distancer dynamic occurs with the therapist as pursuer, often resulting in the family backing away from change (Fogarty, 1976). The skill of the therapist is in increasing the patient's and family's motivation for change.

Sandra and Molly came to therapy because of some mild partner violence (Sandra had slapped Molly on the arm once); both said they wanted to stop this destructive way of relating before it got worse. When the therapist tried to schedule an intake session, neither member of the couple could agree on when to come in. Finally, both said that Wednesday at 8 p.m. would work, though the therapist had stated that she saw patients only until 7 p.m. The therapist was tempted to bend the commitment to herself and her own family out of concern for this couple's problem. However, recognizing a potentially unhelpful pattern at the beginning of therapy, she said she would work hard to schedule them, but it had to be sometime during her regular office hours before 7 p.m. Whitaker and Bumberry (1988) called this the "battle for structure" and insisted the therapist must win this battle for treatment to succeed.

The therapist also asked Sandra and Molly each to take notes anytime either of them began to feel angry and bring the notes into therapy, thereby working to increase their motivation for change. Whitaker and Bumberry (1988) called this the "battle for initiative" and insisted that the family must win this battle for treatment to succeed.

BRIEF AND LONG-TERM STRATEGIES AND TECHNIQUES

The techniques and strategies of family therapy operationalize systems thinking and can be used in single-session therapy or long-term work. Goal setting, in the beginning, allows the family and the therapist to stay focused and measure the progress and outcome of therapy. The use of tools such as the genogram, time lines, and sculpting organizes complex family information so that it is useful to the family and the therapist. Techniques such as positive connotation and listing family strengths help to broaden the assessment of the presenting problem. Circular questions, enactment, and externalizing the problem are techniques that put the presenting complaint in context.

Goal Setting

Family therapy is an active therapy. Early in treatment, the therapist works to define the presenting problem, the people involved with the problem, the interpersonal patterns of behavior related to the problem, and the criteria by which each family member would know if the therapy is successful. Goal setting becomes a group activity, with the therapist working to help the family negotiate common achievable goals in their own words. This is not so easy. (If it were, the family would likely not need therapy!) Sometimes, goal setting can take several sessions, because family members do not agree on the definition of the problem or the desired outcome. Also, many times initial goals are framed in unachievable terms.

Sonia, for example, stated that her goal for couples therapy was to have her husband, Reynolds, never express anger with her. Therapy then focused on psychoeducational principles that normalize anger, so an appropriate goal focused instead on *how* Sonia wishes Reynolds to express his anger to her.

Enactment

In many psychotherapies, patients talk about other relationships and problems. In family therapy, these relationships and problems are brought into the room. After setting a goal about dealing with anger, the therapist asked Reynolds to show how he acts when he's angry with Sonia. "Assume that you had a bad day at work. Then think of something that Sonia does that is sometimes irritating. Turn to her and show me what happens when you're angry."

The in-session enactment allows the therapist and the patients to witness the problem firsthand. The patients can then reflect on the experience, and the therapist can coach them on alternative ways of communicating. "Try telling Sonia when you come in the door, 'Honey, I had a stressful day at work. Let me tell you about it.' Monitor your own internal experience to make sure that you don't take out your difficult day on the person you love the most." After the couple tried out this new way of communicating, the therapist advised, "When expressing your feelings about an irritating habit, be sure to start with, 'When you leave your workout clothes on the floor, it makes me angry. I feel like you want me to do all the cleaning up in the house, even though we both have outside jobs.'"

Circular Questions

Family therapists use interview techniques that reveal the nature of relationships in the family (Selvini Palazzoli, Boscolo, Cecchin, & Prata, 1980). One of those techniques, called circular questions, sometimes brings to light long-standing misunderstandings.

Therapist: Sonia, when Reynolds leaves his clothes on the floor, what is he trying to communicate to you?

Sonia: He wants me to become a better housewife. He's hoping I'll do his chores as part of that. But I'm not!

Reynolds: [looking shocked] This is not a test of your skills! I've always been sloppy in the bedroom. I need to change that now that I have a roommate.

Externalizing the Problem

A family therapy technique introduced by Michael White (White & Epston, 1990) moves the problem outside of one individual or one relationship. Externalizing the problem reduces blaming behavior that can prevent the problem from being resolved.

Bill and Stella came for therapy because Stella was having recurrent spells of blanking out. At first her physician thought she might have epilepsy, but long-term monitoring in the hospital revealed that these spells were psychogenic in origin. The neurologist thought their timing was related to marital stress and referred the couple for therapy. In the second session, after setting goals that included reducing the blanking out spells and improving their marriage, the therapist asked Stella and Bill to consider these spells as something external to both of them.

"What do the spells look like?" the therapist asked. "What color are they? Do they have a name? Are they like an animal, a plant, a person?"

Stella and Bill had surprisingly little disagreement about the nature of the spells. Stella said they were red, "hot like a fire." Bill agreed, adding they were "like a red porcupine, all sharp and bristly." These descriptions gave the therapist valuable information about the possible relationship of these spells to anger in the relationship. When the therapist asked about a name for this porcupine, Stella said, "Porky."

To some extent this exercise served to desensitize both members of the couple to talking about the spells, which had theretofore been mysterious and somewhat scary. The therapist then set about to find out when Porky was likely to come on the scene and to slowly help the couple learn to identify their anger and express it appropriately. Two sessions after externalizing this symptom, Stella revealed that Bill was sometimes emotionally abusive to her. Her Catholic faith, she felt, did not permit her to express anger back. She now noticed that Porky tended to appear in reaction to Bill's emotional tirades. Over time, Bill was placed on antidepressants as an aid to learning self-regulation skills. As his verbal abuse eased, Stella's blanking out spells stopped altogether. Both Stella and Bill continued to work on communication and anger management.

Family Sculpting

Another technique that serves as both assessment and intervention is that of family sculpting (Satir, 1988). Most commonly, the therapist asks one family member to place other family members in a physical pose, as if in a sculpture, to represent the way that sculptor views the family functioning. The therapist may ask for three sculpts: one from an important time in the past, one in the present, and one that shows how the family member would like to see the family functioning in the future. This exercise is often more revealing than verbal description. Each family member may get a chance, so that differing perspectives (e.g., from a married couple) may be illuminated and discussed.

For example, when asked to sculpt how the couple's relationship is at present, Stella set herself in one corner working and Bill in another. Bill's sculpt was similar, except he was playing racquetball while Stella was at home reading. When asked how she wanted it to be, Stella sat herself and Bill side by side, very still, each staring lovingly at their interlocking hands. For his part, Bill walked the couple around a garden pointing out interesting plants and flowers. This exercise revealed the couple's differing temperaments and goals for the relationship much more vividly than had their earlier verbal descriptions.

REFERENCES

Boszormenyi-Nagy, I., & Spark, G. M. (1973). *Invisible loyalties*. New York, NY: Harper & Row.

Fogarty, T. (1976). Marital crisis. In P. Guerin (Ed.), *Family therapy: Theory and practice* (pp. 325–334). New York, NY: Gardner Press.

Satir, V. (1988). *The new peoplemaking*. Palo Alto, CA: Science and Behavior Books.

Selvini Palazzoli, M., Boscolo, L., Cecchin, G., & Prata, G. (1980). Hypothesizing—circularity—neutrality: Three guidelines for the conductor of the session. *Family Process, 19,* 7–19.

Whitaker, C., & Bumberry, W. (1988). *Dancing with the family: A symbolic–experiential approach*. New York, NY: Brunner/Mazel.

White, M., & Epston, D. (1990). *Narrative means to therapeutic ends*. New York, NY: Norton.

APPENDIX 18.1: FAMILY THERAPY TECHNIQUES

Technique	Video title	Video identifying number	Time at which technique occurs
Collaboration	Family Therapy With a Young Couple Having Communication Problems (Session 3 of 6)	777700321-001	29:21–32:29
Drawing a genogram	Family Therapy With a Young Couple Having Communication Problems (Session 2 of 6)	777700319-001	00:48–1:31
Enactment	Family Therapy With a Young Couple Having Communication Problems (Session 4 of 6)	777700323-001	5:00–14:58
Externalizing the problem	Family Therapy With a Young Couple Having Communication Problems (Session 1 of 6)	777700317-001	26:26–28:31
Goal setting	Family Therapy With a Young Couple Having Communication Problems (Session 1 of 6)	777700317-001	34:24–38:39
Miracle question	Couple Power Therapy for Coping With Stress	777700132-001	11:47–12:57
Positive connotation	Family Therapy With a Young Couple Having Communication Problems (Session 1 of 6)	777700317-001	38:40–40:06
Psychoeducation	Family Therapy With a Young Couple Having Communication Problems (Session 4 of 6)	777700323-001	17:45–18:33

19

FEMINIST THERAPY

LAURA S. BROWN

Feminist therapy has as its superordinate goal the empowerment of clients and the creation of feminist consciousness. Much of what is written in this field has to do with developing methodologies for achieving that goal in a diverse set of circumstances. The therapy relationship is construed as a setting in which, because of the norms and boundaries established by the therapist and her or his adherence to certain principles, people can experience the social environment of an egalitarian relationship. Consequently, development of egalitarian and empowering strategies that are tailored to the particular individual seeking assistance is central to feminist therapy practice. Such empowerment is seen as having the important function of subverting patriarchal influences in the lives and psyches of all of those involved in the therapy process, including the therapist. Because both parties, therapist and

Excerpted from *Feminist Therapy* (2010), from Chapter 3, "Theory," pp. 29–37. Copyright 2010 by the American Psychological Association. Used with permission of the author.

http://dx.doi.org/10.1037/14295-019

Psychotherapy Theories and Techniques: A Reader, G. R. VandenBos, E. Meidenbauer, and J. Frank-McNeil (Editors)

Copyright © 2014 by the American Psychological Association. All rights reserved.

client alike, are immersed in patriarchal cultures, the process of uncovering disempowerment and developing strategies toward empowerment is ongoing, with each feminist therapist discovering the deep and subtle ways in which patriarchal assumptions of hierarchy and privilege inform her or his work and the experience of the people who come into the office.

A feminist therapist continuously asks, "What are the power dynamics in this situation? Where am I taking patriarchal assumptions for granted as true?" The answer to these questions might be something as deceptively simple as including a commentary about gender and social class in an assessment report about learning disabilities to unpack the effects of those variables on the problems being evaluated. Or it might be something as complex and subtle as unpacking the minutiae of power dynamics in the arrangement of office furniture to enhance feelings of equality among those participating in therapy or questioning whether the word *client* is itself inherently disempowering (Brown, 2006).

Feminist therapy as a model does not have specific treatment goals as do many other psychotherapies. Instead, the outcomes of treatment, which represent empowerment for the individual client, are determined collaboratively and assessed via client satisfaction and self-report. Feminist therapists ask clients about their goals and propose ways of meeting those goals; therapist and client discuss, negotiate, and renegotiate these agreements, formally and informally, throughout the course of psychotherapy. When clients do not know their goals, the goal of therapy becomes uncovering the client's wishes; feminist therapists do not use the absence of client knowledge of needs and desires as a cue to impose their own sense of what the goals of therapy ought to be.

This client-focused model of determining the defining characteristics of good outcomes and the effectiveness of therapy places feminist therapy in close relationship with other paradigms such as person-centered, narrative, and multicultural, which place power to define outcome in clients' hands as one piece of a larger strategy of client empowerment within the therapy relationship itself. This stance challenges the social construction of outcome as something measured by therapists or predetermined by the treatment approach. It makes clients the authorities. Rather than measuring outcome with an instrument whose scales are determined by an expert's decision as to what is an important change in therapy, feminist therapists ask their clients to say what has changed for them and how those changes matter to them, a qualitative, phenomenological, and client driven, rather than quantitative and expert driven, methodology for assessing outcome.

Because feminist therapy conceptualizes human experience as taking place in four realms of power—somatic, intrapersonal/intrapsychic, intra-personal/social–contextual, and spiritual/existential, all in constant exchange and interaction (see Table 19.1)—disempowerment and empowerment are

TABLE 19.1
The Biopsychosocial/Spiritual–Existential Axes of Personal Power

Somatic Power	Intrapersonal/Intrapsychic Power
In contact with body; body is experienced as a safe place, accepted as it is rather than forced to be larger or smaller than it would be if adequately nourished. If its size or shape creates a lack of safety for a person, change of size or shape happens in the service of safety; connection with bodily desires for food, sexual pleasure, and rest; no intentional harm to one's own body or that of others with no routine violation of value. Does not require the ability to see, hear, walk, or talk, nor is a powerful body necessarily free of pain or illness, nor strong or physically fit. Compassion regarding body.	Knows what one thinks, thinks critically, can change one's mind; flexible, not suggestible. Trusts intuition, able to find external data; knows feelings as they are felt, feelings a useful source of information about here and now. Absence of numbness, feelings about current, not past or possible futures. Ability to experience powerful emotions, to contain affect, able to self-soothe in ways that are not harmful to self or others physically, psychosocially, or spiritually.

Interpersonal/Social–Contextual Power	Spiritual/Existential Power
More interpersonally effective than not, have desired impacts on others more of the time than not; no illusions of control; forgive self and others, self-protective; differentiated, yet flexible. Capable of forming relationships that work more of the time than not with other individuals, groups, and larger systems; able to create and sustain intimacy, to be close without loss of self or engulfment of other, and to be differentiated without being distant or detached; able to decide to end relationships when those become dangerous, toxic, or excessively problematic; able to remain and work out conflict when that is a possibility; enter roles in life—parent, partner, worker—most often from a place of choice, intention, and desire, not accidentally, although serendipity and the opportunity to encounter the new are welcomed.	Have systems of meaning making that assist with responding to the existential challenges of life and that have the potential to give sense of comfort and well-being; sense of own heritage and culture integrated into identity in ways that allow for better understanding of self; are aware of the social context and can engage with it rather than being controlled by it or unaware of its impact; have a raison d'etre and can integrate that into important aspects of daily life; access to capacities for creativity and fantasy, yet have sense of reality.

seen as potentially occurring in any and all of these axes. Feminist therapy consequently defines power, not simply in the usual sense of control of other humans and/or resources, but in a manner identifying the locations, behavioral and intrapsychic, where patriarchal cultures lead people to experience powerlessness and power. Bias, stereotype, and oppression all constitute social forces that create disempowerment; they can be enacted in the large context of society or culture, the smaller context of family and community, and, intra-psychically, internalized and felt as a part of self. Disempowerment and the consequences of powerlessness are construed as central sources of emotional distress and behavioral dysfunction. Feminist therapy asks, in general and in specific, what might constitute a move toward power for a given person in the domains where powerlessness has been experienced. The feminist therapist is tasked with the cocreation, with her or his client, of strategies that will invite and support empowerment for each person.

POWER AND ITS MANY FACES

Power in the Somatic/Biological Realm

Power can be categorized into the four axes of the biopsychosocial/spiritual-existential model. Thus, in the biological realm, power means being in contact with one's body. Power in the bodily realm means that the body is experienced as a safe place and accepted as it is rather than forced to be larger or smaller than it would be if adequately nourished. If its size or shape creates a lack of safety for a person, change of size or shape happens in the service of safety, which is a form of power, or other paths to safety that do not require modification of the body are considered. Power in the body means connection with bodily desires for food, comfort, sexual pleasure, and rest. It also entails access to means of meeting those needs that do not lead to intentional harm to one's own body or that of others and that do not routinely violate a person's values. Note that power in the body does not require the ability to see, hear, walk, or talk; nor is a powerful body necessarily free of pain or illness, nor strong or physically fit. Rather, empowerment at the biological level has to do with the psychosocial/spiritual relationship of self to embodiment and with the creation of a stance of compassion, acceptance, and advocacy, as needed, for one's embodied experiences.

Power in the Intrapersonal/Intrapsychic Realm

In the psychosocial realm, power means that one knows what one thinks and has the ability to critically examine one's own thoughts and those of others. A person can change her or his mind when new data appear that would warrant such a change; in other words, one is flexible without being suggestible. Power entails the capacity to trust in the information available from one's own intuition and inner knowing, and the ability to find sources of information that will expand the range of one's world and capacities. Powerful people know what they feel as they are feeling it and can use their feelings as a useful source of information about what is happening in the here and now. Power in the realm of affect means an absence of numbness, with current feelings reflecting current, not past or possible future, experiences. Psychosocial power includes the ability to experience powerful and intense emotions, to contain affect as needed to function effectively in one's psychosocial world, and to channel emotions into effective interpersonal strategies. Power on this axis includes, as well, the capacity to self-soothe in ways that are not harmful to self or others physically, psychosocially, or spiritually.

Interpersonal/Social–Contextual Power

Powerful people are more interpersonally effective than not, able to have their desired impacts on others more of the time than not. They realize that they do not control others or the physical world and are able to accept the limits of power and control with grace. Powerful people forgive themselves their humanity and are able to forgive the humanity of others, but they do not forget to protect themselves from people who are unsafe emotionally or physically to them. Powerful people are well defined and differentiated, yet flexible when this will increase the likelihood of a desired outcome. Powerful people have access to their capacities for creativity and fantasy as sources of delight and have a sense of reality that assists them to function in their chosen pursuits.

In the interpersonal realm of psychosocial power, powerful people are capable of forming relationships that work more of the time than not with other individuals, groups, and larger systems. Powerful people can create and sustain intimacy, can be close without loss of self or engulfment of other, and are able to be differentiated without being distant or detached. They are able to decide to end relationships when those become dangerous, toxic, or excessively problematic for them, and they are also able to remain and work out conflict with others when that is a possibility. They enter roles in life— parent, partner, worker—most often from a place of choice, intention, and desire, not accidentally, although they welcome serendipity and the opportunity to encounter the new.

Power in the Spiritual Realm

In the realm of spiritual and existential experience, powerful people have systems of meaning making that assist them in responding to the existential challenges of life and that have the potential to give them a sense of comfort and well-being. They have a sense of their heritage and culture and can integrate it into their identity in ways that allow them to better understand themselves. They are aware of the social context and can engage with it rather than being controlled by it or unaware of its impact. Powerful people have a raison d'être and are able to integrate that into important aspects of their daily lives.

PATRIARCHY AND DISEMPOWERMENT: CAUSES OF DISTRESS

Feminist therapy asserts that patriarchal systems surrounding most human life intentionally and unintentionally disempower almost all people on one or more of these variables, such that this paradigm of the powerful person is entirely aspirational. At the same time, the theory behind feminist therapy argues that much powerlessness can be transformed, even within the material constraints of patriarchal realities, and that one disempowerment strategy of patriarchies has been the creation of a trance of powerlessness that is both cultural and personal, in which various messages are conveyed that most people cannot empower themselves. The wide-scale disempowering messages conveyed by patriarchies about the inevitability of hierarchies, the impossibility of effecting real social change, and the immutability of gendered and other socially constructed roles and relationships all contribute to this societal trance. Feminist therapy subverts and interrupts the trance of powerlessness by inviting its participants to notice where and how greater power is actually available to them. Feminist analysis exposes how power, both intrapersonal and interpersonal, is not truly constrained by sex, phenotype, social class, body, or any of the usual rationales given by the larger context as to why someone cannot do or be a particular thing. By instituting and sustaining challenges to cultural messages suggesting that to give up and go along is the only available option, feminist therapy and its practitioners undermine what is dangerous in patriarchy and create hope, which is a necessary ingredient of the change process.

Within this broad aspirational construct of what constitutes inter- and intrapersonal power, feminist therapists invite clients to discover strategies for becoming more powerful, using the tools of psychotherapy and the relationship of therapist and client as the womb in which such power can grow. It is more usual than not for most people entering therapy to have their power be invisible and unavailable to them and the notion that they might have power at all frankly risible. When the feminist therapist first asks in a therapy session, "What is the powerful thing you could do now?" many people's response is a variation on, "There is no powerful thing." Offering the model of power described previously to clients and framing power as being a continuous variable, rather than a matter of having or not having, breaks the trance of powerlessness, as people begin to understand that they have already been powerful innumerable times and in a wide range of ways.

Gary, a working-class Euro American man in his early thirties, had been diagnosed at a young age with Asperger syndrome (AS), placed in special education classes, and teased and bullied by peers because of his socially odd behaviors. His parents, who had each attended community college for training in the skilled trades, were compliant with the medical and psychological authorities who told them that their son would never be capable of normal relationships and thus responded to his complaints about mistreatment by peers by implying that it was all due to his AS. When he sought psychotherapy for the persistent posttraumatic responses to the peer violence of his childhood, he expressed surprise when Bill, his feminist therapist, asked him about what powerful thing he could do. He responded that he was and always had been powerless. But Gary came to his third session with a printout of several online thesaurus entries about the word *power*, telling Bill, "I think that if I study these, I will find a powerful thing to do." The therapist reflected to Gary that he had just done a powerful thing—he had used his considerable skills and talents as an online researcher to begin to unpack and subvert what he had been told about power.

Frequently, prior to the feminist therapist offering this frame for power, when that power has been apprehended by the individual, it has more often felt negative and dangerous than self-affirming. For people who have been abused by power, power may have become confused with abusiveness, including abusiveness toward self. Many people who enter therapy perceive their strategies for responding to disempowerment—strategies in which creativity, talent, and desperation have combined to now-problematic outcomes—as what is wrong with them, evidence of their powerlessness and failure. "I failed to protect myself," says the woman who was horrifically abused by her parents from her earliest memory, not seeing her dissociation as the way in which she protected herself when no other models of self-protection were available. "I'm not smart enough for graduate school," says the man who dropped out of high school at age 16 to help support his struggling family and who acquired his subsequent education in settings that failed to offer him the study skills available to the children of the middle class with whom he must now compete in his master's program. Often, people have experienced extreme violations of body, mind, thought, feeling, spirit, culture, or some combination of all of these, and have protected themselves by developing strategies of passivity; dissociation from body, affect, or memory; or self-inflicted violence (Brown & Bryan, 2007; Rivera, 2002). For the feminist therapist, all of these strategies and struggles to maintain the capacity to be alive are evidence of a person's previous struggles to achieve power in the face of patriarchy. The pain a person feels is seen, not as psychopathology, but as evidence of an already present and active capacity in the struggling person to move toward the model of powerful individual. The first step of empowerment involves reframing pain as the sign of the desire to become that powerful person.

REFERENCES

Brown, L. S. (2006). Still subversive after all these years: The relevance of feminist therapy in the age of evidence-based practice. *Psychology of Women Quarterly, 30,* 15–24. doi:10.1111/j.1471-6402.2006.00258.x

Brown, L. S. (2006, May). *Feminist therapy with difficult and challenging clients.* Invited workshop presented for the Chinese Guidance and Counseling Association, Taipei, Taiwan.

Brown, L. S. (2006, August). *Swimming as a feminist.* Invited presentation at the meeting of the American Psychological Association, New Orleans, LA.

Brown, L. S. (2010). *Feminist therapy.* Washington, DC: American Psychological Association.

Brown, L. S., & Bryan, T. C. (2007). Feminist therapy with people who self-inflict violence. *Journal of Clinical Psychology, 63,* 1121–1133. doi:10.1002/jclp.20419

Rivera, M. (2002). The Chrysalis Program: A feminist treatment community for individuals diagnosed as personality disordered. In M. Ballou & L. S. Brown (Eds.), *Rethinking mental health and disorder: Feminist perspectives* (pp. 231–261). New York, NY: Guilford Press.

20

FEMINIST THERAPY PROCESS

LAURA S. BROWN

Feminist therapy's vision of humans as biopsychosocial/spiritual/ existential entities extends into the development of feminist strategies for transformation via psychotherapy. Feminist therapists will engage with a very wide and diverse range of change strategies with clients. So long as the superordinate goals of empowerment, egalitarianism, and analysis of power, gender, and social location can be integrated, feminist therapy offers a protean integrative model of practice that has allowed it to be utilized with very different individuals in settings ranging from refugee camps on the Thailand–Burma border (Norsworthy, 2007) to a prison in Washington State (Cole, Sarlund-Heinrich, & Brown, 2007) to mainstream dominant culture men receiving psychotherapy in a private practice office (Brooks, 1998).

Excerpted from *Feminist Therapy* (2010), from Chapter 4, "The Therapy Process," pp. 78–81. Copyright 2010 by the American Psychological Association. Used with permission of the author.

http://dx.doi.org/10.1037/14295-020
Psychotherapy Theories and Techniques: A Reader, G. R. VandenBos, E. Meidenbauer, and J. Frank-McNeil (Editors)
Copyright © 2014 by the American Psychological Association. All rights reserved.

Feminist therapy, and the induction into the egalitarian model, begins with the process of consent, which I have previously referred to as "empowered consent" (Brown, 1994). My clients are offered a five-page, single-spaced document to take home and review in which the basic frameworks of feminist practice are outlined, with an emphasis on the relational nature of therapy, the rights of clients, and the responsibilities of the therapist (a copy of this document is available at http://www.drlaurabrown.com). This document, and those written by other feminist therapists for their clients, serves as an initial invitation for discussions about the nature of feminist therapy practice. The client's ownership of the therapy and her or his right to determine its goals and directions provide a powerful catalyst and jumping-off point for the development of an egalitarian relationship at all steps of therapy.

Although in practice no aspect of psychotherapy is purely somatic, interpersonal, contextual, or spiritual, each exchange will have a particular focus and core on one of these axes. The following section discusses strategies for feminist empowerment models on the somatic axis of power.

SOMATIC INTERVENTIONS

Feminist therapy values somatic interventions as one integrated component of treatment. A feminist therapist will consider ways in which a client is disempowered on the biological axis and notice how apparent disempowerment may actually represent resistance strategies employed in the service of survival or safety. Feminist therapists practice empowerment at this juncture by framing each of these ways of being as what was available to the person as a way of being in the body that best allowed her or him to function and that was congruent with her or his identity. This is a first step toward inviting that person to consider, then explore, ways of being differently and in a more empowered manner in her or his body.

Alicia, a Euro American heterosexual woman in her mid-30s, had been bullied by her peers while a child because she walked with a limp, the aftereffects of a childhood accident in which she fell off a playground structure. Her family had no health insurance coverage and was unable to pay for physical therapy after her bones knitted. Alicia had done two things with these experiences. First, the accident had taken on enormous negative salience, representing "the day my life changed for the worse forever." Second, she had developed shame about how her body moved. The ultimate result of these two important experiences was that she had become physically very immobile. She came into therapy to deal with depressed mood and a loss of motivation for working on her master's thesis. In the course of exploring how her class background and her being the first in her family to go to college were factors in her fears of inadequacy as a professional and her feelings of disloyalty to her family, her therapist suggested the notion of using exercise as a means of improving mood.

Both therapist and client were surprised at the vehemence of Alicia's response. "I don't do that, I don't have a body," she told Katarina, the therapist. Katarina invited Alicia to consider how not having a body was a part of her identity. Together they explored the importance to Alicia of this identity marker, which emerged as having two functions that were temporarily empowering to her. Dissociation from her body reduced intrusive memories of the fall and distanced Alicia from her grief over the loss of the active body she had been in before that day. It also allowed her to be as invisible to others as possible, so that her limp would be minimally visible. Each of these was an important safety strategy for Alicia. She told Katarina that for the present she would rather take medication for her mood, as she was not yet ready to stop using these strategies, "and I'm not sure if I ever will be."

Katarina's response was to validate Alicia as the person in charge of her therapy process; they continued to explore other strategies for Alicia to accomplish her goals. Six months later Alicia told Katarina that she was ready to approach the topic of her accident, now seeing it linked to her difficulties with her thesis. "Being frozen is something I know how to do; being frozen was the best I could do. I didn't want my family to see me as a stuck-up, overeducated person, or my professors to see me as the working-class kid that I am, and I didn't want to see me as disabled, or the other kids to see my limp. So I freeze. Maybe it's time to be visible and thaw. Or not. But let's talk about it."

Feminist therapists will integrate a variety of strategies aimed at increasing power on the biological/somatic axis into their work with clients. They may invite clients to consider learning about strengthening or increasing flexibility of body; to develop greater stamina; to discover how to feed themselves in a loving way; to consider tai chi or yoga; to use bodywork treatments such as massage, Feldenkrais, or Hellerwork; and to explore the usefulness of formal medications. No one of these approaches to engaging with the body will be privileged by a feminist therapist; whichever pathway toward somatic empowerment is a fit for the client is the one that the client and therapist will explore.

Feminist psychopharmacology (Jensvold, Halbreich, & Hamilton, 1996) has studied how sex differences in hormones and responses to drugs, though often little known by those prescribing them, need to be taken into account if prescribing is to happen in a nonoppressive and empowering manner. Many modern psychotropic medications, although effective somatic interventions for some people, also carry risks of side effects that dull sexuality, increase risk of weight gain and diabetes, and have unknown consequences for children who are in utero when pregnant women use them. Feminist psychopharmacology supports clients in exercising judgment and autonomy regarding these and other somatic interventions, rather than defaulting to the prescription of a pill.

Kristina was severely depressed after the birth of her first child. She was nursing and unwilling to take medication that might pass through breast milk to her son. She was generally uncomfortable with Western medicine and wanted to do without pills if possible for everything in her life. She was also so depressed that she could barely relate to her baby and was frightened that he would be emotionally harmed by her tears and lethargy. Paralyzed with indecision by her depression and terrified of making the wrong choice, she told Jeneen, her therapist, that she was tempted to just take a pill and be done with it. "But then I'll hate myself." Jeneen asked Kris if she would like her to be "more pushy" about what to do, and when Kris assented, Jeneen suggested a stepwise process for making a decision about whether and how to take medication. Kris did a consultation with a physician expert in nutritional foundations for mood, with the understanding that this would work more slowly than medication. If, after a period of time, she was not feeling able to parent well, the next step would be to try an antidepressant medication that her physician had carefully researched as to its safety for nursing mothers and their babies. Kris and Jeneen also worked out a "panic button" strategy by which either one could raise the alarm about the safety of parent and child and speed up the process. With the pressure to make a decision off, Kris improved slightly with the nutritional intervention, sufficiently for her to become more active again in the decision-making process. She eventually decided to take the offered antidepressant from a position of more power than she had initially been able to muster.

PSYCHOSOCIAL INTERVENTIONS

Because it is a technically integrative approach to psychotherapy, feminist therapy does not prescribe particular psychosocial interventions. The emphasis, as noted throughout this volume, is on tailoring interventions to meet clients at their strengths, skills, and capacities, all with the goal of increasing the client's movement toward personal power on the four axes and evoking feminist consciousness in the process. In a given day, across sessions, a feminist therapist may utilize tools and strategies from psychodynamic psychotherapies, cognitive therapies, mindfulness-based paradigms, humanistic psychotherapies, expressive and movement therapies, and others. Feminist therapists will offer options to clients when these are available within their own repertoire of skills.

REFERENCES

Brooks, G. (1998). *A new psychotherapy for traditional men*. San Francisco, CA: Jossey-Bass.

Brown, L. S. (1994). *Subversive dialogues: Theory in feminist therapy*. New York, NY: Basic Books.

Cole, K. L., Sarlund-Heinrich, P., & Brown, L. S. (2007). Developing and assessing effectiveness of a time-limited therapy group for incarcerated women survivors of childhood sexual abuse. *Journal of Trauma and Dissociation, 8*, 97–121. doi:10.1300/J229v08n02_07

Jensvold, M. F., Halbreich, U., & Hamilton, J. A. (Eds.). (1996). *Psychopharmacology and women: Sex, gender, and hormones*. Arlington, VA: American Psychiatric Association.

Norsworthy, K. (2007, August). Multicultural feminist collaboration and healing from gender-based violence in Burma. In E. N. Williams (Chair), *International perspectives on feminist multicultural psychotherapy—Content and connection*. Symposium presented at the meeting of the American Psychological Association, San Francisco, CA.

APPENDIX 20.1: FEMINIST THERAPY TECHNIQUES

Technique	Video title	Video identifying number	Time at which technique occurs
Agenda setting (collaborative)	Feminist Therapy for Treating Anger in a Young Adult Male (Session 3 of 6)	777700289-001	2:16–3:40
Challenge to cultural messages of power	Feminist Therapy for Treating Anger in a Young Adult Male (Session 3 of 6)	777700289-001	32:29–34:01
Promoting awareness of privilege	Feminist Therapy for Treating Anger in a Young Adult Male (Session 3 of 6)	777700289-001	27:58–32:05
Somatic interventions (meditation)	Feminist Therapy for Treating Anger in a Young Adult Male (Session 3 of 6)	777700289-001	20:54–26:21
Use of nonjudgmental language	Feminist Therapy for Treating Anger in a Young Adult Male (Session 3 of 6)	777700289-001	34:01–35:44
Validation of client rights	Feminist Therapy for Treating Anger in a Young Adult Male (Session 3 of 6)	777700289-001	42:49–43:30

21

GESTALT THERAPY

DEREK TRUSCOTT

Frederick Perls (1893–1970)—known to all as "Fritz"—was the charismatic and controversial founder of gestalt therapy. Gestalt therapy—like person-centered therapy—flourished during the North American human potential movement of the 1960s and will probably always be associated with that historical period and the flamboyant Fritz. It endures as a therapeutic system, however, because of its unique incorporation of the "whole person" into therapy.

Fritz was born and raised in Berlin. After serving as a medical corpsman in World War I, he earned his doctor of medicine degree, specializing in psychiatry. He then moved to Vienna to undertake training in psychoanalysis, and he studied there with Karen Horney and Wilhelm Reich. Reich

Excerpted from *Becoming an Effective Psychotherapist: Adopting a Theory of Psychotherapy That's Right for You and Your Client* (2010), from Chapter 6, "Gestalt," pp. 83–90. Copyright 2010 by the American Psychological Association. Used with permission of the author.

http://dx.doi.org/10.1037/14295-021

Psychotherapy Theories and Techniques: A Reader, G. R. VandenBos, E. Meidenbauer, and J. Frank-McNeil (Editors)
Copyright © 2014 by the American Psychological Association. All rights reserved.

(1897–1957) was a student of Freud who was influential in introducing such central ideas to what would become gestalt therapy as *organismic self-regulation* and *character armor*, although he went on to have a controversial career. Fritz later worked with Kurt Goldstein, a principal figure of the holistic school of psychology who is best known for coining the term *self-actualization* (Goldstein, 1939).

While working with Goldstein, Fritz met and later married Laura Perls (née Lore Posner; 1905–1990). Laura studied psychology at Frankfurt University and received a doctorate in science. Among her teachers were psychologists Kurt Goldstein and Max Wertheimer (one of the founders of Gestalt psychology) and existential philosophers Paul Tillich and Martin Buber. Fritz and Laura later fled Western Europe, just ahead of the Nazis, to South Africa, where they established a psychoanalytic institute.

Fritz and Laura cowrote *Ego, Hunger and Aggression: A Revision of Freud's Theory and Method* (Perls, 1947)—although Laura was not given authorship credit—during this period of upheaval, and the book presaged many gestalt therapy concepts. In it they reevaluated the psychoanalytic conceptualization of aggression and suggested that Sigmund Freud had underestimated the importance of basic bodily functions like eating and digestion. They also discussed holistic and existential perspectives and described therapeutic exercises designed to promote physical awareness rather than cognitive insight.

In response to the rise of apartheid in South Africa, Fritz and Laura immigrated to the United States and established the New York Institute for Gestalt Therapy in 1952. Several years of collaboration with members of this group resulted in a comprehensive formulation of the theory and practice for their approach. Paul Goodman (1911–1972) is generally credited with writing *Gestalt Therapy: Excitement and Growth in the Human Personality* (Perls, Hefferline, & Goodman, 1951), the seminal book on the theory and practice of gestalt therapy. Best known for his 1960 book *Growing Up Absurd: Problems of Youth in Organized Society*, Goodman was the prototypical starving artist, discouraged and marginalized, rarely making ends meet to support his wife and two children. During a period in his life when he was particularly distraught, he met Fritz and Laura and became a founding member of the New York Institute.

Half of *Gestalt Therapy* consisted of reports of the results of exercises in awareness that Ralph Hefferline (1910–1974) administered with his students at the institute. The other half was a statement of their new approach. Although a rather dense read and not initially well received, *Gestalt Therapy* remains a cornerstone of the gestalt approach.

Fritz spent the rest of his life training, giving workshops, and establishing gestalt training centers. After establishing the New York Institute, he established the Cleveland Institute of Gestalt Therapy in 1954; then the Esalen Institute in Big Sur, California, in 1962; and, finally, one on Vancouver Island, British Columbia, Canada, shortly before his death in 1970. Most of his writings from the latter part of his life were transcribed from his workshops. Laura remained in New York, where she continued to lead long-term training groups for gestalt therapists until the mid-1980s.

Gestalt therapy drew influences from a number of sources. First is psychoanalysis, from which the rationalist concern with the inner life was drawn and adapted. As it is for the psychodynamic therapist, for the gestalt therapist the fundamental material with which to work is subjective phenomena—what is going on inside the client. Rejected were the construct-laden theory that Freud and his followers developed and their reductionistic worldview. Gestalt therapy adopted instead the humanistic emphasis on holism and growth.

Existentialism also informs gestalt therapy. The existentialist view that Western societies have exalted intellectual reason over subjective experience is turned into the imperative used by Fritz to "lose your mind and come to your senses" (Perls, 1969, p. 69). Another influence from existentialism is the gestalt therapist's encouragement of individuals to make choices about how they will live on the basis of their own experience, rather than living according to established habits or unquestioningly accepting the norms of society. They also turned away from Freud's rationalist search for the reason *why* a person behaves a certain way and toward the existential *how* a person lives. Gestalt therapy is concerned with what *is*—the present, subjective experience. To gestalt therapists, "why" the client is the way he or she is is of no consequence to helping choose healthy behavior. What "caused" clients to become the way they are is assumed to be irrelevant.

Finally, Gestalt psychology gave to gestalt therapy more than its name. Although gestalt therapy is not directly an application or extension of Gestalt psychology, the latter's focus on interaction and process and many of its important experimental observations and conclusions inform gestalt therapy. In particular, gestalt therapy incorporates the Gestalt psychology concept of *homeostasis*. Needs are understood as disturbing of an individual's homeostasis. A healthy person, when aware of a need, acts to satisfy the need and thus returns to balance. Distress arises when a person is unable to act to regain homeostasis. For example, where displays of grieving are frowned on, emotions might be channeled into a psychosomatic illness. In this way, awareness is directed away from the grief and transferred onto concern about the illness—a concern the society will allow the person to take action to deal with.

Gestalt therapy also draws from Gestalt psychology language to describe this process of needs arising as *figure/ground* (gestalt) formation. The figure is whatever is the focus of attention for an individual within the entire *field*. The field encompasses other people, the environment, and the individual as a whole (i.e., mind, body, and emotions). The ground is everything else in the field except the figure. Whatever need is most disturbing of an individual's homeostasis becomes figural for that person. With the need is satisfied, it merges back into the ground to make way for the next figure to emerge and so on.

GESTALT RATIONALE

A human being is a unified whole that cannot be reduced to a simple summation of physical, biological, psychological, or conceptual properties. We are different from the mere sum of our parts. We all have a heart, kidneys, lungs, and a brain and also emotions, sexuality, memories, hopes, and dreams. Gestalt therapy strives to enlist our innate homeostatic tendency toward becoming a whole that is as healthy as we are able to be. Distress is understood as withdrawal from awareness of our experience of body, self, and environment. This withdrawal arises out of the lessons we learned in childhood when we were dependent on others for our survival. We learned to deny certain aspects of our experience because they were literally life threatening. Often, clients who seek help through psychotherapy are in a state in which thoughts and feelings associated with distinct memories and fantasies about the past linger in the background of their experience. This state is associated with an inauthentic existence that results in preoccupations (e.g., worrying), compulsive behavior, wariness, and self-defeating behavior.

Because contact and withdrawal change from moment to moment as a need is met or an interest is pursued and other needs and interests are allowed to arise, healthy functioning results from contact with our experience in the present. Answers to questions of how and why development may have been arrested in a client's childhood are not germane to current health. Instead, growth takes place as we let go of distractions that prevent personal growth from taking place. When these distractions are gone, a focused experience remains. With this uncluttered awareness, concentration is deepened, leading us into wholehearted functioning. In a world gone mad with complexity, the simplicity of immediate experience allows us to shed debilitating habits of mind that distract us from contact with our true selves. Life happens in the present—not in the past or the future—and when we are dwelling on the past or fantasizing about the future, we are not truly living. Our past informs our present; it does not determine it. Our future can inspire us; it need not dominate us. Through contact with our present experience, we are able to take responsibility for our actions and find the excitement, energy, and courage to live life fully and with intention.

GESTALT GOALS

In gestalt therapy, the singular goal is *awareness:* awareness of the contact between our physical bodies, our environment, and our selves. Ideally, this awareness progresses to deeper levels as therapy proceeds and becomes a state that clients can experience more often in their life. This deepened awareness allows greater capacity for self-regulation and more opportunity for self-determination. Awareness allows clients to better accept responsibility for their actions and reactions and to freely choose how to live their lives. Awareness also facilitates personal growth. Rather than attempting to help clients solve their problems, the gestalt therapist strives to show clients that awareness is a means for them to find their own solutions. Symptoms that prompt someone to seek therapy are understood as processes resulting from personal growth that has been thwarted. With awareness of how unacknowledged feelings are active in our experience, growth is released and symptoms resolve.

GESTALT CHANGE PROCESSES

From a gestalt perspective, change is paradoxical. This is because the more one tries to be who one is not, the more one stays the same (Beisser, 1970). If, instead, clients are encouraged to focus on the here and now of their experience, they will find that any point of contact becomes a portent of exciting new possibilities (Polster & Polster, 1973). Change then occurs spontaneously and without effort through awareness of what and how we are thinking, feeling, and doing—through awareness of the field of our present moment. The ensuing process leads to changes in the entire field that is the client's existence. It is this experience that is essential for change—not thinking or talking about the experience. Most of us tend to talk *about* ourselves, our past, our problems, our dreams, our ideas. The more aware we are of the full extent of our experience, the more able we are to integrate and accept all aspects of our self. In addition, the more thorough the exploration, the more intense the reorganization, allowing us to accept responsibility for our actions and reactions and thereby make choices that are based on a more authentic appreciation of environmental demands and of our true needs and desires.

GESTALT CHANGE TASKS

Historically, Fritz discouraged preestablished techniques and encouraged therapists instead to design "games" or "experiments" that are individually tailored to each client (Levitsky & Perls, 1970). Yet, the use of classic gestalt techniques has persisted, perhaps because they are just so intriguing and in part because it is actually very difficult to propose unique change tasks for each client in each unique circumstance. Gestalt change tasks are called *games* to emphasize the interpersonal nature of the task and to highlight the "as if" quality of the undertaking. If the client experiences reluctance, this too is honored as an opportunity for learning. In fact, how we resist contact in the here and now can be a rich resource from which the therapist draws to propose original, individualized tasks.

The aim of gestalt exercises is to help clients learn about themselves from immediate experience—not from the therapist's conceptualizations. The exercises aim to heighten an individual's awareness of deadened feelings and sensations, reawakening knowledge of personal agency in shaping what is taken for granted as a fixed reality. Thus, the client is given a high degree of control over how and what is learned from psychotherapy.

Such experiments, properly undertaken, are part of the collaborative give-and-take between client and therapist in a psychotherapy session. The use of the present moment for therapeutic leverage is isomorphic of living in the here and now. When designing an experiment, the therapist pays particular attention to the client's nonverbal language and proposes a task designed to intensify the client's current experience in order to expand awareness of the here and now. Ideally, each individualized experiment grows out of the therapist's responsive interaction with the client. Because the experience can be very emotional and unsettling, it is best if clients are prepared for experiments (Greenwald, 1976) and a strong therapeutic relationship is established beforehand. The following paragraphs describe some of the games proposed by gestalt therapists.

Internal dialogue exercises are probably the most famous of the gestalt experiments. They are intended to address internal conflicts caused by uncritical acceptance of others' opinions and promote an integration of all aspects of self. The client plays each role and engages in a dialogue by moving back and forth between two chairs. From each chair, the client speaks directly to the imagined person–entity in the empty chair. The most common conflict is the *top dog–underdog*. The top dog is the inner dictator who tells us what we should do. The underdog plays the victim–rebel and schemes to thwart and avoid doing as the top dog demands.

Making the rounds is a group-based task that involves asking the client to speak to or do something with the other members of a group. Group members take turns giving the client feedback about what they have observed. This allows the client to take interpersonal risks, present newly owned aspects of the self, and confirm or disconfirm assumptions in relation to others.

Reversal exercises invite the client to behave in a manner opposite of his or her usual presentation, such as having a shy person behave in an extroverted way. This is helpful for denial of latent aspects of the self. The client is thrust into experiencing what at first feels strange and alien but eventually whole and authentic.

Rehearsal exercises have the client say aloud the inner thinking we all rehearse in preparation for behaving in expected ways. Our internal rehearsals tend to result in inhibitions of spontaneity and genuineness. By saying them aloud, the client can take ownership of his or her intentions to please others and consciously choose to meet those expectations or not.

Exaggeration exercises are used when the client appears to be unaware of some aspect of his or her experience. The client is invited to amplify a subtle behavior—such as a vocal tone or a gesture—to heighten awareness. Exaggeration exercises can also be used with verbal statements in which some important experience is glossed over. This allows the client to experience something that he or she had been avoiding, thereby facilitating integration.

Dream analysis in gestalt therapy considers all parts of a dream to be parts of the dreamer. Dreams are seen as very useful because they are the most spontaneous and uninhibited expression a person can make. To work with a dream, the client retells the dream as though experiencing it here and now. The therapist then uses what is revealed by the dream to raise the client's awareness of self. This may mean the client acts out the dream's different elements—be they people or objects. Alternatively, dream analysis might involve finishing the dream in a different manner, or the therapist might ask the client to do an internal dialogue exercise with the dream to determine what it has to tell the person.

Using the *language of responsibility* involves encouraging clients to say what they mean and mean what they say. In other words, clients use language that injects real feeling into their words. The language of responsibility has three important aspects: (a) *directness*—talking directly to the therapist or another group member rather than alluding to matters by being indirect (e.g., "Smoking is harmful to the environment" may be replaced by "I cannot breathe properly, and you are killing me by smoking when I am with you!"); (b) *checking things out*—encouraging the client to ask directly, "How do you feel about that?" instead of guessing what another person thinks or feels; and (c) *first person, active speech*—allowing the speaker to own what is being said and imbue it with personal meaning and emotion (e.g., "It is not good for people to live alone" contrasts with "I do not like to live alone").

REFERENCES

Beisser, A. (1970). Paradoxical theory of change. In J. Fagan & I. Shepherd (Eds.), *Gestalt therapy now* (pp. 77–80). New York, NY: Harper & Row.

Goldstein, K. (1939). *The organism: A holistic approach derived from pathological data in man*. New York, NY: American Books.

Goodman, P. (1960). *Growing up absurd: Problems of youth in the organized society*. New York, NY: Vintage.

Levitsky, A., & Perls, F. (1970). Rules and games of gestalt therapy. In J. Fagan & I. L. Shepherd (Eds.), *Gestalt therapy now* (pp. 140–149). Palo Alto, CA: Science and Behavior Books.

Perls, F., Hefferline, R., & Goodman, P. (1951). *Gestalt therapy: Excitement and growth in the human personality*. New York, NY: Julian Press.

Perls, F. S. (1947). *Ego, hunger and aggression: A revision of Freud's theory and method*. Durban, South Africa: Knox.

Perls, F. S. (1969). *Gestalt therapy verbatim*. Lafayette, CA: Real People Press.

22

GESTALT THERAPY PROCESS

UWE STRÜMPFEL AND RHONDA GOLDMAN

Isadore From (1984) warned decisively against reductionist methods wherein Gestalt therapy is represented as the sum of its various techniques. However, although this is a holistic approach, distinct methods and interventions can be identified (From, 1984). The therapist discourages the client from making on-the-spot interpretations, as well as thinking and rationalizing that prevent awareness of emotions and sensory experience. An emphasis away from plans for the future, talking about the past, or thinking in abstractions is encouraged. Awareness can also be achieved by experimenting with the expression of impulses and feelings (Naranjo, 1993). As Gestalt therapy evolved, a number of micro- and macrotechniques have been developed. Microtechniques describe what the therapist does on a moment-to-moment

Excerpted from David J. Cain and Julius Seeman (Eds.), *Humanistic Psychotherapies: Handbook of Research and Practice* (2002) from Chapter 6, "Contacting Gestalt Therapy," pp. 205–211. Copyright 2002 by the American Psychological Association. Used with permission of the authors.

http://dx.doi.org/10.1037/14295-022
Psychotherapy Theories and Techniques: A Reader, G. R. VandenBos, E. Meidenbauer, and J. Frank-McNeil (Editors)
Copyright © 2014 by the American Psychological Association. All rights reserved.

basis, whereas macrotechniques are experiments such as two-chair and empty-chair interventions. We describe some of the most salient types of microtechniques below.

In repetition responses, the therapist suggests that the client repeat a gesture, verbal expression, or particular aspect of body language. For example, a client with depression who has no access to his or her feelings might shrug his or her shoulders often. The therapist may ask the client to repeat this gesture several times, while at the same time asking the client about his or her feelings. This may help the client to share with the therapist his or her feelings of profound resignation.

Exaggeration and elaboration techniques are based on the same principles of awareness. Clients are asked to repeat and intensify a particular behavior to bring unconscious emotional processes into awareness. Automated aspects of functioning that are not processed in awareness can be brought to the client's attention in this way. If a client tends to grin, the therapist may ask the client to concentrate on his or her facial expression and exaggerate it.

Identification involves the client concentrating on a sensory experience, such as a headache, a feeling of tension, sickness in the stomach, or an element within a dream. This is one of the earliest techniques of Gestalt therapy and can be introduced by the therapist in a number of ways, such as "What do your tears say?" or "Can you give your loneliness a voice?" Identification may be regarded as a projective technique in which primary emotions or reactions like disgust and contempt are discovered and symbolized.

Representing or dramatizing is a technique in which clients are asked, for example, to assume the roles of influential people in their lives in staging a family scene. This technique is often practiced in groups in which different roles may be adopted by different people, but it is also effective in individual therapy. This technique is partially informed by psychodrama practices, and the possibilities for dramatization are limitless. The enactment of inner conflict helps activate emotional processes and provides a tangible, living stage for the client. Habitual patterns of conflict that have been rigidly repeated over a lifetime become conscious, enabling the client to break the chain of repeated dysfunctional behavior. Dramatizations are also practiced within the context of both the empty-chair and the two-chair method. For a more full description of Gestalt therapy techniques, see Greenberg, Rice, and Elliott (1993).

The following case example illustrates the macrointervention of the empty-chair and two-chair dialogues; the microinterventions are embedded within the dialogues. The following dialogues are excerpts from a case with a 27-year-old woman with depression. She has two young children, and her husband is a compulsive gambler. She initially feels both responsible and abandoned when he goes out to gamble, leaving her alone with the children and draining the family of financial assets. Her father was also a compulsive gambler, and her mother had always "put up with it," silently suffering with her pain. On two occasions prior to therapy, the client had left her husband, and her family had basically responded with the message that a good wife "stands by her man." The following dialogue illustrates a sample of an empty-chair dialogue used by the therapist (T) in which the client (C) is working with unfinished business with her mother and in which she eventually forgives her mother (microinterventions are identified throughout in brackets).

C: (toward mother) You expected so much from me; you made me believe that you knew what was right for me, that I should always take care of the children, my younger brothers.

T: Tell her what you missed out on. [identification]

C: (crying) I wanted to be myself. I wanted you to accept me as an individual.

T: Tell your mom what you wanted to hear. [expression of need]

C: (crying) I wanted to hear you say you loved me.

T: Tell her what it was like for you.

C: (crying) It was lonely and confusing, knowing that I did as you said, and I always tried to please you but you never expressed your love. [identification]

T: You feel a lot of sadness with her love not coming to you.

C: I also believe that at the time, it was hard for her. I know what she was going through with my father 'cause of what I went through, um . . . just being stuck in her own confusion because of his gambling.

T: Okay, come over here, and be your mom and tell her how it was for you that you were not able to love her. [dramatization]

C: I was uh very occupied by your father's gambling.

Later in dialogue, as her mother again:

C: (crying) I was wanting something I wasn't getting from your father. I wanted to make him see that his family was important. I just felt despair.

T: You felt desperate to try to turn things around.

C: (crying) and um . . . I'm sorry that I didn't allow you to do other things, to have other relationships with your friends or anyone, I needed your help at home . . . as much as you needed your own time with your friends.

In this dialogue, the therapist is encouraging the client to fully express her sadness and acknowledge her unmet need for approval and love from her mother. This allows her to achieve a new understanding of her mother's struggles and how those may have contributed to her inability to be more giving with her daughter. The therapist is encouraging the client's construction of new meaning particularly in relationship to her mother.

What follows is a two-chair work dialogue in which the same client is working with a self-evaluative split. In this excerpt, a shift (softening of the critic or harsh topdog) begins to take shape. (Microinterventions are identified throughout in brackets.)

C: I feel I don't count, that I don't know anything, that I am stupid.

T: OK, come back over here (to critic chair). Make her feel stupid. [dramatizing]

C: You don't count, you're stupid, you are worthless.

T: Again, make her not count. [exaggeration]

C: You're stupid. It doesn't matter what you say, there's no meaning to what you say; you just don't know anything.

T: OK, come back to this chair. How do you feel when she puts you down and ridicules you? [encouraging emotional expression]

C: Oh (sigh), I just feel like she is right and that is just the way it is.

T: Do you notice when you say this that your shoulders kind of hunch and you slump in your chair. Hunch over like that some more. What is it like to feel so hopeless? [repetition]

C: I just feel so alone (client begins to cry).

T: Yeah, it hurts, give the loneliness a voice. What do you want to say to her? [identification and encouraging emotional expression]

C: It hurts when you talk to me like this (sobbing).

T: Yeah, it hurts when she talks to you like this. What do you want from her? [encouraging emotional expression]

C: I want you to accept me unconditionally. I want you to listen to me.

Later in the dialogue,

T: Now change back over here (to critic chair). She says she wants to feel she counts and she wants to be heard, accepted. What do you say?

C: Okay, um, yes that is fair. [beginning of softening of critic]

T: So, what are you saying, that you understand her need?

C: (crying) Um, yeah, I'm sorry. You don't deserve to be treated like that. [elaboration of softening]

In this dialogue, the therapist helps the client move beyond her feelings of hopelessness to access her primary feelings of sadness and loneliness and accompanying need for approval. Identification and validation of these emotions help to strengthen the self, which allows her to stand up to her critical self. Later in the dialogue, when the client moves into the other chair, her critical self softens and becomes more accepting. As the dialogue ends, the client is beginning to access underlying needs for nurturance.

By the end of a 16-week therapy, the client was no longer depressed and did not feel guilty or responsible when her husband gambled. She showed significant improvement in her self-esteem and interpersonal relationships.

DREAMWORK

A survey conducted in Florida on the use of dreamwork by psychotherapists (Keller et al., 1995) showed that the Gestalt method is used more often than the Freudian approach. Prominent Gestalt therapists, such as Polster and Polster (1973), give work with dreams a central place in Gestalt therapy. A number of techniques are used to give dreamwork immediacy. The client is asked to start by telling the dream as if it is occurring in the present, which helps the dreamer relate more directly to the dream's content. The client may also be asked to act out the dream, to identify with a figure or a mood, and to narrate his or her dream experiences from a subjective perspective.

The following dialogue excerpt, extracted from a dream seminar by Fritz Perls (P), exemplifies this type of dreamwork. The participant, Nora (N), is a member of the seminar and is familiar with Gestalt interventions such as identification and dramatization.

N: In my dream I was in an incomplete house and the stairs have no rails. I climb up the stairs and get very high, but they go nowhere. I know that in reality it would be awful to climb that high on these stairs. In the dream it's bad enough, but it's not that awful, and I always wonder how I could endure it.

P: Okay. Be this incomplete house, and repeat the dream again. (Although familiar with Gestalt methods, Nora shows difficulty getting into the method of identification.)

Later in the dialogue,

N: I am the house and I'm incomplete. And I have only the skeleton, the parts and hardly the floors. But the stairs are there. And I don't have the rails to protect me. And yet I do climb and—

P: No, no. You're the house. You don't climb.

N: Yet I'm climbed on. And I end somewhere on the top, and it—and it leads nowhere and—

P: Say this to Nora. You're the house and talk to Nora.

N: You're climbing on me and you're getting nowhere. And you might fall. Usually you fall.

P: . . . Now say the same thing to some people here, as the house. "If you try to climb on me . . . "

N: If you try to climb on me, you'll fall.

P: Can you tell me more what you're doing to them if they're trying to live in you and so on . . . . (Nora sighs) Are you a comfortable house to live in?

N: No, I am open and unprotected and there are winds blowing inside. (voice sinks to whisper) And if you climb on me you'll fall. And if you'll judge me . . . I'll fall.

P: You begin to experience something? What do you feel?

N: I want to fight.

P: Say this to the house.

N: I want to fight you. I don't care about you. I do. I don't want to. (crying) . . . I don't want to cry and I don't want you—I don't even want you to see me cry. (cries) . . . I'm afraid of you . . . I don't want you to pity me.

P: Say this again.

N: I don't want you to pity me. I'm strong enough without you, too. I don't need you and—I, I wish I don't need you.

Emotions that arise in the course of the telling of the dream are an important source of information that provide insight for the dreamer. Dreams are understood as clients' projections, representing the functioning of the self and the dreamer's existential situation in life. In this example, the client describes an incomplete house and becomes sad and later angry while she identifies with this element. The reworking of dreams offers an opportunity for the client to reintegrate neglected aspects of the self. Perls (1969) commented on Nora's dream:

Nora's projection is the incomplete house. She does not experience herself at the beginning as an incomplete house. It's projected as if she is living in this house. But she herself is the incomplete house. . . . If you're capable of projecting yourself totally into every little bit of the dream—and really become that thing—then you begin to reassimilate, to reown what you have disowned, given away. The more you disown, the more impoverished you get. Here is an opportunity to take back. The projection often appears as something unpleasant. . . . But if you realize, "This is my dream. I'm responsible for the dream. I painted this picture. Every part is me," then things begin to function and to come together, instead of being incomplete and fragmented. (p. 98)

Later in the session, Perls helps the client contact her self-support functions. Through the method of identification, Nora starts to realize that she, as the house, has the potential for solid foundations and surroundings.

P: Can you tell this to the group. That you have solid foundations?

N: You can walk and it's safe, and you could live with it if you don't mind being a little bit uncomfortable. I'm dependable.

P: So what do you need to be complete?

N: I don't know. I . . . I don't think I need, I . . . I just feel I . . . I want more.

P: Aha. How can we make the house a bit warmer?

N: Well, cover it, close—put windows in it; put walls, curtains, nice colors—nice warm colors.

Working with the client's experience is characteristic of Gestalt therapy. Experiencing is indivisible from emotional processes. On both a micro and macro level, Gestalt therapy has a range of interventions aimed at confronting spontaneously arising emotions in the contact process and thereby supporting clients in deepening their experience.

REFERENCES

From, I. (1984). Reflections on Gestalt therapy after thirty-two years of practice: A requiem for Gestalt. *Gestalt Journal, 7,* 4–12.

Greenberg, L. S., Rice, L. N., & Elliott, R. (1993). *Facilitating emotional change: The moment-by-moment process.* New York, NY: Guilford Press.

Keller, J. W., Brown, G., Maier, K., Steinfurth, K., Hall, S., & Piotrowski, C. (1995). Use of dreams in therapy: A survey of clinicians in private practice. *Psychological Reports, 76,* 1288–1290. doi:10.2466/pr0.1995.76.3c.1288

Naranjo, C. (1993). *Gestalt therapy: The attitude and practice of an atheoretical experimentalism.* Nevada City, CA: Gateways/IDHHB.

Perls, F. S. (1969). *Gestalt therapy verbatim.* Moab, UT: Real People Press.

Polster, E., & Polster, M. (1973). *Gestalt therapy integrated: Contours of theory and practice.* New York, NY: Brunner/Mazel.

APPENDIX 22.1: GESTALT THERAPY TECHNIQUES

Technique	Video title	Video identifying number	Time at which technique occurs
Dreamwork	Self-Directed Dream Work for Hearing Loss	777700175-001	4:51–6:36
Identification	Self-Directed Dream Therapy for Work Anxiety	777700176-001	15:43–16:54
Representing or dramatizing	Working Through Depression With Emotion-Focused Therapy	777700053-001	30:45–36:12

23

MULTICULTURAL THERAPY

LILLIAN COMAS-DÍAZ

Exploration of clients' ethnocultural heritage elicits ancestry, history, genetics, biology, and sociopolitical legacy. More specifically, clinicians obtain contextual information on clients' maternal and paternal cultures of origin, religions, social class, gender and family roles, languages, and other variables. As you examine your clients'' multiple contexts, make sure to consider the larger historical and sociopolitical factors that inform their lives. In addition to eliciting collective narratives, you can assess generational experiences such as disconnection; dislocation; and trauma, including sociopolitical trauma, such as a group history of slavery, colonization, the Holocaust, and others. Moreover, you can inquire about history of *collective formative events*. These may include natural disasters, political violence, terrorism, and social cataclysms, such as the

Excerpted from *Multicultural Care: A Clinician's Guide to Cultural Competence* (2012), from Chapter 3, "Multicultural Assessment: Understanding Lives in Context," pp. 67–74. Copyright 2012 by the American Psychological Association. Used with permission of the author.

http://dx.doi.org/10.1037/14295-023
Psychotherapy Theories and Techniques: A Reader, G. R. VandenBos, E. Meidenbauer, and J. Frank-McNeil (Editors)
Copyright © 2014 by the American Psychological Association. All rights reserved.

Great Depression, that tend to lead to an enduring and distinguishing membership affiliation (Elder, 1979). Such affiliation engenders feelings of shared participation in social experiences that create firm bonds, distinguishing persons who have endured these events from those who have not. For example, a bonding experience for many baby boomers is the Vietnam War. Likewise, clinicians can explore experiences with collective oppression and trauma. For instance, whereas many women feel connected by experiences of sexism, many people of color feel bonded by experiences of racism, and many women of color are "branded" by sexist racism. Moreover, having lived through collective bonding events tends to shape responses to subsequent events. These bonding experiences can lead to sympathetic trauma or feeling secondhand (vicarious) trauma if one witnesses a trauma inflicted upon a person of one's cultural group. To illustrate, many African Americans experienced traumatic responses to the televised incident in which White policemen were beating African American Rodney King (Shorter-Gooden, 1996). Their sympathetic trauma was akin to a realization that "it could happen to me." This type of indirect trauma goes beyond psychological identification and empathy for the pain of others and relates to the fact that one's membership in an ethnic group predisposes one to potentially become a victim of a hate crime.

It is important to explore the presence of historical and contemporary cultural trauma. *Cultural trauma* refers to the victimization that individuals and groups may experience because of their culture, including their ethnicity, race, gender, sexual orientation, class, religion, or political ideology, and their interaction with other diversity characteristics. These events can have longstanding effects on individuals and groups. For example, individuals with a history of colonization may experience postcolonization stress disorder (PCSD). PCSD results from a historical and generational accumulation of oppression, the struggle with racism, cultural imperialism, and the imposition of mainstream culture as dominant and superior (Comas-Díaz, 2000; Duran & Duran, 1995). As a form of posttraumatic stress disorder, however, PCSD is an entity unto itself. Contemporary exposure to racism, xenophobia, homophobia, hate crimes, and other forms of oppression causes cultural trauma. Moreover, many individuals experience cultural trauma individually, collectively, vicariously, intergenerationally, or all of these ways. The following vignette illustrates the usefulness of exploring clients' ethnocultural heritage.

An upper-middle-class married woman, Laura, sought treatment for anxiety after Sister Mary, her spiritual adviser, suggested psychotherapy to her. Laura's symptoms included sweaty palms, heart palpitations, nervousness, and dizziness during social interactions with her husband's colleagues. As an attorney, Laura did not experience dysfunctional symptoms in her professional role. Her husband, John, was a White philanthropist who could trace his ancestral origins back to the *Mayflower*. Laura's clinician, Dr. Cross, was a psychologist with cross-cultural experience (he spent a year in Sicily as an American field student) and a White American man of British ancestry. After completing a clinical assessment, Dr. Cross decided to conduct a multicultural assessment to further explore the source of Laura's anxiety. In exploring Laura's ethnocultural heritage, he found out that her mother, Clara, was a Mexican sculptor who grew up in a working-class neighborhood in Arizona, where Clara suffered severe ethnic and gender discrimination. Laura's father, Don, a lawyer who is a White American and whose ancestry is British, met Clara at an art exhibition. In discussing her maternal ethnocultural heritage, Laura realized that she felt like an impostor and harbored fears of being "found out" as half Mexican. Consequently, she was able to identify the dread of being rejected by her husband's social and business circle as the source of her anxiety. Laura was a tall, blonde, fair-skinned woman who many believed "did not look stereotypically Mexican." Even though Laura did not report being the victim of direct ethnic prejudice, her mother's stories about being called a "wetback" (a pejorative term used to designate Mexicans without a legal residence status) were vivid in her mind and in her nightmares. It appeared that Laura was experiencing an intergenerational trauma (Danieli, 1998) arising from her mother's exposure to racism and xenophobia in Arizona. The succession of traumatic events and oppression that members of a cultural group endure, *historical trauma* has intergenerational effects (Evans-Campbell, 2008). Unfortunately, the intergenerational trauma continues to affect subsequent generations because when the cultural trauma is not resolved, it becomes internalized.

SOCIOPOLITICAL TIMELINES

To explore the effects of history and cultural trauma on clients, clinicians can chart a sociopolitical timeline. This process helps individuals to connect their history to the present and to envision a future.

You can complement the examination of the effects of sociopolitical and historical factors through the exploration of your client's sociopolitical timeline. A timeline helps to identify your client's personal, family, and historical events.

Laura's sociopolitical timeline is as follows:

- April 25, 1846: Mexican–American War begins
- January 1848: Peace agreement and Treaty of Guadalupe Hidalgo
- 1950: Clara, Laura's mother, is born
- 1955: Clara immigrated to the United States
- 1964: Civil Rights Act

- 1960s: Chicano movement
- 1970s: Women's movement
- 1975: Laura's parents are married
- 1980: Laura is born
- 2008: Barack Obama, the first person of color (mixed race, White and Black African) to become president of the United States, is elected
- April 28, 2010: Arizona anti-immigration law (see Arizona State Senate, 2010)

BIOCULTURAL AND ECOLOGICAL CONTEXTS

The meaning of pain and suffering has cross-cultural variations. Consequently, when you delineate your client's ethnocultural heritage, you can explore *biocultural* variables—the physical factors grounded in a cultural context. When you adopt a physical health mode during the first stage of the assessment, you can examine your client's health and illness belief systems. For instance, a belief in mind–body–spirit unity is relevant to an understanding of culture-bound syndromes as coping skills, particularly anger management. To illustrate, *mal de pelea* among Latinos and *hwa-byung* among Koreans are syndromes related to anger management within a culturally specific context (American Psychiatric Association, 2000).

When you promote health as a holistic construct, you help to cement a multicultural therapeutic alliance. Assessing biological functioning is congruent with culturally diverse clients who are familiar with the U.S. medical or public health model. Moreover, you can explore your clients' biocultural genetic predispositions to illnesses. As an illustration, one in four Ashkenazi Jews carries a genetic predisposition to develop Tay–Sachs disease, Canavan disease, Niemann–Pick disease, Gaucher disease, familial dysautonomia, Bloom syndrome, Fanconi anemia, cystic fibrosis, and mucolipidosis IV (see Jewish Virtual Library, 2011). Likewise, lower rates of Alzheimer's dementia are present in African Americans, Japanese (with autopsy confirmation), and Cree Indians than in White populations (Sakauye, 1996). As a clinical implication of these findings, if a Japanese American presents with Alzheimer's-related symptoms, clinicians may want to explore the existence of other types of disorders, such as multi-infarct dementia.

Exploring a client's biocultural background can provide useful information. For example, Laura reported that her maternal uncle had died of diabetes-related complications. After learning about Laura's maternal Mexican ancestry, Dr. Cross inquired about Laura's propensity to develop diabetes. A physical exam revealed that Laura had a prediabetic condition.

Similarly, clinicians can gather information following a wellness perspective. Many sociocentric individuals view wellness as a balance among the physical, emotional, relational, cognitive, ecological, and spiritual dimensions. Therefore, you can examine clients' lifestyle through questions about nutrition (special foods), physical activity, ability or disability status, use of alternative medicine, intake of vitamins and herbs, relaxation practices, spiritual practices, use or abuse of substances, and others. In addition, you can explore clients' ecological contexts, such as living in the northern latitude and being susceptible to seasonal affective disorder, as well as being exposed to higher than normal lithium soil quantities in the U.S. Southwest. Along these lines, you can examine your clients' environmental circumstances. For example, Caspi, Taylor, Moffitt, and Plomin (2000) found that lower income neighborhoods are associated with children's development of behavioral problems. Living in high-density areas forces inner-city individuals to endorse specific survival adaptations—behaviors that become dysfunctional when living in low-crime areas. Although one's clients may not reside in a lower income neighborhood, they may be vicariously affected by having significant others who do.

MULTIGENERATIONAL GENOGRAMS

You can diagram clients' ethnocultural heritage with the use of *multigenerational genograms* (McGoldrick, Gerson, & Petry, 2008; McGoldrick, Gerson, & Shellenberger, 1999). Similar to family trees, genograms present family relationships, issues, and concerns in a multigenerational format. A multigenerational genogram recognizes the centrality of a collective identity, highlighting the connections with intergenerational and historical linkages. It is important to earn a client's trust and credibility before attempting to do a genogram.

When you diagram a genogram, you can use symbols to organize and understand a client's family history and dynamics from a nuclear to an extended genealogical perspective (McGoldrick et al., 1999, 2008). A multigenerational genogram goes back at least three generations and helps you to map a client's patterns and dynamics in a collective context (McGoldrick et al., 1999). See GenoPro (1998–2013) for basic genogram symbols; see also McGoldrick et al. (1999, 2008).

CULTURAL GENOGRAMS

Genograms are particularly useful when you compare your own genealogy with your client's. As a clinical tool, a genogram helps one examine clinician–client similarities and differences. As part of your clinical training or personal therapy, you may have already completed your own genogram. However, when working with multicultural clients, you should diagram your own cultural genogram. Note that clinicians should make sure that they have earned enough cultural credibility before introducing this multicultural tool.

Cultural genograms place individuals within their collective contexts, including but not limited to genealogical, biological, developmental, historical, political, economic, sociological, ethnic, and racial influences (Hardy & Laszloffy, 1995). In short, cultural genograms emphasize the role of context in the lives of individuals. Hardy and Laszloffy advanced the concept of the cultural genogram as an extended genealogical tool to map contextual relationships among heritage, affiliation, history, collective trauma, ecology, place, community, racial socialization, experiences with oppression, ingroup dynamics, outgroup dynamics, relationship with dominant society, relationship with members of other racial ethnic groups, politics, identity, immigration, translocation, adaptation, acculturation, transculturation, ethnic/racial identity development, and many other contextual factors. In particular, cultural genograms examine the management of cultural differences and similarities. Because of the emphasis on ethnocultural heritage, it is important to go at least five generations back when completing a cultural genogram. In addition to charting the regular information obtained through a genogram, cultural genograms (Comas-Díaz, 2011; Hardy & Laszloffy, 1995) chart culture-specific information such as

- activities of daily life;
- birth, marriage, death, and developmental milestone rituals;
- meaning of cultural similarities and differences;
- meaning of leisure;
- ethnocultural heritage;
- cultural translocation;
- cultural adaptation, acculturation, and transculturation;
- dual consciousness, biculturalism, and multiculturalism;
- communication style;
- cultural–racial/ethnic identity development;
- soul wounds;
- historical and contemporary trauma;
- racial socialization;
- gender racial socialization;
- experience with oppression and privilege;
- internalized oppression and privilege;
- orientation to time;
- sense of agency;
- ingroup/outgroup member dynamics;

- relations with dominant society members;
- spirituality and faith;
- geopolitics, ecological influences; and
- psychopolitical influences.

Clinicians should not expect to complete a cultural genogram in a single session. Allow yourself enough time to let clients' cultural genealogical stories emerge. Both an assessment and a treatment instrument, a cultural genogram promotes clients' self-healing because it allows them to reconnect with their cultural heritage. Use your clinical judgment when conducting a cultural genogram with your multicultural clients. Information on cultural genograms is in Hardy and Laszloffy (1995).

Clinicians should complete their own cultural genogram. Figure 23.1 shows an example.

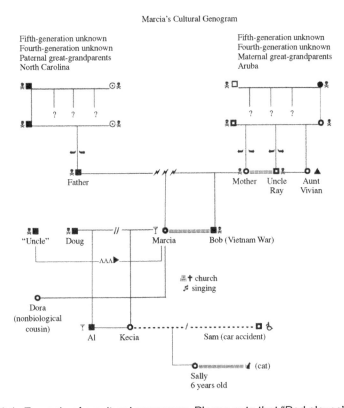

Figure 23.1. Example of a cultural genogram. Please note that "Red slaves" are people who were kidnapped from Goajira (Venezuela) and forced into slavery (see Regional Office for Culture in Latin America and the Caribbean, n.d.). The genogram information here follows the genogram formulation by McGoldrick and colleagues

(continues)

Cultural symbols
- ● Marcia
- ● Mixed-race woman or girl
- ■ African American man or boy
- ■ Mixed-race man or boy
- ☐ Venezuelan Red slave
- ⊙ Native American woman or girl
- ⚣ Deceased
- ↩|↪ Person has lived in 2 cultures
- ☡ Physical disability
- ▲ Family secret
- ⬚✝ Christian Church
- ⚡⚡ Conflict
- ♪ Music
- Υ Alcohol abuse
- ☑ ☒ Pet (cat, dog)

Color (Marcia used the following colors)
- ○ Orange - self-designation
-    Gold - daughter Kecia
- ☐ Blue - son Al
- ◯ Pink - granddaughter Sally
- ⊙ Reddish brown - paternal Cherokee great-grandmother
- ☐ Red - maternal great-grandfather Red slave Venezuelan

Emotional relationship symbols
- ─────────── Good
- ____⚡⚡____ Basically good, some powerful arguments
- ⚡⚡⚡⚡ Conflicted
- ═════════ Close or Enmeshed

Relationship

Married

Cohabiting

Common law marriage

Divorced

Separated

Sexual abuse

Figure 23.1. (*Continued*) (1999, 2008; standard genogram symbols can be viewed at http://courses.wcupa.edu/ttreadwe/courses/02courses/standardsymbols.htm). The essential differences between a genogram and a cultural genogram are that the latter goes back at least five generations, emphasizes ethnoracial identity, acknowledges the sociopolitical and historical contexts, and recognizes sociocentric cultural values. Here, some genogram symbols were modified to reflect racial–ethnic identification and collectivistic cultural values, and "universal" symbols were added to simplify the diagram.

REFERENCES

American Psychiatric Association. (2000). *Diagnostic and statistical manual of mental disorders* (4th ed., text rev.). Washington, DC: Author.

Arizona State Senate. (2010). *Fact sheet for S.B. 1070.* Retrieved from http://www.azleg.gov/legtext/49leg/2r/summary/s.1070pshs.doc.htm

Caspi, A., Taylor, A., Moffitt, T. E., & Plomin, R. (2000). Neighborhood deprivation affects children's mental health: Environmental risks identified in a genetic design. *Psychological Science, 11,* 338–342. doi:10.1111/1467-9280.00267

Comas-Díaz, L. (2000). An ethnopolitical approach to working with people of color. *American Psychologist, 55,* 1319–1325. doi:10.1037/0003-066X.55.11.1319

Comas-Díaz, L. (2011). Multicultural approaches to psychotherapy. In J. C. Norcross, G. R. VandenBos, & D. K. Freedheim (Eds.), *History of psychotherapy: Continuity and change* (2nd ed., pp. 243–267). Washington, DC: American Psychological Association. doi:10.1037/12353-008

Danieli, Y. (Ed.). (1998). *International handbook of multigenerational legacies of trauma.* New York, NY: Plenum Press.

Duran, E., & Duran, B. (1995). *Native American postcolonial psychology*. Albany: State University of New York Press.

Elder, G. (1979). Historical change in life patterns and personality. In P. Baltes & O. G. Brim (Eds.), *Life-span development behavior* (Vol. 2, pp. 117–159). New York, NY: Academic Press.

Evans-Campbell, T. (2008). Historical trauma in American Indian/Native Alaska communities: A multilevel framework for exploring impacts on individuals, families, and communities. *Journal of Interpersonal Violence, 23*, 316–338. doi:10.1177/0886260507312290

GenoPro. (1998–2013). *Rules to build genograms*. Retrieved from http://www.genopro.com/genogram/rules/

Hardy, K. V., & Laszloffy, T. (1995). The cultural genogram: Key to training culturally competent family clinicians. *Journal of Marital and Family Therapy, 21*, 227–237.

Jewish Virtual Library. (2011). *Ashkenazi Jewish genetic diseases*. Retrieved from http://www.jewishvirtuallibrary.org/jsource/Health/genetics.html

McGoldrick, M., Gerson, R., & Petry, S. (2008). *Genograms: Assessment and intervention* (3rd ed.). New York, NY: Norton.

McGoldrick, M., Gerson, R., & Shellenberger, S. (1999). *Genograms: Assessment and intervention*. New York, NY: Norton.

Regional Office for Culture in Latin America and the Caribbean. (n.d.). *Introduction: Breaking the silence, the case of Aruba*. Retrieved from http://www.lacult.org/sitios_memoria/Aruba.php?lanen

Sakauye, K. (1996). Ethnocultural aspects. In J. Sadavoy, L. W. Lazarus, L. F. Jarvik, & G. T. Grossberg (Eds.), *Comprehensive review of geriatric psychiatry* (2nd ed., pp. 197–221). Washington, DC: American Psychiatric Press.

Shorter-Gooden, K. (1996). The Simpson trial: Lessons for mental health practitioners. *Cultural Diversity and Mental Health, 2*, 65–68. doi:10.1037/1099-9809.2.1.65

24

MULTICULTURAL THERAPY PROCESS

LILLIAN COMAS-DÍAZ

Historically, multicultural individuals have resorted to diverse sources of healing. Just to name a few, these sources include empowerment approaches, such as ethnic psychotherapies, folk healing, and spiritual practices. For instance, network family therapy emerged from a Native American context to use individuals' relational network in support of the healing process (Attneave, 1990). As a result, mainstream counselors borrowed and incorporated network therapy into substance abuse treatment (Galanter, 1993).

Multicultural care promotes the incorporation of diverse healing modalities into mainstream treatment. This means that multicultural caring clinicians aim to empower their clients by complementing their treatment

Excerpted from *Multicultural Care: A Clinician's Guide to Cultural Competence* (2012), from Chapter 7, "Multicultural Treatment," pp. 172–187. Copyright 2012 by the American Psychological Association. Used with permission of the author.

http://dx.doi.org/10.1037/14295-024
Psychotherapy Theories and Techniques: A Reader, G. R. VandenBos, E. Meidenbauer, and J. Frank-McNeil (Editors)
Copyright © 2014 by the American Psychological Association. All rights reserved.

orientation with varied approaches. In fact, several multicultural experts recommend the use of a plurality of interventions in clinical practice (Sue & Sue, 2008).

In this chapter, I present multicultural treatment as an empowering approach. First, I present a cultural adaptation of mainstream clinical practice. Then, I discuss empowerment as an example of a culture-centered clinical treatment. A clinical case illustrates the empowering focus of multicultural treatment. I conclude with a discussion of the ethics of being a multicultural caring clinician.

CULTURAL ADAPTATION OF MAINSTREAM MENTAL HEALTH PRACTICE

Seeking mental health services can be a paradox for multicultural individuals. Although people of color have a significant need, unfortunately, the history of service delivery to these populations is fraught with obstacles and missed opportunities. To illustrate, most people of color have to overcome a history of medical research abuses and subsequent mistrust toward the health care delivery. Regrettably, this medical legacy affects those clients of color whose primary care practitioners refer them to mental health treatment. Moreover, numerous multicultural individuals perceive clinical practice as being monocultural, ethnocentric, and insensitive to their cultural and spiritual experiences (Hall, 2001; Sue, Bingham, Porché-Burke, & Vasquez, 1999). As such, clinical practice tends to reflect dominant cultural values and to ignore multicultural worldviews. Consequently, many culturally diverse individuals fear that dominant mental health practice is a stigmatizing and acculturative institution (Ramirez, 1991). In contrast, when multicultural clients encounter clinicians who respect, hear, understand, and care for them, they tend to remain in treatment. Certainly, cultural competence is the key to engage multicultural clients to treatment. For instance, research found clinicians' cultural competence, compassion, and sharing their clients' worldview were more important factors than ethnic matching between client and clinician (Knipscheer & Kleber, 2004). Consequently, clinicians' lack of cultural competence is one reason many multicultural individuals resort to alternative sources of healing.

Although some clinicians have questioned the applicability of dominant clinical practice to multicultural clients (Bernal, Bonilla, & Bellido, 1995; Sue et al., 1999), others have suggested a cultural adaptation to mainstream clinical practice (Altman, 1995; Bernal & Scharrón-del-Río, 2001; Foster, Moskowitz, & Javier, 1996; Kakar, 1985). The cultural adaptation of mainstream psychotherapy consists of both the development of generic cross-cultural skills and the acquisition of culture-specific skills. Because every encounter is multicultural in nature, when you enhance your generic cross-cultural skills, you improve your cultural competence with all clients.

Nonetheless, when you develop culture-specific skills, you enhance your ability to work with particular cultural populations. According to multicultural experts, the development of culture-specific skills includes (a) involvement of culturally diverse people in the development of interventions; (b) inclusion of collectivistic cultural values (such as familism, social cohesion, contextualism); (c) attention to spirituality, religion, and faith; (d) recognition of the relevance of acculturation; and (e) acknowledgment of the effects of oppression on mental health (Muñoz & Mendelson, 2005).

According to Bernal et al. (1995), a cultural adaptation of mainstream psychotherapies needs to include the dimensions of language, persons, metaphors, content, concepts, goals, method, and context. Specifically, the language used in treatment needs to be culturally congruent to the client's worldview; the persons must be engaged in a good therapeutic relationship; metaphors must include symbols and concepts shared by members of the cultural group; the content of the clinician's cultural knowledge must be sufficient (i.e., does your client feel understood by you?); the concepts of the treatment must be congruent with the client's culture; the goals of therapy must be culturally congruent; the methods and instruments of therapy must be culturally adapted and validated; and the context must include the clients' ecology, including historical and sociopolitical circumstances.

An example of the incorporation of cultural factors in treatment is ethnic family therapy. As a field, family therapy has a legacy of incorporating ethnicity and culture into its theory and practice (Ho, 1987; McGoldrick, Giordano, & Garcia-Preto, 2005). Ethnic family therapy emerged out of this tradition to address the cultural context of families and to use ethnic values in treatment. Boyd-Franklin's (2003) multisystemic approach presented in her book *Black Families in Therapy* is a classic example of this perspective. As an illustration of a multicultural care treatment, ethnic family therapy requires clinicians to develop cultural competence. Family clinicians commit to cultural competence by becoming multiculturally aware, avoiding ethnocentric attitudes and behaviors, aiming to achieve an insider/outsider status, and engaging in selective disclosure (Ariel, 1999).

Psychoanalysis has a long-standing tradition of examining the relationship between culture and psyche. This tradition gave birth to psychoanalytic anthropology (Devereux, 1953). Early on, psychoanalysts exhibited an interest in the relationship between oppression and psychological functioning (Kardiner & Ovesey, 1951). Along these lines, proponents of the cultural school of psychoanalysis believed that human development is rooted in environmental factors that vary across cultural contexts and historical periods (Seeley, 2000). Adherents of the cultural school of psychoanalysis, such as Eric Fromm, Karen Horney, and Harry Stack Sullivan, argued that culture shapes behavior because individuals are contextualized and embedded in social interactions (Comas-Díaz, 2011). Some psychoanalysts are responding to the call to culturally adapt their practice through the incorporation of clients' social, communal, and spiritual orientations into psychoanalysis (Foster et al., 1996). As a vivid example, Altman (1995) reported using a modified object relations framework, in which he examines his clients' progress by their ability to use relationships to grow, rather than by the insight that they gain. Similarly, Indian psychoanalyst Kakar (1985) culturally adapted his clinical practice by educating, empathizing, and actively expressing warmth toward his East Indian patients.

And yet, other multicultural clinicians recommended the cultural adaptation of evidence-based practice (EBP) based on commonalities regarding mind–body connection, the role of thoughts in health and illness, and the importance of education in healing (Muñoz & Mendelson, 2005). Lamentably, EBP approaches tend to underemphasize the role of historical and sociopolitical contexts in the delivery of clinical care to people of color and, thus, lack a contextual–ecological viewpoint to examine social and environmental problems (Rogers, 2004). To address these concerns, an American Psychological Association (APA) Presidential Task Force reconceptualized EBP as the "integration of the best available research with clinical expertise in the context of client characteristics, culture, and preferences" (APA Presidential Task Force on Evidence-Based Practice, 2006, p. 273). Although evidence-based treatments tend to lack cultural and ecological validity (Hall, 2001; Rosselló & Bernal, 1999), research on culture-sensitive EBPs has shown benefits for some culturally diverse populations. For example, researchers found positive gains in the areas of depression (Kohn, Oden, Muñoz, Robinson, & Leavitt, 2002; Organista, Muñoz, & González, 1994), anxiety (Sanderson, Rue, & Wetzler, 1998), obsessive disorder (Hatch, Friedman, & Paradis, 1996); attention-deficit/hyperactivity disorder, depression, conduct disorder, substance use, trauma-related disorders, and other clinical problems (Horrell, 2008) among clients of color. (The interested reader can consult Morales & Norcross, 2010, for a report on the conference "Culturally Informed Evidence Based Practices." The conference proceedings are available at http://psychology.ucdavis.edu/aacdr/ciebp08.html.)

Notwithstanding the above-mentioned gains, people of color drop out of mental health treatment more often than their White counterparts (Miranda et al., 2005; Organista et al., 1994). Unfortunately, a decontextualized manualized clinical approach (Carter, 2006; Wampold, 2007) tends to restrict access to treatment of choice (Norcross, Koocher, & Garofalo, 2006; Rupert & Baird, 2004). To bridge this gap, experts recommend that clinicians incorporate culture-centered strategies into their clinical approaches (Bernal & Scharrón-del-Río, 2001). Indeed, empowerment is a central component of culture-centered clinical interventions.

EMPOWERMENT: A CULTURE-CENTERED CLINICAL INTERVENTION

APA Multicultural Guideline 5 (APA, 2003) recommends that clinicians recognize that there are situations in which adapting culture-centered interventions to their practice will increase their clinical effectiveness. In other words, this guideline asks clinicians to focus on clients' cultural contexts and to include a broad range of interventions into their practice. You can comply with this recommendation when you complement your practice with empowering, pluralistic, and holistic approaches. Given the central relationship between health and oppression in the lives of many people of color, numerous clinicians have recognized the need for empowerment approaches in multicultural care (Muñoz, 1996; Sue & Sue, 2008).

To facilitate empowerment, you can acknowledge your clients' experiences with racism, sexism, classism, homophobia, heterosexism, ethnocentrism, ableism, ageism, and other forms of discrimination. For instance, you can open a clinical space to discuss the effects of the oppression on your clients' lives. In such a space, you can become a witness and an interpreter of your clients' maladies. Dr. Cassidy witnessed John's experiences with oppression regarding race and sexual orientation. During their initial session, Dr. Cassidy facilitated the emergence of a working alliance when he examined John's ADDRESSING areas. John's responses to the ADDRESSING tool revealed a conflict with being a gay Black man raised working class with a minister father in a Southern Baptist community. Although John reported no previous personal or family psychiatric history, he agreed to see a psychologist for anger management. John's responses to the explanatory model of distress revealed that the behavior of his White coworkers triggered his anger. He acknowledged being the victim of a combined racist and homophobic discrimination at work. John stated that a White coworker spotted him walking out of a gay bar several days before the harassment at work began. In addition, John described several incidents where he experienced racial microaggressions ("You're an affirmative action baby"). Perhaps John's combined lower social status as an African American gay man made him more of a discrimination target. As a result, John discussed with Dr. Cassidy his plan to file a discrimination complaint at work.

After analyzing the symbolic meaning of John's intended complaint, how would you handle this plan? In other words, should you advocate for, against, or remain neutral on John's plan to file an Equal Employment Opportunity complaint? Although multicultural caring clinicians do not need to be politically active, they recognize that clinical practice is grounded in a political context and, thus, can be a political action. In other words, your clinical orientation can be an instrument of the status quo, or, conversely, it can be an empowering activity. You can conduct a cultural self-assessment to explore your political ideology.

Cultural Self-Assessment: Political Ideology

What is your political ideology—conservative, liberal, centrist, radical, libertarian, apolitical, or none? Do you belong to a political party? How do you feel about clients endorsing political views different from your own? How do you feel about clients endorsing your personal political views? How do you feel about the political issues affecting minority groups? For example, how do you feel about state abortion laws, same-sex marriage, anti-immigration laws, and the Americans With Disabilities Act (1990)? What criteria do you use when you examine political issues in your clinical practice?

Empowerment as a Multicultural Clinical Tool

Regardless of your political orientation, remember that mainstream clinical practice's neglect of sociopolitical contexts can be detrimental to many multicultural clients. In other words, numerous people of color's realities differ from the experience of most majority group members because of their history of collective oppression and trauma (Vasquez, 1998). Moreover, people of color tend to internalize their oppression. Regardless of your political orientation, you can use empowerment approaches to help your clients differentiate functional adaptive responses from dysfunctional ones.

Multicultural caring clinicians use empowering approaches to foster clients' examination of their oppression to promote liberation (Pinderhughes, 1994). Therapeutic empowerment helps clients to increase their self-efficacy, mastery, agency, and control (Dass-Brailsford, 2007). For example, research findings suggested that African American adolescents empowered by cultural pride and racial socialization endorsed fewer depressive behaviors as opposed to those who reported experiences of discrimination (Davis & Stevenson,

2006). Empowerment promotes self-healing by allowing the doctor who resides in each patient a chance to go to work. When you subscribe to an empowerment multicultural model, you recognize your clients' contextual reality, accept their experience as valuable knowledge, affirm their cultural strengths, and acknowledge their perspectives on healing. In summary, a multicultural empowerment helps clients to

- increase their access to resources;
- develop options to exercise choice;
- affirm cultural strengths;
- strengthen support systems;
- promote cultural identity development;
- foster self-healing;
- develop critical consciousness;
- overcome internalized oppression;
- improve individual and collective self-esteem; and
- engage in transformative actions.

The clinical emphasis on empowerment in the United States has political roots. Civil rights movements (e.g., Black power, Chicano/Brown power; gay, lesbian, and bisexual rights) have led to the empowerment of minorities. These movements raised consciousness and attempted to redress the social and political inequities affecting marginalized minority groups. Minority empowerment movements examined the dynamics of power and privilege between dominant group members and individuals from disenfranchised groups. As a result, multiculturalism emerged to promote a critical dialogue on oppression and power and to explore models for healing and liberation.

Critical Consciousness Dialogue

Looking beyond the shores of the United States, multiculturalists found an example of such critical dialogue in Freire's (1970) education for the oppressed. A Brazilian educator, Freire identified his model as *conscientizacion*, or critical consciousness—a process of personal and social liberation through critical thinking. Adherents of critical consciousness teach their clients to critically perceive their circumstances, analyze the causes of their oppression, and discover new ways of action (Freire, 1970). Clinicians using critical consciousness promote clients' agency and ask them to engage in transformative actions. Succinctly put, conscientizacion encourages clients to examine meaning, beliefs, and existential choices to critically analyze their situation, affirm ethnocultural strengths, and promote personal and collective transformation.

Because oppression robs its victims of their capacity for critical thinking, the development of conscientizacion involves asking questions to help clients to make a connection between their concerns and the distribution of power. Asking critical questions, such as What? Why? How? For whom? Against whom? By whom? In favor of whom? In favor of what? To what end? (Freire & Macedo, 2000, p. 7) can raise consciousness and initiate critical reflection and dialogue about individuals' life circumstances. This process facilitates clients' examination of their own issues against the backdrop of sociopolitical realities.

Marcia, the African American client, missed the first part of a lecture because she misplaced her admission ticket. You may remember that the White female clerk denied her entrance to the conference until she found Marcia's name on a second list. Marcia expressed anger at the incident and interpreted the clerk's behavior as racist. My question about alternative explanations seemed to direct her anger toward me ("It's easy for you to ask about alternative explanations. You're not Black."). In addition, you may remember that as a result, we engaged in a discussion about our racial differences ("You're right, I'm not Black. How do you feel about working with a non-Black clinician? Can we talk about your experiences with racism?"). This discussion resulted in a power differential analysis between us.

Let us see what happened when I asked Marcia the following critical consciousness questions:

Lillian: Can we examine the incident from a different perspective?

Marcia: Fine with me.

Lillian: Why do you think the clerk refused to let you in?

Marcia: You tell me . . . .

Lillian: Honestly, I really want to know what you think.

Marcia: I told you she's a racist hypocrite.

Lillian: Who benefits from her behavior?

Marcia: What kind of question is that?

Lillian: Please, can you think about it? Who benefits?

Marcia: Not me!

Lillian: What happened afterward?

Marcia: I already told you, she gave the presenter his badge.

Lillian: Can you tell me more?

Marcia:	Had a late night? [*Laughs*] Your memory isn't so good today.
Lillian:	Come on.
Marcia:	OK. The presenter was standing next to me when he asked the clerk to let him in the room. Where're you going with this?
Lillian:	Please bear with me. I'm trying to help. What was the woman's purpose in letting you wait?
Marcia:	I will not answer that question. [*Moves backwards into her chair.*]
Lillian:	OK. It's natural to be angry.
Marcia:	You may be trying to help, but . . .
Lillian:	But . . . ?
Marcia:	Why don't you help me with my snowballing anger?
Lillian:	Snowballing?
Marcia:	Yeah. My snowballing anger gets everything in its way.
Lillian:	How does it get to you?
Marcia:	[*Takes several deep breaths, straightens her skirt, and moves forward in the chair.*] I'm tired of fighting racism.

I remembered the power analysis I had conducted previously, in which I compared Marcia's areas of privilege and oppression with mine. As a result, the topic of dark skin emerged as both a connection and a disconnection between us. Although I am not White, my skin color is lighter than Marcia's.

Lillian:	I wonder if there is a connection between your snowballing anger and what happened?
Marcia:	I don't know, maybe . . .
Lillian:	What was the presenter's skin color?
Marcia:	Were you there?
Lillian:	I don't understand your question. [*Not addressing Marcia's ironic tone in her question*] No, I wasn't there.
Marcia:	So why are you asking about his color?
Lillian:	Well, a hunch.
Marcia:	He was Indian, you know, from India, and his skin was quite dark.
Lillian:	What do you make out of that?

Marcia moved slowly toward the box of tissues in front of her. She took one tissue. She then grabbed a second one while still holding the box in her left hand. Finally, Marcia took a third tissue. She released the box and bunched the three tissues together. Only then did Marcia's tears began to flow.

RACISM-RELATED DISTRESS

As I indicated previously, the single most common problem underlying psychotherapy with African American women is racism-related distress (Landrine & Klonoff, 1996). Marcia's encounter with the White female clerk was colored by her societal role as a Black woman, the social distance between Blacks and Whites in Washington, DC, and her exposure to personal and collective racial discrimination. Her angry reaction at the clerk's behavior uncovered a racial–gender injury, a response consistent with evidence showing that racism is a pathogen with biological consequences for its victims (Krieger, 1999). To illustrate, research has documented that African Americans show greater increases in blood pressure when exposed to a stressful task than do Whites (Anderson, Lane, Muranaka, Williams, & Houseworth, 1988; Treiber et al., 1993). This racial difference can be understood in the context of African Americans' cumulative exposure to racial discrimination (Sue, Capodilupo, & Holder, 2008). Certainly, racial discrimination has been related to health problems among ethnic minorities (Araújo & Borrell, 2006; Williams, Neighbors, & Jackson, 2008; Williams, Yu, Jackson, & Anderson, 1997). Moreover, African Americans' history of slavery and exposure to microaggressions can result in oversensitivity toward perceived acts of disrespect, as they may be subliminally associated with historical trauma.

Lillian: Can you tell me what is like for you to be a Black woman?

Marcia: It ain't easy . . . too much stress.

Lillian: How can I help?

Marcia: You can't get it. You have light skin.

Lillian: Yes, my skin is lighter than yours. I don't experience what you do as a Black woman.

Marcia: No, you don't. [*Says this in a loud voice as she averted her eyes.*]

Lillian: How can I help? [*Asks this in a soft voice.*]

Marcia: [*Speaks after a long pause.*] Can you help me to separate my legitimate anger from overreactions?

The power differential analysis that I conducted in a previous session offered a safe place for the discussion of racial differences. Marcia identified colorism (preference for light skin over dark skin) as a main difference between us. I attempted to remain "present" and did not shy from exploring our differences as women of color. Furthermore, by answering critical consciousness questions, Marcia confronted the possibility that she may have overreacted to the White clerk's behavior. Marcia associated her cumulative exposure to racial microaggressions with an exacerbation of her irritable bowel syndrome. It seemed that her exposure to racial stress and her "snowballing" anger culminated in physical and psychological symptoms.

Constant exposure to racism increases behavioral exhaustion, psychological distress, and physiological disturbances (Clark, Anderson, Clark, & Williams, 1999). For example, Marcia revealed a history of overreactions to neutral interpersonal situations. She reported a series of conflicts in relationships with her adult offspring, relatives, friends, and neighbors. Marcia's reactions seemed consistent with ethnocultural allodynia, a psychological reaction to cumulative pain. In medicine, *allodynia* refers to exaggerated pain sensitivity in response to neutral or relatively innocuous stimuli, resulting from previous exposure to painful stimuli. I and my partner, Frederick Jacobsen, borrowed the term *allodynia* and coined the concept of ethnocultural allodynia as an increased sensitivity to ethnocultural dynamics associated with exposure to emotionally painful social, racial, and ethnoracial stimuli (Comas-Díaz & Jacobsen, 2001).

Ethnocultural allodynia entails a disturbance in individuals' ability to judge perceived ethnocultural and racial insults and, subsequently, discern defiant and maladaptive responses from adaptive ones. Ethnocultural allodynia describes a pain caused by previous racial and ethnic and cultural injuries as an extreme reaction to neutral or ambiguous stimuli. Therefore, people of color can develop ethnocultural allodynia as a reaction to an increased sensitivity to ethnocultural and racial dynamics associated with past exposure to microaggressions. Marcia's ethnocultural allodynia was a maladaptive response involving an injury to her sense of self that compromised her coping.

Completing Marcia's cultural genogram offered a fuller picture of the context of her historical and contemporary trauma. To aid in this process, Marcia brought a photo album during the completion of her cultural genogram. The essential differences between a regular genogram and a cultural genogram are that the latter goes back at least five generations, emphasizes ethnoracial identity, acknowledges the sociopolitical and historical contexts, and recognizes sociocentric cultural values.

Figure 23.1 shows Marcia's cultural genogram. I included the information suggested by Hardy and Laszloffy (1995) and used the form suggested by McGoldrick and colleagues (McGoldrick, Gerson, & Petry, 2008; McGoldrick, Gerson, & Shellenberger, 1999). I modified some genogram symbols to reflect racial and ethnic identification and collectivistic cultural values. Moreover, I added more universal symbols to simplify the genogram.

REFERENCES

Altman, N. (1995). *The analyst in the inner city: Race, class and culture through a psycho-analytic lens.* New York, NY: Analytic Press.

American Psychological Association. (2003). Guidelines on multicultural education, training, research, practice, and organizational change for psychologists. *American Psychologist, 58,* 377–402. doi:10.1037/0003-066X.58.5.377

American Psychological Association Presidential Task Force on Evidence-Based Practice. (2006). Evidence-based practice in psychology. *American Psychologist, 6,* 271–285. doi:10.1037/0003-066X.61.4.271

Americans With Disabilities Act. (1990). Retrieved from http://www.usdoj.gov/crt/ada/adahom1.htm

Anderson, N. B., Lane, J. D., Muranaka, M., Williams, R. B., Jr., & Houseworth, S. J. (1988). Racial differences in blood pressure and forearm vascular responses to the cold face stimulus. *Psychosomatic Medicine, 50,* 57–63.

Araújo, B. Y., & Borrell, L. N. (2006). Understanding the link between discrimination, mental health outcomes, and life chances among Latinos. *Hispanic Journal of Behavioral Sciences, 28,* 245–266. doi:10.1177/0739986305285825

Ariel, S. (1999). *Culturally competent family therapy: A general model.* Westport, CT: Praeger.

Attneave, C. (1990). Core network intervention: An emerging paradigm. *Journal of Strategic & Systemic Therapies, 9,* 3–10.

Bernal, G., Bonilla, J., & Bellido, C. (1995). Ecological validity and cultural sensitivity for outcome research: Issues for cultural adaptation and development of psychosocial treatments with Hispanics. *Journal of Abnormal Child Psychology, 23,* 67–82. doi:10.1007/BF01447045

Bernal, G., & Scharrón-del-Río, M. R. (2001). Are empirically supported treatments valid for ethnic minorities? Toward an alternative approach for treatment research. *Cultural Diversity and Ethnic Minority Psychology, 7,* 328–342. doi:10.1037/1099-9809.7.4.328

Boyd-Franklin, N. (2003). *Black families in therapy: Understanding the African American experience* (2nd ed.). New York, NY: Guilford Press.

Carter, J. (2006). Theoretical pluralism and technical eclecticism. In C. D. Goodheart, A. E. Kazdin, & R. J. Sternberg (Eds.), *Evidence-based psychotherapy: Where practice and research meet* (pp. 63–79). Washington, DC: American Psychological Association. doi:10.1037/11423-003

Clark, R., Anderson, N. B., Clark, V. R., & Williams, D. R. (1999). Racism as a stressor for African Americans: A biopsychological model. *American Psychologist, 54,* 805–816. doi:10.1037/0003-066X.54.10.805

Comas-Díaz, L. (2011). Interventions with culturally diverse populations. In D. Barlow (Ed.), *The Oxford handbook of clinical psychology* (pp. 868–887). New York, NY: Oxford University Press.

Comas-Díaz, L., & Jacobsen, F. M. (2001). Ethnocultural allodynia. *Journal of Psychotherapy Practice and Research, 10,* 246–252.

Dass-Brailsford, P. (2007). *A practical approach to trauma: Empowering interventions.* Thousand Oaks, CA: Sage.

Davis, G. Y., & Stevenson, H. C. (2006). Racial socialization experiences and symptoms of depression among Black youth. *Journal of Child and Family Studies, 15,* 303–317. doi:10.1007/s10826-006-9039-8

Devereux, G. (1953). Cultural factors in psychoanalytic therapy. *Journal of the American Psychoanalytic Association, 1,* 629–655. doi:10.1177/000306515300100403

Foster, R. F., Moskowitz, M., & Javier, R. (Eds.). (1996). *Reaching across the boundaries of culture and class: Widening the scope of psychotherapy.* New York, NY: Aronson.

Freire, P. (1970). *Pedagogy of the oppressed.* New York, NY: Seabury Press.

Freire, P., & Macedo, D. (2000). *The Paulo Freire reader.* New York, NY: Continuum.

Galanter, M. (1993). Network therapy for addiction: A model for office practice. *American Journal of Psychiatry, 150,* 28–36.

Hall, G. C. N. (2001). Psychotherapy research with ethnic minorities: Empirical, ethical, and conceptual issues. *Journal of Consulting and Clinical Psychology, 69,* 502–510. doi:10.1037/0022-006X.69.3.502

Hardy, K. V., & Laszloffy, T. (1995). The cultural genogram: Key to training culturally competent family clinicians. *Journal of Marital and Family Therapy, 21,* 227–237.

Hatch, M. L., Friedman, S., & Paradis, C. M. (1996). Behavioral treatment of obsessive-compulsive disorder in African Americans. *Cognitive and Behavioral Practice, 3,* 303–315. doi:10.1016/S1077-7229(96)80020-4

Ho, M. K. (1987). *Family therapy with ethnic minorities.* Newbury Park, CA: Sage.

Horrell, S. C. V. (2008). Effectiveness of cognitive–behavioral therapy with adult ethnic minority clients: A review. *Professional Psychology: Research and Practice, 39,* 160–168. doi:10.1037/0735-7028.39.2.160

Kakar, S. (1985). Psychoanalysis and non-Western cultures. *International Review of Psychoanalysis, 12,* 441–448.

Kardiner, A., & Ovesey, L. (1951). *The mark of oppression: A psychosocial study of the American Negro.* New York, NY: Norton.

Knipscheer, J. W., & Kleber, R. J. (2004). A need for ethnic similarity in the therapist–patient interaction? Mediterranean migrants in Dutch mental health care. *Journal of Clinical Psychology, 60,* 543–554. doi:10.1002/jclp.20008

Kohn, L. P., Oden, T., Muñoz, R. F., Robinson, A., & Leavitt, D. (2002). Adapted cognitive behavioral group therapy for depressed low-income African American women. *Community Mental Health Journal, 38,* 497–504. doi:10.1023/A:1020884202677

Krieger, N. (1999). Embodying inequality: A review of concepts, measures, and methods for studying health consequences of discrimination. *International Journal of Health Services, 29,* 295–352. doi:10.2190/M11W-VWXE-KQM9-G97Q

Landrine, H., & Klonoff, E. A. (1996). The Schedule of Racist Events: A measure of racist discrimination and a study of its negative physical and mental health consequences. *Journal of Black Psychology, 22*, 144–168. doi:10.1177/00957984960222002

McGoldrick, M., Gerson, R., & Petry, S. (2008). *Genograms: Assessment and intervention* (3rd ed.). New York, NY: Norton.

McGoldrick, M., Gerson, R., & Shellenberger, S. (1999). *Genograms: Assessment and intervention*. New York, NY: Norton.

McGoldrick, M., Giordano, J., & Garcia-Preto, N. (Eds.). (2005). *Ethnicity and family therapy* (3rd ed.). New York, NY: Guilford Press.

Miranda, J., Bernal, G., Lau, A., Kohn, L., Hwang, W.-C., & LaFramboise, T. (2005). State of the science on psychosocial interventions for ethnic minorities. *Annual Review of Clinical Psychology, 1*, 113–142. doi:10.1146/annurev.clinpsy.1.102803.143822

Morales, E., & Norcross, J. C. (2010). Evidence-based practices with ethnic minorities: Strange bedfellows no more. *Journal of Clinical Psychology, 66*, 821–829. doi:10.1002/jclp.20712

Muñoz, R. F. (1996). *The healthy management of reality*. Retrieved from http://www.medschool.ucsf.edu/latino/pdf/healthy_management.pdf

Muñoz, R. F., & Mendelson, T. (2005). Toward evidence-based interventions for diverse populations: The San Francisco General Hospital prevention and treatment manuals. *Journal of Consulting and Clinical Psychology, 73*, 790–799. doi:10.1037/0022-006X.73.5.790

Norcross, J. C., Koocher, G. P., & Garofalo, A. (2006). Discredited psychological treatments and tests: A Delphi poll. *Professional Psychology: Research and Practice, 37*, 515–522. doi:10.1037/0735-7028.37.5.515

Organista, K. C., Muñoz, R. F., & González, G. (1994). Cognitive-behavioral therapy for depression in low-income and minority medical outpatients: Description of a program and exploratory analyses. *Cognitive Therapy and Research, 18*, 241–259. doi:10.1007/BF02357778

Pinderhughes, E. (1994). Empowerment as an intervention goal: Early ideas. In L. Gutierrez & P. Nurius (Eds.), *Education and research for empowerment practice* (pp. 17–31). Seattle: University of Washington School of Social Work, Center for Policy and Practice Research.

Ramirez, M. (1991). *Psychotherapy and counseling with minorities: A cognitive approach to individual and cultural differences*. New York, NY: Pergamon Press.

Regional Office for Culture in Latin America and the Caribbean. (n.d.). *Introduction: Breaking the silence, the case of Aruba*. Retrieved from http://www.lacult.org/sitios_memoria/Aruba.php?lan-en

Rogers, W. A. (2004). Evidence based medicine and justice: A framework for looking at the impact of EBM upon vulnerable and disadvantage groups. *Journal of Medical Ethics, 30*, 141–145. doi:10.1136/jme.2003.007062

Rosselló, J., & Bernal, G. (1999). The efficacy of cognitive–behavioral and interpersonal treatments for depression in Puerto Rican adolescents. *Journal of Consulting and Clinical Psychology, 67*, 734–745. doi:10.1037/0022-006X.67.5.734

Rupert, P., & Baird, R. (2004). Managed care and the independent practice of psychology. *Professional Psychology: Research and Practice, 35*, 185–193. doi:10.1037/0735-7028.35.2.185

Sanderson, W. C., Rue, P. J., & Wetzler, S. (1998). The generalization of cognitive behavior therapy for panic disorder. *Journal of Cognitive Psychotherapy, 12*, 323–330.

Seeley, K. M. (2000). *Cultural psychotherapy: Working with culture in the clinical encounter.* Northvale, NJ: Aronson.

Sue, D. W., Bingham, R. P., Porché-Burke, L., & Vasquez, M. (1999). The diversification of psychology: A multicultural revolution. *American Psychologist, 54*, 1061–1069. doi:10.1037/0003-066X.54.12.1061

Sue, D. W., Capodilupo, C. M., & Holder, A. M. B. (2008). Racial microaggressions in the life experience of Black Americans. *Professional Psychology: Research and Practice, 39*, 329–336. doi:10.1037/0735-7028.39.3.329

Sue, D. W., & Sue, D. (2008). *Counseling the culturally diverse: Theory and practice* (5th ed.). New York, NY: Wiley.

Treiber, F. A., McCaffrey, F., Musante, L., Rhodes, T., Davis, H., Strong, W. B., & Levy, M. (1993). Ethnicity, family history of hypertension and patterns of hemodynamic reactivity in boys. *Psychosomatic Medicine, 55*, 70–77.

Vasquez, M. J. (1998). Latinos and violence: Mental health implications and strategies for clinicians. *Cultural Diversity and Mental Health, 4*, 319–334. doi:10.1037/1099-9809.4.4.319

Wampold, B. E. (2007). Psychotherapy: The humanistic (and effective) treatment. *American Psychologist, 62*, 857–873. doi:10.1037/0003-066X.62.8.855

Williams, D. R., Neighbors, H. W., & Jackson, J. S. (2008). Racial/ethnic discrimination and health: Findings from community studies. *American Journal of Public Health, 98* (Suppl. 1), S29–S39.

Williams, D. R., Yu, Y., Jackson, J. S., & Anderson, N. B. (1997). Racial differences in physical and mental health: Socioeconomic status, stress, and discrimination. *Journal of Health Psychology, 2*, 335–351. doi:10.1177/135910539700200305

APPENDIX 24.1: MULTICULTURAL THERAPY TECHNIQUES

Technique	Video title	Video identifying number	Time at which technique occurs
Empowerment	Multicultural Therapy for Trust and Intimacy Issues (Session 1 of 6)	777700344-001	37:10–38:11
Facilitate empowerment	A Culturally Competent Approach to Working With Mixed-Race Clients (Client 3)	777700118-001	08:58–10:41
Identify clients as partners	A Culturally Competent Approach to Working With Mixed-Race Clients (Client 3)	777700118-001	37:15–38:52
Multicultural assessment	A Culturally Competent Approach to Working With Mixed-Race Clients (Client 3)	777700118-001	02:00–06:02
Inviting multicultural clients to tell their cultural story	A Culturally Competent Approach to Working With Mixed-Race Clients (Client 2)	777700117-001	30:56–32:44
Model of distress	Multicultural Therapy With a Young Latina	777700066-001	15:07–22:19
The LEARN method			
Listen—the client's perspective of problem	Multicultural Therapy for Trust and Intimacy Issues (Session 1 of 6)	777700344-001	00:17–03:41
Explain—your perceptions of the problem	Multicultural Therapy for Trust and Intimacy Issues (Session 1 of 6)	777700344-001	24:24–25:58
Acknowledge	Multicultural Therapy for Trust and Intimacy Issues (Session 1 of 6)	777700344-001	25:56–31:39
Recommend	Multicultural Therapy for Trust and Intimacy Issues (Session 1 of 6)	777700344-001	35:54–39:04
Negotiate	Multicultural Therapy for Trust and Intimacy Issues (Session 1 of 6)	777700344-001	39:04–42:00
The BELIEF method			
Belief—What caused the problem?	Multicultural Therapy With a Young Latina	777700066-001	02:36–03:44
Explanation—Why did it happen?	Multicultural Therapy With a Young Latina	777700066-001	15:07–15:35

(*continues*)

Technique	Video title	Video identifying number	Time at which technique occurs
Learn—Help me understand?	Multicultural Therapy With a Young Latina	777700066-001	15:35–17:25
Impact—What is the impact on your life?	Multicultural Therapy for Trust and Intimacy Issues (Session 3 of 6)	777700348-001	31:12–32:50
Empathy—must be very difficult	Multicultural Therapy for Trust and Intimacy Issues (Session 3 of 6)	777700348-001	32:50–33:25
Feelings—How are you feeling about it?	Multicultural Therapy for Trust and Intimacy Issues (Session 3 of 6)	777700348-001	33:25–35:28

25

NARRATIVE THERAPY

STEPHEN MADIGAN

There is no power relation without the correlative constitution of a field
of knowledge, nor any knowledge that does not presuppose and constitute
at the same time power relations.
—Michel Foucault (*Discipline and Punish: The Birth of the Prison*)

A MULTISTORIED VERSION OF LIFE

By taking up a poststructural theoretical view, Epston and White proposed that the complexity of life, and how lives are lived, is mediated through
the expression of the stories we tell. Stories are shaped by the surrounding
dominant cultural context; some stories emerge as the long-standing reputa-
tions we live through, and other (often more preferred) stories of who we are
(and might possibly become) can sometimes be restrained and pushed back
to the margins of our remembered experience (Madigan, 1992, 2007). But
whatever the stories are that we tell (and don't tell), they are performed, live
through us, and have abilities to both restrain and liberate our lives (Epston,
2009; Parker, 2008; Turner, 1986; White, 1995, 2002).

Excerpted from *Narrative Therapy* (2011), from Chapter 3, "Theory," pp. 29–38. Copyright 2011 by the
American Psychological Association. Used with permission of the author.

http://dx.doi.org/10.1037/14295-025
Psychotherapy Theories and Techniques: A Reader, G. R. VandenBos, E. Meidenbauer, and J. Frank-McNeil
(Editors)
Copyright © 2014 by the American Psychological Association. All rights reserved.

White and Epston organized their therapy practice around the idea of a multistoried version of life (of what a story/problem-story can mean). This therapeutic concept afforded them the flexibility to view persons and problems not as fixed, fossilized, or under any one unitary description, theory, or label (White, 2002; White & Epston, 1990). Multistoried considerations regarding who a person might be in relation to the problem allowed them to reconsider and resist an isolated or categorized story of a person.[1]

Epston and White's narrative therapy afforded the person and/or problem definition a flexibility for multiple interpretations of what he or she might be—allowing both client and therapist the possibility to re-vise, re-collect, and re-member (McCarthy, personal communication, 1998; Myerhoff, 1986; White, 1979) a story from various and competing perspectives (Madigan, 1996; Madigan & Epston, 1995; White, 2005). It is among these relational re-authoring conversations that change was believed to take place in narrative therapy (Zimmerman & Dickerson, 1996).

Epston and White also believed that a multistoried version of life might include a newly revised re-telling about a person's and/or group's past, present, and future (Denborough, 2008). For example, in 1974, millions of Americans were deemed healthy (literally) overnight when the diagnostic category *homosexuality* was erased from the American Psychiatric Association's *Diagnostic and Statistical Manual of Mental Disorders*. At that time, the American Psychiatric Association made headlines by announcing that it had decided homosexuality was no longer a mental illness. The decision was brought forward as gay activists demonstrated in front of the American Psychiatric Association convention. The 1974 vote showed 5,854 association members supporting and 3,810 opposing the disorder's removal from the manual.

From a narrative therapy perspective, the practice of voting on whether homosexuality constitutes mental illness is not only therapeutically absurd but, needless to say, also highly unscientific and politically motivated (J. Tilsen, personal communication, 2006). Narrative therapists regard the vote on the status of gay identity as a clear example of how illogical it is for professionals in positions of power to be allowed to make arbitrary decisions regarding the mental health identity of others (Caplan, 1995; Nylund, Tilsen, & Grieves, 2007). Nevertheless, with the stroke of a powerfully political pen, these identified homosexual persons, once viewed as sick and/or morally evil by professional members of psychiatry, religion, the law, and so on, were moved

---

[1]Common solitary story lines of people who come to therapy include over-involved mother, under-involved man, despondent immigrant worker, anorexic girl, depressed sole parent, oppositional youth—and any universally agreed-on description acting to harden the categories of what can be storied and/or given relevance.

(at least by the American Psychiatric Association) from one side of the healthy/unhealthy binary to the other (however, they remained unholy and unlawful in the eyes of many religious institutions and legal jurisdictions).

The politics of such a move is quite telling about how psychological decisions regarding healthy/unhealthy identities are willfully created in the fields of mental health. The politics of psychiatry's power-over position also demonstrates the capricious and half-baked intellectual scenery of psychological decision making.

As witnesses to this process of documentation within psychological history, we might now turn our sights toward how other categories of pathology are invented. For example, we might question what institutional processes are involved in turning so-called healthy persons into supposed unhealthy and not "normal" members of society (Nylund & Corsiglia, 1993, 1994, 1996). The answer to this question regarding the legitimacy of a person's identity may depend on who is telling this story, from what set of ethical beliefs they are telling the story from, and with what authority they are telling it. The conclusion is often our realization that not all stories told are equal. However, the power to advise or label someone (and through this process decide who is normal and who is not normal) is often a source of unquestioned authority and privilege by both professionals and those who seek our help.

From the outset, narrative therapy has explored the issue of storytelling rights with people and the influence this may have in constructing a life support system for problems (M. White, personal communication, 1990). Take, for example, the story that a sole parent and immigrant mother recently told me about how, during a 15-minute physical checkup with her new general practitioner, she was informed that she was a "depressed" person. Despite the medical doctor's psychological diagnosis proving to be shocking news for the woman, she did adhere to the culturally sanctioned medical/psychological expertise by purchasing the selective serotonin reuptake inhibitor medication prescribed. It was through the mediated politics of this (somewhat common) power-related medical interchange that she then began to question her own version of herself (as healthy and well functioning). When I asked her how she currently viewed herself, she responded that she had begun the process of performing herself as a depressed person.

By reproducing the professional's opinion of her as a depressed person (as a more relevant and complete story of who she was), the woman began to question her reputation as a community leader within her cultural group, as a strong survivor within her family, as a loving parent to her children, and as a skilled worker to her employer. Unfortunately, these community-supported stories of herself were not accounted for by the doctor during their 15-minute problem-focused depression interview.

Without an exploration by the family doctor into the *intersectionality*[2] of the woman's personhood—living outside the boundaries and confinements of the disembodied category of depression—the relationship between depression and the person was left vastly underexplored. Naming the woman's experience *depression* and having the professional expert's story individually inscribed onto her body did absolutely nothing to account for a relational and contextual exploration of other relevant issues such as gender, race, sexuality, class, and so forth. To a narrative therapist, a noncontextualized therapeutic interview of this kind would be viewed as unethical.

RE-AUTHORING CONVERSATIONS

Psychologist Jerome Bruner[3] (1990) suggested that within our selection of stories expressed, there are always feelings and lived experience left out of the dominant story told. Narrative therapy is organized through the text analogy, with the central idea that it is the stories people tell and hold about their lives that determine the meaning they give to their lives. Therefore, it is what we select out as meaningful from the stories we tell that is given expression. For example, a grade of 80% on a driving test could be expressed through a story of appreciating what was remembered in order to achieve an 80% passing grade or, alternatively, what it was that accounted for all that was forgotten that did not afford a perfect grade—two descriptions and two very different experiences in the telling of these descriptions.

Epston and White relied heavily on the text analogy (Bruner, 1990) as a way to explore re-authoring conversations[4] with the people who came to see them in therapy. Re-authoring conversations were a crucial part of both the philosophical underpinnings of narrative therapy theory as well as the practice work itself. White and Epston found that persons tended to seek out therapy when the narratives they were telling (or were somehow involved in) did not quite represent their lived experience and when there were vital aspects of their experience that contradicted dominant narratives about them

---

[2]Intersectionality is a sociological theory seeking to examine how various socially and culturally constructed categories of discrimination interact on multiple and often simultaneous levels, contributing to systematic social inequality. Intersectionality holds that the classical models of oppression within society, such as those based on race/ethnicity, gender, religion, nationality, sexual orientation, class, or disability, do not act independently of one another; instead, these forms of oppression interrelate, creating a system of oppression that reflects the "intersection" of multiple forms of discrimination.

[3]Bruner suggested that there are two primary modes of thought: the narrative mode and the paradigmatic mode. In narrative thinking, the mind engages in sequential, action-oriented, detail-driven thought. In paradigmatic thinking, the mind transcends particularities to achieve systematic, categorical cognition. In the former case, thinking takes the form of stories and "gripping drama."

[4]The text analogy proposes that meaning is derived from storying our experience. And it is the stories that persons tell that determine meaning about their lives.

(D. Epston, personal communication, 1991). They found that by externalizing problems, the process assisted persons in separating from saturated tellings of these problem stories. Persons then began to identify previously neglected aspects of their lived experience (that contradicted the dominant story told).

Epston and White also found that re-authoring conversations invited people to do what they routinely do, that is, to link events of their lives in sequences through time—according to a theme or a specific plot (Bruner, 1990). It was in this activity of telling/performing their story that people were assisted by the therapist to identify the more neglected events of their lives, named in narrative therapy as *unique outcomes*[5] (Goffman, 1961). People were then encouraged to capture these unique outcomes into alternative story lines named *unique accounts*. For example, when Tom first entered into therapy with me, he initially relayed a version of himself as a "failed" person. It was only after a bit of narrative inquiry that he began a fascinating re-telling of himself that included stories about his life lived as a proud father, fair-minded employer, talented gardener, etc.—stories once restrained through a totalized telling of himself as a resident-psychiatric-ward-chronic-problem person.

White and Epston (1990) felt that unique outcomes provided a starting point for re-authoring conversations that lived outside the restraints of the problem-saturated story being told. Unique outcomes made available a point of entry into the alternative story lines of people's lives that, at the outset of these therapeutic conversations, became visible only as withered traces that were full of gaps and not clearly named. As these conversations proceeded, therapists built a scaffold around the emerging subordinate story (M. White, personal communication, 1991).

As unique outcomes were identified, the narrative therapy conversation plotted them into an alternative story line about the person's lived experience. Unique outcomes were explained by way of unique accounts as the narrative therapist worked to generate questions to produce, locate, and resurrect alternative (and preferred) stories that filled in—and made more sense of— the client's stories of unique outcomes (White, 1988/1989).

Questions were introduced by Epston and White to investigate what these new developments in the story might mean about the person and his or her relationships (stories that lived outside the dominant-problem story being told by the person, family members, or professional). It was then important to the therapeutic conversation for these subordinate stories to be given a thicker description (Geertz, 1983) and plotted into an alternative story about the person's life.

---

[5]Unique outcomes are also referred to as *exceptions*. Unique accounts of these unique outcomes are also referred to as, for example, alternative stories or subordinate storylines.

More questions might be crafted to inspire what White and Epston (1990) called *unique redescription questions*[6] designed to investigate what the new developments might reflect about the person and his or her relationships. Questions also involved the investigation of plot lines to discover unique outcomes, unique accounts, unique possibilities, and unique circulations of the story, as well as experience of experiences, preferences, and historical locations to support the evolving story.

The numerous ways that Epston and White designed narrative therapy's re-authoring conversations acted to re-invigorate people's efforts to understand (a) what it was that was happening in their lives, (b) what it was that had happened, (c) how it had happened, and (d) what it all could possibly mean. In this way, therapeutic conversations encouraged a dramatic reengagement with life and with history and provided options for people to more fully inhabit their lives and their relationships.

Epston and White established that there were some parallels between the skills of re-authoring conversations and the skills required to produce texts of literary merit.[7] Among other things, texts of literary merit encourage (in the reader) a dramatic reengagement with many of their own experiences of life. It is within this dramatic reengagement that the gaps in the story line are filled, and the person lives the story by taking it over as his or her own.

Operating alongside the skills that construct texts of literary merit, White and Epston made it possible for people to address and to fill in the gaps of these alternative landscapes of their experience (Epston, 1998). Their narrative therapy questions were not oriented to the already known in ways that precipitated the sort of thoughtlessness that is the outcome of boredom and an acute familiarity with the subject,[8] and nor were these narrative questions oriented to precipitate the sort of thoughtlessness that is the outcome of fatigue and of failure to identify the unfamiliar.[9]

As re-authoring conversations evolved, they provided conditions under which it became possible for people to step into the near future of the landscapes of action of their lives (Epston & Roth, 1995). Questions were introduced that encouraged people to (a) generate new proposals for action, (b) account for the circumstances likely to be favorable to these proposals for action, and (c) predict the outcome of these proposals.

---

[6]See Chapter 4 of Madigan (2011) on unique redescription questions.

[7]White and Epston's book *Narrative Means to Therapeutic Ends* was originally published in 1990 as *Literary Means to Therapeutic Ends*.

[8]A narrative therapist is interested in having completely new and novel conversations in therapy with the person. This involves a new re-telling of the story of the person/problem and not a parroting of what has been told many times before by the person or by experts commenting on the person/problem relationship.

[9]As in the development of any skills, competence in the expression of these scaffolding questions is acquired through practice, more practice, and then more practice.

Epston and White found that people were likely to respond to questions by generating identity conclusions that were informed by the well-known structuralist categories of identity—these being categories of needs, motives, attributes, traits, strengths, deficits, resources, properties, characteristics, drives, and so on. These structuralist identity conclusions invariably provided a poor basis for knowledge of how to proceed in life. As these conversations further evolved, there were opportunities for people to generate identity conclusions that were informed by nonstructuralist categories of identity—intentions and purposes, values and beliefs, hopes, dreams and visions, commitments to ways of living, and so on (M. White, personal communication, 1992).

It was in the context of the development of these nonstructuralist identity conclusions that people found the opportunity to progressively distance themselves from their problemed lives, and it was from this distance that they became knowledgeful about matters of how to proceed (D. Epston, personal communication, 2009). It was also from this distance that people found the opportunity to have significant dramatic engagements with their own lives and to take further steps in the occupancy and habitation of their life.[10]

REFERENCES

Bruner, J. (1990). *Acts of meaning*. Cambridge, MA: Harvard University Press.

Caplan, P. J. (1995). *They say you're crazy: How the world's most powerful psychiatrists decide who's normal*. Reading, MA: Addison-Wesley.

Denborough, D. (2008). *Collective narrative practice: Responding to individuals, groups, and communities who have experienced trauma*. Adelaide, Australia: Dulwich Centre.

Epston, D. (1998). *Catching up with David Epston: A collection of narrative practice-based papers published between 1991 and 1996*. Adelaide, Australia: Dulwich Centre.

Epston, D. (2009). *Down under and up over: Travels with narrative therapy* (B. Bowen, Ed.). Warrington, England: AFT.

Epston, D., & Roth, S. (1995). In S. Friedman (Ed.), *The reflecting team in action: Collaborative practice in family therapy* (pp. 39–46). New York, NY: Guilford Press.

Geertz, C. (1983). *Local knowledge: Further essays in interpretive anthropology*. New York, NY: Basic Books.

Goffman, E. (1961). *Asylums: Essays in the social situation of mental patients and other inmates*. New York, NY: Doubleday.

---

[10]Some material in this section has been reprinted from *Workshop Notes*, by M. White, September 21, 2005, and retrieved from http://www.dulwichcentre.com.au/michael-white-workshop-notes.pdf. Copyright 2005 by the Dulwich Centre. Reprinted with permission.

Madigan, S. (1992). The application of Michel Foucault's philosophy in the problem externalizing discourse of Michael White [Additional commentary by Deborah Anne Luepnitz, rejoinder by S. Madigan]. *Journal of Family Therapy, 14,* 265–279. doi:10.1046/j..1992.00458.x

Madigan, S. (1996). The politics of identity: Considering community discourse in the externalizing of internalized problem conversations. *Journal of Systemic Therapies, 15,* 47–62.

Madigan, S. (2007). Anticipating hope within written and naming domains of despair. In C. Flaskas, I. McCarthy, & J. Sheehan (Eds.), *Hope and despair in narrative and family therapy: Adversity, forgiveness and reconciliation* (pp. 100–112). Hove, England: Routledge.

Madigan, S. (2011). *Narrative therapy.* Washington, DC: American Psychological Association.

Madigan S., & Epston, D. (1995). From "spy-chiatric gaze" to communities of concern: From professional monologue to dialogue. In S. Friedman (Ed.), *The reflecting team in action: Collaborative practice in family therapy* (257–276). New York, NY: Guilford Press.

Myerhoff, B. (1986). "Life not death in Venice": Its second life. In V. W. Turner & E. M. Bruner (Eds.), *The anthropology of experience* (pp. 261–286). Chicago: University of Illinois Press.

Nylund, D., & Corsiglia, V. (1993). Internalized other questioning with men who are violent. *Dulwich Centre Newsletter, 1993*(2), 29–34.

Nylund, D., & Corsiglia, V. (1994). Attention to the deficits in attention deficit disorder: Deconstructing the diagnosis and bringing forth children's special abilities. *Journal of Collaborative Therapies, 2*(2), 7–16.

Nylund, D., & Corsiglia, V. (1996). From deficits to special abilities: Working narratively with children labeled "ADHD." In M. F. Hoyt (Ed.), *Constructive therapies 2* (pp. 163–183). New York, NY: Guilford Press.

Nylund, D., Tilsen, J., & Grieves, L. (2007). The gender binary: Theory and lived experience. *International Journal of Narrative Therapy and Community Work, 3,* 46–53.

Parker, I. (2008). Constructions, reconstructions and deconstructions of mental health. In A. Morgan (Ed.), *Being human: Reflections on mental distress in society* (pp. 40–53). Ross-on-Wye, England: PCCS Books.

Turner, V. (1986). *The anthropology of performance.* New York, NY: PAJ Books.

White, M. (1979). Structural and strategic approaches to psychodynamic families. *Family Process, 18,* 303–314. doi:10.1111/j.1545-5300.1979.00303.x

White, M. (1988/1989, Summer). *The externalizing of the problem and the re-authoring of lives and relationships* [Special issue]. *Dulwich Centre Newsletter.*

White, M. (1995). Psychotic experience and discourse. In M. White (Ed.), *Re-authoring lives: Interviews and essays* (pp. 45–51). Adelaide, Australia: Dulwich Centre.

White, M. (2002). Addressing personal failure. *International Journal of Narrative Therapy and Community Work, 3,* 33–76.

White, M. (2005). Children, trauma and subordinate storyline development. *International Journal of Narrative Therapy and Community Work, 3/4,* 10–22.

White, M., & Epston, D. (1990). *Narrative means to therapeutic ends.* New York, NY: Norton.

Zimmerman, J. L., & Dickerson, V. C. (1996). *If problems talked: Narrative therapy in action.* New York, NY: Guilford Press.

26

NARRATIVE THERAPY PROCESS

STEPHEN MADIGAN

UNIQUE OUTCOME QUESTIONS

Unique outcome questions invite people to notice actions and intentions that contradict the dominant problem story. These can predate the session, occur within the session itself, or happen in the future.

- Given over-responsibility's encouragement of worry, have there been any times when you have been able to rebel against it and satisfy some of your other desires? Did this bring you despair or pleasure? Why?
- Have there been times when you have thought—even for a moment—that you might step out of worry's prison? What did this landscape free of worry look like?

Excerpted from *Narrative Therapy* (2011), from Chapter 4, "The Therapy Process," pp. 88–95. Copyright 2011 by the American Psychological Association. Used with permission of the author.

http://dx.doi.org/10.1037/14295-026

Psychotherapy Theories and Techniques: A Reader, G. R. VandenBos, E. Meidenbauer, and J. Frank-McNeil (Editors)
Copyright © 2014 by the American Psychological Association. All rights reserved.

- I was wondering if you had to give worry the slip in order to come to the session here today?
- What do you think it may have been that helped support the hope in yourself that helped you sidestep worry?
- Can you imagine a time in the future that you might defy worry and give yourself a bit of a break?

UNIQUE ACCOUNT QUESTIONS

Conversations develop more fully following the identification of unique outcomes and begin to demonstrate how they can become features in a preferred alternative story. Unique account questions invite people to make sense of exceptions/alternatives to the dominant story of the problem being told (e.g., "I always worry"). These exceptions may not be registered as significant or interesting or different; however, once uttered and uncovered, they are held alongside the problem story as part of an emerging and coherent alternative narrative.

Unique account questions/answers use a grammar of agency and locate any unique outcome in its historical frame, and any unique outcome is linked in some coherent way to a history of struggle/protest/resistance to oppression by the problem or an altered relationship with the problem.

- How were you able to get yourself to school and thereby defy worries that want to keep you to themselves at home alone?
- Given everything that worry has got going for it, how did you object to its pushing you around?
- How might you stand up to worry's pressure to get you worried again, to refuse its requirements of you?
- Was it easier to be worry free for those moments when you were simply watching that movie unencumbered?
- Could your coming here today be considered a form of radical disobedience to worry?

UNIQUE RE-DESCRIPTION QUESTIONS

Unique re-description questions invite people to develop meaning from the unique accounts they have identified as they re-describe themselves, others, and their relationships.

- What does this tell you about yourself that you otherwise would not have known?

- By affording yourself some enjoyment, do you think in any way that you are becoming a more enjoyable person?
- Of all the people in your life who might confirm this newly developing picture of yourself as worrying less, who might have noticed this first?
- Who would support this new development in your life as a worry-free person?
- Who would you most want to notice?

UNIQUE POSSIBILITY QUESTIONS

Unique possibility questions are viewed as next-step questions. These questions invite people to speculate about the personal and relational futures that derive from their unique accounts and unique re-descriptions of themselves in relation to the problem.

- Where do you think you will go next now that you have embarked on having a little fun and taking a couple of little risks in your life?
- Is this a direction you see yourself taking in the days/weeks/years to come?
- Do you think it is likely that this might revive your flagging relationship, restore your friendships, or renew your vitality? (This conversation can lead back to unique re-description questions.)

UNIQUE CIRCULATION QUESTIONS

Circulation of the beginning preferred story involves the inclusion of others. Circulating the new story is very important because it fastens down and continues the development of the alternative story (Tomm, 1989).

- Is there anyone you would like to tell about this new direction you are taking?
- Who would you guess would be most pleased to learn about these latest developments in your life?
- Who do you think would be most excited to learn of these new developments?
- Would you be willing to put them in the picture?

Experience of Experience Questions

Experience of experience questions invite people to be an audience to their own story by seeing themselves, in their unique accounts, through the eyes of others.

- What do you think I am appreciating about you as I hear how you have been leaving worry behind and have recently taken up with a bit of fun and risk?
- What do you think this indicates to Hilda (her or his best woman friend) about the significance of the steps you have taken in your new direction?

Questions That Historicize Unique Outcomes

These questions represent any important type of experience of experience questions. Historical accounts of unique outcome allow for a new set of questions to be asked about the historical context. These questions serve to (a) develop the blossoming alternative story, (b) establish the new story as having a memorable history, and (c) increase the likelihood of the story being carried forward into the future. The responses to these produce histories of the alternative present (M. White, personal communication, 1993).

- Of all the people who have known you over the years, who would be least surprised that you have been able to take this step?
- Of the people who knew you growing up, who would have been most likely to predict that you would find a way to get yourself free of worry?
- What would "X" have seen you doing that would have encouraged him or her to predict that you would be able to take this step?
- What qualities would "X" have credited you with that would have led him or her to not be surprised that you have been able to____?[1]

PREFERENCE QUESTIONS

Preference questions are asked all throughout the interview. It is important to intersperse many of the previous questions with preference questions to allow persons to evaluate their responses. This should influence the therapist's

---

[1]Once the therapist begins to get a grasp on the format and the conceptual frame for developing temporal questions (past, present, or future), unique account questions, unique re-description questions, etc., they become a easier to develop and will eventually seem "ordinary" to the interviewer and the context.

further questions and check against the therapist's preferences overtaking the client's preferences.

- Is this your preference for the best way for you to live or not? Why?
- Do you see it as a good or a bad thing for you? Why?
- Do you consider this to your advantage and to the disadvantage of the problem or to the problem's advantage and to your disadvantage? Why?

CONSULTING YOUR CONSULTANTS QUESTIONS

Consulting your consultants questions serve to shift the status of a person from client to consultant. The insider knowledge the person has in relationship to his or her experience with the problem—because of lived experience—is viewed by the therapist as unique and special knowledge. The insider knowledge is documented and can be made available to others struggling with similar issues (Madigan & Epston, 1995).

- Given your expertise in the life-devouring ways of anorexia, what have you learned about its practices that you might want to warn others about?
- As a veteran of anti-anorexia and all that the experience has taught you, what counterpractices of fun and risk would you recommend to other people struggling with anorexia?

The structure of the narrative interview is built through questions that encourage people to fill in the gaps of the alternative story (untold through a repeating of the problem-saturated story). The discursive structure assists people to account for their lived experience, exercise imagination, and circulate the remembered stories as meaning-making resources.

The therapeutic process of narrative therapy engages the person's fascination and curiosity. As a result, the alternative story lines of people's lives are thickened (Turner, 1986) and more deeply rooted in history (i.e., the gaps are filled, and these story lines can be clearly named).

COUNTERVIEWING QUESTIONS

Personally, I only ask questions in therapy, or at least I ask questions 99% of the time.[2] This is the way I was taught by David Epston and Michael White and the way that has always felt the most comfortable.

---

[2] I created the idea of counterviewing questions as a means to explore and explain the deconstructive method involved in narrative therapy interviewing.

For the experienced narrative therapist, questions are not viewed as a transparent medium of otherwise unproblematic communication. It is considered a common practice for narrative therapists to be deeply committed to the ongoing investigation and location of therapeutic questions within community discourse as a way of figuring out the history and location of where our questions come from (Madigan, 1991a, 1993, 2007). The process of discovering the influences that shape therapeutic questions and discussing why we use them with the people we talk with in therapy is viewed as a practice of therapist accountability[3] (Madigan, 1991b, 1992). Questioning therapists about their therapeutic questions is also used as a framework for narrative supervision (Madigan, 1991a).

Experiencing a close-up re-reading of therapy allows the idea of counterviewing questions (Madigan, 2004, 2007) to emerge. A narrative therapy organized around counterviewing questions speaks to narrative therapy's deconstructive therapeutic act. Narrative questions are designed to both respectfully and critically raise suspicions about prevailing problem stories while undermining the modernist, humanist, and individualizing psychological project.[4]

Narrative therapy counterviewing also creates therapeutic conditions to do the following:

- explore and contradict client/problem experience and internalized problem discourse through lines of questions designed to unhinge the finalized talk of repetitive problem dialogues and create more relational and contextual dialogues,
- situate acts of resistance and unique accounts that could not be readily accounted for within the story being told,
- render curious how people could account for these differences,
- appreciate and acknowledge these as acts of cultural resistance, and
- rebuild communities of concern.

Narrative therapy's method of close-up deconstructive counterviewing engages the relational world of therapeutic interviewing in the following ways:

- Counterviewing is an intensely critical mode of reading professional systems of meaning and unraveling the ways these systems work to dominate and name.

---

[3]For further reading on accountability practices, see McLean, White, and Hall (1994) and Tamasese and Waldegrave (1994), *Dulwich Centre Newsletter*, Nos. 1 and 2.

[4]For a clear example of counterviewing, see the American Psychological Association six-part DVD live session set of Stephen Madigan's narrative therapy work, *Narrative Therapy Over Time* (2010).

- Counterviewing views all written professional texts (files) about the client as ways to lure the therapist into taking certain ideas about the person for granted and into privileging certain ways of knowing and being over others.
- Counterviewing is an unraveling of professional and cultural works through a kind of antimethod that resists a prescription—it looks for how a problem is produced and reproduced rather than wanting to pin it down and say this is really what it is.
- Counterviewing looks for ways in which our understanding and room for movement is limited by the lines of persuasion operating in discourse.
- Counterviewing also leads us to explore the ways in which our own therapeutic understandings of problems are located in discourse.
- Counterviewing allows us to reflect on how we make and remake our lives through moral-political projects embedded in a sense of justice rather than in a given psychiatric diagnosis.

REFERENCES

Madigan, S. (1991a). Discursive restraints in therapist practice: Situating therapist questions in the presence of the family—A new model for supervision (Cheryl White, Ed.). *International Journal of Narrative Therapy and Community Work, 3,* 13–21.

Madigan, S. (1991b). A public place for schizophrenia: An interview with C. Christian Beels. *International Journal of Narrative Therapy and Community Work, 2,* 9–11.

Madigan, S. (1992). The application of Michel Foucault's philosophy in the problem externalizing discourse of Michael White [Additional commentary by Deborah Anne Luepnitz, rejoinder by S. Madigan]. *Journal of Family Therapy, 14,* 265–279. doi:10.1046/j..1992.00458.x

Madigan, S. (1993). Questions about questions: Situating the therapist's curiosity in front of the family. In S. G. Gilligan & R. Price (Eds.), *Therapeutic conversations* (pp. 219–236). New York, NY: Norton.

Madigan, S. (2004). Re-writing Tom: Undermining descriptions of chronicity through therapeutic letter writing campaigns. In J. Carlson (Ed.), *My finest hour: Family therapy with the experts* (pp. 65–74). Boston, MA: Allyn and Bacon.

Madigan, S. (2007). Watchers of the watched—Self-surveillance in everyday life. In C. Brown & T. Augusta-Scott (Eds.), *Postmodernism and narrative therapy* (pp. 67–78). New York, NY: Sage.

Madigan S., & Epston, D. (1995). From "spy-chiatric gaze" to communities of concern: From professional monologue to dialogue. In S. Friedman (Ed.), *The reflecting team in action: Collaborative practice in family therapy* (257–276). New York, NY: Guilford Press.

McLean, C., White, C., & Hall, R. (Eds.). (1994). Accountability: New directions for working in partnership [Special issue]. *Dulwich Centre Newsletter, 1994*(2–3).

Tomm, K. (1989). Externalizing problems and internalizing personal agency. *Journal of Strategic and Systemic Therapies, 8*, 16–22.

Turner, V. (1986). *The anthropology of performance*. New York, NY: PAJ Books.

APPENDIX 26.1: NARRATIVE THERAPY TECHNIQUES

Technique	Video title	Video identifying number	Time at which technique occurs
Relative influence questioning	Narrative Therapy for Bulimia (Session 1 of 6)	777700305-001	15:21–15:54
Unique outcome questions	Narrative Therapy for Bulimia (Session 1 of 6)	777700305-001	11:26–12:23
Unique account questions/ answers	Narrative Therapy for Bulimia (Session 1 of 6)	777700305-001	13:34–15:20
Unique redescription questions	Narrative Therapy for Bulimia (Session 4 of 6)	777700311-001	12:20–14:04
Experience of experience questions	Narrative Therapy for Bulimia (Session 2 of 6)	777700307-001	22:52–25:40
Questions that historicize unique outcomes	Narrative Therapy With a Couple (Session 6 of 6)	777700315-001	7:59–8:29
Preference questions	Narrative Therapy With a Couple (Session 3 of 6)	777700308-001	34:24–36:51
Consulting your consultants questions	Narrative Therapy for Bulimia (Session 2 of 6)	777700307-001	45:32–46:35
Counterviewing questions	Narrative Therapy for Bulimia (Session 3 of 6)	777700309-001	36:14–39:13
Insider leagues (this clip references insider leagues)	Narrative Therapy for Bulimia (Session 3 of 6)	777700309-001	44:19–44:45

27

PERSON-CENTERED THERAPY

DAVID J. CAIN

Carl Rogers published the most complete statement of his approach in 1959 and never modified it in any significant way. However, Rogers never considered his theory to be a finished product and anticipated that it would be developed further over time. The most essential concepts of his approach will be identified in this section, followed by variations of person-centered therapy and substantive contemporary developments.

THERAPEUTIC GOALS

The goals of the person-centered therapist are primarily process goals. Therefore, the quality of engagement, moment to moment, between therapist and client is central. The fundamental goal of person-centered therapists is

---

Excerpted from *Person-Centered Psychotherapies* (2010), from Chapter 3, "Theory," pp. 17–26. Copyright 2010 by the American Psychological Association. Used with permission of the author.

http://dx.doi.org/10.1037/14295-027
Psychotherapy Theories and Techniques: A Reader, G. R. VandenBos, E. Meidenbauer, and J. Frank-McNeil (Editors)
Copyright © 2014 by the American Psychological Association. All rights reserved.

the creation of an optimal therapeutic relationship for their clients. As Rogers has eloquently stated: "Individuals have within themselves vast resources for self-understanding, and for altering their self-concepts, basic attitudes, and self-directed behavior; these resources can be tapped if a definable climate of facilitative psychological attitudes can be provided" (1980, p. 115). The "definable climate" includes (a) the therapist's congruence, genuineness, authenticity, or transparency; (b) unconditional positive regard or nonpossessive warmth, acceptance, nonjudgmental caring, liking, prizing, affirmation; and (c) a genuine desire to understand the client's experience and accurate empathic communication of that experience. Toward the end of his life, Rogers also identified therapist *presence* as a powerful and facilitative aspect of the person-centered therapist's manner of being. Rogers (1957) assumed that if the client experienced these therapist qualities or conditions, personal growth would take place.

While Rogers and other person-centered therapists were concerned with clients' achievement of their goals, the emphasis of the therapist is on creating conditions for growth rather than alleviation of symptoms alone. In other words, the emphasis is on the development of the whole person rather than on a specific complaint. For some person-centered therapists, the only goal is to provide the core conditions, while other person-centered therapists believe that the identification of and focus on specific client-generated goals is desirable because it gives the therapy direction and cohesion and assures that the therapist and client are working toward the client's ends.

KEY CONCEPTS

Actualizing Tendency

Rogers defined the *actualizing tendency* as "the inherent tendency of the organism to develop all its capacities in ways which serve to maintain or enhance the organism" (1959, p. 196). This definition suggests that people naturally move toward differentiation, expansion in growth, wholeness, integration, autonomy and self-regulation, and effectiveness in functioning. The actualizing tendency is viewed as a biologically based master motive that subsumes other motives such as a reduction in needs, tensions, and drives as well as an inclination to learn and be creative. It is the bedrock on which person-centered psychotherapy is based. A core belief in an actualizing tendency is the basis for the client-centered therapist's trust and optimism in clients' resourcefulness and capacity to move forward and find solutions to their problems. Art Combs, speaking of the person's fundamental drive toward fulfillment or health, stated, "Clients can, will and *must* move toward health, *if* the way seems open to them to do so" (1999, p. 8, italics in original). Tageson believes that the "living organism . . . will always do the best it can to actualize its potentials . . . and it will do so as a *unit* along all dimensions of its functioning" (1982, p. 35, italics in original). While Rogers viewed the actualizing tendency as primarily constructive and prosocial, he and others (e.g., Bohart, 2007) acknowledged that persons may develop behaviors that are neither moral nor enhancing though they represent persons' attempt to adapt as best they can (e.g., lying or stealing to get something one wants). Although life experiences may weaken the actualizing tendency, it is always assumed to exist as a potential on which clients can draw.

Self, Ideal Self, and Self-Actualization

The *self* (self-concept, self-structure) as defined by Rogers (1959) is the "organized, consistent conceptual gestalt composed of perceptions of characteristics of the 'I' or 'me' . . . together with the values attached to these perceptions" (p. 200). The self is a fluid and changing gestalt that is available to awareness and that is definable at a given time. Though relatively consistent over time, it is also malleable as new experiences alter the ways persons view themselves. The terms *self* and *self-concept* represent persons' views of who they are, while the term *self-structure* represents an external view of the self. The *ideal self* represents the view of self the person would like to be. Often there is a discrepancy between the self one sees one self to be and the person one hopes or strives to be.

As the self-structure is developed, the "general tendency toward actualization expresses itself also in the actualization of that portion of the experience of the organism which is symbolized in the self" (Rogers, 1959, p. 196). Thus, when aspects of experience defined as the self are actualized (e.g., "I am athletic"), the process is one of *self-actualization*. The actualization of the self may be in harmony with the actualizing tendency to maintain and enhance the organism, or it may be at odds with the actualizing tendency, resulting in the development of aspects of the self that may be valued by the person but have adverse consequences. For example, the person may develop his or her capacity to be deceptive, thus gaining desired ends from others while such deception compromises the integrity of the person and therefore does not maintain or enhance the total organism/person.

Congruence and Incongruence

Congruence describes a state in which the person's self-concept and experiences, including thoughts, feelings, and behavior, are in harmony. That is, the person is integrated, whole, or genuine. Rogers believed that congruence represents an optimal state of functioning and a primary quality of mental health. *Incongruence* represents a state of discord between the self-concept and experience. Rogers (1959) described this state as one of "tension and internal confusion" (p. 203) because people cannot reconcile the discrepancy between their thoughts, feelings, or actions and the way they perceive themselves. For example, a person who views himself or herself as having high integrity will likely experience distress when realizing that he or she frequently engages in dishonest behavior. When a person is in a state of incongruence but is unaware of it, the person becomes vulnerable to experiencing anxiety, threat, and disorganization or confusion about the sense of self. At such moments the person may feel a wave of uncertainty or insecurity about who he or she is and experience being out of sorts, troubled by some vague concern, or "off center."

Psychological Adjustment and Maladjustment

In Rogers's theory, optimal *psychological adjustment* "exists when the concept of the self is such that all experiences are or may be assimilated on a symbolic level into the gestalt of the self-structure. Optimal psychological adjustment is thus synonymous with complete congruence of self and experience, or complete openness to experience" (1959, p. 206). Rogers believed that if persons were nondefensively receptive to all experiences, they would likely make good decisions, achieve high levels of adjustment, and function well. In short, a person who is psychologically adjusted is congruent and integrated and functions well because he or she has taken in and assessed all experiences and information that may be relevant to living effectively.

On the other hand, "*psychological maladjustment* exists when the organism denies to awareness, or distorts in awareness, significant experiences, which consequently are not accurately symbolized and organized into the gestalt of the self-structure, thus creating an incongruence between self and experience" (Rogers, 1959, p. 204). Thus, maladaptation is essentially a state of incongruence between one's self and one's experience. The person is likely to experience *threat* when "an experience is perceived . . . as incongruent with the structure of the self" (p. 204). Consequently, the person cannot integrate some experiences or corresponding actions with the self because they don't fit. For example, a man confidently entering a talent show (seeing himself as talented) may get feedback from credible judges that he has little or no talent. The person is thrown into a state of threat and disillusionment because he cannot reconcile the disheartening feedback with a view of himself as talented. He may be inclined to deny or distort such threatening information in an attempt to maintain the integrity of the self as perceived. Thus, after a period of time, the man who received feedback that he was not talented may revise the view of self by denying that the judges were fair or competent in perceiving the person's "real" talent. By doing so, he remains maladjusted because his decisions are based on incomplete or distorted information.

Experience and Openness to Experience

By *experience*, Rogers referred to

all that is going on within the envelope of the organism at any given moment which is potentially available to awareness. It includes events of which the individual is unaware, as well as all the phenomena which are in consciousness. . . . It includes the influence of memory and past experience, as these are active in the moment, in restricting or broadening the meaning given to various stimuli. It also includes all that is present in immediate awareness or consciousness. (1959, p. 197)

Experience includes the person's awareness of his or her behavior. Synonyms include the *experiential field* and *phenomenal field*, and this concept encompasses thoughts, feelings, sensations, and images.

When the person is *open to experience*, he or she readily takes in information arising from within or from the external environment without defensiveness. Openness to experience is critical to optimal functioning because it enables the person to receive and process any and all experiences and draw from those experiences to make effective decisions in daily life. Conversely, defensiveness reduces the person's receptivity to experience, capacity to process, make sense of, and act on experience that may be threatening to the self. Simply put, sometimes what one may benefit from knowing is not necessarily what one may be willing or able to know and examine. A woman who makes excuses for her boyfriend's failure to make time for her or show much interest in her may be failing to access information critical to her dealing effectively with him. Failing to do so renders her vulnerable to self-blame, insecurity, anxiety, or depression.

Positive Regard and Unconditional Positive Regard

People experience *positive regard* when they perceive that some aspect of their self-experience (e.g., feelings, beliefs) or behavior makes a positive difference to or is valued by someone else. In this state the person is likely to feel warmth, liking, respect, and acceptance from others. Rogers (1959) views the need for positive regard as a basic need that is essential to one's well-being. We experience *unconditional positive regard* when we perceive that any experience or behavior is accepted without conditions by another person. Thus, a person may act in ways of which he or she is not proud but still find that he or she is accepted by another. Rogers (1959) states, "This means to value the person, irrespective of the differential values which one may place on his specific behaviors" (p. 208). When clients experience unconditional positive regard from their therapists, they are likely to feel accepted and prized, which in turn enables them to develop more tolerant and accepting feelings toward themselves. While unconditional positive regard is theoretically possible, some have argued that it is an unachievable ideal. However, when clients feel predominantly accepted and consistently valued for who they are by their therapists or significant others, they are likely to develop positive and accepting views of themselves. This desire to be seen accurately and be accepted seems to be a powerful and universal need in people. Therapists display unconditional positive regard toward their clients when they are accepting toward experiences or behaviors of which clients may sometimes be proud and, at other times, ashamed. Consequently, clients learn to accept themselves as flawed but worthy persons.

Clients experience *positive self-regard* when they are accepting of their behavior independently of whether the behavior is accepted or prized by others. *Unconditional self-regard* is experienced when an "individual perceives himself in such a way that no self-experience can be discriminated as more or less worthy of positive regard than any other" (Rogers, 1959, p. 209). That is, the person continues to value himself or herself regardless of his or her experiences or behavior. Again, while unconditional self-regard is theoretically possible, it is more likely that persons generally accept themselves while being aware they sometimes fail to live up to their own standards.

Conditions of Worth

Conditions of worth exist in the person "when a self-experience . . . is either avoided or sought solely because the individual discriminates it as being less or more worthy of self-regard" (Rogers, 1959, p. 209). Simply put, this means that an individual may engage in or avoid a behavior based on whether it brings him or her acceptance or regard from another person. The approval of another may take on such importance that the person disregards whether or not the behavior enhances his or her self, growth, or well-being. Children are especially vulnerable to the conditions of worth communicated by their parents and significant others and therefore may value an experience or behavior "positively or negatively solely because of these conditions of worth which he has taken over from others, not because the experience enhances or fails to enhance his organism" (p. 209). Consequently, an experience "may be perceived as organismically satisfying, when in fact this is not true" (p. 210). For example, a young boy may be proud that he does not cry when he is hurt because he has learned from his parents that crying is weak while stifling one's tears means he is a "big boy." If his parents did not disapprove of crying, the boy would likely cry when distressed and experience this behavior as natural and acceptable.

As primarily social beings, people are constantly concerned about how others see them and whether others like or approve of them. Consequently, most people engage in frequent "image management" to achieve others' approval and whatever benefits accompany such approval. The dilemma of image management and approval seeking is that, even though people may avoid rejection by important others, they become alienated from themselves and fearful of being the natural, spontaneous selves they are. Internally, they know they are not being true to themselves and sometimes feel like frauds. However, this need to be liked and accepted can be so powerful as to compromise one's values, integrity, and self. It does indeed take courage to be and reveal one's true self since the risks of disapproval and rejection may be real. Conversely, living authentically and being true to one's self brings the satisfaction that comes from standing somewhere for something. It enables one to live with integrity even though it may create discord with others. As Rogers has said, "it's risky to live."

Locus of Evaluation

Locus of evaluation refers to the source of the person's values. If the source is internal, the person is "the center of the valuing process, the evidence being supplied by his own senses. When the locus of evaluation resides in others, their judgment as to the value of an . . . experience becomes the criterion of value for the individual" (Rogers, 1959, p. 209). Rogers viewed functioning from an internal locus of evaluation as a sign of autonomy or self-governance and mental health. When the locus of evaluation is external, the person relies on the views of others, especially persons of authority or other authoritative sources (e.g., Bible, parents) to guide their lives. People often prefer to allow others to guide or influence their choices in hope that it will lead to a sound and safe decision while removing full responsibility from themselves for their decisions (e.g., "I followed the advice of my therapist"). Conversely, making choices based on one's own beliefs, values, and senses may be experienced as more risky but may also result in a feeling of pride, confidence, and self-reliance.

Organismic Valuing Process

This process suggests that persons have a built-in, trustworthy, evaluative mechanism that enables them to experience "satisfaction in those . . . behaviors which maintain and enhance the organism and the self" (Rogers, 1959,

p. 209). As an ongoing process, experiences are viewed freshly and valued in terms of how well they serve the person's sense of well-being and potential growth. Person-centered therapists' belief in the organismic valuing process enables them to trust that clients will act in their best interests when guided by this bodily felt source of wisdom. Consequently, person-centered therapists facilitate the client's attending to all experiences, external and internal, to guide them. For persons to benefit from the guidance and wisdom of their organismic valuing processes, they must pay attention to their inner voices, feelings, and intuitions and discriminate which of these is likely to enhance their choices for healthy living. Clients, of course, may choose to ignore the inherent wisdom of their organismic valuing processes and make life decisions based on other factors that they perceive to serve them at a given time. For example, a wife's allegiance to her abusing spouse may be harmful to her well-being and growth but chosen nevertheless because the spouse provides for her basic needs (e.g., food and dwelling) and even some of her emotional needs (e.g., periodic love and affection).

Internal and External Frame of Reference

The client's *internal frame of reference* refers to "all of the realm of experience which is available to the awareness of the individual at a given moment" (Rogers, 1959, p. 209). It is the subjective experience of the person and can only be known fully by the person. This frame of reference includes thoughts, feelings, perceptions, sensations, meanings, memories, and fantasies. Therapist empathy enables the therapist to grasp the client's inner world through inference, though the accuracy of the therapist's understanding is confirmed or disconfirmed by the client. To view another person from an *external frame of reference* means to "perceive solely from one's own subjective internal frame of reference without empathizing with the observed person" (1959, p. 211). For example, a man who spends long hours at work each day may perceive himself as dedicated to his family (internal frame of reference), while his wife may view him as neglecting his family (external frame of reference).

REFERENCES

Bohart, A. C. (2007). The actualizing person. In M. Cooper, M. O'Hara, P. F. Schmid, & G. Wyatt (Eds.), *The handbook of person-centered psychotherapy and counselling* (pp. 47–63). New York, NY: Palgrave Macmillan.

Combs, A. W. (1999). *Being and becoming: A field approach to psychology.* New York, NY: Springer.

Rogers, C. R. (1957). The necessary and sufficient conditions of therapeutic personality change. *Journal of Consulting Psychology, 21*, 95–103. doi:10.1037/h0045357

Rogers, C. R. (1959). A theory of therapy, personality, and interpersonal relationships as developed in the client-centered framework. In S. Koch (Ed.), *Psychology: A study of science, Vol. 3. Formulations of the person and the social context* (pp. 184–256). New York, NY: McGraw-Hill.

Rogers, C. R. (1977). *Carl Rogers on personal power.* New York, NY: Delacorte.

Rogers, C. R. (1980). *A way of being.* Boston, MA: Houghton Mifflin.

Tageson, C. W. (1982). *Humanistic psychology: A synthesis.* Homewood, IL: Dorsey Press.

28

PERSON-CENTERED THERAPY PROCESS

DAVID J. CAIN

THE VARIETIES OF EMPATHY

In this section I will identify some of the various forms empathy might take. *Silent listening* often has a comforting effect on clients, allowing them to say what's on their mind in their own pace and manner. Cindy was a client who wanted me to listen without responding while she told me the entire story of her marriage and divorce. And so I did, for several weeks, carefully recording everything she said. Later, we returned to her story and processed the experience in detail. In an evaluation of my therapy with her, she described me as a "fantastic listener." Intent and patient listening is a form of attending to or ministering to another. This is an involved form of listening, not a passive one, that is often therapeutic in and of itself.

Excerpted from *Person-Centered Psychotherapies* (2010), from Chapter 4, "The Therapy Process," pp. 94–103. Copyright 2010 by the American Psychological Association. Used with permission of the author.

http://dx.doi.org/10.1037/14295-028
Psychotherapy Theories and Techniques: A Reader, G. R. VandenBos, E. Meidenbauer, and J. Frank-McNeil (Editors)
Copyright © 2014 by the American Psychological Association. All rights reserved.

The primary limitations of silent empathy are that therapists do not give their clients a response to interact with, nor do clients know if they have truly been understood.

Empathic understanding responses are the staple of the person-centered therapist in that they attempt to grasp and accurately communicate the client's basic message. This is the fundamental or basic form of empathy upon which more complex forms of empathy are built. These deceptively simple responses often lead clients to explore further what is currently present for them. They help set in motion and sustain clients' attention to relevant aspects of their experience.

C: I am just dragging today.

T: Just no energy for anything.

C: No, I just feel like staying home and avoiding everything I have to do.

Clarification is a form of empathy in which the therapist articulates clearly what the client is attempting to say, struggling to find words for, or expresses in a vague way. It brings into focus what the client means. Using a musical metaphor, it is as if the client hits a note off key and the therapist hits the right note. The client experiences a "ring of truth" and clarity.

C: I'm really out of sorts.

T: You seem angry.

C: I guess I am. Nothing is going right today!

Affective empathy focuses on the client's emotion or bodily felt sense of a problem. It goes beyond the content of the client's messages and articulates the feeling that is expressed or implied.

C: I just can't believe my mother is dead.

T: You're feeling sad and lost that she's no longer with you.

C: Terribly.

Explorative empathy uses a probing and tentative style as the therapist attempts to assist the client to locate, explore, unfold, examine, and reflect on unclear or hidden aspects of experience. The exploration might take the form or broadening or deepening the clients' understandings of their realities.

C: I can't quite put my finger on it, but I feel anxious about my upcoming wedding to Jim.

T: So there's some vague sense of doubt or fear about marrying Jim?

C: Yes. Like I'm not sure that he and I have the same hopes for our life together.

Evocative empathic responses are designed to heighten, make more vivid, amplify, and bring to life clients' experiences. The therapist uses rich, penetrating, connotative language, feeling words and imagery, and a dramatic expressive manner that heightens the client's experience. Accurately capturing the full feeling tone is especially important as the therapist strives to grasp the full impact of the client's experience.

C: (recalling being mugged)

T: You were scared to death he was going to shoot you. The hairs on your neck stood up as you felt the cold gun barrel on your neck and heard a threatening voice saying "Give me your wallet or you will never see another day."

C: That still sends shivers down my spine.

Inferential empathy endeavors to infer the meaning of something the client has hinted at or has stated at a more superficial level; it articulates the tacit or implicit in what is said. In this form of empathy, the therapist often articulates what is unspoken but at the edge of awareness, relying on his or her intuition and therapeutic judgment to do so. The veracity of the understanding is confirmed by the client's sense of its rightness.

C: (a professional tennis player) I played the worst game of my life in the final of my last tournament.

T: I know that leaves you profoundly disappointed in yourself, and I sense that you have tapped into your worst fears that you cannot perform under pressure.

C: Ugh. That's it! I just couldn't overcome my fear that I was going to screw up. Then I tightened up and lost all confidence. And *did* play poorly.

Affirmative empathic responses validate the client's experience or sense of self, whether positive or negative. To be optimally effective, such responses require credible evidence from the therapist's and client's knowledge of the client.

C: I am so proud of how my children are doing. I think I'm a good mother.

T: You are a good mother.

C: I think I've been neglectful of my husband.

T: From what you've said, I can see that you have been neglectful lately.

Empathic challenges are responses by therapists that address clients' perceptions and assumptions. While still acknowledging and remaining within the client's frame of reference, empathic challenges gently offer an alternative understanding or perspective—a different way of viewing the client's world, offering an opportunity for the client and therapist to work toward the best understanding possible.

C: I don't want to go to work today.

T: I think you *do* want to go to work but just not have to deal with your boss.

C: I guess that's true. I do like my work, just not working for my boss.

Conjectural or hypothetic empathy expresses the therapist's attempt to get at that which is out of or at the fuzzy edge of the client's awareness. The therapist provides an interpretation of the client's reality but does not attempt to provide new information. The therapist's response is grounded in the client's disclosures even though the information may not be in the foreground of the client's consciousness. Such responses often reflect something the therapist grasps that has not yet been articulated by the client but which is easily recognizable if accurate. Adlerian therapists have identified a mechanism called the *recognition reflex* that suggests that people naturally recognize a personal truth when it is clearly presented. The therapist might offer a hypothesis by saying something like "I have an idea of what might be going on. Would you like to hear my understanding?" The client almost inevitably is curious to hear what the therapist sees and readily accepts the invitation. The therapist then frames the response in a tentative manner by saying "Could it be that . . . ?" or "Is it possible that . . . ?" and then offers his or her understanding. By framing the conjecture or hypothesis in this manner, it is easily rejected if inaccurate. When it is accurate, the client resonates with it and confirms it.

C: I just don't know what to make of Kate's irritability toward me lately.

T: I have a thought about what may be going on. Would you like to hear my conjecture?

C: Yes.

T: Could it be that you have some fears that she doesn't accept you as you are?

C: Yes. That's it. I guess I didn't want to admit that.

Observational empathy is a response to nonverbal modes of communication such as facial expression, vocal tone, and body language. Observational empathy often takes the form of process observations regarding the client's manner of expression. Such responses often heighten clients' self-awareness and help them recognize that what they experience and communicate often goes beyond their words.

C: I can't believe how mean my mother can be.

T: I notice that your hand is all balled up in a fist as you talk about your mother.

C: I guess I am very angry at her.

Self-disclosure may serve to show that therapists grasp their clients' realities by sharing their own experiences. Such responses are often desirable when clients experience something that they doubt anyone else can possibly understand and often concern something powerful, like the feeling of the loss of a cherished pet.

C: When my dog died, I felt like a large piece of me died with him.

T: I think I do have some sense of how devastating that still is for you. When my dog died, I felt a terrible sense of sadness and loss. Like one of my best friends was gone.

C: Exactly.

First person empathy is a style in which the therapist speaks in the first person as if he or she were the client. Such responses have the effect of being more personal and impactful since clients hear their own voices spoken.

C: I am so depressed I can barely get out of bed.

T: I feel almost completely immobilized.

C: I just have no energy or desire to do anything.

A variation of first-person empathy is similar to the psychodrama method of "doubling" in which the therapist tries to inhabit the person of the client. It has its roots in an acting approach in which the actor seemingly *becomes* the person he or she is playing. In this approach to empathy, the therapist sits next to the client, with minimal eye contact in order to focus completely on the immediate, lived experiences of the client. In such moments, the therapist essentially is the client and speaks the client's voice. The therapist also allows himself or herself some "creative license" to express something outside of or on the edge of the client's awareness or to express something in a more dramatic way that the client has understated. Clients often report the powerful impact of hearing themselves speak; they say they get a more poignant sense of themselves. One of my clients expressed her appreciation for having the opportunity to have a "clone" of herself. She felt her true self was brought to life, and this enabled her to see and hear herself in a fresh way. In this style the therapist continuously checks with the client to verify the accuracy of his or her articulated understanding of the client.

C: I can't believe my husband cheated on me.

T: I feel crushed and betrayed.

C: That bastard! How could he do that?

T: I hate him for violating my trust.

C: I guess I do. I'm furious.

There are many other ways to communicate understanding to our clients, limited only by the therapist's imagination, creativity, and use of self. Sometimes empathy emerges from the therapist's intuitive sense of how to respond and takes unusual forms. For example, a therapist hears a client's feeling of being overwhelmed and comments, "Stop the world. I want to get off." Improvisational forms of empathy are often spontaneous and novel expressions of understanding. On many occasions I have sung a verse from a song to a client that captures the essence of the experience. A client of mine was talking about the difficulty of living with her boyfriend and I sang, "I don't know how to love him." Empathy might take simple forms such as offering a client a cup of tea when the therapist notices how stressed the client feels. Sometimes the form of empathy might be surprising and penetrating. For example, respected client-centered therapist John Shlien told of a client who was struggling with painful issues regarding his mother, to which Shlien responded, "Mama! Mama!" The client resonated strongly to Shlien's response. In sum, therapists and clients may find a wide variety of empathic responses to be effective.

EMPATHY AND EMOTION

Working empathically with clients' emotions is at the heart of effective therapy. Most of the problems clients experience are emotional in nature (e.g., depression, anxiety) or have a strong emotional component (e.g., conflicted relationships, low self-esteem). The "body knows" more than can be articulated, and finding the potential wisdom contained in clients' feelings often leads them forward. Our emotions have a number of important functions. They (a) reflect the body's interpretation of a situation or experience; (b) alert us to what's wrong or right, good or bad for us and orient us toward what's needed for our well-being; (c) represent impulses to act and serve to energize and prioritize action; (d) contain personal wisdom essential to effective functioning and growth; (e) reveal a meaning system that informs us of the importance of events in our lives; (f) often serve as precognitive means of adaptation enabling us to respond quickly to events; (g) help identify core beliefs or schemas; (h) help us clarify our motivation; (i) often serve as "wake-up calls" to attend to how one's life is not working; and (j) are critical to sound decision making.

Rather than view emotion primarily as something that interferes with functioning, person-centered/humanistic therapists have embraced the importance of understanding the adaptive nature of emotion in effective decision making and functioning. Neuroscientist Antonio Damasio, author of *Descartes' Error*, provides evidence that "certain aspects of the process of emotion and feeling are indispensable for rationality [and] . . . take us to the appropriate place in a decision-making space, where we may put the instruments of logic to good use" (1994, p. xiii). One cannot know oneself or function well in the world without paying attention to one's feelings. Conversely, an impairment in persons' ability to access emotional information disconnects them from one of their most adaptive meaning production systems and impairs their ability to make sense of the world.

A sizable and growing body of research shows that working with client emotion, and that depth of experiencing in particular, is consistently related to good client outcome (e.g., Greenberg, Korman, & Paivio, 2002). However, most clients do not tend to process their feelings uninvited, while some prefer to avoid them. Since clients often express emotions without attending to them, it is especially important for the therapist to point to what is felt, or on the edge of awareness, and invite the client to attend to it with curiosity and discover its personal meaning and implications. Further, as Sachse and Elliott (2002) have reported, the quality of the therapist's empathic response to the client may deepen, maintain, or diminish client's experiential processing and self-exploration. In short, when therapists deepen their responses, clients deepen theirs, but when therapists flatten their responses to emotion, so do clients. Finally, it is important to underscore that both *emotional expression and reflection* on the experienced emotion are critical for client change. The mere expression of emotion, while possibly cathartic, typically does not lead to functional learning unless the client cognitively processes the implied meaning of the emotion and its implications for more effective living.

ROLE OF THE CLIENT

When Rogers articulated his "necessary and sufficient conditions" hypothesis, he specified only two conditions for the client: that the client and therapist are in psychological contact and that the client be "in a state of incongruence, being vulnerable or anxious" (1957, p. 96). Rogers believed that if clients experienced anxiety, or incongruence between their experiences and self-concepts, they would be sufficiently motivated to alleviate distress. This belief is also grounded in Rogers's assumption of an inherent master motivation, the actualizing tendency, which serves to maintain and enhance the organism. Rogers's concept of an organismic valuing process, a trustworthy evaluative mechanism that enables persons to experience satisfaction in behaviors that serve the person's growth, was seen as a source of wisdom in the client. The concept of "psychological contact" meant to Rogers that at least a minimal relationship between therapist and client existed, one in which therapist and client make a perceived difference in the field of the other.

He stated his belief that "significant personality change does not occur except in a relationship" (1957, p. 96). Rogers's faith was that *if* certain specifiable therapist qualities were experienced by the client, *then* the actualizing tendency would propel the client toward growth and psychological health.

As in any therapy, the client's responsibility is to identify and discuss meaningful concerns and problems. As clients do so and experience their therapists' nonjudgmental empathy, they tend to elucidate their issues further, explore and reflect on them, and assess how new learnings and insights might be applied to their daily lives. Since person-centered therapy is fundamentally nondirective, it is the client's responsibility to determine the direction of therapy and how to participate. Since person-centered therapy is basically a relational therapy, clients are likely to benefit to the degree that they engage effectively with their therapists. Clients' willingness to express their feelings and process them is also a critical client task. In addition, it is the client's responsibility to make the choice to change and the effort to incorporate change in their daily lives.

Clients of person-centered therapists sometimes need to adjust to the reality that their therapist will not guide, suggest, direct, or otherwise attempt to influence their decisions. Although this may create discomfort and uncertainty, clients of person-centered therapists often benefit ultimately by learning how to make choices and direct their lives. By doing so, they eventually become their own locus of evaluation and the authors of their lives. Most clients who find the person-centered therapist's nondirectiveness to be uncomfortable usually come to understand its purpose and adapt to it reasonably well. Person-centered therapy's effectiveness is, to a large degree, dependent on the client's inclination toward and capacity for self-reflection, something that can be cultivated to varying degrees in most clients.

REFERENCES

Damasio, A. R. (1994). *Descartes' error: Emotion, reason, and the human brain*. New York, NY: Putnam.

Greenberg, L. S., Korman, L. M., & Paivio, S. C. (2002). Emotion in humanistic psychotherapy. In D. J. Cain & J. Seeman (Eds.), *Humanistic psychotherapies: Handbook of research and practice* (pp. 499–530). Washington, DC: American Psychological Association. doi:10.1037/10439-016

Rogers, C. R. (1957). The necessary and sufficient conditions of therapeutic personality change. *Journal of Consulting Psychology, 21*, 95–103. doi:10.1037/h0045357

Sachse, R., & Elliott, R. (2002). Process–outcome research on humanistic therapy variables. In D. J. Cain & J. Seeman (Eds.), *Humanistic psychotherapies: Handbook of research and practice* (pp. 83–115). Washington, DC: American Psychological Association. doi:10.1037/10439-003

APPENDIX 28.1: PERSON-CENTERED THERAPY TECHNIQUES

Technique	Video title	Video identifying number	Time at which technique occurs
Mirroring	Collaborative Person-Centered Psycho-therapy for Divorce (Session 1 of 6)	777700294-001	00:00–00:26
Empathic under-standing (similar to simple reflection)	Collaborative Person-Centered Psycho-therapy for Stress (Session 1 of 5)	777700293-001	10:38–12:11
Clarification	Collaborative Person-Centered Psycho-therapy for Stress (Session 1 of 5)	777700293-001	23:53–24:37
Affective empathy	Collaborative Person-Centered Psycho-therapy for Stress (Session 1 of 5)	777700293-001	29:01–29:16
Explorative empathy (similar to complex reflection)	Collaborative Person-Centered Psycho-therapy for Stress (Session 1 of 5)	777700293-001	01:20–02:28
Evocative empathic responses	Collaborative Person-Centered Psycho-therapy for Stress (Session 1 of 5)	777700293-001	07:56–09:06
Inferential empathy	Collaborative Person-Centered Psycho-therapy for Stress (Session 1 of 5)	777700293-001	07:12–07:46
Affirmative empathic responses	Collaborative Person-Centered Psycho-therapy for Stress (Session 4 of 5)	777700299-001	29:02–31:44
Conjectural or hypothetic empathy (Interpretation)	Collaborative Person-Centered Psycho-therapy for Stress (Session 2 of 5)	777700295-001	21:47–24:46
Observational empathy	Collaborative Person-Centered Psycho-therapy for Stress (Session 1 of 5)	777700293-001	05:17–05:54
First-person empathy	Collaborative Person-Centered Psycho-therapy for Stress (Session 1 of 5)	777700293-001	25:11–26:20

29

PSYCHOANALYTIC THERAPY

JEREMY D. SAFRAN

To begin thinking about the goals of psychotherapy, it is essential to make some assumptions about what psychological health looks like. And these assumptions are inevitably influenced by values and beliefs about the nature of what constitutes the "good life." Different forms of psychotherapy and different psychoanalytic traditions hold different assumptions about the nature of the good life and by implication the goals of psychoanalysis. Freud's oft-quoted remark that "psychoanalysis transforms neurotic misery into ordinary unhappiness" is seen by some as reflecting a pessimistic perspective on life. But it can also be seen as embodying a certain form of wisdom. Freud believed that life by its very nature involves various forms of suffering: illness, loss of loved ones and friends, disappointments, and ultimately death. It is essential, however, to distinguish what might be termed *existential suffering*

Excerpted from *Psychoanalysis and Psychoanalytic Therapies* (2012), from Chapter 3, "Theory," pp. 48–56. Copyright 2012 by the American Psychological Association. Used with permission of the author.

http://dx.doi.org/10.1037/14295-029

Psychotherapy Theories and Techniques: A Reader, G. R. VandenBos, E. Meidenbauer, and J. Frank-McNeil (Editors)
Copyright © 2014 by the American Psychological Association. All rights reserved.

from self-imposed neurotic suffering. From Freud's perspective, one of the goals of psychoanalysis is to help people learn to grapple with life's inevitabilities with a certain degree of equanimity and dignity.

As I discuss in greater detail later in this chapter, many contemporary psychoanalysts have emphasized the goal of living life with vitality. Dimen (2010), paraphrasing the author Andrew Solomon, said that "good treatment restores vitality, not happiness" (p. 264). In addition, for many contemporary psychoanalysts there is also an emphasis on challenging potentially oppressive normative emphases on singular and conventional definitions of "mental health" and on replacing them with a respect for and appreciation of the infinite number of different ways of being in this world and a celebration of this diversity (e.g., Corbett, 2009; Dimen, 2010; Harris, 2008). In the words of the influential British psychoanalyst, Donald Winnicott (1958): "We are poor indeed if we are only sane" (p. 150).

As Cushman and Gilford (2000) argued, in many respects psychoanalysis goes against the grain of many values that are characteristic of our culture and that are reflected in such developments as the managed care system and the evidence-based treatment movement. According to them, the advent of the managed care system, the evidence-based treatment system, and the dominance of the health care system by the cognitive–behavioral tradition reflect such values as clarity, activity, speed, concreteness, practicality, realism, efficiency, systematization, consistency, independence, and self-responsibility.

Psychoanalysis, in contrast, tends to value such dimensions as complexity, depth, nuance, and patience. This emphasis on patience, acceptance, and allowing things to unfold in their own way can be traced back to some aspects of Freud's early thinking and is an important thread that is expressed in different ways in different psychoanalytic traditions. Freud cautioned analysts that the "furor sanandi" (an excessive zeal to cure) could interfere with the therapist's ability to assume the kind of attitude of patience and acceptance that is necessary to be truly helpful. Wilfred Bion (1970) is famous for speaking about the importance of approaching every session "without memory or desire" in order to allow the "emotional truth" of what is taking place to emerge (p. 57).

The downside of this type of perspective is that it can lend itself to the type of never-ending analysis that is caricatured in Woody Allen movies and that clients have valid reasons to be concerned about. In fact, some very prominent analysts have argued that this attitude can too often degenerate into a failure to grapple with the question of what is genuinely helpful to clients and is one of the factors that has led to the declining popularity of psychoanalysis (Renik, 2006). On the other hand, there is a certain wisdom embodied in this emphasis that can serve as a valuable corrective to the contemporary Western tendency to overestimate our capacity for individual efficacy and mastery and that fails to recognize the limitation of our ability to "have it all."

COMPLEXITY, AMBIGUITY, AND CURIOSITY

Psychoanalysis tends toward the view that at a fundamental level, human beings are complex creatures whose experience and actions are shaped by multiple and often conflicting conscious and unconscious determinants, as well as by social and cultural forces. Related to this is an emphasis on the importance of tolerance of ambiguity. Psychoanalytic thinking assumes that given the complexity of human experience, there is a fundamental ambiguity to the therapeutic process. This sense of ambiguity forecloses the possibility of pat understandings of what is going on with one's client or in the therapeutic process. This can lead to a fair amount of anxiety for novice therapists who want to feel that they can understand what is going on in a definitive fashion and have clear guidelines for practice. The positive side of this fundamental ambiguity is a genuine curiosity in watching the process emerge and allowing one's understanding to unfold and evolve over time (McWilliams, 2004). This can be associated with a genuine respect for the complexity of human nature and a feeling of humility in the face of the ultimate unknowability of things.

THE ETHIC OF HONESTY

Freud believed in the importance of shedding one's illusions and coming to accept the inevitabilities of life. He believed that self-deception is ubiquitous, and he valued the process of self-reflection and truth seeking (in the sense of searching for one's real motives). In a sense, one could say that psychoanalysis is associated with an ethic of honesty (e.g., McWilliams, 2004; Thompson, 2004). Clients are encouraged to strive to be truthful with themselves about their own motives, and this type of honesty is expected of therapists as well.

Once we accept the idea of unconscious motivation, we begin to recognize that we are all at some level strangers to ourselves. We begin to see that we therapists are just as susceptible to self-deception as our clients are. It is not unusual for trainees in supervision to find out that they were intervening in a certain way because of feelings that they were completely unaware of (e.g., competitiveness, insecurity, irritation, a desire for control) and that our rational or theoretical understanding of why we are acting as we are as therapists is often only part of the story or an after-the-fact justification.

Conducting psychotherapy from a psychoanalytic perspective thus inevitably involves an ongoing process of self-discovery and personal growth for therapists. It is difficult to work with clients, especially challenging ones, without being willing to explore one's own contribution to what is going on in the therapeutic relationship in an ongoing fashion and a willingness to reflect on why we are doing what we are doing in a given session. Many contemporary psychoanalysts believe that in many successful treatments, both the client and the therapist change. Practicing psychoanalysis is thus not for the faint of heart.

A SEARCH FOR MEANING, VITALITY, AND AUTHENTICITY

Freud's emphasis was on becoming aware of our irrational, instinctually based wishes and then renouncing or taming them through our rational faculties. One important shift in the goals of psychoanalytic thinking, especially in North America, involves an emphasis on the importance of creating meaning and revitalizing the self. This shift may in part be a result of changing cultural and historical conditions. This shift in cultural sensibility corresponds to an important shift in the cultural landscape from Freud's time to ours. Psychoanalysis was born during an era when individualism was in the process of becoming more pronounced. In the Victorian culture of Freud's time, the self was viewed as dangerous and an emphasis was placed on self-mastery and self-control (Cushman, 1995). Over the last century, the culture of individualism has continued to evolve, and the individual has become increasingly isolated from the community. This is a double-edged sword. On the one hand, the more individuated person of contemporary culture is freer of the potentially suffocating influence of community. On the other hand, he or she is cut off from the sense of meaning and well-being that potentially flows from being integrated with a wider community.

The disintegration of the unifying web of beliefs and values that traditionally held people together and that give life its meaning has resulted in the emergence of what Philip Cushman (1995) referred to as the *empty self*. This empty self experiences the lack of tradition, community, and shared meaning as an internal hollowness; a lack of personal conviction and worth; and a chronic, undifferentiated emotional hunger. In contemporary Western culture, psychological conflicts are thus more likely to involve a search for meaning and a hunger for intimate and meaningful relationships than a conflict between sexual instincts and cultural norms (Mitchell, 1993; Safran, 2003).

This search for meaning is linked to a process of individuation—a process of both discovering and deciding what one really believes in, rather than simply accepting consensual social values. Philosophers and historians tell us that the concept of authenticity is a relatively novel invention that emerged in 18th-century Europe (Guignon, 2004; Taylor, 1992). Its emergence was associated with the rise of the culture of Romanticism. The Romantic movement can be understood as a backlash against the Enlightenment. It was an attempt to recover a sense of oneness and wholeness lost with the rise of modernity. The Romantic movement holds that truth is discovered not through scientific investigation or by logic but through immersion in one's deepest feelings. There is a distrust of society in the Romantic movement and an implicit belief in the existence of an inner "true self" that is in harmony with nature. Conventional social rituals are seen as artificial and empty, and as potentially stifling authenticity. Consistent with this sensibility, there is an important thread in contemporary psychoanalytic thinking that views the therapist's authentic responsiveness to the client as an important element in the change process. The therapist's ability to act spontaneously or to improvise in response to the demands of the moment is viewed as a potential antidote to the devitalizing effects of social ritual and conformity in people's lives (e.g., Ringstrom, 2007; Stern et al., 1998). Irwin Hoffman has persuasively argued that it is important not to emphasize the value of spontaneity at the expense of ritual, and vice versa. He argues instead for the value of thinking in terms of the dialectical interplay between ritual and spontaneity in the therapeutic process. A detailed discussion of Hoffman's perspective is beyond the scope of this book, but the interested reader is referred to Hoffman (1998).

REFLECTION-IN-ACTION VERSUS TECHNICAL RATIONALITY

At a time when there is a growing emphasis in the psychotherapy field on the importance of developing evidence-based practices that can be delivered in a standardized fashion, there is an important trend in contemporary psychoanalytic thinking that emphasizes the unique nature of every therapeutic encounter and the impossibility of developing "standardized" interventions or principles of intervention. The idea that professional knowledge consists of "instrumental problem solving made rigorous by the application of scientific theory and technique" is referred to as *technical rationality* by Schön (1983, p. 21). Interestingly, Schön (1983) and others conducting research on differences in the problem-solving styles of experts versus novices (e.g., Dreyfus & Dreyfus, 1986) have found that skilled practitioners across a wide range of disciplines (musicians, architects, engineers, managers, psychotherapists) do not problem-solve in a manner consistent with this model of technical rationality. Instead, they engage in a process of what Schön termed *reflection-in-action*. This involves an ongoing appraisal of the evolving situation in a rapid, holistic, and (at least partially) tacit fashion. It involves a reflective conversation with the relevant situation that allows for modification of one's understanding and actions in response to ongoing feedback.

It has become increasingly common for contemporary psychoanalytic thinkers to argue that this notion of reflection-in-action provides a better framework for conceptualizing the therapeutic activities of a skilled therapist than does the model of technical rationality (Aron, 1999; Hoffman, 2009; Safran & Muran, 2000). The therapist can no longer look toward a unitary and universal set of principles to guide his actions. Instead, he is confronted with a multiplicity of theoretical perspectives that he can use to help him reflect on how best to act in this particular moment with this particular client. Any guidelines derived from theory must ultimately be integrated with the therapist's own irreducible subjectivity (Renik, 1993) and with the unique subjectivity of the client to find a way of being that is facilitative in a given moment.

KEY CONCEPTS

In this section, I outline some of the central concepts of psychoanalytic thinking. Most, if not all, of these concepts have evolved over time. In addition, whereas some of these concepts originated in the early days of psychoanalytic thinking, others emerged at later stages in the evolution of psychoanalytic theory.

The Unconscious

The concept of the unconscious is central to psychoanalytic theory. Over time psychoanalytic conceptualizations have evolved, and these days different models of the unconscious are emphasized by different psychoanalytic schools. Freud's original model of the unconscious was that certain memories and associated affects are split off from consciousness because they are too threatening to the individual.

As Freud's thinking about the unconscious evolved, he began to distinguish between two different principles of psychic functioning that are always taking place at the same time: secondary process and primary process. *Secondary process* is associated with consciousness and is the foundation for rational, reflective thinking. It is logical, sequential and orderly. *Primary process*, which operates at an unconscious level, is more primitive in nature than secondary process. In primary process, there is no distinction between past, present, and future. Different feelings and experiences can be condensed together into one image or symbol, feelings can be expressed metaphorically, and the identities of different people can be merged. The "language" of primary process does not operate in accordance with the rational, sequential rules of secondary process or consciousness. Primary process can be seen operating in dreams and fantasy.

Over time Freud came to think of the unconscious not only in terms of traumatic memories that had been split off but also in terms of instinctual impulses and associated wishes that are not allowed into awareness because we have learned that they are unacceptable through cultural conditioning. These instincts and associated wishes are often related to the areas of sexuality and aggression. For example, a woman has sexual feelings toward her sister's husband but disavows them or pushes them out of awareness because she experiences them as too threatening. A man has angry feelings toward his boss but pushes them out of awareness because they are too threatening. Freud referred to the process through which unacceptable wishes are kept out of awareness as *repression*.

This perspective ultimately became formalized and elaborated further by Freud with his distinction between the id, the ego, and the superego. It is important to point out, however, that although this conceptualization had an important influence on the development of subsequent psychoanalytic theory, many contemporary psychoanalysts no longer find it to be particularly useful. Charles Brenner, one of the major architects of mainstream American ego psychology in the 1950s, explicitly rejected the usefulness of this model of the mind as early as the mid-1990s (Brenner, 1994) in favor of a model that simply sees intrapsychic conflict as ubiquitous.

Many contemporary interpersonal and relational psychoanalysts find it more useful to think of the mind as consisting of multiple self-states that may to varying degrees be in conflict with one another and that emerge in different relational contexts (e.g., Bromberg, 1998, 2006; Davies, 1996; Harris, 2008; Mitchell, 1993; Pizer, 1998). In this perspective, there is no central executive control in the form of the ego. Consciousness is a function of a coalition of different self-states. It is thus an emergent product of a self-organizing system that is influenced in an ongoing fashion by current interpersonal context. From a developmental perspective, experience taking place in the context of interpersonal transactions that are intensely anxiety provoking or traumatic can be kept out of awareness. But there is no hypothetical psychic agency keeping it out of awareness. Instead, there is a failure to attend to the experience and construct a narrative about it (Stern, 1997, 2010). It is thus this failure of attention and construction that leads to the splitting off or dissociation of aspects of experience. And just as the interpersonal context leads to the dissociation of experience in the first place, we need others to help us attend to and construct a narrative about it. As Donnel Stern (2010) put it in his most recent book, the therapist thus serves as an essential "partner in thought" for the client.

Whether the unconscious is conceptualized in traditional Freudian terms, or in terms of aspects of experience that are not symbolized (or self-states that are dissociated), the concept of the unconscious is central to psychoanalytic thinking. For most psychoanalysts, one of Freud's most important insights is that "we are not masters of our own house." We are all motivated by forces outside of our awareness.

Fantasy

Psychoanalytic theory holds that people's fantasies play an important role in their psychic functioning and the way in which they relate to external experience, especially their relationships with other people. These fantasies vary in the extent to which they are part of conscious awareness—ranging from daydreams and fleeting fantasies on the edge of awareness to deeply unconscious fantasies that are defended against. In Freud's early thinking, these fantasies were linked to instinctually derived wishes and served the function of a type of imaginary wish fulfillment. In this view of fantasies, they are typically linked to sexuality or aggression. Over time Freud and other analysts developed a more elaborate view of the nature of fantasy that sees fantasies as serving a number of psychic functions, including the need for the regulation of self-esteem, the need for a feeling of safety, the need for regulating affect, and the need to master trauma. Because fantasies are viewed as motivating our behavior and shaping our experience, yet for the most part operate outside of focal awareness, exploring and interpreting clients' fantasies is viewed as an important part of the psychoanalytic process.

REFERENCES

Aron, L. (1999). Clinical choices and the relational matrix. *Psychoanalytic Dialogues*, 9, 1–29. doi:10.1080/10481889909539301

Bion, W. R. (1970). *Attention and interpretation*. London, England: Routledge.

Brenner, C. (1994). The mind as conflict and compromise formation. *Journal of Clinical Psychoanalysis*, 3, 473–488.

Bromberg, P. M. (1998). *Standing in the spaces: Essays on clinical process, trauma and dissociation*. Hillsdale, NJ: Analytic Press.

Bromberg, P. M. (2006). *Awakening the dreamer: Clinical journeys*. Hillsdale, NJ: Analytic Press.

Corbett, K. (2009). *Boyhoods: Rethinking masculinities*. New Haven, CT: Yale University Press.

Cushman, P. (1995). *Constructing the self, constructing America: A cultural history of psychotherapy*. Reading, MA: Addison-Wesley.

Cushman, P., & Gilford, P. (2000). Will managed care change our way of being? *American Psychologist*, 55, 985–996. doi:10.1037/0003-066X.55.9.985

Davies, J. M. (1996). Linking the "pre-analytic" with the postclassical: Integration, dissociation, and the multiplicity of unconscious process. *Contemporary Psychoanalysis*, 32, 553–576.

Dimen, M. (2010). Reflections on cure, or "I/thou/it." *Psychoanalytic Dialogues*, 20, 254–268. doi:10.1080/10481885.2010.481612

Dreyfus, H. E., & Dreyfus, S. E. (1986). *Mind over machine: The power of human intuition and expertise in the era of the computer.* New York, NY: Free Press.

Guignon, C. (2004). *On being authentic.* London, England: Routledge.

Harris, A. (2008). *Gender as soft assembly.* Hillsdale, NJ: Analytic Press.

Hoffman, I. Z. (1998). *Ritual and spontaneity in the psychoanalytic process: A dialectical-constructivist view.* Hillsdale, NJ: Analytic Press.

Hoffman, I. Z. (2009). Doublethinking our way to "scientific" legitimacy: The desiccation of human experience. *Journal of the American Psychoanalytic Association, 57,* 1043–1069. doi:10.1177/0003065109343925

McWilliams, N. (2004). *Psychoanalytic psychotherapy: A practitioner's guide.* New York, NY: Guilford Press.

Mitchell, S. A. (1993). *Hope and dread in psychoanalysis.* New York, NY: Basic Books.

Pizer, S. A. (1998). *Building bridges: The negotiation paradox in psychoanalysis.* Hillsdale, NJ: Analytic Press.

Renik, O. (1993). Analytic interaction: Conceptualizing technique in light of the analyst's irreducible subjectivity. *Psychoanalytic Quarterly, 62,* 553–571.

Renik, O. (2006). *Practical psychoanalysis for therapists and patients.* New York, NY: Other Press.

Ringstrom, P. A. (2007). Scenes that write themselves: Improvisational moments in relational psychoanalysis. *Psychoanalytic Dialogues, 17,* 69–99. doi:10.1080/10481880701301303

Safran, J. D. (2003). The relational turn, the therapeutic alliance and psychotherapy research: Strange bedfellows or postmodern marriage? *Contemporary Psychoanalysis, 39,* 449–475.

Safran, J. D., & Muran, J. C. (2000). *Negotiating the therapeutic alliance: A relational treatment guide.* New York, NY: Guilford Press.

Schön, D. A. (1983). *The reflective practitioner: How professionals think in action.* New York, NY: Basic Books.

Stern, D. B. (1997). *Unformulated experience: From dissociation to imagination in psychoanalysis.* Hillsdale, NJ: Analytic Press.

Stern, D. B. (2010). *Partners in thought: Working with unformulated experience, dissociation, and enactment.* New York, NY: Routledge.

Stern, D. N., Sander, L. W., Nahum, J. P., Harrison, A. M., Lyons-Ruth, K., Morgan, A. C., . . . Tronick, E. Z. (1998). Non-interpretive mechanisms in psychoanalytic therapy: The "something more" than interpretation. *International Journal of Psychoanalysis, 79,* 903–921.

Taylor, C. (1992). *The ethics of authenticity.* Cambridge, MA: Harvard University Press.

Thompson, M. G. (2004). *The ethic of honesty: The fundamental rule of psychoanalysis.* New York, NY: Rodopi.

Winnicott, D. W. (1958). *Through paediatrics to psycho-analysis: Collected papers.* New York, NY: Basic Books.

30

PSYCHOANALYTIC THERAPY PROCESS

JEREMY D. SAFRAN

INTERPRETATION OF TRANSFERENCE
AND COUNTERTRANSFERENCE

One of the most important forms of interpretation is referred to as a *transference interpretation*. This is an interpretation that focuses on the here and now of the therapeutic relationship between the client and the therapist. The reason that transference interpretations are considered to be particularly important is that they have the advantage of drawing the client's attention to something that is happening in the moment. A transference interpretation thus has an immediate and experiential quality to it. By drawing the client's attention to the way in which their perceptions and actions are shaping their

Excerpted from *Psychoanalysis and Psychoanalytic Therapies* (2012), from Chapter 4, "The Therapy Process," pp. 85–91. Copyright 2012 by the American Psychological Association. Used with permission of the author.

http://dx.doi.org/10.1037/14295-030
Psychotherapy Theories and Techniques: A Reader, G. R. VandenBos, E. Meidenbauer, and J. Frank-McNeil (Editors)
Copyright © 2014 by the American Psychological Association. All rights reserved.

experience of things in the here and now, therapists provides them with an opportunity to actually observe themselves in the process of shaping their experience of the situation. They thus begin to experience themselves as agents in the construction of reality. Transference interpretations can focus exclusively on the therapeutic relationship or explore similarities between what is taking place in the therapeutic relationship and other relationships in the client's life (both present and past). For example, Doris, a divorced woman in her mid-30s, consistently complains about romantic partners being emotionally unavailable and has just been speaking about her supervisor as not being sufficiently supportive. For the last few sessions (including this one), I have had the sense that Doris is feeling frustrated with me, so I say, "I wonder if there is any similarity between your experience with your supervisor and the way in which you are experiencing our relationship in this moment?" Interpretations that do not involve a focus on the here and now of the therapeutic relationship can run the risk of leading to an intellectualized understanding. It is one thing to conceptually or intellectually understand one's own role in a self-defeating pattern and another to have an experientially grounded, emotionally immediate understanding.

For many contemporary psychoanalytic therapists, transference interpretations have become inseparable from the process of the exploration of the transference/countertransference matrix. Consistent with an emphasis on a two-person psychology, transference is not conceptualized as a distorted perception arising in a vacuum but as one element in an ongoing transference/countertransference enactment. In practice, then, transference interpretations often involve an ongoing collaborative exploration of who is contributing what to the relationship. In my own writing, I have used the term *metacommunication* to designate this process of collaborative exploration (e.g., Safran & Muran, 2000). Metacommunication consists of an attempt to step outside of the relational cycle that is currently being enacted by treating it as the focus of collaborative exploration, a process of communicating or commenting on the relational transaction or implicit communication that is taking place. It is an attempt to bring ongoing awareness to bear on the interaction as it unfolds. There are many different forms of metacommunication. A therapist can offer a tentative observation about what is taking place between him or her and the client (e.g., "It seems to me that we're both being cautious with each other right now . . . does that fit with your experience?"). A therapist can convey a subjective impression of something the client is doing (e.g., "My impression is that you're pulling away from me right now"). Or the therapist can disclose some aspect of his or her own experience as a point of departure for exploring something that might be taking place in the therapeutic relationship (e.g., "I'm aware of feeling powerless to say anything that you might feel is useful right now"). Any disclosure of this type must be considered the very first step in an ongoing process of exploring the transference/countertransference cycle. The therapist does not begin by assuming that his or her feelings are in any way caused or evoked by the client, but rather that they may offer clues as to something that is unconsciously being enacted in the relationship.

It is also important to bear in mind that clients can experience straightforward traditional interpretations of the transference as a criticism or as a form of one-upmanship, especially in situations in which the therapeutic alliance is strained. In other words, they can be experienced by clients as the therapist's attempt to take himself or herself out of the equation by insinuating something to the effect of "The tension we're having in our relationship right now is your fault and I've got nothing to do with it." This is particularly likely to occur in situations in which the therapist is caught in an enactment and is unconsciously using the interpretation to deny any responsibility for what is going on or is defensively blaming the client for a mutually constructed pattern in the therapeutic relationship.

NONTRANSFERENCE INTERPRETATIONS

Although I have been emphasizing the value of transference interpretations because of their emotional immediacy, it is important not to minimize the potential value of interpretations that don't make reference to the therapeutic relationship. In some situations, making a well-timed, well-worded interpretation about an event taking place in the person's relationships outside of the therapy situation can be particularly useful. This is especially true if the client is confused about what is taking place in the situation and is receptive to considering the possibility that a specific unconscious conflict is playing a role. For the interpretation to be helpful, however, the context has to be such that the client really does experience the interpretation as a new and emotionally meaningful way of looking at the situation, rather than just as an intellectualized and arid attempt to understand what is going on. It is difficult to specify exactly what type of context facilitates this sense of newness other than to say that the client needs to be experiencing a genuine sense of confusion and a search for understanding, and the interpretation must be phrased in such a way that it facilitates further exploration rather than shutting down. For example, Peter, a successful professional in his 40s, began treatment after his wife discovered that he was having an affair with a female coworker and threatened to leave him. He immediately ended the affair and sought therapy in the hope of understanding what had led him to have an affair in the first place. This was the only time he had ever had an affair, and he experienced it as completely out of character for himself and a form of compulsion or addiction that he had no control over. After spending several sessions getting to know him, I began to get a sense of a man with considerable disowned anger who was feeling devalued by and emotionally isolated from his wife. I began to interpret his affair as an attempt on his part to reaffirm his sense of potency and lovability and as an expression of disowned anger at his wife. He experienced this interpretation, combined with the process of beginning to develop greater ownership of his needs for validation and for emotional intimacy and of his anger, as extremely helpful.

Another reason that extratransference interpretations can be valuable is that clients are coming to treatment to deal with problems in their everyday lives, not with problems in their relationships with their therapists. To the extent that the therapist focuses exclusively on transference interpretations, the client may have difficulty finding relevance to his or her everyday life. Of course in practice, this potential problem is often reduced by making transference interpretations that involve establishing a link between what is taking place in the therapeutic relationship and what is taking place in the client's everyday relationships. Although this type of interpretation can be extremely helpful, as previously indicated the potential danger is that the client will experience this linking of the two relationships as an attempt to blame him or her for what is going on in the therapeutic relationship by saying, in essence, "You're doing the same thing with me that you do with everyone else in your life." The therapist thereby refuses to accept responsibility for his or her own contribution to what is taking place in the therapeutic relationship. This can be especially likely to happen if the alliance is tenuous or there is a therapeutic impasse. In such situations, it can be useful to carefully explore what is taking place in the therapeutic relationship on its own terms, with a genuine openness to understanding how each partner is contributing to what is taking place, rather than to rush to establish links with relationships in the client's everyday life.

GENETIC TRANSFERENCE INTERPRETATIONS AND HISTORICAL RECONSTRUCTION

A third major type of interpretation is referred to as a *genetic transference interpretation*. A genetic transference interpretation involves conveying a hypothesis about the role that one's developmental experiences have played in shaping one's current conflicts. For example, the therapist may interpret the client's tendency to be overprotective of other people, thereby denying his or her own needs, as stemming from the client's history of protecting a depressed and fragile mother.

Because psychoanalysis originated with the exploration of the client's past, there has been a tendency at different points in psychoanalytic thinking to overestimate the importance of making genetic transference interpretations. The problem with an excessive emphasis on interpretations of this type is that it can lead to an intellectualized understanding of the potential influence of the past on the present without resulting in a real change. Notwithstanding this potential problem, a good genetic transference interpretation can play a valuable role in helping the client to begin to replace a sense of confusion and perplexity with some sense of meaning and understanding. It can also help to reduce the client's tendency to excessive self-blame by helping him or her to see that current problems are a meaningful and understandable result of an attempt to cope with a difficult or traumatic childhood situation. For example, Howard, a male client in his mid-20s, experienced a lack of direction in his life, a chronic low-level depression, and a sense of inadequacy. His father was an extremely successful business executive whom my client described as charismatic and always the center of attention. When Howard was 8 years old, his father and mother divorced. Although Howard maintained a relationship with his father, he felt he was never able to obtain his approval. Over time, it emerged that whenever Howard would tell his father about something he had accomplished or was excited about, he had the impression that his father belittled him. In one session, I suggested to Howard that perhaps his father felt the need to "put him down" because of his own need to be the center of attention and an associated feeling of being threatened by any success his son might have. Howard found this interpretation extremely helpful, and it opened the door for exploring important associated feelings.

Of course, too much emphasis on tracing the historical roots of one's current self-defeating patterns can lead to a type of preoccupation with the past and a tendency to blame others rather than to develop a sense of agency that can promote change. This is, however, by no means inevitable, and to the extent that it does take place it can and should be explored in the same way that any defense is explored.

THE USE OF DREAMS

Dream interpretation was once considered central to psychoanalytic practice. Freud referred to dreams as the "royal road to the unconscious," and some of his most important early breakthroughs in psychoanalytic theory and practice emerged out of the interpretation of his own dreams and the dreams of clients. Freud considered dreams to be a form of wish fulfillment and had a well-worked-out methodology for working with dreams. Since Freud's time, a variety of different psychoanalytic models have been developed for conceptualizing the meaning of dreams and for working with them. One particularly useful approach to dream interpretation was developed by Fairbairn, who conceptualized all figures in a dream to represent different aspects of the self. For example, I once had a female client who was terrified to sleep at home alone when her husband was away. At such times it was common for her to have dreams in which she was being chased by an axe murderer. When I suggested that she experiment or play around with the possibility of seeing herself in the role of the axe murderer, she was able to contact some of the aggressive feelings associated with being in the role and ultimately to contact disowned feelings of anger toward her husband for abandoning her during his frequent business trips.

Although a variety of different psychoanalytic approaches to the interpretation of dreams have developed over time, I think it is fair to say that dream interpretation no longer plays the central role in North American psychoanalytic theory and practice that it once did. To some extent the exploration of transference/countertransference enactments has become more central. Nevertheless, most psychoanalysts and psychoanalytic therapists including myself do find it particularly useful to work with dreams under certain circumstances. One situation in which dreams can be particularly useful is when clients have difficulty contacting and expressing their inner life during treatment. In this type of situation, suggesting to clients that they begin to pay attention to and write down their dreams is a way of providing material for the treatment that emerges spontaneously while the client is asleep and is not subject to the same type of defensive processes that otherwise can drastically constrain the range of experiences. Of course, the client's recording of the dream and subsequent recounting of it in the session involves a process of reconstruction, but the fashion in which it is reconstructed can be of interest in and of itself. Another situation in which working with dreams can be particularly interesting is one in which the client reports a particular vivid dream or one with striking or startling imagery and associated affect.

REFERENCE

Safran, J. D., & Muran, J. C. (2000). *Negotiating the therapeutic alliance: A relational treatment guide*. New York, NY: Guilford Press.

APPENDIX 30.1: PSYCHOANALYTIC THERAPY TECHNIQUES

Technique	Video title	Video identifying number	Time at which technique occurs
Empathy	Psychoanalytic Therapy With a Pattern of Broken Relationships (Session 1 of 6)	777700256-001	22:47–24:29
Metacommunication	Psychoanalytic Therapy With a Pattern of Broken Relationships (Session 2 of 6)	777700260-001	28:25–30:25
Exploration of defenses	Psychoanalytic Therapy With a Pattern of Broken Relationships (Session 2 of 6)	777700260-001	43:17–44:35
Interpretation	A Psychodynamic Approach to Spirituality in Psychotherapy (Client 1)	777700122-001	11:23–12:40
Transference interpretation	Psychoanalytic Therapy With a Pattern of Broken Relationships (Session 4 of 6)	777700265-001	26:41–35:36
Dream interpretation	Brief Dynamic Therapy With a Young Woman, Messer	777700043-001	11:21–14:18

31

RATIONAL EMOTIVE
BEHAVIOR THERAPY

ALBERT ELLIS AND DEBBIE JOFFE ELLIS

THE ABC (OR ABCDE) THEORY

The ABC (or ABCDE) theory of rational emotive behavior therapy (REBT) clarifies the connection between an *activating event* and its *consequences* by identifying the *beliefs* involved, and it provides the means for replacing irrational beliefs with rational ones through *disputation* and the emergence of *effective* new philosophies. It simplifies the process of illuminating how we self-disturb and shows the way to *un*-self-disturb. Clients benefit when their therapists teach them the procedure by doing it with them, and individuals benefit from doing it on their own, particularly through writing, in the early days of their learning the REBT technique.

Excerpted from *Rational Emotive Behavior Therapy* (2011), from Chapter 3, "Theory," pp. 23–32. Copyright 2011 by the American Psychological Association. Used with permission of the authors.

http://dx.doi.org/10.1037/14295-031
Psychotherapy Theories and Techniques: A Reader, G. R. VandenBos, E. Meidenbauer, and J. Frank-McNeil (Editors)
Copyright © 2014 by the American Psychological Association. All rights reserved.

A stands for *activating events* or *adversities*. We identify clearly what happened.

C stands for *consequences*. They may be both emotional and behavioral.

Although the Bs precede the Cs, when doing the procedure, it is helpful to identify the Cs first and to notice which of the emotional ones are "unhealthy" negative emotions, such as anxiety, depression, rage, shame, guilt, jealousy, and hurt. REBT does not seek to change "healthy" negative emotions, such as annoyance and frustration, regret, and disappointment, because these are often appropriate responses to difficult circumstances and do not debilitate a person as the unhealthy ones can frequently do.

B stands for *beliefs* or *belief system*. People's belief systems include functional or rational beliefs (RBs) and dysfunctional or irrational beliefs (IBs) and includes them strongly (emotionally) and behaviorally (activity-wise). Their RBs, as noted earlier, tend to be preferences and wishes (e.g., "I *want* to perform well and be approved of by significant others"), and IBs tend to include absolutistic musts, shoulds, and demands (e.g., "I *should/must/ought to/ have to* perform well and be approved by significant others"). It is important to remember that when people want to change their IBs (which lead to self-defeating consequences) to RBs (which lead to self-helping consequences), they had better work on their believing-emoting-behaving, and not merely on their believing. This means, more specifically, that they had better vigorously and forcefully (that is, emotively) change their dysfunctional Bs and, at the same time, forcefully and persistently feel and act against them. Why? Because, as already noted, their believing invariably includes their emoting and their behaving and is integrally related to these.

D stands for *disputing*. After distinguishing rational from irrational beliefs, one keeps one's preferences and forms effective and healthy new philosophies. People achieve this by changing their demands through arguing with and vigorously disputing them. There are three main forms of disputing and rational questioning:

1. Realistic disputing. In this form of disputing, the IBs are challenged by investigating the truth or factual reality behind them. Typical questions that are asked include: Why *must* I perform well? Where is the evidence that I *must* be approved by significant others? Where is it written? Is it really awful, terrible, and as bad as it could be? Can I really not stand it?

2. Logical disputing. In this form of disputing, the logic underlying the IBs is investigated. Typical questions include: Are my beliefs logical? Do they follow from my preferences? Does it follow that if I perform badly and lose approval of others then that makes me an inadequate person?

3. Pragmatic disputing. In this form of disputing, one investigates the pragmatic outcome of holding the IBs. Typical questions include: Will holding this belief help me or hurt me? What results will I get if I believe that I absolutely *must* perform well and always be approved of by significant others? Do I want these results?

When people persistently dispute their IBs, and retain their RBs, the outcome is E, which stands for *effective new philosophies*. These are healthy, functional, and realistic positions from which to perceive oneself, others, and one's world. Examples of effective new philosophies are the following: "No matter how badly I acted, I am not a bad person—just a person who acted badly that time" and "Although some circumstances in my life are difficult and unfortunate at present, that does not mean that the world is all bad or that my whole life is rotten. Nor will these circumstances last forever." At this point, people can create additional and appropriate coping statements.

To enjoy and maintain healthy preferences and to continue to surrender dysfunctional demands, ongoing application of REBT techniques is required. This takes us to the next key concept of REBT.

WORK AND PRACTICE

Work and practice lead to the most lasting of changes and not only to feeling better but also to *getting* better. In the following pages are several thinking, feeling, and action REBT techniques, which are also described in many other REBT writings. REBT recommends trying the ones that seem most appropriate for the person and the disturbances he or she wishes to be free of. It recommends giving each technique a solid trial. If one doesn't work, it recommends using another, and another, and still another! Even when one works, it pushes for trying some of the others as well. REBT recommends using each method many times. Assess and reassess progress (or lack of it). Keep on doing, doing, doing the methods earnestly, forcefully, and vigorously.

THE MULTIMODAL NATURE OF REBT

REBT is multimodal—it has created intellectual, affective, and action techniques and has adapted some methods from other therapies, which have been comfortably integrated with the REBT ones.

REBT was pioneering in that it integrated emotive and behavior with thinking methods. Cognitive, emotive, and behavioral methods have been used for centuries to help people with disturbances by philosophers, religious and spiritual leaders, and therapists. Many of these techniques were adopted and adapted by therapists such as Pierre Janet (1898), Paul Dubois (1907), and Alfred Adler (1929). When, in the 1950s, these methods were falling into disuse, George Kelly (1955) and I (AE) independently revived them, and in the 1960s and 1970s, Aaron Beck (1976), Donald Meichenbaum (1977), William Glasser (1965), David Barlow (1988), and others repeated this revival in using many kinds of cognitive behavior therapy.

Following are some of the main REBT cognitive, emotive, and behavioral techniques.

Cognitive Techniques

ABC (or ABCDE) Method for Emotional and Behavioral Disturbance

This method was described earlier in this chapter.

Possible Secondary Symptoms

Possible secondary symptoms include anxiety *about* anxiety, depression *about* depression, and so forth. Acknowledge any self-castigation and accept it as failing to be helpful in changing the primary disturbance, but be aware that does not make *you* a failure. Then go back to using the ABC approach to remedy the secondary symptoms.

Assessing the Cost–Benefit Ratio

This relates to one's unconditional acceptance of self, others, and life on an ongoing basis—of one's behaviors and of one's activities in life. Make lists of the plusses and minuses in each case and assess where changes may be beneficial.

Distraction Methods

These include activities such as meditation, yoga, other relaxation techniques, and exercising, which are often palliative and may only work for a while. Although not elegant solutions, they can be helpful in allowing you to step back, refresh, and possibly assess the issues of disturbance more objectively and helpfully.

Modeling

Albert Bandura (1997) and other psychologists have used modeling to help children and adults to acquire learning skills, and REBT and cognitive behavioral therapists have often taught their clients how to use it successfully

(J. S. Beck, 1995; Ellis, 2001a, 2001b, 2003a, 2003b, 2005). Some ways of using this technique are as follows:

- Find people you know who exhibit the attitudes, emotional well-being, and behaviors you aspire to develop and ask them how they do so. Use their relevant thoughts, feelings, and actions to model yours.
- Investigate people you do not know—perhaps famous ones, whether living or dead—and use them as models. Some of our clients felt inspired by hearing the famous story of Epictetus, a Roman slave who warned his master not to tighten the ball and chain on his leg because he might break Epictetus' leg. The master ignored him, tightened the chain, and actually broke the leg. Whereupon, *without feeling hurt and angry*, Epictetus calmly said, "See, I was right. You broke my leg." His master was so impressed with Epictetus' *self-acceptance and lack of anger* that he freed him to become the leading Stoic philosopher of Rome. I incorporated aspects of his philosophy into REBT theory and particularly like his wise statement, written in the first century AD in *The Enchiridion:* "Men are not disturbed by things, but by the views which they take of them" (Ellis, 1962, p. 54). Some of our clients used Epictetus as a model of accepting and unangry demeanor and helped themselves by choosing to act this way more of the time. The actor Christopher Reeve was rendered paralyzed in a horse-riding accident. We read newspaper articles that described how he used his remaining years of life to campaign for stem cell research and other causes; he made an impact and was productive despite his severe disabilities (Christopher and Dana Reeve Foundation, 2010). Many consider him a model of acceptance of adversity and of constructive action despite limitations. Many other models of advantageous behaviors and attitudes can be found.

Biblio–Audio–Video Therapies

Books and recorded sources of information on REBT, on some of the other cognitive behavioral therapies, and on various life-enhancing philosophies—current and past—may be helpful for repetitively pursuing the rational practices that are appropriate and reinforcing.

Talking About REBT With Others

Helping others by using REBT principles with them reinforces its principles. Talking people out of their rigid irrationalities helps people talk themselves out of their own irrationalities. This is particularly applicable in a group therapy setting.

Problem Solving

REBT encourages practical problem solving. This includes looking at the adversity one faces and figuring out action plans worth trying.

Philosophic Discussion

REBT may also include considerable philosophic discussion with clients and students.

Emotive–Evocative Techniques

Rational Emotive Imagery

This can be done in a brief period of time each day and is an effective exercise for quickly changing unhealthy negative emotions to healthy ones. It involves cognizing, as using imagery does. In addition to doing it with clients, and teaching them to do it on their own, we regularly use it with volunteers from audiences at workshops, and I (AE) particularly have been using it in my famous Friday Night Workshops for more than 40 years. Both volunteers and audience observers have consistently reported back, as have clients, that it helped them get in touch with, and change, strong dysfunctional feelings. The approach was created by Maxie Maultsby Jr. in 1971 after he studied with me in 1968. A number of therapists have advocated it (Lazarus, 1997).

Rational emotive imagery helps people vividly experience one of the fundamental concepts of REBT: That when people are faced with adversity, negative emotions are almost always healthy and appropriate when they consist of feelings of sorrow, disappointment, frustration, annoyance, and displeasure. It would actually be aberrant for a person to feel happy or neutral when these events occurred. Having certain negative emotions is fundamental in helping people to deal with unpleasant reality and motivate themselves to try to change it. The problem is that practically the whole human race can easily transmute the healthy negative feelings of disappointment and regret into disturbed feelings such as anxiety, depression, rage, and self-pity. These are legitimate emotions in the sense that all emotions are legitimate; however, they usually sabotage rather than help people. Therefore, it is preferable that in using rational emotive imagery, one thinks of something that he or she sees as very unpleasant and strongly feels the kinds of unhealthy, negative feelings that one would frequently experience in reaction to it. The person gets in touch with these feelings, feels them strongly, and then works on changing them to healthy negative feelings by changing their thinking about the same unfortunate situation. When individuals have changed their feelings to healthy (rather than unhealthy) negative ones, they are then to keep practicing, preferably at least once a day, for the next 30 days, until they have trained themselves to experience, automatically or unconsciously, the *healthy* negative feeling whenever they imagine this adversity or when it actually happens. They usually can manage to bring on their healthy negative feelings within 2 or 3 minutes and within a few weeks are usually able to automatically bring them on. Many people have achieved excellent results in changing dysfunctional anxiety, guilt, depression, and anger throughout our years of practice.

Shame-Attacking Exercises

This popular emotive–evocative, as well as behavioral, exercise is famous in REBT. It recognizes that shame is suffered by many who wrongly and demandingly tell themselves that they *should* never act in foolish ways or appear foolish, wrong, or stupid to others. When they demand that they "should not" or "must not" have erred, then they feel ashamed, embarrassed, humiliated, or depressed (or any combination of the above). Shame is created from judging one's act *and* oneself—and from the false interpretation that one's deed represents oneself and that when a deed is rotten and worthless, so is the person. This is false. The shame-attacking exercise does not discourage people from assessing the success or failure of what they do, but does encourage the removal of self-damning. It consists of doing something one considers shameful and would normally avoid doing—something one would severely put oneself down for doing. An example is wearing "inappropriate" clothing to a formal occasion, and while doing this "shameful" act, one works on one's thoughts and emotions so that one doesn't feel embarrassed—one is intentionally doing a foolish thing while focusing on not putting oneself down while doing it. One of the many suggestions I (AE) have shared over the years is to yell out the stops in the subway or on a bus while remaining on the vehicle as it moves on from each of these stops. People may stare—an excellent opportunity to practice unconditional self-acceptance and cessation of self-damning!

Strongly Using Coping Statements

Since the early years of REBT, I have recommended that clients and members of the public identify and dispute strongly their irrational beliefs and devise instead rational coping statements. By the 1970s, cognitive behavioral therapists such as Aaron Beck (1976), Donald Meichenbaum (1977), Maxie Maultsby Jr. (1971), and David Burns (1980) were also encouraging their clients to do so. We have already described how successful disputing leads to healthy coping statements. What makes this emotive is the vigor and strength we use while repeating them over and over to ourselves, so that with time, we genuinely are convinced of the truth and benefit of them. So one *forcefully* repeats them, choosing relevant coping statements. Some general ones that many find helpful:

- I *can* stand what I don't like. I just don't like it.
- Even if I fail at something, *I* am never, never, never a failure.
- Nothing is *awful*, just inconvenient.

Role Playing

In therapy, workshops, and group therapy, role playing can be helpful for evoking disturbing emotions to dispute the contributing beliefs to feel undisturbed. Among friends, relatives, or group therapy members with whom one role-plays, situations considered difficult are enacted. If the situation, for example, is a risky job interview, the role player gives the fearful person a hard time in the interview, and the person wanting to overcome the fear does his or her best to succeed at it. When others are present and observing the role play, they are then invited to critique the interview. Then the role play is tried again. If the person feels anxious during this next role play, he or she and the "interviewer" (as well as any others present) look for the "shoulds, oughts, and musts" that are creating the anxiety and insecurity. These demands are then vigorously disputed. The goal is to help the person achieve healthful concern but not unhealthy anxiety. Also helpful is reverse role playing in which another voices the anxiety-creating beliefs and the person who wants to get rid of them persists in disputing and talking the other out of them.

Make Strong Disputing Tapes

In this exercise, a person tape-records some of his or her IBs, such as, "I must always succeed and be approved of by others." The individual then disputes the IBs on the same tape, realistically, logically, and pragmatically, making the disputing as forceful and emotive as possible. The disputing tape can then be listened to with critical friends, who give constructive feedback and note how forceful it is. It is repeated until it feels solidly convincing.

Use of Humor

People are encouraged to keep things in healthy perspective by not taking themselves, others, and the actions of oneself and by others too seriously.

I (AE) have written hundreds of rational humorous songs, which are helpful in this regard.

Behavioral Techniques

Reading the previous two sections on cognitive and emotive techniques, you may have noticed that there is some overlap of cognitive, emotive, and behavioral—and in the following techniques, which are largely behavioral, you will see overlap again. We remind you of a pioneering REBT theme from 1955 that continues to the present—and will continue: Human thinking, feeling, and behaving are integrated and include important aspects of each other.

REFERENCES

Adler, A. (1929). *The science of living.* New York, NY: Greenberg.

Bandura, A. (1997). *Self-efficacy: The exercise of control.* New York, NY: Freeman.

Barlow, D. H. (1988). *Anxiety and its disorders: The nature and treatment of anxiety and panic.* New York, NY: Guilford Press.

Beck, A. T. (1976). *Cognitive therapy and the emotional disorders.* New York, NY: International Universities Press.

Beck, J. S. (1995). *Cognitive therapy: Basics and beyond.* New York, NY: Guilford Press.

Burns, D. D. (1980). *Feeling good: The new mood therapy.* New York, NY: Morrow.

Christopher and Dana Reeve Foundation. (2010). *Christopher Reeve: Biography.* Retrieved from http://www.christopherreeve.org/site/c.ddJFKRNoFiG/b.4431483/

Dubois, P. (1907). *The psychic treatment of nervous disorders.* New York, NY: Funk and Wagnalls.

Ellis, A. (1962). *Reason and emotion in psychotherapy.* Secaucus, NJ: Citadel.

Ellis, A. (2001a). *Feeling better, getting better, staying better: Profound self-help therapy for your emotions.* Atascadero, CA: Impact.

Ellis, A. (2001b). *Overcoming destructive beliefs, feelings, and behaviors: New directions for rational emotive behavior therapy.* Amherst, NY: Prometheus Books.

Ellis, A. (2003a). *Anger: How to live with and without it* (Rev. ed.). New York, NY: Citadel Press.

Ellis, A. (2003b). *Sex without guilt in the twenty-first century.* Teaneck, NJ: Barricade Books.

Ellis, A. (2005). *The myth of self-esteem: How rational emotive behavior therapy can change your life forever.* Amherst, NY: Prometheus Books.

Ellis, A. (2010). *All out! An autobiography*. Amherst, NY: Prometheus Books.

Glasser, W. (1965). *Reality therapy: A new approach to psychiatry*. New York, NY: Harper.

Janet, P. (1898). *Névroses et idées fixes* [Neuroses and fixed ideas]. Paris, France: Alcan.

Kelly, G. (1955). *The psychology of personal constructs*. New York, NY: Norton.

Lazarus, A. A. (1997). *Brief but comprehensive therapy: The multimodal way*. New York, NY: Springer.

Maultsby, M. C., Jr. (1971). Rational emotive imagery. *Rational Living, 6*, 24–27.

Meichenbaum, D. (1977). *Cognitive-behavior modification: An integrative approach*. New York, NY: Plenum Press.

32

RATIONAL EMOTIVE BEHAVIOR THERAPY PROCESS

ALBERT ELLIS AND DEBBIE JOFFE ELLIS

BRIEF AND LONG-TERM STRATEGIES AND TECHNIQUES

Brief Therapy

When I (AE) originated rational emotive behavior therapy (REBT), it was designed as a therapy that could be effective and brief for many clients. After my experience working as a psychoanalyst from 1947 to 1953, during which I found that most forms of psychoanalysis were too drawn-out, long-winded, and inefficient, I (with my "gene for efficiency") started using REBT, both briefly and in more prolonged treatment. Clients who are severely disturbed, for biological as well as environmental reasons, usually benefit more from longer term and more intensive treatment, but many individuals who

Excerpted from *Rational Emotive Behavior Therapy* (2011), from Chapter 4, "The Therapy Process," pp. 47–54. Copyright 2011 by the American Psychological Association. Used with permission of the authors.

http://dx.doi.org/10.1037/14295-032
*i*McNeil (Editors)
Copyright © 2014 by the American Psychological Association. All rights reserved.

self-disturb or self-neuroticize can be significantly helped in five to 12 sessions, and in some cases even fewer sessions.

When clients understand the REBT principles of how they disturb themselves, of how they can undisturb themselves and of how they can choose to maintain healthy thinking, feeling, and behaving, they are well on the way to stability and greater fulfillment. They have learned that they can maintain their gains by continuing to practice REBT principles—and they make the effort to do so. Effective therapy with lasting results is a lifelong process, initiated with a therapist and maintained by self-therapy and ongoing effort (and follow-up and refresher sessions when appropriate).

Thus, in effective REBT brief therapy, the client soon grasps that

- their emotional disturbances are largely created as a result of irrational thinking and the tendency to escalate preferences into absolutistic shoulds, oughts, and musts;
- by actively and vigorously disputing their absolutistic demands— while maintaining their preferences—with thinking, feeling, and acting methods, the demands can be changed to healthy preferences;
- dysfunctional thinking, feeling, and actions can easily return and ongoing effort will be required to prevent that from happening;
- if a relapse occurs, they can unconditionally accept themselves with the relapse, recognizing that it is a human tendency to fall back at times and that all humans are fallible—then they can return to the methods that worked for them before; and
- they had better willingly do "homework" for the rest of their lives.

One of my (AE) famous lines is: "Life has inevitable suffering as well as pleasure. By realistically thinking, feeling, and acting to enjoy what you can, and unangrily and unwhiningly accepting painful aspects that cannot be changed, you open yourself to much joy." When remembering this, clients can experience healthy perspective.

Some of our clients, usually those who are highly motivated and particularly bright, effected healthy transformations in their lives after only one or two sessions. Many were already quite self-aware and had read a great deal of useful literature, and the REBT seemed to succinctly formulate in easy-to-do form some of what they had already been contemplating. A good number of people familiar with Buddhism, and some of them who practiced it, took quickly and easily to the ABCs of REBT. Some of the similarities between Buddhist and REBT principles were described earlier in this book.

And talk about *brief* therapy: In a study by the authors, published in the *Journal of Rational-Emotive and Cognitive Behavior Therapy* (Ellis & Joffe, 2002) and titled "A Study of Volunteer Clients Who Experienced Live Sessions of Rational Emotive Behavior Therapy in Front of a Public Audience," 97 of the 100 respondents found their session helpful. Volunteers agreed to a 30-minute demonstration—quite a brief time indeed. It is hoped that they carried out their homework and that they continue to remember REBT principles and to act on them.

Long-Term Therapy

This section focuses on REBT group therapy because it is an excellent example of the application of REBT therapy that continues on a long-term basis. As already mentioned, clients with greater endogenous disturbances and poor learning skills can benefit more from long-term individual REBT therapy—and from long-term group therapy. Additionally, less disadvantaged clients who have significantly benefited from individual therapy may wisely elect to replace it with long-term REBT group therapy. Some clients choose to do both.

Let's now look at aspects of REBT group therapy. Some clients go directly into group therapy without having had individual sessions; others join group therapy on the recommendation of their therapist while still attending individual sessions or after a period of individual sessions has concluded. Several methods of psychotherapy use group therapy for expediency reasons—because it is more practical and cheaper for the clients and not because it fits in with the theory that ostensibly underlies these methods.

REBT basically uses an elegant and educational rather than a medical or psychodynamic model. Consequently, like most teaching, it is almost inevitable that it be done in group as well as individual sessions. It is usually used in small group sessions, with from eight to 12 clients on a once-a-week basis, but it is done at times with much larger groups, such as a class of 20 or 30 students or a public workshop at which more than 100 people may be present. Its group aspects are also adaptable to audiovisual presentations because it can be taught and practiced with the use of CDs, DVDs, webcasts, live radio and TV presentations, bibliotherapy, programmed instruction, and other forms of mass media presentations. As much or more than any other contemporary form of psychotherapy, therefore, it is truly group oriented, and frequently the REBT practitioner uses group processes as the method of choice rather than because special circumstances practically force him or her to do so.

In small-scale group therapy of eight to 12 clients, the participants are interested in getting to the roots of their emotional disturbances, understanding the difficulties of the other members of the group, and helping themselves and their fellow group members to (a) rid themselves of their current symptoms and function better in their intrapersonal and interpersonal affairs and (b) minimize their basic disturbability, so that for the rest of their lives, they will tend to feel appropriate rather than inappropriate emotions and to reduce (and preferably remove) the tendency to upset themselves needlessly. In REBT groups, the therapeutic goal is partly symptom removal, but, more important, it is for each of the members to achieve a profound philosophic change and (more specifically) to accept (although not necessarily like) reality; to give up all kinds of magical thinking; to stop awfulizing, catastrophizing, and demonizing about life's misfortunes and frustrations; to take full responsibility for their own emotional difficulties; and to stop all forms of self-rating and fully and unconditionally accept oneself and others as being fallible and human.

The main goals of REBT group therapy are the same as those of REBT individual therapy: namely, teaching clients that *they* are responsible for their own emotional upsets or disturbances; that they can change their dysfunctional or debilitating emotions and behavior by changing their irrational beliefs and self-defeating philosophies; and that if they acquire radically new and profoundly held rational belief systems, many may healthfully cope with almost any unfortunate activating events that may arise in their lives and keep themselves, at worst, deeply sorrowful and regretful but not anxious, depressed, or enraged about these activators. Some of the important group-oriented goals and methods that are used in REBT include the following.

Because REBT teaches individuals how to accept the existence of suffering and grim circumstances in life, and how to change what they can through effort instead of by whining and demandingness, all group members are encouraged to reveal and discourage the presenting individual's perfectionism, rigidity, and demands. Leaders educate members to make suggestions and constructively criticize any self-defeating or unhelpful thoughts, behaviors, and emotions that come up, and to learn from them. However, they are taught not to criticize, damn, or feel hopeless about oneself, others, or life itself. Group leaders do their best to model the REBT attitudes and behaviors. All members are also taught to dispute—logically, realistically, pragmatically, and empirically—the disturbance-creating thinking of the other members.

The therapist usually is appropriately active, probing, challenging, confronting, and directive. He or she persistently models rational thinking and appropriate emoting. He or she is not only a trained therapist but also teaches the scientific, or logicoempirical, method to the group members, so that they can apply it effectively to their personal and emotional lives.

Both the therapist and the group consistently give activity-oriented therapy session and homework assignments to group members. Some of these assignments (e.g., speaking up in group itself) may be carried out and monitored during the regular sessions. Other assignments (e.g., making social contacts) are to be carried on outside the group but regularly reported and discussed during group sessions. We have observed that such assignments are more effectively given and followed up when given by a group than by an individual therapist.

REBT includes a number of behavioral methods (as already explained earlier), including assertion training, in vivo risk taking, role playing, and behavior rehearsal, which can partly be done in individual sessions but are more effective in group. Thus, if a member is usually afraid to tell people what he thinks of their behavior, he may be induced to do so with other group members.

The group deliberately encourages observing emotions and behaviors rather than obtaining information through the client's secondhand reports. Angry or anxious individuals, who might feel at home with an individual therapist and hide their feelings in therapy, can often reveal much in group, where they interact with several of their peers.

In REBT, some clients fill out written homework report forms and give them to the therapist to go over. In group sessions, a few homework forms are often read and corrected so that all the members of the group, and not merely the individual handing in the form, may be helped to see specifically what unhealthy negative emotional consequence was experienced (at point C); what activating events occurred to spark it (at point A); what rational and irrational beliefs the individual told himself or herself (at point B) to create the dysfunctional consequences; and what kind of effective disputing could be done (at point D) to minimize or eradicate the irrational beliefs that led to the self-defeating consequences. By hearing about other group members' main problems and how they dealt with them on the homework report, clients are helped to use these reports more efficiently themselves.

Individuals receive valuable feedback from the group as to how they malfunction and what they are probably foolishly telling themselves to create their disturbances. They also learn to view others and to give feedback. More important, they gain practice in talking themselves out of their irrational beliefs and therefore in consciously and unconsciously talking themselves out of their own self-defeating irrational beliefs.

One main purpose of REBT group sessions is to offer members a wider range of possible solutions to their problems than they might normally receive in individual sessions. Out of 10 people present at a given session, one may finally zero in on a presenter's central problem (after several others have failed), and another may offer an elegant solution to it (after various ineffectual, inelegant, symptom-focused solutions have hitherto been offered). Whereas a single would-be helper may give up on a difficult issue (or person), some group members may persist and finally prove to be quite helpful.

Revealing intimate problems to a group of people may itself be therapeutic for the client. In regular REBT small-group therapy, he or she discloses many ordinarily usually hidden events and feelings to a dozen or so peers. In REBT public workshops, individuals may reveal themselves to a hundred or more people. Especially if they are usually shy and inhibited, this kind of disclosure may be a most useful risk-taking experience, which the therapist will often emphasize by showing the inhibited person that he or she has opened up and actually received little, if any, criticism or an attack that he or she predicted. Further, even if one is disapproved or laughed at, he or she can still accept oneself and find this censure *unfortunate* rather than *awful*.

Group members are of all ages, usually ranging from about 20 to 70, and including all kinds of diagnostic categories. Groups usually have a fairly equal number of males and females or may intentionally include one gender only. After a member joins a group, he or she may have concomitant individual therapy sessions regularly or irregularly. Most group members choose to have them irregularly and therefore mainly learn the principles and practices of REBT in the course of the group process. Clients who are distinctly shy or who have problems relating to others are particularly encouraged to join a group because working out their difficulties with their peers may be better for them than only working with an individual therapist (who has a particular role with them and therefore is not representative of the people they associate with in real life).

All groups are open-ended. That is, once a member joins, he or she can attend group for a minimum of 6 weeks and then (after giving 2 weeks' notice) drop out at any time. Those who drop out are usually soon replaced by new members. When a member joins, he or she comes into a group that is filled mostly with long-term members who have been in attendance for a period of several months to some years and who help teach "some of the ropes" of REBT, during regular sessions, after sessions, and in private contacts that they may have during the week. New members are also prepared for the group process by (a) having had one or more individual REBT sessions, (b) reading various books on REBT, and (c) attending workshops and lectures.

REBT group therapy has some disadvantages and limitations, especially when compared with more individualized REBT processes. In small-group procedures, for example, group members can easily, out of overzealousness and ignorance, mislead other members and at times even present them with harmful directives and views. They can give poor or inelegant solutions, for example, continuing to show a disturbed person the "practical" methods he or she can use to make oneself more successful in life, rather than what deeper philosophic changes he or she can make in disturbance-creating outlooks.

Some difficult, and even some well-intentioned, group members can waste time in irrelevancies. Some may try to dominate, neglect doing homework assignments, lead the problem presenter "down the garden path," or sidetrack and defuse some of the therapist's main points. Some may hold back because they inordinately look for the approval of other group members; others bring out their own and others' minor instead of major difficulties and otherwise get off on various nontherapeutic limbs. Group members can also bombard a presenter with so many and such powerful suggestions that he or she feels overwhelmed. They can give poor homework assignments or keep presenting so many new problems that old assignments are not sufficiently checked up on. They can allow a member, if the therapist does not actively intervene, to get away with minimal participation and hence make minimal change in his or her disordered behavior. They can become overly frustrated and hostile and can irrationally condemn a participant for his or her symptoms or continuing resistance to working at giving up those symptoms. The well-trained REBT group therapist is vigilant about attending to any of these occurrences and brings the group back on track.

REBT group therapy, consequently, is hardly a panacea for all ills, nor is it suitable for all individuals who feel emotionally disturbed and come for help. Some clients are not ready for it and would better continue with individual REBT before entering a group. Others, such as some compulsive talkers or hypomanic individuals, may benefit considerably from group work but can be too disruptive and require too much monitoring and training. Hence, it may be best to exclude them and have them work out their problems in other modes of treatment. We believe, however, that many disturbed clients can benefit as much, and probably more, from group therapy than from individual treatment alone.

To conclude this section on brief and long-term strategies and techniques, we remind readers about REBT's goals of helping people not merely to feel better but to *get better* for the long term. Hence, both short- and long-term clients are encouraged and taught how to maintain and enhance their REBT gains after they leave therapy and are urged not to hesitate to return for booster individual sessions or to rejoin their therapy group if they backslide, relapse, or think they are progressing too slowly.

REFERENCE

Ellis, A., & Joffe, D. (2002). A study of volunteer clients who experienced live sessions of rational emotive behavior therapy in front of a public audience. *Journal of Rational-Emotive and Cognitive-Behavior Therapy, 20,* 151–158. doi:10.1023/A:1019828718532

APPENDIX 32.1: RATIONAL EMOTIVE BEHAVIOR THERAPY TECHNIQUES

Technique	Video title	Video identifying number	Time at which technique occurs
Realistic disputing	REBT for Coping With Divorce Transition (Session 1 of 6)	777700352-001	19:49–23:37
Logical disputing	REBT for Coping With Divorce Transition (Session 1 of 6)	777700352-001	12:34–16:33
Using humor	REBT for Coping With Divorce Transition (Session 1 of 6)	777700352-001	09:59–10:42
Pragmatic disputing	REBT for Coping With Divorce Transition (Session 2 of 6)	777700354-001	06:29–07:41
Strongly using coping statements	REBT for Coping With Divorce Transition (Session 1 of 6)	777700352-001	24:45–26:34
Rational coping statements	REBT for Coping With Divorce Transition (Session 5 of 6)	777700362-001	34:23–35:59
Problem solving	REBT for Coping With Divorce Transition (Session 1 of 6)	777700352-001	33:24–38:10
Role playing	REBT for Coping With Divorce Transition (Session 5 of 6)	777700362-001	10:50–13:18
Assessing the cost–benefit ratio	REBT for Considering Divorce (Session 1 of 6)	777700353-001	38:50–40:45
Rational emotive imagery	REBT for Coping With Divorce Transition (Session 2 of 6)	777700354-001	26:00–27:29
Philosophic discussion	REBT for Coping With Divorce Transition (Session 2 of 6)	777700354-001	33:54–36:32
Skill training (Assertiveness)	REBT for Coping With Divorce Transition (Session 4 of 6)	777700358-002	43:38–45:06
Distraction methods	REBT for Coping With Divorce Transition (Session 6 of 6)	777700360-001	11:31–14:13
Using reinforcements	REBT for Coping With Divorce Transition (Session 1 of 6)	777700352-001	24:01–26:27
Relapse prevention	REBT for Coping With Divorce Transition (Session 6 of 6)	777700360-001	36:00–47:00

33

REALITY THERAPY

ROBERT E. WUBBOLDING

Choice theory provides a comprehensive explanation of human behavior. Its purview ranges from effective behaviors often described as mentally healthy, in-control, and self-actualizing to minimally and severely ineffective or out-of-control behaviors, such as those described in the *DSM–IV–TR*. Contrary to current criticism (Sue & Sue, 1999) that counseling and psychotherapy theories founded in a Euro-American context are culture bound, choice theory addresses behaviors of individuals and groups representing cultures from every continent. The delivery system reality therapy, summarized in the acronym WDEP, applies to individuals and groups from virtually every ethnicity (Mickel, 2005; Wubbolding, 1989, 1991, 2000b; Wubbolding

Excerpted from *Reality Therapy* (2011), from Chapter 3, "Choice Theory," pp. 31–39. Copyright 2011 by the American Psychological Association. Used with permission of the author.

http://dx.doi.org/10.1037/14295-033
Psychotherapy Theories and Techniques: A Reader, G. R. VandenBos, E. Meidenbauer, and J. Frank-McNeil (Editors)
Copyright © 2014 by the American Psychological Association. All rights reserved.

et al., 2004). In speaking of reality therapy as used in Korea, Kim and Hwang (2006) state,

> Since 1986 reality therapy and choice theory have been introduced to the counseling and business fields in Korea followed with much research. . . . It is embraced by professionals, including counselors, educators, psychologists, psychiatrists, social workers and others, as well as parents. (p. 25)

Citing several research studies in the Malaysian language, Jusoh, Mahmud, and Ishak (2008) state, "These works are testimony that reality therapy, when applied in suitable modules, can be beneficial for clients of various backgrounds" (p. 5).

Because of the emphasis on human behavior as chosen and due to major expansions in control theory, Glasser renamed the foundational principles and the developments of control theory *choice theory*. It remains an internal control system in that behavior is not thrust on human beings from the external environment or culture nor determined by past experiences or parental persuasion. Though these influences can leave their imprint, they do not nullify free choice.

Choice theory is based on the principle that human motivation is a "here and now" phenomenon. As a psychological explanation, choice theory posits five human needs from which springs choice (Glasser, 1998, 2005, 2008). These needs are seen as genetic and therefore universal. They are not culture bound, not limited to any racial or ethnic group. Rather, they are motivators that drive the behavior of all human beings.

SURVIVAL OR SELF-PRESERVATION

The psychological needs described below are housed in the cerebral cortex, sometimes referred to as the "new brain" because of its more recent development in the history of humankind. It sometimes receives a help-me signal from the autonomic nervous system that houses the "old brain," the place of the survival or self-preservation need. It causes the system to resist disease, to feel hunger and thirst, to seek physical homeostasis, and to pursue sexual gratification. Characteristic of all biological sensate creatures, the need for self-preservation drives the organism to maintain life. And yet, human living is more complicated than mere self-preservation. The satisfaction of survival often occurs not in isolation but as a motivation interdependent with the satisfaction of other needs. Twenty-first century survival requires at least some human interaction, successful endeavors, and effective choices. Enjoying life also provides need satisfaction and is often an additional benefit. Glasser

(1998) states, "It is these additional lifelong needs beyond survival that make our lives so complicated, so different from those of animals" (p. 33).

BELONGING, LOVE, AFFILIATION

Human beings possess an innate need for human closeness and for interdependence. While the genetic origin of this need remains hypothetical, belonging and other needs provide a basis and a pathway for effective therapy. Two examples illustrating the efficacy of satisfying the need for belonging in a constructive manner can be found in stories of forced confinement and captivity.

Nien Cheng's Interrogations

Cheng (1986) tells the story of her 6-year solitary confinement during the Maoist regime in China and how she coped with her almost overwhelming loneliness and isolation and the accompanying passivity and depression. Within the rigid restrictions imposed upon her, she gained a sense of belonging by shouting her answers during her interrogations. She satisfied her need for belonging as best she could, believing that other prisoners in the same building could hear her voice. Thus, her shouting was her way of gaining a sense of belonging with them as well as communicating a source of courage to them. She also tells of an increased sense of power accompanying this deep feeling of belonging.

Fred and Porter's Bond

Hirsch (2004) presents a story of heroic courage and human bonding. Fred Cherry and Porter Halyburton, fighter pilots and prisoners of war in Vietnam, suffered unspeakable psychological and physical tortures during their nearly seven years' internment. Major Fred Cherry, an African American Air Force pilot, was raised in a segregated world. Shot down and wounded, he suffered additional torture at the hands of his captors, adding to his pain and suffering. U.S. Navy Lieutenant Junior Grade Porter Halyburton, a White man raised in the South in the 1940s and '50s, became Fred's cellmate. Their legendary closeness saved both of them. Porter nursed Fred, who received extremely primitive treatment for his injuries, including several operations and poor postoperative treatment. He helped Fred by bathing and exercising him, while Fred supported him psychologically for 7 months. Fred taught Porter the lessons of heroism, loyalty, and a bias-free worldview. Because of their synergistic union, they both survived and carried with them during the rest of their imprisonment the desire to survive, not only to rejoin their families, but to see each other again and resume their friendship. Another prisoner, Giles Norrington, a Navy pilot shot down in 1968, recalled,

> By the time I arrived, Porter and Fred had already achieved legendary status. . . . The respect, mutual support, and affection that had developed between them were the stuff of sagas. Their stories, as individuals and as a team, were a great source of inspiration. (Hirsch, 2004, pp. 9–10)

As Hirsch noted,

> Many of the POWs had to cross racial, cultural, or social boundaries to exist in such close confines. But Halyburton and Cherry did more than coexist—they rescued each other. Each man credits the other with saving his life. One needed to be saved physically; the other, emotionally. In doing so, they forged a brotherhood that no enemy could shatter. (p. 10)

In November 2004 Fred and Porter appeared on C-SPAN. They once again stated that they would do the same again for each other. Parenthetically, Fred stated that he has never once dreamed about Vietnam, illustrating a principle crucial to reality therapy: Human relationships alleviate pain and can even lessen posttraumatic stress.

These anecdotes illustrate the life-sustaining nature of the human effort to satisfy the need for belonging. On the operational level, reality therapists see belonging as the most prominent need. Regardless of the presenting issue, the effective use of reality therapy includes a therapeutic alliance as a foundation for assisting clients to improve their interpersonal relationships. Wubbolding (2005) states, "Enhanced acquaintanceships, friendships and intimacies provide the royal road to mental health and quality living" (p. 44).

INNER CONTROL, POWER, ACHIEVEMENT, SELF-ESTEEM, RECOGNITION

Originally referred to as power, the third human motivator or source of behavior covers a variety of concepts. Satisfying the need for power does not equate with dominating or controlling other human beings. Fulfilling this need is not a zero-sum game. There need not be winners and losers in the quest for power. Rather, individuals choose activities aimed at helping them gain a sense of inner control, the perception that they are in charge of their lives, that they have achieved or accomplished something. For instance, upon being released from the hospital after a successful surgical procedure, the patient experiences a sense of inner control, a feeling of being in charge of her own life.

Even competitors often feel an intense sense of accomplishment not merely because they have triumphed over others but because they have demonstrated to themselves and others their highest level of achievement. At the 2008 Olympics in Beijing, Carol Huynh won the first Canadian gold medal in wrestling. Hawthorn (2008) described how the Huynh family arrived in Canada after fleeing from Vietnam in 1978. Carol's parents watched her from the stands, weeping and cheering. Neither they nor Carol herself described this accomplishment as defeating an opponent. Rather, they spoke of the discipline required as well as the support she received from her coach, her family, and the people from Hazelton, British Columbia, and from her current home in Calgary, Alberta. Her coach, Debbie Brauer, stated, "Kinship is very strong. It's a community that, despite its problems, really does pull together. It's not what you do for a living, or what color your skin is, but who you are that matters" (Hawthorn, 2008, p. 7).

On the other hand, the urge to triumph in competition also satisfies the power need. The desire to win an election, to defeat the opponent, to triumph over the other team creates the feeling of power and achievement. Some people choose to satisfy their need for power by conquering and exploiting others emotionally, intellectually, and even physically. Fulfilling this need with little concern for the needs of others explains antisocial and even Axis II behaviors, often providing a substitute for a person's inability to satisfy belonging in an appropriate manner.

Human beings desire the self-perception of being capable of achieving, of accomplishing something, of pride, status, and importance. For the most part, they seek these inner satisfactions in a positive, effective, or mentally healthy manner. But they sometimes attempt to fulfill these needs in ways that are self-destructive or harmful to others. In discussing choice theory applied to juvenile delinquents and their need for recognition, Myers and Jackson (2002) state,

> The juveniles have been lectured by the best. What they have not gotten is praise for doing a good job. They have not received approval from those they love and respect. They have not been rewarded for a job well done. And, the touch they have received may have been the back of someone's hand. Let juveniles know when they do well. (p. 199)

Many people attempt need satisfaction, especially fulfilling their need for status or importance, by the abuse of drugs, which consequently creates the illusion of need satisfaction. They gain the momentary perception of being in charge of their own lives, but they have deluded themselves. When the illusion fades, the feeling of power or achievement disintegrates, often resulting in a deepening sense of powerlessness.

FREEDOM, INDEPENDENCE, AUTONOMY

The fourth human motivator urges people to search for options, to select among possibilities, and to make specific choices. Depending on culture and experience, human beings seek independence or autonomy in varying degrees and in diverse ways, either life enhancing or damaging to self or others. Uncovering satisfactory options constitutes a primary goal in the practice of reality therapy. As with other needs, the external world imposes natural or environmental limits on human choice. Still, the practitioner of reality therapy avoids falling into the trap of agreeing with the oft-stated refrain, "I have no choice." As Glasser (1998) states, "There is always a choice."

Viktor Frankl (1984) based his logotherapy on the principle that no matter how dire the circumstances, the human person has a choice. During his 3 years of imprisonment at Auschwitz, he believed he had a choice, not regarding actions but how he would *perceive* the diabolical world of the concentration camp. Carl Rogers frequently described a hypothetical prisoner in solitary confinement tapping on the wall in Morse code, "Is anybody out there?" After years of engaging in the only choice available, he hears a response: "Yes, I am on the other side of the wall." The prisoner must have experienced an intense feeling of liberation and even exhilaration.

People express and fulfill the need for freedom in a variety of ways. Some people have a high need for freedom and seem to tolerate little restriction or structure. Others feel free when they are required to conform to a predictable routine. When asking participants in training sessions "What do you like about your job?" many respond that they know what to expect on their jobs. Others state, "No two days are alike." Clearly, some individuals enjoy a maximum amount of variety, while others find need satisfaction in a more organized work environment.

FUN, ENJOYMENT

Aristotle defined a human as a creature that is risible—that is, it can laugh. Choice theory embraces the principle that people have an innate need or motivation that directs but does not compel their behavior toward fun or at least enjoyment. From the cradle to the grave, human beings find ways to be comfortable and to enjoy their surroundings. Moreover, Glasser (1998) connects the need for fun with learning:

> We are the only land-based creatures who play all our lives and because we learn all our lives, the day we stop playing is the day we stop learning. People who fall in love are learning a lot about each other and they find themselves laughing almost continually. One of the first times infants laugh is when someone plays peek-a-boo with them. I believe they laugh

because that game teaches them something very useful. They learn, I am I and you are you. (p. 41)

Wubbolding (2000b) states, "The developmental task of differentiating oneself from others involves the deep inner need for fun" (p. 16). Other developmental tasks are facilitated by enjoyment. Adolescents and adults, young and old, seek personal adjustment by redirecting their thoughts and actions from life's problems to pleasant endeavors. A major task for a therapist implementing choice theory is helping clients make positive and often delectable choices leading to a sense of inner joy.

When counseling couples and families, the effective reality therapist assists them in planning to have fun together, suggests Wubbolding (2000a, 2000b). He also states, "If they have achieved a high degree of intimacy, they have spent time together learning. A therapist, using reality therapy, helps clients have fun together, do enjoyable activities as a [unit], laugh at themselves and at the foibles of others. The comedian Victor Borge has said that the shortest distance between two people is a laugh" (Wubbolding, 2000b, p. 16).

At first glance the role of fun in mental health might seem shallow and superficial. In discussing the role of enjoyment in a client's life, it might appear that the therapist is facilitating an avoidance of deeper issues. The opposite, however, is true: A discussion of positive mental health provides an alternative to major and minor disorders. For example, diagnostic criteria for dysthymic disorders include low energy or fatigue and feelings of hopelessness. In terms of choice theory needs, these individuals do not effectively satisfy their need for fun.

Questioning clients about their need for fun is a useful starting point in the process of therapy with many clients. With oppositional adolescents, the reality therapist frequently asks them to "describe the last time you did something that was fun without getting in trouble or did something that would not have gotten you in trouble if your parents, teachers or police observed you doing it." This approach coincides with the Eriksonian axiom, "There is not a one-to-one correlation between the problem and the solution." To discuss fun with clients exemplifies reality therapy as a mental health system, not merely a system for remediating mental disorders. Sometimes the solution seems to have little to do with the problem.

IS THERE A HUMAN NEED FOR SPIRITUALITY, FAITH, MEANING, OR PURPOSE?

Staub and Pearlman (2002) describe a need for spirituality—that is, transcendence of the self. They state that in later life this need becomes more significant, "but the groundwork for its satisfaction is laid all through life. We can fulfill it through spiritual experiences or connection to God or other spiritual entities. . . . We can fulfill it by creating higher, more universal meaning in our lives" (p. 1).

In reviewing the literature on human needs, Litwack (2007) states,

> If one studies the history of mankind, it is difficult to dismiss the power of spirituality. Whether called a formal religion, humanism or a belief in nature, throughout history mankind seems to have had the need to believe in something other (higher, different) than oneself. (p. 30)

Frankl's logotherapy (1984) shares the emphasis on human decision and choice as a theoretical cornerstone. He also emphasizes meaning and purpose as a foundational principle for therapy and even for daily living. Frankl attributes his own sense of purpose, meaning, and faith as reasons for his surviving Auschwitz. He further associates the need for purpose and meaning with prisoners' survival more than their athletic and physical strength.

The use of reality therapy has been applied to spirituality in helping clients deepen their faith in the divine, to live a spiritually oriented life, and to focus on issues outside and larger than themselves (Carleton, 1994; Linnenberg, 1997; Tabata, 1999; Wubbolding, 1992). Many clients perceive that their problems and issues have a spiritual and moral dimension (Mickel & Liddie-Hamilton, 1996). In discussing family therapy, Mickel and Hall (2006) describe love as expressed in family life as holistic and spiritual. They assert that love is beyond the physical and mental world in that it lasts forever.

Choice theory as articulated by William Glasser places faith and spirituality as behaviors chosen to satisfy needs. On the other hand, he allows for faith as a need but not one of *his* formulations. He emphasizes that anyone instructing others about choice theory is free to add needs to the basic five, but it should be emphasized that the additional needs are beyond the original theory (Glasser, 2008).

REFERENCES

Carleton, R. (1994). *Reality therapy in the Christian context* [Audio cassette]. Montgomery, AL: Private Publication.

Cheng, N. (1986). *Life and death in Shanghai*. New York, NY: Grafton Books.

Frankl, V. (1984). *Man's search for meaning*. New York, NY: Washington Square Press.

Glasser, W. (1998). *Choice theory*. New York, NY: HarperCollins.

Glasser, W. (2005). *Defining mental health as a public health issue*. Chatsworth, CA: William Glasser Institute.

Glasser, W. (2008, July 16). *Back to the basics*. Keynote address to annual international conference of the William Glasser Institute, Colorado Springs, CO.

Hawthorn, T. (2008, August 18). A golden day for a village that reached out to a family. *Globe and Mail*, pp. 1, 7.

Hirsch, J. (2004). *Two souls indivisible*. New York, NY: Houghton Mifflin.

Jusoh, A. J., Mahmud, Z., & Ishak, N. M. (2008). The patterns of reality therapy usage among Malaysian counselors. *International Journal of Reality Therapy, 28*(1), 5–14.

Kim, R.-I., & Hwang, M. (2006). A meta-analysis of reality therapy and choice theory group programs for self-esteem and locus of control in Korea. *International Journal of Choice Theory, 1*(1), 25–30.

Linnenberg, D. (1997). Religion, spirituality and the counseling process. *International Journal of Reality Therapy, 17*(1), 55–59.

Litwack, L. (2007). Basic needs—a retrospective. *International Journal of Reality Therapy, 16*(2), 28–30.

Mickel, E. (2005). *Africa centered reality therapy and choice theory*. Trenton, NJ: Africa World Press.

Mickel, E., & Hall, C. (2006). Family therapy in transition: Love is a healing behavior. *International Journal of Reality Therapy, 15*(2), 32–35.

Mickel, L., & Liddie-Hamilton, B. (1996). Family therapy in transition: Social constructivism and control theory. *Journal of Reality Therapy, 16*(1), 95–100.

Myers, L., & Jackson, D. (2002). *Reality therapy and choice theory*. Lanham, MD: American Correctional Association.

Staub, E., & Pearlman, L. (2002). Understanding basic psychological needs. Retrieved from http://www.heal-reconcile-rwanda.org/lec_needs.htm

Sue, D. W., & Sue, D. (1999). *Counseling the culturally different: Theory and practice* (3rd ed.). New York, NY: Wiley.

Tabata, M. (1999). The usefulness of reality therapy for biblical counseling. *Japanese Journal of Reality Therapy, 5*(1), 30–34.

Wubbolding, R. (1989). Radio station WDEP and other metaphors used in teaching reality therapy. *Journal of Reality Therapy, 8*(2), 74–79.

Wubbolding, R. (1991). *Understanding reality therapy*. New York, NY: HarperCollins.

Wubbolding, R. (1992). *You steer* [CD]. Cincinnati, OH: Center for Reality Therapy.

Wubbolding, R. (2000a). Reality therapy. In A. Horne (Ed.), *Family counseling and therapy* (3rd ed., pp. 420–453). Itasca, IL: Peacock.

Wubbolding, R. (2000b). *Reality therapy for the 21st century*. Philadelphia, PA: Brunner Routledge.

Wubbolding, R. (2005). The power of belonging. *International Journal of Reality Therapy, 24*(2), 43–44.

Wubbolding, R. E., Brickell, J., Imhof, L., Kim, R. I., Lojk, L., & Al-Rashidi, B. (2004). Reality therapy: A global perspective. *International Journal for the Advancement of Counselling, 26*(3), 219–228.

34

REALITY THERAPY PROCESS

ROBERT E. WUBBOLDING

Many of the skills for establishing a constructive atmosphere in the therapeutic relationship are common to other theories and are characteristic of healthy human relationships. Consequently, they serve as an appropriate foundation for reality therapy interventions based on choice theory. Most typical of reality therapy is a systematic series of interventions summarized by the acronym WDEP (Wubbolding, 1989, 1991, 2000, 2008). Each letter represents a cluster of possible ways to help clients become increasingly aware of the various elements of their internal control systems, examine a broader spectrum of opportunities, and thereby make more effective choices. These four letters focus the theory on clinical practice and provide its delivery system, making it usable for the therapist and for the client. In speaking of the WDEP system, Glasser stated, "It is an eminently usable tool that can be

Excerpted from *Reality Therapy* (2011), from Chapter 4, "The Therapy Process," pp. 76–82. Copyright 2011 by the American Psychological Association. Used with permission of the author.

http://dx.doi.org/10.1037/14295-034
Psychotherapy Theories and Techniques: A Reader, G. R. VandenBos, E. Meidenbauer, and J. Frank-McNeil (Editors)
Copyright © 2014 by the American Psychological Association. All rights reserved.

learned by readers, used in agencies and schools, and taught in classrooms. I hope that this system will become a household phrase and used by therapists, counselors, teachers and parents" (Wubbolding, 1991, p. xii).

EXPLORING WANTS

The key question under the W of the WDEP system is

WHAT DO YOU WANT?

The user of reality therapy is aware of the theoretical concept of the quality world. Its contents are everything highly valued: core beliefs, ideas, and treasured possessions and relationships. The question "What do you want?" summarizes quality world interventions made by the therapist. In exploring the quality world, the therapist assists clients to formulate, clarify, and prioritize the pictures in their mental picture albums—that is, their wants. This process serves as the foundation for other interventions based on the WDEP system and requires much attention in the therapeutic process. Its importance is illustrated in the well-known caution to "be careful what you wish for." An employee desiring early retirement might be well advised to avoid nurturing "medical retirement" as a quality world picture. This desire might result not in the satisfaction of the freedom need; it might result in a threat to the survival need.

Levels of Wants

Because of the primary importance of wants, the quality world is often referred to as the "world of wants." Though the quality world is rich in content, the common denominator of the various ingredients of the quality world—and therefore the focus of therapy—consists in the *wants* of the client. Everything in the quality world appears desirable. However, these wants are not constant or standardized. They exist at various levels of desirability and are changeable.

Nonnegotiable demand. Some wants, such as the desire for oxygen, nourishment, or the freedom from torture, are so intensely desired that clients cannot function without them. Some clients rigidly cling to wants that, in fact, damage relationships. However, with skillful counseling and negotiation, clients can move toward more fluid wants and better relationships. For example, an unyielding parent insists that an adolescent conform to the same rules that were in force during childhood.

Pursued goal. Clients expressing the positive symptom "I want to improve" formulate goals that are backed up by behaviors. Going to school, developing a positive relationship, finding a job, and joining a 12-step program are examples. A more intense want could replace a pursued goal, as when a young person enlists in military service and leaves behind a relationship.

Wish. Some effort is made to achieve the wish, but its satisfaction requires little exertion. Taking a chance on the lottery entails less than overwhelming effort. Sometimes a wish focuses on something impossible to achieve. A resident of northern Minnesota might wish for Caribbean-like weather in January, or a resident of Jamaica might wish for snow to practice tobogganing for the Winter Olympics.

Weak whim. Fulfilling this want is slightly desirable but of little importance. A man selects a tie to wear for work but cares little about the exact color or design. In counseling couples, one person expresses the pursued goal of a happier relationship, while the other says that it would be nice but it is of little value.

Double bind. Sabotaging a want with ineffective behaviors sends the signal "I want it but I don't want it." A person genuinely wants to lose weight but undermines the effort by consistently overeating. Habitual bickering in a relationship damages the achievement of a genuine want expressed by couples, "We want our marriage to improve."

Reluctant passive acceptance. Clients on their own or through therapy learn to accept the inevitable. Many people gain an acceptance of a disease, handicap, situation, or event that is not desired. A person feels pain at rejection by a lover. Someone contracts a fatal illness or is injured in an accident. Another person experiences a loss of physical prowess or even faces death. Though the unavoidable may be undesirable, human beings learn to accept it.

Nondesired active acceptance. People often formulate clearly defined wants knowing that a side effect or consequence of its fulfillment will be an undesirable result. The pain of childbirth is hardly desirable, yet women accept it as an unavoidable corollary of the joy of giving birth. A battered woman living in a shelter desires to visit her father, knowing that there is a high likelihood of being abused. These side effects are not quality world pictures, but they unavoidably accompany the highly desired want.

Fantasy dream. Even though there is overwhelming evidence that the attainment of the dream is impossible, a person might fantasize about having a family like the Cosby TV family or the Brady Bunch. These wants are out of reach, unattainable, but they remain expressed as "Wouldn't it be nice?"

Though it is not necessary to categorize precisely every want during the process of therapy, it is useful to help clients determine the degree of intensity of a want. Helpful questions include, "How intensely do you want it?" "Is your want a nonnegotiable desire or a weak whim?" "Is it something you intend to pursue relentlessly, or is it something 'it would be nice to have'?" From the perspective of choice theory, the quality worlds of some clients lack priorities among wants. For many people recovering from addictions and members of codependent families, all wants appear to be equally important and urgent. A major part of the reality therapy process with such individuals entails helping them realize that some wants are of greater consequence than others.

Level of Commitment

Asking clients questions focusing on how hard they want to work at achieving their goals or how much energy they wish to exert to satisfy their wants and needs helps them move from Stage I "I want to improve" to Stage II "Positive symptoms." When clients decide that behavioral change is to their advantage, they are ready to make more effective choices, and therapy can proceed more rapidly when therapists help them raise their level of commitment. Wubbolding (2000a) has identified five levels of commitment.

1. *"I don't want to be here. Leave me alone. Get off my back."* Clients coerced to attend therapy sessions by family or court often display resistance, reluctance, and even hostility toward change and toward the therapist. This level, in fact, represents no commitment. Yet it is commonly heard by private practitioners, probation officers, child care workers, and practitioners in university counseling centers when clients have experienced an intervention and are *sent* to receive help.

2. *"I want the outcome, but I don't want to make the effort."* Some clients seek better relationships with family members, a job promotion, weight reduction, freedom from oversight by law enforcement, or a myriad of other wants. Failing to exert effort places their behavior at this second level of commitment. Though slightly higher than the first level, it contains resistance to action planning. The reality therapist helps clients evaluate this level of commitment and its lack of efficacy in effecting want and need fulfillment.

3. *"I'll try." "I might." "I could." "Maybe." "Probably."* The middle level of commitment shows some willingness to take more effective control of one's own behavior. However, change is not immutably linked to an "I'll try" commitment. "Trying" allows room for excuses and failure. The reality therapist can point to an airline customer's question, "When does your flight leave for Los Angeles?" If the ticket agent responds, "We will try to depart at 9:15 a.m.," the customer would ask for a higher level of commitment. Still, the middle level of commitment represents more resolve than Levels 1 or 2.

4. *"I will do my best."* Though containing an escape hatch to failure expressed as "I did my best, but I didn't follow through," doing one's best points toward action planning. It represents a step beyond mere wanting and trying and a willingness to choose positive symptoms.

5. *"I will do whatever it takes."* Efficacious choices and follow-through behaviors characterize the highest level of commitment. Clients consistently follow through on plans and even accept the responsibility for less than desired outcomes. For instance, an employee chooses behaviors designed to ensure a promotion. However, the employer does not bestow the honor desired by the worker. The employee makes no excuses, places no blame, and looks to the future.

The levels of commitment are best seen as developmental. Even though Level 3 is not as efficacious as Level 5, it can represent a client's improvement in that he or she has moved from resistance and apathy to a higher level of motivation for change.

Exploring the Perceptual System

Contained in the perceptual system are two components. Three perceptual filters constitute the first component, whereby human beings acknowledge the world, see relationships, and place a value on incoming information. The second component is the perceived world, a storehouse of perceptions of self and the external world.

When discussing the three perceptual filters, the therapist seeks information and clarification for ascertaining how clients see the world around them. To what degree do they see the world without putting a value on their perceptions? What do they believe is high value for them? Do they see a relationship between how their own behavior impacts the world around them and the incoming information received from it? For example, does a client perceive any connection between treating coworkers rudely and the perception that they don't like him? Does a specific client believe that her use of drugs has a relationship to her loss of family, loss of job, or loss of status? How much does a client value effective, altruistic, or legal behaviors purposely chosen to satisfy needs? Or does the client see value only in behaviors that are an attempt to satisfy needs regardless of whether they are unsuccessful, harmful to others, or even outside the law?

Connected with this exploration is the discussion of locus of control. First formulated by the social learning theorist Rotter (1954), the notions of internal place of control versus a sense of external control coincide with the principles of internal control psychology, more specifically choice theory. In speaking of Rotter's work, Mearns (2008) states,

> People with a strong internal locus of control believe that the responsibility for whether or not they get reinforced lies within themselves. Internals believe that success or failure is due to their own efforts. In contrast, externals believe that the reinforcers in life are controlled by luck, chance or powerful others. Therefore, they see little impact of their own efforts on the amount of reinforcement they receive. (p. 4)

The single difference between Rotter's principle and choice theory is that in choice theory the payoff for behavior is not seen as reinforcing but rather as satisfying the internal motivation, or general needs and specific wants.

Reality therapists help clients ascertain their perceived degree of internal versus external control. People depressing themselves believe that they are at the mercy of external circumstances, that they are powerless because of events beyond their control. Others adopt the self-talk, "I can't because they won't let me." Consequently, one of the goals of reality therapy is to help clients change their perception of victimization by changing their actions. The principle of internal control entails application beyond psychology and therapy. Burnett (1995) states that society is "tired of people claiming to be a victim every time someone confronts them for an antisocial behavior" (p. i). He provides the example of Bart Simpson: "I didn't do it." "Nobody saw me do it." And finally, "You can't prove anything."

Embracing the principle of internal control rather than external control does not imply that every limitation, problem, defeat, or pathology is within a person's ability to control. Many assaults from the external world are unavoidable and are direct attacks against one or more human need: self-preservation, belonging, power or inner control, freedom, and fun. When threatened, it is often difficult and sometimes impossible to generate a need-satisfying behavior. The driver of a car skidding out of control on an icy street is likely to *feel* out of control and unable to choose a relaxed, calm, and self-confidencing behavior. Choice theory does not teach that changing perceptions from external to internal is easy; nor is the perception of internal control easily accessible. Therefore, a principle of internal control congruent with choice theory is *Human beings (clients) have more control than they often perceive.*

REFERENCES

Burnett, D. (1995). *Raising responsible kids*. Laguna Niguel, CA: FunAgain Press.

Mearns, J. (2008). The social learning theory of Julian B. Rotter. Retrieved from http://psych.fullerton.edu/jmearns/rotter.htm

Rotter, J. B. (1954). *Social learning and clinical psychology*. New York, NY: Prentice Hall.

Wubbolding, R. (1989). Radio station WDEP and other metaphors used in teaching reality therapy. *Journal of Reality Therapy, 8*(2), 74–79.

Wubbolding, R. (1991). *Understanding reality therapy*. New York, NY: HarperCollins.

Wubbolding, R. (2000). *Reality therapy for the 21st century*. Philadelphia, PA: Brunner Routledge.

Wubbolding, R. (2008). Reality therapy. In J. Frew & M. Spiegler (Eds.), *Contemporary psychotherapies for a diverse world* (pp. 360–396). Boston, MA: Houghton Mifflin.

APPENDIX 34.1: REALITY THERAPY TECHNIQUES

Technique	Video title	Video identifying number	Time at which technique occurs
Exploring wants	Reality Therapy for a Woman Dealing with Divorce	777700167-001	11:53–12:56
What are you doing?	Reality Therapy for Returning to the Workforce	777700168-001	23:32–26:04
Describe a typical day	Reality Therapy for a Woman Dealing with Divorce	777700167-001	24:53–28:00
Evaluating current controllable behaviors	Reality Therapy for Returning to the Workforce	777700168-001	5:55–6:53
Self-evaluation	Reality Therapy for Returning to the Workforce	777700168-001	4:10–4:25
Is what you are doing helping you?	Reality Therapy for a Woman Dealing with Divorce	777700167-001	14:11–19:38
Self-evaluation questions	Reality Therapy for a Woman Dealing with Divorce	777700167-001	34:14–35:45
Instructing in planning	Reality Therapy for a Woman Dealing with Divorce	777700167-001	39:40–41:20

35

RELATIONAL–CULTURAL THERAPY

JUDITH V. JORDAN

Relational–cultural theory (RCT) arose from an effort to better understand the importance of growth-fostering relationships in people's lives. It seeks to lessen the suffering caused by chronic disconnection and isolation, whether at an individual or societal level, to increase the capacity for relational resilience, and to foster social justice. Walker (2002) notes that the connections and disconnections that characterize relationships occur in a context that has been "raced, engendered, sexualized and stratified along dimensions of class, physical ability, religion or whatever constructions carry ontological significance in the culture" (p. 2). The effects of privilege, marginalization, and cultural forces are seen by RCT as central to psychological development. Relational–cultural theorists have "depicted culture as more than the scenic backdrop for the unfolding of

Excerpted from *Relational–Cultural Therapy* (2010), from Chapter 3, "Theory," pp. 23–32. Copyright 2010 by the American Psychological Association. Used with permission of the author.

http://dx.doi.org/10.1037/14295-035
Psychotherapy Theories and Techniques: A Reader, G. R. VandenBos, E. Meidenbauer, and J. Frank-McNeil (Editors)
Copyright © 2014 by the American Psychological Association. All rights reserved.

development; rather, culture is viewed as an active agent in relational processes that shape human possibility" (Walker, 2005, p. 48). The insight that relational development is always completely suffused with social and cultural identities has been central to the development and practice of RCT.

While the RCT model was originally developed to better represent women's experiences, it has become clear that men's psychological growth has also been distorted by the lenses used to study it. Men's desires and needs for connection have been denied and made invisible. The dominant culture has insistently demanded that men achieve the goals of independence, autonomy, and individualistic competitive achievement. The denial of vulnerability, the need for a strong and separate self, and the reliance on power over others as the path to safety have exacted enormous costs for men (Pollack, 1998). Bill Pollack (1998) has written about what he calls the normative trauma of male socialization, and Ron Levant has outlined what he calls normative alexithymia in men schooled in a "strong," stiff-upper-lip, tough, hard, nonfeminine masculinity (Levant, 1992). Today, RCT hopes to better represent both women's and men's psychological experience as it seeks transformation of chronic disconnection into connection and empowerment for individuals of both genders and for society as a whole.

CORE CONCEPTS

The core concepts of RCT (Jordan, 2000) include the following:

1. People grow through and toward relationship throughout the life span.
2. Movement toward mutuality rather than separation characterizes mature functioning.
3. Relationship differentiation and elaboration characterize growth.
4. Mutual empathy and mutual empowerment are at the core of growth-fostering relationships.
5. Authenticity is necessary for real engagement and full participation in growth-fostering relationship.
6. In growth-fostering relationships, all people contribute and grow or benefit. Development is not a one-way street.
7. One of the goals of development from a relational perspective is the development of increased relational competence and capacities over the life span.

MUTUAL EMPATHY AND GROWTH-FOSTERING RELATIONSHIPS

In sum, rather than moving toward greater separateness and independence, the goal is to increase our capacity for relational resilience, mutual empathy, and mutual empowerment. Mutual empathy is the core process that allows for growth in relationship. In a dyad, it involves the responsiveness of two people, but it can occur between more people as well. In this movement of empathy, with each person affected by and seeing her impact on the other, the individual sees the possibility for change and for connection. Thus, aspects of one's experience that have been split off and seen as unacceptable or threatening begin to come back into relationship. When protective strategies of disconnection are operating, people remain stuck in old patterns of disconnection. Under these conditions there is not much room for growth. In mutual empathy, people begin to see that they can bring more and more of themselves into relationship. In this process, they become more present, more open to change and learning.

The need for connection in which growth is a priority is the core motivation in people's lives. In growth-fostering relationships, people are able to bring themselves most fully and authentically into connection. Jean Baker Miller suggested that these relationships have five outcomes ("the five good things"): a sense of zest; a better understanding of self, other, and the relationship (clarity); a sense of worth; an enhanced capacity to act or be productive; and an increased desire for more connection (Miller & Stiver, 1997).

DISCONNECTION

RCT sees disconnections as normative in relationships; they occur when one person misunderstands, invalidates, excludes, humiliates, or injures the other person in some way. Acute disconnections occur frequently in all relationships. If they can be addressed and reworked, they are not problematic; in fact, they become places of enormous growth. When an injured person, particularly one who has less power, can represent her or his experience of disconnection or pain to the more powerful person and be responded to, with interest or concern, the less powerful, hurt person has a sense of "mattering," of having an effect on the other. This strengthens connection as well as a sense of relational competence. Thus, places of empathic failure can become places of increasing trust and strength in relationships.

If, however, the less powerful person is not allowed or encouraged to voice her or his hurt or anger, that person will learn to suppress that aspect of her or his experience. She or he learns to move into hiding and inauthenticity to stay in relationship. Often with shame or withdrawal, the person moves out of genuine, growth-producing relationship. Furthermore, the person twists herself or himself to fit in, to be acceptable to this powerful other person. The person feels profoundly disempowered and unseen. The relationship itself is diminished by these exchanges, and if they occur repeatedly, a condition of chronic disconnection develops. In this situation the less powerful, injured person feels she or he is to blame for the disconnection and feels immobilized and increasingly isolated. The injured person brings less and less of her or his real experience into the relationship and often loses touch with her or his own feelings and inner experience. While this dynamic creates isolation and disempowerment at the personal level, it also preserves the politics of dominance. In this way the personal is political, the political is personal, and the rewriting of a psychological paradigm becomes an act of social justice.

RELATIONAL IMAGES

Relational images (RI) are the inner constructions and expectations we each create out of our experience in relationships (Miller & Stiver, 1997). They develop early in life and are carried from one relationship to another, sometimes subject to modification (growth) and sometimes limiting our expectations in ways that anchor us in the relational past. Our expectations of relationships are held in these relational images. Chronic disconnections lead to negative relational images. When relational images are flexible, they can be modified and do not generate inappropriate generalizations. However, when they are rigidified and overly generalized, they keep us from participating fully in the actual relationship at hand. In this way they operate similarly to what many psychodynamic models refer to as transference in therapy, bringing expectations from the past to bear on the present in a way that distorts current reality.

While Freud believed that therapist neutrality and objectivity were necessary for transference to develop (Freud, 1912/1958), RCT sees "transference" phenomena emerging in all relationships. In this context, "Replication becomes problematic when it keeps people 'stuck in the past' and not free to engage in new relationships in the present" (Miller & Stiver, 1997, p. 138). RCT further suggests that "neutrality" and distance on the part of the therapist can interfere with moving into a new and different relational experience in therapy. Instead, the therapist can actively participate in helping to reshape relational images: "Memories of one's past relationships, with their history of connections and disconnections, shape the content and complexities of the relational images people bring into therapy. These images inform the expectations people have about relationships in general, but in therapy they become the focus of exploration" (Miller & Stiver, 1997, p. 139).

In therapy, the therapist and client also search for exceptions to the dominant relational image known as discrepant relational images. If a core relational image is "Whenever I make my needs known, I will be abandoned," a discrepant relational image might be "My Aunt Cathy was really there for me whenever I needed her." The negative relational image "When I get angry at people they retaliate by rejecting me" could be contradicted by the discrepant relational image "My brother used to stick with me and validate my anger." If negative relational images contribute to a sense of hopelessness and isolation, these discrepant relational images challenge their "pathological certainty"; they are places of hope and relational possibility upon which therapists can help expand.

Often, profound reworking of these negative relational images occurs around empathic failures in the therapy relationship itself. If one assumes that negative relational images and a sense of woundedness and self-blame arose in situations where the individual was unable to represent the pain of her experience to the other, more powerful person, being able to represent the pain of being misunderstood or not seen by the therapist to the therapist and having that representation acknowledged and addressed can open previously closed doors. The repair of these disconnections is at the heart of therapy. In these repairs, the individual's sense of insignificance, relational incompetence, and isolation shifts. Relational expectations and neurological circuits are modified as the therapist responds to the client in ways that disconfirm the entrenched and limiting relational images. Negative relational images begin to change, relational expectations are altered, and the effects of shame and self-blame give way to self-empathy and hope. These transformations, while sometimes incremental, are profound, and they bring the client into current reality with the ability to develop current relationships. We have referred to this condition as relational mindfulness (Surrey, 2005; Surrey & Eldridge, 2007) or relational awareness (Jordan, 1995).

Jean Baker Miller developed the notion of "condemned isolation" (Miller, 1989) to capture the fixedness and pain of the relational images that keep us locked out of relationship and therefore out of hope. In condemned isolation we feel immobilized, unworthy, and alone, and we feel that we have created this reality. The individual feels that she or he is to blame for her or his powerlessness and hopelessness and there is something intrinsically "wrong" with her or him. Under such conditions, she or he will not risk the vulnerability necessary to make connections. The threat of further isolation is simply too great. Miller and Stiver (1997) coined the term *central relational paradox* to capture what happens in this situation. Though we deeply desire and need connections, we are terrified of what will happen if we move into the vulnerability necessary to make deep connection, so we keep large aspects of ourselves out of connection. We develop strategies of disconnection, trying to protect ourselves by disconnecting, keeping parts of ourselves split off. We develop these strategies to avoid isolation, but paradoxically they contribute to our sense of isolation and being unseen. In her research with adolescent girls, Gilligan formulated an almost identical paradox (Gilligan, 1990). She documents the ways in which girls in early adolescence seem to lose certain outspoken and insightful parts of themselves as they attempt to fit into the kinds of relationships the culture prescribes for them. The extreme of this dissociation from one's own inner experience occurs in sexual and physical abuse (Herman, 1992). We thus see how these strategies and their consequences can result from social forces, as well as from individual experiences.

CONTROLLING IMAGES AND SHAME

Controlling images also create patterns of isolation and disempowerment. African American sociologist Patricia Hill Collins (2000) has explored the ways society creates controlling images to shame and disempower certain groups. They define who we are, what is acceptable, and what we can do. Collins notes that controlling images—like stereotypes of "mammies, matriarchs, welfare mothers"—are actually lies that hold people in their "place" and induce the notion that change cannot happen. These defining images feel real and immutable. It is hard for people to stay with their own truth when they are immersed in a sea of distorting and controlling images. Often, these societal controlling images become part of an individual's relational images: "From a relational–cultural perspective, strategies of disconnection give rise to internalized oppression, a complex of relational images grounded in the distortions and disinformation required to normalize the inequalities of a power-over culture" (Walker, 2005, p. 54).

Strategies of disconnection frequently arise around shame and a sense of unworthiness. Shame is a contributing factor to much immobilization and a major source of chronic disconnection: "In shame, one feels disconnected, that one's being is at fault, that one is unworthy of empathic response, or that one is unlovable. Often in shame people move out of connection, lose their sense of efficacy and lose their ability to authentically represent their experience" (Jordan, 2000, p. 1008). Shame arises naturally when people feel that their "being" is unworthy, that if people knew them more fully, they would reject or scorn them. Shame is named by Tomkins (1987) as one of the original affects, present from birth and reflected in gaze aversion. But shame is also imposed upon people to control and disempower them.

Shaming is a powerful way to silence and isolate individuals, but it also plays a large role in silencing and disempowering marginalized groups whose members are strategically, if often invisibly, shamed in order to reinforce their isolation and thus their subordination: "Isolation is the glue that holds oppression in place" (Laing, 1998). A dominant group's authority can be maintained by the widespread power tactic of silencing those who present differing views of reality. Microaggressions, in which seemingly small acts of violence or disrespect go unnamed and unchallenged, are a part of the invisibility of these power tactics (Jenkins, 1993). In particular, when the dominant group inevitably and strategically discourages open conflict and expression of difference by the nondominant groups, differences are framed as signs of deficiency. The marginalized groups often internalize the dominant group's standards, and internalized oppression (Lipsky, 1984) functions to perpetuate the shame and disempowerment.

Often, moving from group shame to a sense of worth is based on the effects of creating cohesive group pride (gay pride, Black pride, girl power). Creating or joining a community buffers individuals from the disempowerment of marginalization. In these collective, empowering movements out of shame, people reclaim their dignity and their right to be respected by others. In *The Skin We're In*, Janie Ward (2000) has written about the importance to Black adolescent girls of actively creating healthy resistance (liberation resistance) to the dominant White norms that threaten to silence and isolate them. She points to the importance of thinking critically about the dominant realities, naming them, and opposing them with alternative versions of reality. This creates a sense of positive identity and undermines the notion of *THE reality* or *THE truth*, which often is only a panoply of "controlling images" (Collins, 2000; Robinson & Ward, 1991; Ward, 2000).

It is essential that clinicians recognize the multiple sources of shame that bring people into therapy. Helen Block Lewis coded transcripts of hundreds of psychotherapy sessions and found that shame was by far the most common emotion patients expressed (Lewis, 1987). RCT's focus on helping individuals build and rebuild their capacity for growth-fostering relationships calls for taking into account any and all forces affecting that capacity, including, especially, oppressive social systems. Racial identity models (Helms & Cook, 1999) allow us to understand how deeply racial/ethnic identity issues are woven into our social fabric and how profoundly they affect relational possibilities. Controlling images and shame have a profound impact on development: "How one is regarded by the culture influences one's ability to negotiate developmental tasks" (Walker, 2005, p. 50). Therapists and clients can work together to understand and address the effect of controlling images, shame, and oppression: "Given the foundational premise [of RCT] that healthy development occurs through action-in-relationship, it follows that developmental potential is enhanced when an individual can function free of the inhibiting objectifications that limit the range of growth and possibility" (Walker, 2005, p. 50). The dynamics of shame and oppression can also pertain to dyadic relationships, particularly abuse situations where the perpetrator often shames and isolates the target.

The central relational paradox suggests that when a person has been humiliated, hurt, or violated in early relationships, the yearning for connection actually increases. But at the same time the person develops an exaggerated sense that the vulnerability necessary to enter authentic relationship is not safe. Thus there is an enhanced desire for connection and an increased fear of seeking connection. In therapy it becomes very important for the therapist to honor this central relational paradox. The therapist must be respectful of the strategies of disconnection and must deeply understand why these strategies of disconnection were developed and how they helped keep the person alive at crucial times in unresponsive or violating relationships. The therapist must "feel with" the client in the sense of really "getting it," developing a contextual empathy that helps her or him see the conditions that created this need for self-protection through disconnection. At the same time, the therapist must hold the overarching, even if tentatively embraced, desire for more real connection. In moving from chronic disconnection to connection, supported by the therapist, the client will begin to relinquish strategies of disconnection and in so doing will have to experience a certain sense of vulnerability and risk. As the client begins to relinquish the strategies of disconnection, the therapist will need to expect sudden disconnects following increased closeness or authenticity, as the client leaps to old patterns of safety. In part, the work of therapy involves differentiating current relational possibilities from old relational images. It involves introducing uncertainty into the client's overly generalized and fixed negative relational images (e.g., shifting "When I show my tenderness, I get beaten up" to "When I was vulnerable as a child my stepfather beat me, but my current boyfriend is there for me") and helping the client experience new relationships for her- or himself.

REFERENCES

Collins, P. H. (2000). *Black feminist thought* (2nd ed.). New York, NY: Routledge.

Freud, S. (1958). Recommendations to physicians practicing psychoanalysis. In J. Strachey (Ed.), *The standard edition of the complete psychological works of Sigmund Freud* (Vol. 12, pp. 111–120). London, England: Hogarth Press. (Original work published 1912)

Gilligan, C. (1990). Joining the resistance: Psychology, politics, girls and women. *Michigan Quarterly Review, 29,* 501–536.

Helms, J. E., & Cook, D. (1999). *Using race and culture in counseling and psychotherapy: Therapy and process.* Boston, MA: Allyn & Bacon.

Herman, J. (1992). *Trauma and recovery.* New York, NY: Basic Books.

Jenkins, Y. M. (1993). Diversity and social esteem. In J. L. Chin, V. De La Cancela, & Y. M. Jenkins (Eds.), *Diversity in psychotherapy: The politics of race, ethnicity, and gender.* (pp. 45–64). Westport, CT: Praeger.

Jordan, J. V. (1995). Boundaries: A relational perspective. *Psychotherapy Forum, 1*(2), 1–4.

Jordan, J. V. (2000). The role of mutual empathy in relational/cultural therapy. *Journal of Clinical Psychology, 56,* 1005–1016. doi:10.1002/1097-4679(200008)56:8<1005::AID-JCLP2>3.0.CO;2-L

Laing, K. (1998). Katalyst leadership workshop presented at In Pursuit of Parity: Teachers as Liberators, Boston, MA.

Levant, R. F. (1992). Toward the reconstruction of masculinity. *Journal of Family Psychology, 5,* 379–402. doi:10.1037/0893-3200.5.3-4.379

Lewis, H. B. (Ed.). (1987). *The role of shame in symptom formation.* Hillsdale, NJ: Erlbaum.

Lipsky, S. (1984). Unpublished and untitled manuscript.

Miller, J. B. (1989). Connections, disconnections and violations. *Work in Progress, No. 33.* Wellesley, MA: Stone Center Working Paper Series.

Miller, J. B., & Stiver, I. (1997). *The healing connection: How women form relationships in therapy and in life.* Boston, MA: Beacon Press.

Pollack, W. (1998). *Real boys: Rescuing our sons from the myths of boyhood.* New York, NY: Random House.

Robinson, T., & Ward, J. V. (1991). A belief in self far greater than anyone's disbelief: Cultivating resistance among African American female adolescents. In C. Gilligan, A. G. Rogers, & D. Tolman (Eds.), *Women, girls and psychotherapy: Reframing resistance* (pp. 87–103). New York, NY: Harrington Park Press.

Surrey, J. (2005). Relational psychotherapy, relational mindfulness. In C. K. Germer, R. D. Siegel, & P. R. Fulton (Eds.), *Mindfulness and psychotherapy* (pp. 91–110). New York, NY: Guilford Press.

Surrey, J., & Eldridge, N. (2007). *Relational–cultural mindfulness.* Presentation at the Jean Baker Miller Training Institute Workshop, Wellesley College, Wellesley, MA.

Tomkins, S. S. (1987). Shame. In D. Nathanson (Ed.), *The many faces of shame* (pp. 133–161). New York, NY: Guilford Press.

Walker, M. (2002). Power and effectiveness: Envisioning an alternate paradigm. *Work in Progress, No. 94.* Wellesley, MA: Stone Center Working Paper Series.

Walker, M. (2005). Critical thinking: Challenging developmental myths, stigmas, and stereotypes. In D. Comstock (Ed.), *Diversity and development: Critical contexts that shape our lives and relationships* (pp. 47–67). Belmont, CA: Brooks Cole.

Ward, J. V. (2000). *The skin we're in: Teaching our children to be emotionally strong, socially smart, spiritually connected.* New York, NY: Free Press.

36

RELATIONAL–CULTURAL
THERAPY PROCESS

JUDITH V. JORDAN

Relational–cultural theory (RCT) appreciates that therapy unfolds in a complex and often unpredictable way. Initially the therapy relationship must become "safe enough" to allow the exposure and exploration of vulnerability. With the client, the therapist explores what might get in the way of asking for support and affirms the wisdom of the client's existing strategies of disconnection. Therapists should not try to dismantle these strategies of disconnection but rather take a respectful approach to them, appreciating their necessity. This period of therapy can be difficult and can last a long time if there has been significant neglect or violation in early relationships. When, over time, the therapy relationship does not replicate the pain of earlier relationships, relational discrepancies are experienced and noticed, and change becomes possible. The client's new understanding of her or his

Excerpted from *Relational–Cultural Therapy* (2010), from Chapter 4, "The Therapy Process," pp. 38–51. Copyright 2010 by the American Psychological Association. Used with permission of the author.

http://dx.doi.org/10.1037/14295-036

Psychotherapy Theories and Techniques: A Reader, G. R. VandenBos, E. Meidenbauer, and J. Frank-McNeil (Editors)
Copyright © 2014 by the American Psychological Association. All rights reserved.

own and others' contribution to the relationship becomes more nuanced and differentiated.

One day Lisa, a client with posttraumatic stress disorder (PTSD), saw frustration in my face and asked, "Do you just want to throw me out or maybe kill me?" Because we had experienced other crises like this, she could hear me when I answered that I was indeed feeling frustrated, but in no way did I want to throw her out or kill her, that if anything my frustration made me get a little too intense about trying to understand better. She could see that I was not her rageful father who had repeatedly assaulted her when he was angry. Her relational images were beginning to shift and a more differentiated experience of affect was coming into being.

As the client comes to expect more authentic connection, she or he begins to take small risks in the area of dealing with the inevitable conflicts that occur in relationships. Rather than moving into avoidance or inauthenticity, the client may begin to try out stating a difference or disagreement. Clients develop more relational confidence and resilience. Relational confidence involves seeing that one has the capacity to move another person, effect a change in a relationship, or affect the well-being of all participants in the relationship. The negative relational images that have limited the client to an expectation that she does not "matter," that she cannot have an impact, and that she is relationally incompetent begin to alter when she sees her own relational competence emerge. Seeing, feeling, and knowing the experience of impact on the therapist moves the client back into relationship.

Relational awareness or mindfulness involves bringing a kind of attunement and consciousness to relationships themselves in addition to each participant in the relationship. Questions like "What does the relationship need?" "How strong is the relationship?" and "What will support the relationship?" begin to be important. Getting through things together is part of the work. And staying in the uncertainty of the process is more easily said than done. One useful therapy mantra is "listening with curiosity rather than reaching for certainty."

I remember when Lisa, who was extremely critical of me even after we had established a good record of working through disconnections, walked into my office one day and said, "This has been a pretty tough relationship for both of us, hasn't it? I remember when you called my sister by the wrong name and I decided that was it, we were done. I said you were losing your marbles or maybe you just didn't care. And you sputtered an apology that I tried to believe. And then remember when I told you later that you weren't the smartest therapist I'd ever had but you weren't the dumbest? And I thought I was giving you a present with that? Yeah, we've been through a lot and we're still here talking to each other. . . . Amazing. I guess we both deserve some credit for that!" This acknowledgment was, in itself, a therapeutic milestone.

Together, over time, the therapist and client create a relationship in which the client can include more of herself, her experience, and her feelings, especially those parts of her experience she has had to keep out of relationship. The therapist is empathic with how terrifying it is for the client to express yearnings for connection and relinquish strategies to stay out of connection. In therapy with an emotionally present therapist who is committed to responsively reworking relational failures, isolation lessens and the brain changes. In what RCT refers to as the *corrective relational experiences* where relational images are reworked, it is highly likely that neuronal shifts occur as well.

It is also useful if the therapist can grasp how therapy actually "threatens" a client's strategies of disconnection. It is essential that the therapist appreciate how dangerous it feels to the client to give up these strategies of disconnection; without them, she or he may feel powerless and out of control. The therapist works on being empathic with the central relational paradox, whereby the client at once yearns to move into authentic, safe relationship and fears relinquishing the strategies of disconnection to do so. This push–pull can sometimes result in impasses. When such an impasse occurs, the therapist needs to refocus on following the client's lead and help titrate the movement toward connection appropriately, in such a way that the client is not triggered into terror.

RCT psychotherapy outcomes include greater freedom to express yearnings for connection without feeling helpless. Strategies of staying out of connection decrease. The client experiences greater confidence in her or his capacity to bear her or his feelings, knowing that she or he need not be alone. Complex feelings and cognitions replace "all or nothing" functioning. Pathological certainty shifts. The client develops an enlarged sense of relational resources in her or his life. Feeling connected and empowered, the client begins to experience more of the "five good things": zest, clarity, worth, productivity, and desire for more connection. Thus as the client's relational skill shifts, her or his energy can move into productive and creative work.

Because RCT therapy enhances the client's desire for connection, it is an approach that is intrinsically about building networks and community. With an appreciation of the sociopolitical forces that create chronic disconnection and disempowerment, the individual often feels empowered to begin to challenge limiting social conditions. Thus RCT therapy does not simply aim to help people "adjust" to disempowering social circumstances. Such an approach would support the notion that the problem is "in the individual," a model of thinking intrinsically embedded in separation psychology. Rather, by naming destructive social practices, empathizing with the impossibility of making change alone, reinforcing the importance of finding allies, and examining ways to resist shaming practices at both a collective and a personal level, RCT therapy supports skills that create both personal well-being and social justice. In her work with African American adolescent girls, Janie Ward (2000) provides a beautiful model for building this resistance to isolating and disempowering cultural forces. As isolation and shame are lessened, energy becomes available for building more enlivening connections and constructive community.

In sum, compared to many therapeutic approaches, RCT therapy does not offer a vast array of specific techniques. Its major contribution to the therapist's toolbox is its insistence on the use of mutual empathy and radical respect for the client and its emphasis on understanding and reworking chronic disconnections and dysfunctional relational images. The therapy relationship itself creates healing and change.

THE ELEMENTS OF THERAPY

Working With Connections and Disconnections

A disconnection occurs in an interaction when one person does not feel heard, understood, or responded to by another person, and there is a loss of empathic responsiveness. Disconnections occur all the time in relationships. Most of them are minor, and they can often become places to work on building stronger connection. If the hurt or "injured" person can represent her or his feelings to the other person and be responded to empathically, disconnection leads to stronger connection. Working toward reconnection requires a commitment to better understanding and the effort of repair. If therapists get invested in maintaining images of themselves as totally empathic, caring healers, or people who have moved beyond the human condition of uncertainty, suffering, and stumbling in their own journeys, they will undoubtedly abandon clients at their moments of greatest honesty and vulnerability. When a client takes the risk of voicing a criticism or doubt about the therapist, the therapist who needs to be right or "in control" may well resort to a distancing or demeaning understanding of this honesty, such as "She's confusing me with her father," "He's resisting my interpretation," or "She's expressing her hostility toward me." It is always easier for therapists to bring their empathy to bear on the client's experience when the client's hurt is from others. When therapists themselves are the source of the injury, they must make a special effort to avoid defensiveness and thus blame or abandon the client.

RCT therapy suggests that when therapists learn that their misattunements are part of a disconnection, they need to try hard to stay present and take in whatever the complaint or injury is. This can entail being nondefensive and responding in a manner that affirms the client's experience—that is, offering a response that presumably was not there when the client was hurt or injured by others as a child. Thus, the therapist might apologize for failures in memory or lapses in attention or suggest that indeed she or he didn't "get" something and try to go back over it to see how to do better this time. When an empathic failure occurs, the most important question is What happens next? Is the client offered a relational milieu that says that understanding the client and the client's healing is more important than the therapist's pride or ego? Is the therapist dedicated to really understanding and being with the client's experience? If the therapist sends the message that she or he can receive and work on feedback about her or his own limitations and fallibility, then chronic disconnection need not ensue. Unlike in past relationships, clients do not have to go into shame or protective inauthenticity but can stay with their own experience as the therapist stays with them. This relational repair brings about healing and rekindles hope.

VIGNETTE

The Struggle to Stay Connected

Diana, a 20-year-old woman, was one of my most challenging clients and also one of my most valued teachers. She had been in treatment with several therapists before she arrived at my office. Although some of her therapists "gave up on her," she had fired others for being too "shrinky and cold." At that time I was practicing in a psychiatric teaching hospital where Diana was hospitalized. She began treatment with some hope and also caution. It didn't take her long to find me disappointing. She found me far too conventional and "stiff." She also was quick to notice the ways that I didn't "get" her. In response to my empathic failures, Diana would call her former therapists to report on the latest "dumb" thing I had said. Many of these therapists happened to be esteemed former supervisors of mine. Diana was an accurate recorder of my mistakes so when I would encounter one of these people in the cafeteria or elsewhere, they would let me know that she had called and then ask, with some surprise, if I had really said such and such (with a roll of the eyes to indicate how ridiculous it would have been if I had). Of course I had.

I was filled with a sense of shame, exposure, and some irritation that Diana was exposing my failings to so many people. My images of myself as a kind, empathic therapist were being substantially challenged. I had to struggle with my own tendency to disconnect. I was defensive and had little understanding of her pattern of doing this. At first I traveled the traditional route of seeing her actions as being about her veiled hostility toward me. I tried to get her to talk about this. Mostly, I think, I was trying to find a way to get her to stop exposing my incompetence. But over time I came to appreciate that Diana had developed an intelligent and effective way to stay in treatment with me. For her as a trauma survivor, therapy behind closed doors, where she was invited to share her vulnerability with a powerful other person, was in no way a safe situation. In fact it was triggering. She had been sexually abused, behind closed doors, by a supposedly trustworthy powerful person (her stepfather). The therapy situation did not offer her safety. Each time I made a mistake or failed her empathically, she experienced an "amygdala hijack." In other words, what might have been perceived as a small error by others signaled to her that she was unsafe and that potentially she would be violated. Thus, that small error caused a big reaction.

In response to this reaction, Diana did something brilliant. She brought the therapy out from behind the closed doors and said, "Listen to this. Look at this. Look at what my therapist is saying and doing. Witness this relationship." In this way she could feel safe enough to stay in the work. While I struggled with this dynamic and was blind to its meaning for way too long, I finally did understand that she was indeed doing what she had to do to overcome the terror that the situation created for her. When I finally could appreciate this with her and demonstrated that I could get beyond my own uncertainty, shame, and sense of exposure to stay with her needs and help her be safe, she began to feel safe enough to trust that we would work on the misunderstandings and failures together; she no longer had to go into high alert when an empathic failure occurred. But she also knew that if she needed to bring in witnesses, she had that option.

Together Diana and I built enough trust to take the next step of talking together about the hurts, disappointments, and disconnections she experienced in therapy with me. She contributed a great deal to establishing a relationship that was safe enough for both of us that we could facilitate her healing.

The therapist's ability to work with disconnections—those occurring in the therapy and outside it—is crucial to the movement of the therapy. Very importantly, the therapist does not want to abandon people to their repetitive expectations of nonresponsiveness from others or push them toward connection when connections have not been experienced as safe. Both the desire to connect and the strategies of disconnection that have developed to protect an individual's vulnerability in a nonempathic milieu must be honored. The therapist must attend carefully to the disconnections in therapy and be ready to renegotiate them to effectively expand the possibility for future change. Sometimes that means pointing out a particular pattern of disconnection; sometimes that means quietly allowing retreat from vulnerability, without a word. For in those moments of extreme vulnerability, there is the possibility that any comment could be perceived as shaming. When the therapist hurts the client—whether through thoughtlessness, misunderstanding, or defensiveness—the hurt must be addressed: with acknowledgment and sometimes even an apology, conveying a clear sense that it is not okay for the therapist to hurt the client, but also pointing out that such misunderstandings may be inevitable at times. Often the therapist needs to show the pain she or he feels at having created pain for the client. Contrary to the commonly expressed fear that showing this will lead to a constriction of feeling or will invite the client to "take care of the therapist," this open acknowledgment often leads to a sense that the therapist cares and is strong enough to show her or his vulnerability.

People who suffer with chronic disconnection and hold negative relational images often misattribute blame to themselves for their isolation. They feel in some way defective, that they have caused the isolation, they are bad or boring or not deserving of love. So it is especially important that therapists take appropriate responsibility for their contributions to disconnections.

Once in therapy I was a bit preoccupied with a project I was working on. A client I had been seeing for some time was talking about how important writing in her journal was. But as I listened, I couldn't really follow her and I was feeling a bit lost. I commented, "Things seem to be getting unclear in here today." She quickly responded: "With you or with me?" In that moment she helped me see that my own drifting attention was leaving her feeling alone and in that isolation she was beginning to slip away. I acknowledged that I thought I was a bit preoccupied and that she had probably been feeling like I had left her alone and that perhaps a journal was a more reliable place to communicate. It was not necessary to say what exactly preoccupied me; this is part of the difference between experiential validation and full disclosure.

When a disconnection occurs, whatever the relationship has been or is moving toward shifts. There is uncertainty. Accompanying uncertainty is often anxiety and fear. It is a moment of possibility and risk. This moment can be an opportunity to forge stronger connection or to close down around pain and fear. When there is nonresponsiveness, a holding of images of what should be, or clinging to some illusion of certainty, therapist and client move out of the open space of relatedness into guarding their separateness or self-images. When the situation is indeed unsafe, this represents appropriate protectiveness. If people cannot take the small risks to test out how safe the relationship would be for open curiosity and learning, they cannot move toward each other. Questions to ask include: Can we do something about this difficulty in our relationship? Is there sufficient mutuality and safety to undertake the necessary vulnerability to work through the difficulty together? Through asking and answering questions like these, therapist and client together build a new template for negotiating hard places in relationship.

WORKING WITH EMPATHY

Empathy is a crucial element in rebuilding relational images and creating connection. Empathy is a complex cognitive affective skill; it is the ability to put oneself in the others' shoes, to "feel with" the other, to understand the other's experience. It is crucial to the felt experience of connectedness and is therefore crucial to healing in therapy. It demands clarity of the source of the affect (where does the affect first arise?), and it creates increasing clarity about the meaning of the client's experience. It also lessens the experiential distance between client and therapist. Empathy is not just a means to better understand the client; in mutually empathic exchanges, the isolation of the client is altered. The client feels less alone, more joined with the therapist. It is likely that in these moments of empathy and resonance, there is active brain resonance between therapist and client (Schore, 1994), which can alter the landscape and functioning of the brain. Thus, those areas of the brain that register isolation and exclusion fire less and those areas that indicate empathic responsiveness begin to activate. The orbitofrontal cortex is quite plastic and subject to relational reworking throughout most of life. Empathic responsiveness in therapy can help develop new neuronal pathways and shift old patterns of firing.

Mutual empathy is based on the notion that in order for empathy to "make a difference," to create healing and lessen isolation, the client must be able to see, know, and feel the therapist's empathic response. Chronic disconnection leads to demoralization and a loss of hope for empathic responsiveness from the other person; indeed, from all others. Only by bringing oneself more fully into empathic relationship can one learn new responses and begin to discard the old, fixed, overly generalized expectations of relational failure.

Mutual empathy, based in respect, allows both people to see the impact they have on one another. The therapist's responsiveness to the client's feelings gives the client a firsthand experience of being "felt" (*really* understood) by the other, of having impact. When the client notices the therapist tearing up as she herself is tearfully recounting her mother's painful death, she knows her pain is received and felt, that her suffering matters. The client feels less isolated and hopeless. Whereas in prior relationships, the client may have felt closed down and not responded to, she or he now sees how she or he emotionally affects the other person. There is a deepening sense of trust in these exchanges—in oneself, in the other, and in the relationship—and an expanding belief in the possibility that relationships and individuals can make a difference in the surrounding world. The client's cognitive capacities also come alive, with more clarity and creativity. Finding growth-fostering relationships does not lead to withdrawal from the world in a cocoon of warm and gratifying connection. Rather, it leads to an increased investment in the world and in others' well-being.

The separate self model overemphasizes the "taking in" of supplies and the building of a separate sense of well-being. RCT contends that one's own growth need not be pitted against another's; participating in growth-fostering relationships enables mutual growth. Empathy for oneself and others is enlarged. Overly personalized and distorted understandings of past relationships begin to shift.

REFERENCES

Schore, A. (1994). *Affect regulation and the origin of the self: The neurobiology of emotional development.* Hillsdale, NJ: Erlbaum.

Ward, J. V. (2000). *The skin we're in: Teaching our children to be emotionally strong, socially smart, spiritually connected.* New York, NY: Free Press.

APPENDIX 36.1: RELATIONAL–CULTURAL THERAPY TECHNIQUES

Technique	Video title	Video identifying number	Time at which technique occurs
Mutual empathy	Using RCT to Treat the Grief and Sadness Over a Breakup	777700197-001	09:26–11:13
Radical respect for client	Treating Fear of Intimacy With Relational–Cultural Therapy (Session 3 of 5)	777700279-001	25:28–26:38
Understanding and reworking chronic disconnections	Treating Fear of Intimacy With Relational–Cultural Therapy (Session 1 of 5)	777700273-001	23:43–27:54
Identifying dysfunctional relational images	Using RCT to Treat the Grief and Sadness Over a Breakup	777700197-001	32:31–33:53
Identifying controlling images and shame	Treating a Middle-Aged Woman With Low Self Esteem With Relational–Cultural Therapy	777700198-001	15:09–17:06
Assessing disconnection	Treating Fear of Intimacy With Relational–Cultural Therapy (Session 2 of 5)	777700277-001	30:27–32:26
Affirming the wisdom of the client's existing strategies of disconnection	Treating Fear of Intimacy With Relational–Cultural Therapy (Session 1 of 5)	777700273-001	31:58–33:44
Empathizing with the impossibility of making change alone	Treating a Middle-Aged Woman With Low Self Esteem With Relational–Cultural Therapy	777700198-001	33:34–36:06
Reinforcing the importance of allies	Treating Fear of Intimacy With Relational–Cultural Therapy (Session 4 of 5)	777700281-001	22:27–24:35
Exploring what blocks the client from asking for support	Treating a Middle-Aged Woman With Low Self Esteem With Relational–Cultural Therapy	777700198-001	30:53–32:24
Examining ways to resist shaming practices	Treating Fear of Intimacy With Relational–Cultural Therapy (Session 2 of 5)	777700277-001	09:52–12:33
Encouraging–empowering	Using RCT to Treat the Grief and Sadness Over a Breakup	777700197-001	35:42–38:11
Affirming the client's experience	Using RCT to Treat the Grief and Sadness Over a Breakup	777700197-001	30:46–32:35
Therapeutic authenticity/empathy	Treating a Middle-Aged Woman With Low Self Esteem With Relational–Cultural Therapy	777700198-001	27:08–29:06
Acknowledging the power of social context	Treating a Middle-Aged Woman With Low Self Esteem With Relational–Cultural Therapy	777700198-001	21:35–24:15

" Can I stress you a little bit today? "

37

SCHEMA THERAPY

LAWRENCE P. RISO AND CAROLINA McBRIDE

More than 30 years ago, Aaron T. Beck (1967, 1976) emphasized the operation of cognitive schemas as the most fundamental factor in his theories of emotional disorders. Schemas, accordingly, played a principal role in the development and maintenance of psychological disorders as well as in the recurrence and relapse of episodes.

Despite the central place of cognitive schemas in the earliest writings of cognitive therapy, the cognitive techniques and therapeutic approaches that later emerged tended to address cognition at the level of automatic negative thoughts, intermediate beliefs, and attributional style. In a similar way, the psychotherapy protocols that developed tended to be short term. Relatively less attention was paid to schema-level processes.

Excerpted from Lawrence P. Riso, Pieter L. du Toit, Dan J. Stein, and Jeffrey E. Young (Eds.), *Cognitive Schemas and Core Beliefs in Psychological Problems: A Scientist–Practitioner Guide* (2007), from Chapter 1, "Introduction: A Return to a Focus on Cognitive Schemas," pp. 3–6. Copyright 2007 by the American Psychological Association. Used with permission of the authors.

http://dx.doi.org/10.1037/14295-037
Psychotherapy Theories and Techniques: A Reader, G. R. VandenBos, E. Meidenbauer, and J. Frank-McNeil (Editors)
Copyright © 2014 by the American Psychological Association. All rights reserved.

In most accounts of clinical cognitive theory, cognition can be divided into different levels of generality (Clark & Beck, 1999). Automatic thoughts (ATs) are at the most specific or superficial level. Automatic thoughts are moment-to-moment cognitions that occur without effort, or spontaneously, in response to specific situations. They are readily accessible and represent conscious cognitions. Examples of ATs include "I'm going to fail this test," "She thinks I'm really boring," or "Now I'll never get a job." ATs are often negatively distorted, representing, for instance, catastrophizing, personalization, or minimization. They are significant in that they are tightly linked to both the individual's mood and his or her behavioral responses to situations.

Beliefs at an intermediate level (termed intermediate beliefs or conditional assumptions) are in the form of "if . . . then" rules. Examples of intermediate beliefs include "If I do whatever people want, then they will like me" and "If I trust others, I'll get hurt."

At the highest level of generality are cognitive schemas. Negative automatic thoughts and intermediate beliefs are heavily influenced by underlying cognitive schemas, particularly when these schemas are activated. In cognitive psychology, the notion of cognitive schemas has played an important role in the understanding of learning and memory. For clinical contexts, A. T. Beck (1967) described a cognitive schema as "a cognitive structure for screening, coding, and evaluating the stimuli that impinge on the organism" (p. 283).

A number of authors have returned recently to Beck's original notions of the need to conceptualize patients in terms of their cognitive schemas (see, for instance, Young, 1995, and Safran, Vallis, Segal, & Shaw, 1986). Jeffrey Young (1995; Young, Klosko, & Weishaar, 2003) has been one of the more influential proponents of a schema-focused clinical approach. Noting limitations of traditional cognitive therapy, Young (1995) suggested that a focus on schemas was often necessary because some patients have poor access to moment-to-moment changes in affect, making a primary focus on ATs unproductive. Other patients are readily able to recognize the irrationality of their thoughts in therapy but then report that they still "feel" bad. Still others are unable to establish a productive and collaborative working alliance that is required for more symptom-focused work. Finally, Young noted that patients seen in the community are often much more complex and chronic than are those enrolled in clinical trials with 3-month cognitive therapy protocols. As a consequence, the need to focus on underlying schemas has begun to influence the practice of cognitive therapy. In this volume, we have compiled work by a number of authors who tailor the schema-focused approach to the understanding and treatment of specific clinical problems.

The increased interest in cognitive schemas parallels the search for underlying dimensions of vulnerability to psychopathology. The search for these underlying processes includes factors such as temperament, personality, and personality disorders. Schema-focused approaches also represent a return to an interest in developmental antecedents of psychopathology.

The concept of schemas has a rich ancestry in psychology deriving from cognitive psychology, cognitive development, self-psychology, and attachment theory. Within the cognitive therapy literature, the term *cognitive schema* has had multiple meanings (James, Southam, & Blackburn, 2004; Segal, 1988; Young et al., 2003). These definitions vary in the extent to which schemas are accessible or inaccessible cognitive structures. Nearly all definitions, however, maintain that cognitive schemas represent highly generalized superordinate-level cognition, that schemas are resistant to change, and that they exert a powerful influence over cognition and affect. As in psychoanalytic theory, the notion of cognitive schemas suggests the power of unconscious processes in influencing thought, affect, and behavior. However, unlike the psychodynamic unconscious, schemas exert their influence through unconscious information processing, rather than through unconscious motivation and instinctual drives.

Early attempts to study cognitive schemas used paper-and-pencil measures such as the Dysfunctional Attitudes Scale (Weissman & Beck, 1978). Numerous studies found that currently ill individuals consistently scored higher on self-report inventories purportedly measuring dysfunctional schemas than did control participants who were never depressed (see Segal, 1988, for review). However, subsequent research demonstrated that these elevated scores normalized with symptomatic recovery (Blackburn, Jones, & Lewin, 1986; Giles & Rush, 1983; Haaga, Dyck, & Ernst, 1991; Hollon, Kendall, & Lumry, 1986; Silverman, Silverman, & Eardley, 1984). The explanation for these findings, from a schema-theory perspective, was that following recovery, cognitive schemas became dormant and thus difficult to detect.

Therefore, the next generation of research examined cognitive schemas using information-processing tasks. It was assumed that information tasks would be less prone to reporting biases and more able to detect latent schemas, particularly when these tasks were accompanied by an effort to prime or activate the schema. In one such task, individuals made judgments of whether a number of positive and negative personal adjectives were self-descriptive, followed by an incidental recall test. Results indicated that not only were individuals with depression biased toward recall of negative self-referent information (Derry & Kuiper, 1981; Dobson & Shaw, 1987) but also, and perhaps more importantly, these formerly depressed individuals were biased in their recall after undergoing a sad mood induction (Hedlund & Rude, 1995; Teasdale & Dent, 1987). In other work, individuals who had recovered from depression made more tracking errors during dichotic listening tasks than did control participants, who were never depressed, after they underwent a sad mood induction (Ingram, Bernet, & McLaughlin, 1994). Finally, Miranda and colleagues (Miranda, Gross, Persons, & Hahn, 1998; Miranda, Persons,

& Byers, 1990) assessed dysfunctional attitudes in formerly depressed versus never depressed individuals. Although the groups exhibited similar levels of dysfunctional attitudes before any mood induction, following the mood induction procedure only the formerly depressed group showed increases in their reporting of dysfunctional attitudes. These and other studies substantiated the notion that schemas are latent during nonsymptomatic periods and become accessible and impact cognitive processing when they are activated.

The importance of schemas in the development and maintenance of psychopathology, as well as the role of schemas in treatment resistance, has much in common with the *Diagnostic and Statistical Manual of Mental Disorders* (4th ed.; *DSM–IV*; American Psychiatric Association, 1994) Axis II personality disorders. Like personality disorders, schemas represent purportedly stable generalized themes that develop early in life and are important considerations for understanding and treating a wide range of psychopathological conditions. Unlike personality disorders, however, schemas are dimensional rather than categorical, are more cognitive–affective than behavioral, and were derived from the traditions of personality psychology and cognitive phenomenology, rather than the traditions of operationalized psychiatric nomenclature and descriptive psychopathology.

REFERENCES

American Psychiatric Association. (1994). *Diagnostic and statistical manual of mental disorders* (4th ed.). Washington, DC: Author.

Beck, A. T. (1967). *Depression: Clinical, experimental, and theoretical aspects*. New York, NY: Harper & Row.

Beck, A. T. (1976). *Cognitive therapy and the emotional disorders*. New York, NY: International Universities Press.

Blackburn, I. M., Jones, S., & Lewin, R. J. (1986). Cognitive style in depression. *British Journal of Clinical Psychology, 25*, 241–251.

Clark, D. A., & Beck, A. T. (1999). *Scientific foundations of cognitive theory and therapy of depression*. New York, NY: Wiley.

Derry, P. A., & Kuiper, N. A. (1981). Schematic processing and self-reference in clinical depression. *Journal of Abnormal Psychology, 90*, 286–297. doi:10.1037/0021-843X.90.4.286

Dobson, K. S., & Shaw, B. F. (1987). Specificity and stability of self-referent encoding in clinical depression. *Journal of Abnormal Psychology, 96*, 34–40. doi:10.1037/0021-843X.96.1.34

Giles, D. E., & Rush, A. J. (1983). Cognitions, schemas, and depressive symptomatology. In M. Rosenbaum, C. M. Franks, & Y. Jaffe (Eds.), *Perspectives on behavior therapy* (pp. 184–199). New York, NY: Springer.

Haaga, D. A., Dyck, M. J., & Ernst, D. (1991). Empirical status of cognitive theory of depression. *Psychological Bulletin, 110*, 215–236. doi:10.1037/0033-2909. 110.2.215

Hedlund, S., & Rude, S. S. (1995). Evidence of latent depressive schemas in formerly depressed individuals. *Journal of Abnormal Psychology, 104*, 517–525. doi:10.1037/ 0021-843X.104.3.517

Hollon, S. D., Kendall, P. C., & Lumry, A. (1986). Specificity of depressotypic cognitions in clinical depression. *Journal of Abnormal Psychology, 95*, 52–59. doi:10.1037/0021-843X.95.1.52

Ingram, R. E., Bernet, C. Z., & McLaughlin, S. C. (1994). Attentional allocation processes in individuals at risk for depression. *Cognitive Therapy and Research, 18*, 317–332.

James, I. A., Southam, L., & Blackburn, I. M. (2004). Schemas revisited. *Clinical Psychology & Psychotherapy, 11*, 369–377. doi:10.1002/cpp.423

Miranda, J., Gross, J. J., Persons, J. B., & Hahn, J. (1998). Mood matters: Negative mood induction activates dysfunctional attitudes in women vulnerable to depression. *Cognitive Therapy and Research, 22*, 363–376. doi:10.1023/A:1018709212986

Miranda, J., Persons, J. B., & Byers, C. N. (1990). Endorsement of dysfunctional beliefs depends on current mood state. *Journal of Abnormal Psychology, 99*, 237–241. doi:10.1037/0021-843X.99.3.237

Safran, J. D., Vallis, T. M., Segal, Z. V., & Shaw, B. F. (1986). Assessment of core cognitive processes in cognitive therapy. *Cognitive Therapy and Research, 10*, 509–526. doi:10.1007/BF01177815

Segal, Z. V. (1988). Appraisal of the self-schema construct in cognitive models of depression. *Psychological Bulletin, 103*, 147–162. doi:10.1037/0033-2909. 103.2.147

Silverman, J. S., Silverman, J. A., & Eardley, D. A. (1984). Do maladaptive attitudes cause depression? *Archives of General Psychiatry, 41*, 28–30.

Teasdale, J. D., & Dent, J. (1987). Cognitive vulnerability to depression: An investigation of two hypotheses. *British Journal of Clinical Psychology, 26*, 113–126.

Weissman, A. N., & Beck, A. T. (1978). *Development and validation of the Dysfunctional Attitude Scale: A preliminary investigation.* Paper presented at the meeting of the American Educational Research Association, Toronto, Ontario, Canada.

Young, J. E. (1995). *Cognitive therapy for personality disorders: A schema-focused approach.* Sarasota, FL: Professional Resource Exchange.

Young, J. E., Klosko, J. S., & Weishaar, M. E. (2003). *Schema therapy: A practitioner's guide.* New York, NY: Guilford Press.

38

SCHEMA THERAPY PROCESS

LAWRENCE P. RISO, RACHEL E. MADDUX,
AND NOELLE TURINI SANTORELLI

Years of unrelenting depression can render chronic patients hopeless about their future and their prospects for improving during therapy. Therefore, along with a focus on schemas, early symptom reduction is extremely important. The lack of any tangible sign of improvement in the first few weeks of therapy can reinforce the patient's hopelessness and defectiveness schemas. Thus, early on, behavioral activation strategies such as activity scheduling and assertiveness training along with targeted sleep interventions should be considered.

Once a schema has been identified, the therapist can assist the patient in examining the validity and usefulness of the schema, as well as arriving at alternative or more realistic beliefs. The Core Belief Worksheet (CBW; Beck,

Excerpted from Lawrence P. Riso, Pieter L. du Toit, Dan J. Stein, and Jeffrey E. Young (Eds.), *Cognitive Schemas and Core Beliefs in Psychological Problems: A Scientist–Practitioner Guide* (2007), from Chapter 3, "Early Maladaptive Schemas in Chronic Depression," pp. 47–50. Copyright 2007 by the American Psychological Association. Used with permission of the authors.

http://dx.doi.org/10.1037/14295-038
Psychotherapy Theories and Techniques: A Reader, G. R. VandenBos, E. Meidenbauer, and J. Frank-McNeil (Editors)
Copyright © 2014 by the American Psychological Association. All rights reserved.

1995) is a useful format for weighing the evidence for and against a schema and its related core belief. The CBW helps patients to articulate the core belief (or schema), rate the extent to which they agree with it, and systematically evaluate the data that support or refute it. The level of confidence in the belief is rerated after the data are examined, and the process is often continued over many sessions. The CBW helps patients discover how they exaggerate the "truthfulness" of the belief and establish some distance from inaccurate and destructive ideas. Over time, the CBW will help patients develop more accurate and functional alternative beliefs.

Another useful technique in addressing negative schemas is guided imagery. We have found the descriptions of guided imagery provided by Beck (1995); Edwards (1990); and Layden, Newman, Freeman, and Morse (1993) to be particularly helpful. Imagery exercises can be emotionally evocative and powerful vehicles for corrective experiences, although they must be handled with the utmost sensitivity. Patients who believe they are defective and unlovable because of the sexual abuse they once experienced may need to reprocess the trauma via imagery, actively and rationally responding to the faulty conclusions they had drawn about themselves. Of course, great care and caution needs to be exercised in such a situation to ensure that the patient understands the nature of and rationale for the procedure, and that he or she agrees to it in a collaborative discussion. In addition, care must be taken to ensure sufficient time is allotted in the session for the debriefing that follows. The imagery and reprocessing may be repeated over many sessions, until the patient is better equipped to rationally respond to the negative beliefs and connotations that the sexual abuse once engendered.

Guided imagery may be used in other ways. For example, patients can deliberately manipulate their images to "rewrite" a distressing outcome. One patient's image involved being helplessly berated by his intensely critical father when he was 9 years old (described later in the case illustration). By walking into the image as an adult, he could explain to the boy (i.e., himself at age 9) that his father was an extremely volatile person in the midst of an outburst, possibly related to his alcoholism. His criticisms and rantings at that moment, or any other for that matter, could hardly be construed as an accurate appraisal of anyone's character or abilities.

Role playing is another useful method of undermining problematic core beliefs and schemas. Therapist and patient can take turns playing the role of the schema, versus that of the healthy alternative viewpoint. This point–counterpoint technique (Young, 1995) allows for the brainstorming of many rational responses to the schema, under conditions of high affect and high sensory involvement. In a similar way, therapist and patient can role play important interpersonal situations in the patient's life that typically evoke schematic reactions (e.g., arguments with a parent; being criticized by a colleague). Such an exercise affords patients the chance to practice more adaptive cognitive and behavioral responses while validating the emotions that have been evoked by the high-risk situation. Through repetitions and constructive corrections, the patient learns to counteract even well-established schemas and their concomitant emotions and behaviors, thus providing vital new interpersonal skills.

Patients with chronic depression often have schemas of helplessness, weakness, and inadequacy that lead to passivity during treatment. Thus, therapists must guard against a tendency to become overly directive and dominant during sessions, which will only breed more passivity. According to the interpersonal theory of Donald Kiesler (1983, 1996), dominance and submission are reciprocal tendencies. That is, patients who are submissive in session present an interpersonal pull for therapists to become more dominant (see also McCullough, 2000). However, this is an interpersonal trap in therapy, because becoming more directive brings on the reciprocal tendency for patients to be even more passive and submissive. Consider this example:

> *Patient:* There's really nowhere to turn. You know, nobody who really cares. I just don't know how to climb out of this. I'm totally at a loss.
>
> *Therapist:* I'm sure your wife still cares. You really need to talk to her.
>
> *Patient:* You think so?
>
> *Therapist:* Yes. You need to be really honest and straightforward. This is no time to mince words.
>
> *Patient:* So the direct approach, huh? I guess you're right. But what should I say? I'd probably screw it up.

In this example, the therapist is getting deeper and deeper into telling the patient how to solve problems and is setting the stage for more and more passivity from the patient.

Other patients exhibit hostility toward therapists, which pulls for more hostility from the therapist. This dynamic occurs because friendliness and hostility are corresponding interpersonal tendencies (friendliness pulls for friendliness and hostility pulls for hostility). Remaining cognizant of the reciprocal and corresponding dynamics will help therapists recognize and respond to these challenging interpersonal pulls. At times, the therapist can even strategically vary his or her interpersonal stance. For instance, a therapist can actually take a passive stance (e.g., "I feel a little stumped myself") to pull for a more active and problem-solving approach from patients (e.g., "Well, I guess one thing I can do is talk to my wife").

RETAINING THE BASIC PRINCIPLES OF COGNITIVE THERAPY

A focus on schemas in the treatment of chronic depression differs from traditional cognitive therapy by placing a greater emphasis on early childhood experiences, making greater use of emotive techniques such as guided imagery, using the therapeutic relationship as a vehicle of change, and conducting a lengthier course of therapy because of the resistance to change of underlying schemas. Despite the somewhat different emphasis, it is essential to maintain the basic elements of traditional cognitive therapy including keeping the therapy active and directive, using cognitive therapy techniques, emphasizing self-help homework, and conducting structured sessions (Young, 1995). Most of all, it is essential to develop a list of clear therapeutic goals. Vague and global ideas are in need of specifics to decrease the chronic patient's confusion, hopelessness, and feelings of being overwhelmed with problems.

REFERENCES

Beck, J. S. (1995). *Cognitive therapy: Basics and beyond.* New York, NY: Guilford Press.

Edwards, D. J. A. (1990). Cognitive therapy and the restructuring of early memories through guided imagery. *Journal of Cognitive Psychotherapy, 4,* 33–50.

Kiesler, D. J. (1983). The 1982 Interpersonal Circle: A taxonomy for complementarity in human transactions. *Psychological Review, 90,* 185–214. doi:10.1037/0033-295X. 90.3.185

Kiesler, D. J. (1996). *Contemporary interpersonal theory and research: Personality, psychopathology, and psychotherapy.* New York, NY: Wiley.

Layden, M. A., Newman, C. F., Freeman, A., & Morse, S. B. (1993). *Cognitive therapy of borderline personality disorder.* Needham Heights, MA: Allyn & Bacon.

McCullough, J. P. (2000). *Treatment for chronic depression: Cognitive behavioral analysis system of psychotherapy.* New York, NY: Guilford Press.

Young, J. E. (1995). *Cognitive therapy for personality disorders: A schema-focused approach.* Sarasota, FL: Professional Resource Exchange.

APPENDIX 38.1: SCHEMA THERAPY TECHNIQUES

Technique	Video title	Video identifying number	Time at which technique occurs
Emphasis on early childhood experiences	Schema Therapy With a Client Suffering From Anxiety	777700173-001	4:40–8:20
Guided imagery	Schema Therapy With a Client Suffering From Anxiety	777700173-001	30:22–42:11
Active/directive methodology	Schema Therapy With a Client Suffering From Anxiety	777700173-001	40:44–41:23
Development of clear therapeutic goals	Schema Therapy With a Client Suffering From Anxiety	777700173-001	0:09–3:17
Role playing	Schema Therapy With a Client Suffering From Anxiety	777700173-001	23:57–30:00

INDEX

Abandonment fears, 132
ABC/ABCDE theory (rational emotive behavior therapy), 289–292
Acceptance and commitment therapy (ACT), 3–9
    cognitive fusion and defusion in, 4–9
    goal of, 3
    psychological flexibility in, 3–9
Acceptance and commitment therapy (ACT) process, 11–17
    automaticity in, 14–16
    literality in, 13–14
    ubiquitous thoughts in, 12–13
Achievement, 310–311
ACT. *See* Acceptance and commitment therapy
Activating events (rational emotive behavior therapy), 289, 290
Active engagement, 21
Actualizing tendency, 252–253
Adaptability, 157–158
Adaptive strategies, 24–25
Adolescents, 313, 330, 338
Adult attachment, 39–40, 103
Adult Attachment Interview, 40
Adversities (rational emotive behavior therapy), 290
Affect, 129. *See also* Emotion(s)
Affective empathy, 262
Affiliation, 309–310
Affirmative empathic responses, 263
African Americans, 222, 331, 338
Agoraphobia, 30
Ainsworth, M. D. S., 37
Allodynia, 223
Alternative-based interventions (cognitive therapy), 72–75
Altman, N., 216
American Psychological Association (APA) Multicultural Guideline 5, 217
American Psychological Association (APA) Presidential Task Force, 216
Amygdala, 118

Anger, 132, 133
Anxiety, 145
Anxiety disorders
    classical conditioning principles behind, 81–82
    exposure-based strategies for, 29
Anxious–ambivalent attachment, 38
APA (American Psychological Association) Multicultural Guideline 5, 217
APA (American Psychological Association) Presidential Task Force, 216
Aristotle, 312
Assertiveness training, 91–93
Associative learning, 23–26
ATs. *See* Automatic thoughts
Attachment, 36–41
Attachment patterns, 37–38
Attachment theory, 36–37, 40–41
Audiotherapy, 293
Authenticity, 274–275, 326
Autobiographical competence, 40
Autobiographical memory, 59–60
Automaticity, 14–16
Automatic thoughts (ATs)
    evidence-based interventions for, 68–72
    in information processing model of cognition, 63
    in schema therapy, 346
Autonomy, 312
Avoidant attachment, 38
Awareness
    in emotion-focused therapy, 127–129
    in Gestalt therapy, 191, 195
Axis II personality disorders, 348

Bandura, A., 292
Bartlett, E. C., 107
Beck, A. T., 61–63, 295–296, 345, 346, 352
Behavioral activation strategies, 351
Behavioral techniques, 297

Behavior therapy, 19–26
  goals of, 19–21
  key concepts in, 21–23
  role of learning in, 23–26
Behavior therapy process, 29–32, 34
  exposure-based strategies in, 29–31
  exposure hierarchies in, 31–32
  guidelines for effective exposure
    in, 31
  response prevention in, 32
Beijing Olympics (2008), 311
Beliefs, 289, 346
  Core Belief Worksheet, 351–352
  family belief systems, 160
  rational and irrational, 290
  religious, 313–314
Belonging, 309–310
Bernal, G., 215
Bernstein, D. A., 89
Bibliotherapy, 293
Binder, J. L., 41, 45
Biocultural variables, 206–207
Bion, W. R., 272
Black Families in Therapy
  (N. Boyd-Franklin), 215
Borge, Victor, 313
Borkovec, T. D., 89
Boszormenyi-Nagy, I., 159–160, 165
Boundaries, 158
Bouton, M. E., 25, 84
Bowen, M., 156, 158–161
Bowlby, J.
  on importance of attachment, 36–37
  on internal working models, 38
  on lifelong effects of attachment, 39
  therapeutic tasks outlined by,
    40–41
Boyd-Franklin, N., 215
Brauer, Debbie, 311
Brief dynamic therapy, 35–41
  adult attachment in, 39–40
  and attachment patterns, 37–38
  and attachment theory, 36–37,
    40–41
  internal working models in, 38–39
Brief dynamic therapy process,
    43–52, 55
  accessing and processing emotion in,
    44–45
  empathic exploration in, 45

exploration of maladaptive cyclical
    patterns in, 48–49
  focused inquiry in, 45–46
  promotion of change directly in,
    49–50
  relational focus in, 46–48
  therapeutic alliance in, 43–44
  time constraints in, 51–52
Brief rational emotive behavior therapy
    (REBT), 299–301
Bruner, J., 234
Buber, M., 144, 188
Buddhism, 300
Bugental, J. F. T., 142, 149–150
Bumberry, W., 167
Burnett, D., 322

Carter, B., 161
Caspi, A., 207
CBT. *See* Cognitive-behavioral therapy
CBW (Core Belief Worksheet),
    351–352
Character armor, 188
Cheng, N., 309
Cherry, Fred, 309–310
Choice theory, 307, 308, 314, 322
Circular questions, 169
Civil rights movements, 219
Clarfield, L. E., 113
Clarification, 262
Classical conditioning
  and behavior therapy, 23–25
  and cognitive–behavioral therapy,
    81–84
Cleveland Institute of Gestalt Therapy,
    189
CMP (cyclical maladaptive pattern), 45
Coalitions, family, 159
Cognition
  cognitive model of, 61–62
  in emotion-focused therapy, 129
  information-processing model of,
    59–61, 63
  levels of generality with, 346
Cognitive appraisal theory, 79
Cognitive–behavioral therapy (CBT),
    79–86. *See also* Cognitive therapy
  coping statements in, 295–296
  dominance of, 272
  goals of, 80–81

learning theory in, 79, 81–85
treatment principles of, 84–86
Cognitive–behavioral therapy (CBT)
    process, 87–94, 96
    problem-solving training in, 93–94
    rehearsal of social skills and
        assertiveness in, 91–93
    relaxation techniques in, 89–91
    self-monitoring techniques in,
        87–89
Cognitive content, 60
Cognitive defusion, 4–9, 11–16
    automaticity in, 14–16
    literality in, 13–14
    ubiquitous thoughts in, 12–13
Cognitive fusion, 4–9, 12
Cognitive products, 61
Cognitive schemas, 347. *See also*
        Schema *entries*
Cognitive structures
        (constructivism), 111
Cognitive techniques, 292–294
Cognitive therapy, 57–64. *See also*
        Cognitive–behavioral therapy
        (CBT)
    cognitive model of cognition, 61–62
    and information-processing model of
        cognition, 59–61, 63
    realist viewpoint in, 57–58
    schemas in, 61–64, 68, 345
    schema therapy vs., 354
Cognitive therapy process, 67–77
    alternative-based interventions in,
        72–75
    evidence-based interventions in,
        68–72
Cohesion, family, 157
Collective formative events, 203
Collins, P. H., 330
Combs, A., 252
Compulsions, 32
Conditional compensatory response
        model, 83
Conditional responses (CRs), 80, 81, 92
Conditioned appetitive motivational
        model of craving, 83
Conditioned stimuli (CS)
    and behavior therapy, 24–25
    and cognitive–behavioral therapy,
        80, 84

Conditioning
    and behavior therapy, 23–25
    and cognitive–behavioral therapy,
        81–84
Conditions of worth, 256–257
Congruence (person-centered therapy),
        253–254
Conjectural empathy, 264
Connections (relational–cultural
        therapy), 338–339
Consequences (rational emotive
        behavior therapy), 290
Constantine, L., 160
Constructivism, 58
Constructivist therapy, 97–104
    experiencing and explaining in,
        98–99
    goal of, 98
    individual life-span development
        in, 102
    self and intersubjectivity in, 100–102
Constructivist therapy process, 107–
        114, 116
    conducting exploration in, 112–114
    conjuring a world in, 110–112
    therapeutic relationship in, 108–110
Consulting your consultants questions
        (narrative therapy), 245
Context of literality, 13–14
Coping statements, 295–296
Core Belief Worksheet (CBW),
        351–352
Core ordering processes, 111
Corrective relational experiences, 337
Cost–benefit ratio (rational emotive
        behavior therapy), 292
Countertransference, 41
Countertransference interpretation,
        281–283
Counterviewing questions (narrative
        therapy), 245–247
Couples therapy
    emotional expression in, 118
    having fun in, 313
"Credulous approach," 109
Critical consciousness dialogue,
        219–222
CRs. *See* Conditional responses
CS. *See* Conditioned stimuli
Cultural competence, 214

Cultural genograms, 207–210
Cultural issues, 92–93, 160. *See also*
    Multicultural therapy;
    Relational–cultural therapy
Cultural trauma, 204–205
Culture-bound syndromes, 206
Cushman, P., 272, 274
Cyclical maladaptive pattern
    (CMP), 45

Damasio, A., 266–267
Defusion, cognitive. *See* Cognitive
    defusion
Delusions, 70–71
Dependent personality disorder, 62
Depression, 347–348, 351, 353
Destructive entitlement, 159–160
Detouring (family therapy), 159
Diagnostic and Statistical Manual of
    Mental Disorders (DSM–IV)
    Axis II personality disorders in, 348
    ineffective behaviors described
        in, 307
    removal of homosexuality from, 232
Diaries, 88
Diathesis–stress models, 63
Dimen, M., 272
Disconnection (relational–cultural
    therapy), 327–328, 338–339, 341
Disempowerment, 174–176, 178–180
Disputing, in rational emotive behavior
    therapy, 290–291
Distraction methods, 292
Distress
    patriarchy as source of, 178–180
    racism-related, 222–224
Dominance, 353
Double binds, 319
Dramatization, 195
Dreamwork, 193
    in Gestalt therapy process, 199–201
    in psychoanalytic therapy process,
        285–286
DSM–IV. See Diagnostic and Statistical
    Manual of Mental Disorders
DTR (dysfunctional thought record),
    75–76
Dyadic regulation, 44
Dysfunctional attitudes, 347–348
Dysfunctional Attitudes Scale, 347

Dysfunctional thinking, 300
Dysfunctional thought record (DTR),
    75–76
D'Zurilla, T. J., 93

Early maladaptive schemas (EMSs), 62
EBP (evidence-based practice), 216
Edwards, D. J. A., 352
Effective new philosophies, 291
Efran, J. S., 113
EFT. *See* Emotion-focused therapy
Egalitarianism, 181
Ego, Hunger and Aggression
    (Fritz Perls), 188
E–H (existential–humanistic) therapy.
    See Existential therapy
Elaboration exercises, 195
Elliott, R., 267
Ellis, A., 297
Emery, G., 61, 62
Emotion(s)
    in brief dynamic therapy process,
        44–45
    in exposure techniques, 31
    and intersubjectivity, 100–102
    in person-centered therapy, 266–267
    types of, 122–123
Emotional expression, 129–130, 267
Emotional memories, 118
Emotional reasoning, 74
Emotional reflection, 267
Emotion-focused therapy (EFT),
    117–123
    emotion generation in, 121–122
    emotion schemes in, 118–120
    role of client emotions in, 118
    and types of emotion, 122–123
Emotion-focused therapy (EFT) process,
    125–134, 137
    awareness in, 127–129
    corrective emotional experiences
        in, 134
    expression in, 129–130
    reflection in, 131
    regulation in, 130–131
    role of therapist in, 126
    transformation in, 131–134
Emotion generation, 121–122
Emotion regulation, 130–131
Emotion schematic memory, 119

Emotion schemes, 118–120
Emotive–evocative techniques, 294–297
Empathic challenges, 263–264
Empathic conjectures (emotion-focused therapy), 128
Empathic understanding, 262
Empathy
in brief dynamic therapy process, 45
in emotion-focused therapy, 126
in person-centered therapy, 261–267
in relational–cultural therapy, 326, 327, 342–343
Empirical study, 22
Empowered consent, 182
Empowerment
in feminist therapy, 173–174, 176, 181–183
in multicultural therapy process, 217–222
Empty-chair dialogues, 192, 195–198
EMSs (early maladaptive schemas), 62
Enactment, 168
Episodic memory, 59
Epstein, N., 62
Epston, D., 231–232, 234–237
Ethnicity, 331
Ethnocultural allodynia, 223
Evidence-based interventions (cognitive therapy), 68–72
Evidence-based practice (EBP), 216
Evidence-based treatment, 272
Evocative empathic responses, 263
Exaggeration exercises, 193, 195
Existential–humanistic (E–H) therapy. See Existential therapy
Existentialism, 189
Existential suffering, 271–272
Existential therapy, 139–146
core aims of, 144–145
cultivation of presence in, 143–144
experiential mode in, 142–143
freedom as key theme in, 139–141
present moment in, 143
sense of self in, 145–146
Existential therapy process, 149–152, 154
therapeutic guiding in, 150–153
therapeutic listening in, 149–151
Experience (person-centered therapy), 255

Experience of experience questions, 244
Experiencing
in constructivist therapy, 98–99
in existential therapy, 142–143
Explorative empathy, 262
Exposure
in behavior therapy process, 29–32
in cognitive-behavioral therapy, 84–85
External frame of reference, 258
Extinction (learning), 25–26, 84, 92

Facial recognition, 100
Faith, 313–314
Family belief systems, 160
Family life cycle models, 161–162
Family sculpting, 170
Family systems, 156
Family therapy, 155–162
classic concepts in, 157–162
core questions of, 155–156
having fun in, 313
Family therapy process, 165–170
circular questions in, 169
enactment in, 168
externalizing problems in, 169–170
family sculpting in, 170
family's role in, 167
goal setting in, 168
multilateral partiality in, 165–166
patient's role in, 167
therapist's role in, 166–167
Fantasy, 278
Fantasy dreams, 319
Fear, 122, 132
Feeling Good (D. D. Burns), 73
Felt security, 39
Feminist therapy, 173–180. See also Relational–cultural theory
determination of outcomes in, 174
evaluation of power dynamics in, 174–176
and patriarchy as source of distress, 178–180
realms of power examined in, 174–178
Feminist therapy process, 181–184, 186
psychosocial interventions in, 184
somatic interventions in, 182–184
Figure/ground formation, 189–190

First person empathy, 265
Fixed-role therapy, 114
Flooding (exposure techniques), 30
Focused inquiry, 45–46
Foucault, M., 231
Framo, J., 160
Frankl, V., 312, 314
Freedom, 139–141, 312
Freeman, A., 352
Freire, P., 219
Freud, S.
    dynamic model of mental
        functioning, 151
    and fantasy, 278
    and irrationality, 274
    and neutrality, 328
    and suffering, 271–272
    and unconscious forces, 277
Friedman, M., 142
Friendship, 310, 311
From, I., 195
Fun, 312–313
Functional analysis
    in behavior therapy, 20
    in cognitive–behavioral therapy, 80
Functional context, 4
Fusion, cognitive, 4–9, 12

Gadamer, H. G., 100–101
Gaze aversion, 330
Gender, 326
Gendlin, E. T., 142
Genetic transference interpretation,
    284–285
Genograms, 207–210
Gestalt psychology, 189–190
Gestalt therapy, 187–193
    change processes in, 191
    change tasks in, 192–193
    goals of, 191
    history of, 187–189
    theoretical foundations of, 189–191
Gestalt Therapy (Paul Goodman), 188
Gestalt therapy process, 195–202
    case example, 196–199
    dreamwork in, 193, 199–201
    macrotechniques in, 195–196
    microtechniques in, 195–196
Gilford, P., 272
Gilligan, C., 330

Glasser, W., 308–309, 312–314, 317–318
Goal setting, 168
Goldstein, K., 188
Goodman, P., 188
Group rational emotive behavior
    therapy, 301–305
Group shame, 331
Growing Up Absurd (Paul Goodman), 188
Guidano, V. E., 112
Guided imagery, 352
Guided meditation, 151–152
Guiding, 150–151

Habituation, 29–30. *See also* Exposure
Halyburton, Porter, 309–310
Hardy, K. V., 208
Harrison, R. P., 62
Hawthorn, T., 311
Hayes, S. C., 5
Hefferline, R., 188
Helplessness, 353
Here and now
    in brief dynamic therapy, 41, 44, 47
    in family therapy, 156
Hill, C. E., 47
Hirsch, J., 309–310
Hoffman, Irwin, 275
Homeostasis, 189
Homework
    in cognitive–behavioral therapy, 91
    in cognitive therapy, 72–73
Homosexuality, 232
Honesty, 273–274
Horney, K., 187
Hoyt, M. F., 52
Humor, 73, 296–297
Huynh, Carol, 311
Hwa-byung, 206
Hwang, M., 308
Hypothesis, language of, 111–112
Hypothetic empathy, 264

IBs (irrational beliefs), 290
Ideal self, 253
Identification techniques
    (Gestalt therapy), 195
Identity formation, 145
Imaginal exposure, 30
Incongruence (person-centered
    therapy), 253–254

Independence, 312
Individual differences, 82
Individuation
    in family therapy, 157
    and intersubjectivity, 100
    in psychoanalytic therapy, 274
Infancy, attachment in, 36–37
Inferential empathy, 263
Information processing, 347–348
Information-processing model of
        cognition, 59–61, 63
Inner control, 310–311
Insecure attachment, 38, 39
Insight-oriented therapy, 129
Instrumental emotions, 123
Intergenerational transmission, 159–160
Internal dialogue exercises, 192
Internal frame of reference, 258
Internal working models, 38–39
Interoceptive exposure, 30
Interpersonal–relational theory, 35
Interpersonal/social–contextual power,
        174, 175, 177
Interpretation
    countertransference, 281–283
    dream, 285–286
    genetic transference, 284–285
    nontransference, 283–284
    transference, 47–48, 281–283
Intersectionality, 234
Intersubjectivity, 100–102
Intrapersonal/intrapsychic power,
        174–177
In vivo exposure, 30
Irrational beliefs (IBs), 290
Ishak, N. M., 308

Jackson, D., 311
Jordan, J. V., 330
Jusoh, A. J., 308

Kakar, S., 216
Kantor, D., 160
Kasper, L. B., 47
Kelly, G. A., 108, 109, 111, 113, 114
Kierkegaard, S., 152
Kiesler, D. J., 353
Kim, R.-L., 308
King, Rodney, 204
Kivlighan, D. M., 47

Knowledge, 99
Korean populations, 308

Labeling (cognitive distortion), 70
Laing, R. D., 142
Language of responsibility, 193
Laszloffy, T., 208
Layden, M. A., 352
Learning
    in behavior therapy, 23–26
    emotion schematic, 119
Learning theory, 79, 81–85
Le Doux, J., 118
Lehr, W., 160
Levant, R., 326
Levenson, H., 46
Lewis, H. B., 331
Life-span development
    in constructivist therapy, 102
    in relational–cultural therapy, 326
Liotti, G., 111
Listening, 150–151
Literality, 13–14
Litwack, L., 314
Locus of control, 321–322
Locus of evaluation (person-centered
        therapy), 257
Logical disputing, 290
Logotherapy, 314
Long-term rational emotive behavior
        therapy (REBT), 301–305
Love, 309–310

Mahmud, Z., 308
Mahoney, M. J., 108, 112
Main, M., 40
Making the rounds (Gestalt task),
        192–193
Maladaptive patterns, 48–49, 127
Maladaptive primary emotions, 123,
        131–132
Mal de pelea, 206
Managed care system, 272
Manipulative feelings, 123
Marcel, G., 144
Marginalization, 325
Maturana, H., 99
May, R., 141–143, 146, 150
McGoldrick, M., 161
Meaning, 274–275

Mearns, J., 321
Meditation, 151–152
Memories, 118, 328
Mentalization, 40
Metacommunication, 47, 282
Microaggressions, 331
Mikulincer, M., 37
Milan model of family therapy, 160
Miller, J. B., 327–329
Mindfulness exercises, 13
Minuchin, S., 156, 158
Miranda, J., 347–348
Modeling, 91, 292–293
Moffitt, T. E., 207
Morse, S. B., 352
Multicultural therapy, 203–210
    biocultural and ecological contexts
        for, 206–207
    factors in, 203–204
    sociopolitical timelines for use in,
        205–206
    for treatment of cultural trauma,
        204–205
    use of genograms in, 207–210
Multicultural therapy process, 213–224,
    229–230
    cultural adaptation techniques for,
        214–217
    empowerment in, 217–222
    goals of, 213–214
    and racism-related distress, 222–224
Multigenerational genograms, 207–210
Multilateral partiality, 165–166
Muran, J. C., 47
Mutual empathy, 326, 327, 342–343
Mutual feedback loop, 36
Mutuality, 326
Myers, L., 311

Narrative therapy, 231–237
    foundations of, 231–232
    re-authoring conversations in,
        234–237
    unique outcomes and unique
        accounts in, 235
    unique redescription questions in,
        236
Narrative therapy process, 241–247, 249
    consulting your consultants
        questions in, 245

counterviewing questions in,
    245–247
preference questions in, 244–245
unique account questions in, 242
unique circulation questions in,
    243–244
unique outcome questions in,
    241–242
unique possibility questions in, 243
unique redescription questions in,
    242–243
Native Americans, 213
Negative attribution, 70
Negative fortune-telling, 69–70
Neocortex pathway, 118
Network family therapy, 213
Newman, C. F., 352
New York Institute for Gestalt Therapy,
    188
Nezu, A. M., 93
Nondesired active acceptance (reality
    therapy), 319
Nonnegotiable demand, 318

Objectivism, 97
Object relations theory, 160–161
Observational empathy, 264–265
Obsessive–compulsive disorder (OCD)
    exposure treatment for, 30
    ritual prevention in treatment of, 32
Olson, D. H., 158
Open-ended questions, 45
Orbitofrontal cortex, 342
Organismic self-regulation, 188

PCSD (postcolonization stress
    disorder), 204
Pearlman, L., 313–314
Perceptual system, 321–322
Perls, F., 187–189, 192, 199–201
Perls, L., 188
Personal construct systems, 111
Personality disorders, 348
Personal meaning organizations, 111
Person-centered therapy, 251–258
    actualizing tendency in, 252–253
    conditions of worth in, 256–257
    congruence and incongruence in,
        253–254
    experience in, 255

internal and external frames of
reference in, 258
locus of evaluation in, 257
organismic valuing process in,
257–258
positive self-regard in, 255–256
psychological adjustment and
maladjustment in, 254–255
self concept in, 253
therapeutic goals of, 251–252
Person-centered therapy process,
261–269
client's role in, 267–268
emotion in, 266–267
empathy's role in, 261–267
Philosophic discussion, 294
Phobias, 30, 81
Plomin, R., 207
Political ideology, 218
Pollack, B., 326
Polster, E., 199
Polster, M., 199
Positive self-regard, 255–256
Postcolonization stress disorder
(PCSD), 204
Posttraumatic stress disorder (PTSD),
30
Power, 310–311. *See also* Empowerment
Pragmatic disputing, 291
Preference questions (narrative
therapy), 244–245
Preparedness, 82
Presence (existential therapy), 143–144
Pride, 331
Primary adaptive emotions, 122–123
Primary process, 276
Privilege, 325
Proactive schemas, 61
Problem solving, 294
Problem-solving therapy, 73
Problem-solving training, 93–94
Progressive muscle relaxation, 89
Proximity-seeking behavior, 37
Psychoanalysis, 189
Psychoanalytic therapy, 271–278
complexity, ambiguity, and curiosity
in, 273
fantasy in, 278
goals of, 272
honesty in, 273–274

meaning, vitality, and authenticity
in, 274–275
reflection-in-action vs. technical
rationality in, 275–276
the unconscious in, 276–278
Psychoanalytic therapy process,
281–287
dream interpretation in, 285–286
genetic transference interpretation
in, 284–285
nontransference interpretation in,
283–284
transference and countertransference
interpretation in, 281–283
Psychological adjustment and
maladjustment, 254–255
Psychopharmacology, 183–184
PsycTHERAPY, xiii–xiv
PTSD (posttraumatic stress disorder), 30
Pursued goals (reality therapy), 318–319

Racial identity models, 331
Racism
collective oppression resulting
from, 204
distress related to, 222–224
Racket feelings, 123
Radical constructivism, 58
Rational beliefs (RBs), 290
Rational emotive behavior therapy
(REBT), 289–297
ABC/ABCDE theory of, 289–292
behavioral techniques in, 297
cognitive techniques in, 292–294
emotive–evocative techniques in,
294–297
multimodal nature of, 291–292
work and practice in, 291
Rational emotive behavior therapy
(REBT) process, 299–306
brief, 299–301
long-term, 301–305
Rational emotive imagery, 294–295
Rationalism, 97
RBs (rational beliefs), 290
RCT. *See* Relational–cultural theory
Reacquisition (learning theory), 85
Reactive schemas, 61
Realism, 57–58, 97
Realistic disputing, 290

Reality therapy, 307–314
    and achievement, 310–311
    belonging, love, and affiliation in,
        309–310
    freedom, independence, and
        autonomy in, 312
    fun and enjoyment in, 312–313
    inner control in, 310–311
    power in, 310–311
    recognition in, 310–311
    self-esteem in, 310–311
    and spirituality, 313–314
    and survival instincts, 308–309
Reality therapy process, 317–323
    exploring wants in, 318–321
    level of commitment in, 320–321
    perceptual system in, 321–322
    skills in, 317
REBT. See Rational emotive behavior
        therapy
Recognition, 310–311
Recognition reflex, 264
Reflection-in-action, 275–276
Rehearsal exercises, 193
Reich, W., 187–188
Reinstatement (learning theory), 85
Relational context, 4
Relational–cultural theory (RCT),
        325, 335
Relational–cultural therapy, 325–332
    controlling images and shame in,
        330–332
    core concepts in, 326
    disconnection as normative in,
        327–328
    mutual empathy and growth-
        fostering relationships in,
        327
    relational images in, 328–330
    societal contexts in, 325–326
Relational–cultural therapy process,
        335–344
    case examples, 336, 339–341
    complexity in, 335–336
    connection and disconnection in,
        338–339, 341
    empathy in, 342–343
    outcomes with, 337
Relational frame theory (RFT), 4
Relational images (RIs), 328–330

Relationships
    as focus in brief dynamic therapy,
        46–48
    in relational–cultural therapy,
        327–328, 337, 342–343
    therapeutic, 327. See also
        Therapeutic alliance
Relaxation techniques, 89–91
Religious beliefs, 313–314
Reluctant passive acceptance (reality
        therapy), 319
Repetition exercises, 195
Rescorla, R. A., 25
Resistance, 44
Response prevention, 32
Reversal exercises, 193
RFT (relational frame theory), 4
RIs (relational images), 328–330
Ritual prevention, 32
Rogers, C. R., 251–258, 267–268, 312.
        See also Person-centered therapy
Role playing
    in constructivist therapy, 112
    in rational emotive behavior
        therapy, 296
    in schema therapy process, 352–353
Romanticism, 274–275
Rotter, J. B., 321–322
Rush, A. J., 61

Sachse, R., 267
"Safe haven" (attachment theory), 39
Safety signals, 85
SAS (Sociotropy–Autonomy Scale), 62
Schema Questionnaire, 63
Schemas, 61–64, 68
Schema therapy, 345–348
    automatic thoughts in, 346
    history of, 345
    and information processing, 347–348
    underlying processes in, 346–347
Schema therapy process, 351–355
    guided imagery in, 352
    role playing in, 352–353
    traditional cognitive therapy vs., 354
    use of Core Belief Worksheet in,
        351–352
Schneider, K. J., 151–152
Schwartz, R., 161
Secondary process, 276

Secondary reactive emotions, 123, 128
Secondary shame, 123
Secondary symptoms, 292
Secure attachment
    classification of, 38
    positive effects of, 40
A *Secure Base* (J. Bowlby), 37, 41
Self
    in constructivist therapy, 100–102
    in existential therapy, 145–146
    in person-centered therapy, 253
    in Victorian era, 274
Self-actualization, 188
Self-concept, 253
Self-disclosure, 46, 265
Self-esteem, 310–311
Self-monitoring techniques, 87–89
Self-preservation, 308–309
Self processes, 160–161
Self-soothing, 130–131
Self-structure, 253
Semantic memory, 59
Sexism, 204. *See also* Feminist therapy
Shame
    controlling, 330–332
    in emotion-focused therapy, 122–
        123, 132–133
    exercises attacking, 295
Shaver, P. R., 37
Shaw, B. F., 61
Siegel, S., 83
Silence, 150
Silent listening, 261
The Skin We're In (Janie Ward), 331
Social anxiety disorder, 30
Social skills, 91–93
Social support, 310, 311
Sociotropy–Autonomy Scale (SAS), 62
Solomon, A., 272
Somatic power, 174–176
Spark, G., 165
Spiritual/existential power, 174, 175,
    177–178
Spirituality, 313–314
Staub, E., 313–314
Stern, D. N., 277
Stiver, I., 328, 329
Strange Situation Procedure, 37–38, 40
Strupp, H. H., 41, 48
Subjectivity, 276

Submission, 353
Substance use disorders, 83
Suffering, 271–272
Survival instincts, 308–309

Tageson, C. W., 253
Taylor, A., 207
Technical rationality, 275–276
Therapeutic alliance
    in brief dynamic therapy, 43–44
    in constructivist therapy, 108–110
    multicultural, 206
    in reality therapy, 310
    in schema therapy, 346
    strained, 283, 284
Therapeutic relationship, 327
Thought records, 75–76
Thoughts
    automatic. *See* Automatic
        thoughts (ATs)
    ubiquitous, 12–13
Thoughts on Clouds exercise, 13
Threat, 254
TIC-TOC technique, 75
Tillich, P., 142, 188
Time constraints, 51–52
Time-limited dynamic psychotherapy
    (TLDP). *See* Brief dynamic
        therapy
Tomkins, S. S., 330
Transference, 41
Transference interpretation, 47–48,
    281–283
Trauma, 204–205
Triads, family, 158–159
Triangulation, 159

Ubiquitous thoughts, 12–13
Unconditional self-regard, 255–256
Unconditioned stimuli (US)
    and behavior therapy, 24–26
    and cognitive-behavioral therapy,
        81, 83
Unconscious, 276–278
Unique account questions (narrative
    therapy), 242
Unique circulation questions (narrative
    therapy), 243–244
Unique outcome questions (narrative
    therapy), 241–242

Unique possibility questions (narrative
    therapy), 243
Unique redescription questions (narrative
    therapy), 236, 242–243
US. *See* Unconditioned stimuli

Videotherapy, 293
Vitality, 274–275

Wachtel, P. L., 39
Wagner, A. R., 25
Walker, M., 325, 326, 331
Wants (reality therapy), 318–321
Ward, Janie, 331, 338
Watson, J., 37

WDEP (reality therapy), 307, 317
Weak whims (reality therapy), 319
Wertheimer, M., 188
What Are the Numbers? exercise, 8–9,
    15–16
Whitaker, C., 167
White, M., 169, 231–232, 234–237
Whitehead, A. N., 145–146
Winnicott, D. W., 272
Wishes, 319
Word repletion, 4, 9
Wubbolding, R., 310, 313, 320

Yalom, I., 142, 151, 152
Young, J. E., 63, 346